MY STUDIO IS A DUNGEON
IS THE STUDIO

NAYLAND BLAKE

MY STUDIO IS
A DUNGEON IS
THE STUDIO

WRITINGS AND INTERVIEWS,
1983–2024

EDITED AND WITH AN INTRODUCTION
BY JARRETT EARNEST

DUKE UNIVERSITY PRESS
Durham and London
2025

Printed in the United States of America on acid-free paper ∞
Project Editor: Bird Williams
Typeset in Untitled Serif and Copperplate Gothic Std
by Westchester Publishing Services

Library of Congress Cataloging-in-Publication Data
Names: Blake, Nayland, 1960- author | Earnest, Jarrett editor
writer of introduction
Title: My studio is a dungeon is the studio : writings and interviews,
1983–2024 / Nayland Blake ; edited and with an introduction by
JarrettEarnest.
Description: Durham ; London : Duke University Press, 2025. |
Includes index.
Identifiers: LCCN 2025009448 (print)
LCCN 2025009449 (ebook)
ISBN 9781478032502 paperback
ISBN 9781478029083 hardcover
ISBN 9781478061335 ebook
Subjects: LCSH: Homosexuality and art | Homosexuality in art |
Sexual minority culture
Classification: LCC N72.H64 B 59 2025 (print)
LCC N72.H64 (ebook)
DDC 704/.08664—dc23/eng/20250619
LC record available at https://lccn.loc.gov/2025009448
LC ebook record available at https://lccn.loc.gov/2025009449

Cover art: Nayland Blake in Tivoli, New York, 2024. Photograph by
Nayland Blake.

If this collection is dedicated to anything, it is to the hope that reading it will help you make something. Please do. We all need to hear from you.

CONTENTS

xi   *List of Illustrations*

xiii   *Acknowledgments*

1   A Fan Writes . . . :
         An Introduction by Jarrett Earnest

15   The Difficulties That Afflict Us in Art School

18   Assessing My Work

21   Tom of Finland: An Appreciation

32   The ABCs of Art Institutions

37   Performance Script

49   The Saddest Story I Know

58   Schreber, Roussel, Duchamp

64   Performance Script

71   The Secret Square

85   One Hand Clapping: Porn Reviews

102   Bay Area Conceptualism: Two Generations

109   Queer Mysteries

114   Interview by John Gange and Stephen Johnstone

133   City of Hares: A Proposal

136   Curating "In a Different Light"

165   The Story of H (Excerpt)

169   Hare Follies

190   Jack Smith: The Message from Atlantis

205   Ray Johnson: Correspondences

210   Top Ten

214   James Gobel

219   Matthew Benedict: Shroud of Truro

225   Judie Bamber: Further Horizons

230   Seven Quick Notes on Writing an Artist's Statement

233   Kathy Acker: "Because I Want to Live Forever in Wonder"

245   Jim Hodges: "Theme from Mantrap"

250   Interview by Jesse Pearson

260   Nancy Grossman: Misrecognized

265   *Free! Love! Tool! Box!* Workbook

267   Anthony Friedkin: "And *I'm* Carmen Miranda"—What Liberation Looks Like

274   Queer at CAA

280   Samwise Gamgee Cries, with Padding

284   Interview by Tina Horn

289   100 Assignments: Toward a Curriculum

297   Shambling Monstrosity Seeks Mad Scientist

300   Embarrass, Humiliate, Degrade, Objectify:
        Basics of Psychological Status Play

307   In My Dream Body: For Jorge Zontal
        and General Idea

312   Yummy, Slurp! The Pippa Garner Story

319   My Studio Is a Dungeon Is the Studio

335   *Contributors*

337   *Index*

ILLUSTRATIONS

16   Studio, Valencia, California, 1984

19   Studio, San Francisco, California, 1993

30   Dungeon, New York, New York, 1994

35   Studio, San Francisco, California, 1995

47   Museum, Baltimore, Maryland, 1994

56   Studio, San Francisco, California, 1995

62   Museum, Baltimore, Maryland, 1994

69   Theater, Portland, Oregon, 1997

83   Museum, New York, New York, 2003

107   Studio, San Francisco, California, 1993

112   Studio, Tivoli, New York, 2005

131   Studio, Brooklyn, New York, 2007

134   Studio, Brooklyn, New York, 2007

163   Dungeon, Boston, Massachusetts, 2009

167   Dungeon, Boston, Massachusetts, 2008

188   Museum, New York, New York, 2010

203   Museum, New York, New York, 2010

208   Dungeon, withheld, Pennsylvania, 2011

212   Dungeon, withheld, Maryland, 2012

217   Dungeon, withheld, Pennsylvania, 2012

223   Dungeon, withheld, Maryland, 2012

228   Dungeon, withheld, Pennsylvania, 2013

231   Studio, Manhattan, New York, 2011

243   Museum, San Francisco, California, 2012

248   Dungeon, withheld, Maryland, 2012

258   Dungeon, withheld, Maryland, 2014

263   Dungeon, withheld, Pennsylvania, 2015

266   Studio, Manhattan, New York, 2015

272   Museum, Manhattan, New York, 2013

278   Home, Brooklyn, New York, 2016

282   Museum, Manhattan, New York, 2017

287   Studio, Queens, New York, 2018

295   Studio, Peterborough, New Hampshire, 2017

298   Studio, online, 2020

305   Gallery, Los Angeles, California, 2019

308   Dungeon, online, 2020

310   Studio, Queens, New York, 2020

313   Dungeon, Brooklyn, New York, 2020

317   Museum, Manhattan, New York, 2022

320   Museum, Manhattan, New York, 2022

332   Museum, Manhattan, New York, 2024

ACKNOWLEDGMENTS

The life I've led and the career I've had would not have been possible without many, many people. I am grateful to them all, but most especially:

My parents and sister: Joan, Nayland, and Courtney.

My teachers: Deborah Pearson-Feinn, Nancy Mitchnick, Jim Sullivan, Jake Grossberg, and Catherine Lord.

The curators and folks who in various ways gave me the invaluable gift of time and space to work: Renny Pritikin and Judy Moran, John McCarron, Anne MacDonald, Larry Rinder, John Caldwell, Thelma Golden, Ian Berry, Maurice Berger, Maura Reilly, Betti-Sue Hertz, Anne Philbin, and Jamillah James.

And Rick Jacobsen, who embodied the best of what an art world could be.

Dealers: Patricia Davidson, Michelle Mincher and Tessa Wilcox, Richard Kuhlenschmidt, Clarissa Dalrymple, Jack Hanley, Paule Anglim and Ed Gilbert, Fred Mann.

And especially the people I have worked with at Matthew Marks Gallery: Jeffrey Peabody, Cory Nomura, Alex Fang, and particularly Matthew, who has provided wisdom and material support beyond any expectation and friendship that I will always be grateful for.

The commissioners, collaborators, and brilliant minds that I have had the pleasure of being in communication with: Chris Cochrane, Jeff Preiss, Jonathan Hammer, Glen Helfand, Amy Scholder, Dennis Cooper, Lynne Tillman, Robert Gluck, D-L Alvarez, Vincent Fecteau, Robert Crouch, Kevin Killian, Amy Sillman, Dodie Bellamy, David Yarritu, Ishmael Houston-Jones, Patricia Hoffbauer, Dirk Dehner, David Deitcher, Suzanne Nicholas, Nancy

Davenport, Justine Kurland, Marvin Heiferman, AA Bronson, Amy Sadao, Nelson Santos, Mike Smith, Liz Collins, Jeffrey Costello, Robert Tagliapietra, Hrag Vartanian, and Thor Stockman.

My delightful coconspirators who have shared their open hearts and delicious embodiments with me: Phil, Dominic, Lolita, Mike, MJ, and Rae.

The professionals who created this publication: our style editor, Kimberly Kruge, and Ken Wissoker and Ryan Kendall at Duke University Press.

And, finally, this book would not exist without the patience and brilliance of Jarrett Earnest. I came to him hapless with a vague set of barely connected suppositions, rambling monologues, and a title, and over the years of work, he has given me the gift of realizing this volume. He has been a guide, a friend, a sounding board, and the gentlest taskmaster I could hope for. Thank you, Jarrett, for all of it.

I would also like to acknowledge and thank the following publications for having first printed or otherwise given space to these pieces, in the form found herein or another: *Artforum*; *Bay Area Reporter*; *Bay Area Conceptualism: Two Generations* (Hallwalls); *Bunny Butt*; *Dear World*; *Flaming Creature: Jack Smith, His Amazing Life and Times* (Serpent's Tail); *In a Different Light: Visual Culture, Sexual Identity, Queer Practice* (City Lights Books/Institute for Contemporary Art/PS1 Museum); *Lust for Life: On the Writings of Kathy Acker* (Verso); *Nancy Grossman: Tough Life Diary* (Frances Young Tang Teaching Museum and Art Gallery/Skidmore College Press); *New Formations*; *1991, 1992: Jim Hodges* (CRG Gallery); *OUT/ LOOK*; Pomona College Project 26; UCLA Hammer Museum; *Vice*; Walter McBean Gallery (San Francisco Art Institute); *Anthony Friedkin: The Gay Essay* (Yale University Press); Yerba Buena Center for the Arts; and *Pippa Garner: $ELL YOUR $ELF* (Pioneer Works Press /Art Omi).

"Tom of Finland: An Appreciation." *OUT/LOOK*, Fall 1988, 36–45.

"One Hand Clapping." *Bay Area Reporter*, August 22, 1991.

"There Ain't No Cure for the . . ." *Bay Area Reporter*, September 12, 1991.

"America's Funniest Homo Videos." *Bay Area Reporter*, September 26, 1991.

"Authority Figures." *Bay Area Reporter*, October 26, 1991.

"Wow! I Could've Had a . . ." *Bay Area Reporter*, November 14, 1991.

"Blast from the Past." *Bay Area Reporter*, January 2, 1992.

"Bay Area Conceptualism: Two Generations" *Bay Area Conceptualism: Two Generations*, 99–109. Buffalo, NY: Hallwalls, 1992.

"Believe Me, Everybody Has Something Pierced in California: An Interview with Nayland Blake," by Stephen Johnstone and John Gage. *New Formations*, no. 19 (Spring 1993): 50–68.

"Queer Mysteries: David Cannon Dasheill." Walter McBean Gallery, San Francisco Art Institute, 1993, exhibition brochure, unpaginated.

"The Story of H (Excerpt)." *Bunny Butt*, 1994.

"Curating *In a Different Light*." In *In a Different Light: Visual Culture, Sexual Identity, Queer Practice*, edited by Nayland Blake, Lawrence Rinder, and Amy Scholder, 9–43. San Francisco: City Lights Books, 1995.

"The Message from Atlantis." In *Flaming Creature: Jack Smith, His Amazing Life and Times*, edited by Edward Leffingwell, Carole Kismaric, and Marvin Heiferman, 169–83. London: Serpent's Tail; Long Island City, NY: Institute for Contemporary Art/PS1 Museum, 1997.

"Ray Johnson." *Artforum*, March 1999, 107–8.

"Top Ten." *Artforum,* September 2000, 36.

Hammer Projects: James Gobel. Los Angeles, California: UCLA Hammer Museum, 2000, unpaginated.

"Judie Bamber: New Horizons." Exhibition brochure, Pomona College Project 26 (2005): 5–9.

"Kathy Acker: Because I Want to Live Forever in Wonder." In *Lust for Life: On the Writings of Kathy Acker*, edited by Carla Harryman, Avital Ronell, and Amy Scholder, 99–109. London: Verso, 2006.

"Theme from 'Mantrap.'" In *Jim Hodges: 1991,1992,* edited by Alex Dodge, 30–33. New York: CRG Gallery, 2007.

"Shroud of Truro: The Art of Matthew Benedict." *Artforum*, March 2001, 128–33.

"Nayland Blake." *Vice* 15, no. 10 (2008): 111–18.

Free! Love! Tool! Box! Interactive exhibition by Nayland Blake in San Francisco at the Yerba Buena Center for the Arts, (12 October 2012–27 January 2013).

"Misrecognized." In *Nancy Grossman: Tough Life Diary*, edited by Ian Berry, 105–7. Saratoga Springs, NY: Frances Young Tang Teaching Museum and Art Gallery, Skidmore College, 2012.

"'And *I'm* Carmen Miranda'—What Liberation Looks Like." In *The Gay Essay*, by Anthony Friedkin, 25–29. San Francisco: Fine Arts Museum of San Francisco; New Haven, CT: Yale University Press, 2014.

"Interview with Tina Horn" originally appeared as "What a 6 Foot Bear Bison Furry Can Teach Us About Gender Identity" *Mel Magazine*,

2018, accessed 16 January 2025, https://melmagazine.com/en-us
/story/what-a-6-foot-bear-bison-furry-can-teach-us-about-gender
-identity.

Roy, Camille, ed., and Nayland Blake, coed. "The Secret Square." *Dear World*, 1991, 74–79.

"Yummy, Slurp! The Pippa Garner Story" In *Pippa Garner: $ELL YOUR $ELF,* edited by Sara O'Keeffe, Brooklyn, NY: Pioneer Works Press/Art Omi, 2024, 33–38.

A FAN WRITES . . .

AN INTRODUCTION BY JARRETT EARNEST

In a cache of Nayland Blake's childhood papers, there is a binder labeled "Program," an ambitious twenty-page science-fiction story they wrote at the age of twelve. Its dystopia finds human beings effectively imprisoned in heavily medicated comfort, strapped into chairs, and dominated by screens, regulated by artificial intelligence. "He readily accepted anything the machine told him; he allowed it to dictate what to do and when to do it. For example, the door to his small bathroom only opened on regular half-hour intervals. This meant that he had been trained since the time-of-coming-into-being to only need to use it on half-hour periods. In this way, the machine controlled the very workings of his body," prefiguring Blake's lifelong analysis of how social control is enacted on the physical body and on the spaces we inhabit.

Blake's parents met in racially segregated New Bedford, Massachusetts, in 1959, when Nayland Sr., a Black Navy veteran, caught the eye of Joan, a young white woman, while he was working at a record store. Soon she was pregnant, and they fled disapproving families, relocating to Manhattan and eloping at city hall. Young Nayland, named after their father, was born the following year. The elder Blake worked as the super of their building at 101st Street and Riverside Drive, their mother as a secretary at the American Bible Society. A dripping abstract painting four-year-old Blake made in collaboration with their father evidences a loving, creative home, as do their early writings, fastidiously typed by their mother and kept safe for decades.

Throughout the 1960s the Blakes visited museums (the parents quizzing their child after the fact with postcards about the artworks they saw) and the theater: *You're a Good Man, Charlie Brown*; *Jesus Christ Superstar*;

and *Hair*. A ravenous diet of science fiction and fantasy fueled Blake's ambitions to write until they confronted William Burroughs's *Naked Lunch* as a teenager. An artistic revelation—its effect, writer's block. They couldn't figure out how the language worked like it did, and not being able to think their way through it, Blake abandoned writing in high school, shifting their attention to theater and performance. By the mid-1970s, Blake and their slightly older classmates were going downtown to screenings and performances, such as Charlotte Moorman's avant-garde festivals, Jack Smith's films, and Richard Foreman's plays—*Book of Splendors: Part Two* (1977) was especially defining. Foreman's article about his eccentric, recursive methods of composition also transformed Blake's thinking. Foreman writes, "It's a style of living, at certain moments folded back on itself to produce a style of thinking; at certain moments folded back upon itself, which leaves a residue (look, look! The hand moved over the paper and left something!) of a certain style of writing."[1]

Blake attended Bard College in 1978, initially intent on becoming a filmmaker but soon switching to the visual art program. Being an artist seemed to mean being a painter, the horizons heavily circumscribed by the endgame of Jasper Johns and minimal abstraction. The installations of Jonathan Borofsky and a lecture by Judy Pfaff opened, for Blake, a path that further broadened when they saw Colab's shambling experiment *The Times Square Show* (1980). Blake began to create provisional spaces—arrangements of stuff, stage sets without a simple narrative where the viewer moved around like an actor in a scene. One fun-house installation included an altar to the Vodou *loa* Bawon Samdi, engaging with ideas they drew from filmmaker Maya Deren's groundbreaking book *Divine Horseman: The Living Gods of Haiti* (1953). Deren's account focuses on the integrated Haitian Vodou practices and the meeting of signs and rituals (visible and invisible), as well as the highly sophisticated, racially charged syncretism of Indigenous, West African, and Catholic beliefs. Deren attempted to experience Vodou as a participant, describing her own possession by Erzulie, *loa* of love and beauty. For young Blake, Deren provided an early model of the artist who does embodied research in the world, who writes and makes and thinks and lives in ways that cannot be disentangled.

In 1982 Blake moved to Southern California to attend graduate school at the California Institute of the Arts (CalArts). At Bard their investigative installations were considered "brainy," but within the theory-driven culture of CalArts, their commitment to *making* was considered goofy and romantic. Blake identifies the effects of the toxic atmosphere in a text they wrote in their second year, "The Difficulties That Afflict Us in Art School." The young artist argued that there was a fundamental and painful misrecognition of each other's intentions and actions, a context that produced a deformation of language: "We produce a language of defense to hide that knowledge from others and a language of attack to deride that knowledge when we find it elsewhere."

At Bard, Blake had attempted to cure their writer's block by taking a tutorial with poet Robert Kelly. Observing Blake's sensibilities, Kelly suggested the work of Kathy Acker. Finding *The Childlike Life of the Black Tarantula* (1973), Blake later said that Acker's early novels felt like "letters written to me," though they weren't clear yet on how to move forward with their own writing. They attended a reading Acker gave at CalArts from her novella *My Death My Life by Pier Paolo Pasolini* (1984), in which a first-person account of the murdered intellectual is shamelessly ventriloquized and intercut with all kinds of alternate voices, pastiches, and quotations without clear attribution. At one point the novella peels into a burlesque retelling of the plot of the James Bond movie *To Live and Let Die* (1973): "Because he's white, James is a dope and dopiness is his intelligence. He walks into a black bar in Harlem which every white man knows is a dumb thing to do. Of course the wall against which he's sitting flips around so he's down in black bestial animal hell voodoo where black man says 'Mr. Big gonna take care of woo.' James cause he's stupid tries an identity bluff."[2] Acker's style of metacommentary on the pop cultural text, as well as the confrontation with racist and sexist stereotypes, would have lasting echoes in Blake's work.

In their second year at CalArts, Blake's work took a decisive turn, examining the representational codes of gay men by making photographic self-portraits costumed in various personas, like a "clone" in an Izod shirt, smoking a cigarette and sporting a mustache. This married certain operations of the Pictures Generation with their own queer coming of age, looking at the commodification and formation of the self as a subject at odds with their gender presentation and appearance. By graduation Blake's work had expanded into a series of seemingly disparate practices that would take years to understand in relation. In a summary from 1984 included here as "Assessing My Work," Blake narrates in a daze, "Things that I was able to point to as interests and pleasures have become blurred and difficult to locate."

In the pursuit of these inchoate "interests and pleasures" as both an artist and sexual being, Blake moved up to San Francisco, the reigning capital of the queer world, instead of New York or Los Angeles, the typical destinations of their classmates eager for art careers. There Blake published their first piece of writing for the radical queer publication *OUT/LOOK* in 1988. "Tom of Finland: An Appreciation" was also the first critical engagement with the famed gay pornographer whose distinctive drawings of muscular hunks became synonymous with leather and gay bar culture in the second half of the twentieth century: "Tom's work has been left on the sidelines of any debate about gay sensibility because it is pornography. Pornography remains a taboo: We consume it but will not commit to it. Yet when the history of gay images and representations is written, it will contain a large section on our pornographers. In a milieu that has produced a new connoisseurship of sexual acts, what we arouse ourselves with speaks eloquently about who we are." In eight sections Blakes goes on to discuss Tom of Finland from different vantages, as a pornographer, artist, craftsman, narrator, sensualist, voyeur, fascist, sadist, and physique artist. The resulting multidimensional portrait kept the work's contradictions intact and produced what remains the defining critical text on the artist. It also inaugurated a type of essay Blake would continue to write: considerations of artists who had an outsized influence on the formation of queer history and helped define the parameters of Blake's own artistic work.

In a public talk titled "The ABCs of Art Institutions" (1989), Blake noted the way artists, especially queer artists, were taking on the task of criticism for themselves. Citing the failures of contemporary art magazines to address their work in the necessary ways, the text questions how the particular economics of the galleries and audiences produce kinds of discourse. It ends by posing three questions:

How do we as producers use critical writing?
Where do we encounter it?
What do its modes of production and distribution mean?

Attempting to answer these questions to their own satisfaction, Blake would further their argument on pornographers' importance in shaping "gay identity" by becoming a porn reviewer for the burgeoning VHS market, writing for the *Bay Area Reporter*—a gay newspaper.

These pieces take off from the semiotic analysis of erotic imagination with funny narrative recaps and bits of mise-en-scène ("As Matt neared the climax he had been telling us about for five minutes, the camera began a bizarre zoom toward a stack of books in the background. The only readable title was *Native American Architecture*."). While historical analysis shimmers in these chatty pieces, erotic intent motivates the consistently applied criterion circling these images: As they put it in one piece, "Can you beat off to them?" There is an ongoing critique of the normalization of and assimilation within this supposed sexual freedom, always advocating for *queer* as a verb that unsettles. Take the opening of this review of a collection of vintage porn from the 1950s, 1960s, and 1970s: "If you're like me (not that there's any reason you should be), you sometimes find yourself frustrated with the sameness of contemporary pornography. In the past, people have accused me of not liking porn at all, but this is hardly the case. I just don't like run-of-the-mill porn—the kind of porn that doesn't offer the viewer a variety of bodies, positions, and attitudes. Too many porn films show the same things in the same ways."

Blake's engagement with pornography took place within a particularly heated and heady landscape: the feminist sex wars of the 1980s. There were charged disagreements about the ethics of pornography, whether it was always exploitive of women, reifying their oppression by men, or whether there was a potential for liberation in female and queer pornography rooted within pleasure. The increased availability of commercial pornography was also paralleled by the proliferation of self-published alternative porn made for and about sexual cultures that sought to represent their own tastes and experiences. For instance, in 1981 Samois, the lesbian-feminist BDSM organization, published the book *Coming to Power: Writing and Graphics on Lesbian S/M*, and the porn magazine *On Our Backs* was founded in San Francisco in 1984, both controversially celebrating the lesbian S&M community. Three years later, *BEAR* appeared, staking out the sexual paradigm of bigger, hairier gay men as a viable alternative to the stereotypical dyad of skinny twink and muscular clones. In fact, Blake collaborated with D-L Alvarez on their own one-off porn zine, *Brains: The Journal of Egghead Sexuality* (1990), featuring the spectacled smirking cartoon genius-dog Mr. Peabody on the cover and photos of naked guys making out in a bookstore.

The impulses of these underground publications were similar to the culture of zines that circulated in the punk music world and the quixotic facsimiles of the mail art scene, all tightly circling questions of fandom and cultural value. Important theoretical work was also being done to problematize the hierarchy between high and popular culture, typified by Dick Hebdige's study *Subculture: The Meaning of Style* (1979). Reading feminist critic Johanna Russ's analysis of erotic *Star Trek* fan fiction, "Pornography by Women for Women, with Love" (1985), catalyzed Blake's conception of how art engages its audiences. Russ argues that these stories about baroque imagined romances between the television series' two protagonists (the human Captain Kirk and the alien Spock) "ingeniously, tenaciously, and very creatively . . . sexualized our female situation and training, and made out of the restrictions of the patriarchy our own sexual cues."[3] That is, pop cultural iconography could function as a complex, capacitating cipher. It proposes reception as itself a creative act, in which audiences collaborate on new, more idiosyncratic meanings. Like the alternative porn zines, these quirky stories coalesce communities of desire.

The insurgent theoretical work of the journal *Semiotext(e)* mirrored the impact of this fan-driven theorization within underground scenes that Russ describes. The 1981 special issue "Polysexuality," edited by the Canadian psychoanalyst François Peraldi, became a subcultural touchstone for how kink as a "technology of the self" might splinter, proliferate, and transform. On the occasion of Blake's installation of *The Schreber Suite* (1989) at the Berkeley Art Museum, they delivered a fascinating lecture which brings together Raymond Roussel, Marcel Duchamp, and the famous analysand Daniel Paul Schreber within fluctuating trans identifications through a collision of texts, in a drive they call *unmanning*. "I would like, at this point, to suggest a line of inquiry about homosexuality and meaning. I see in the homosexual, as well, certain aspects of a refusal of the phallus, and I wonder if this refusal can be the genesis for a different type of meaning—one that is aleatory, connective, and diffuse, rather than centralized." It should be noted that while Blake describes themself as a "gay man" in these early writings (later identifying as nonbinary with *they/them* pronouns in the early twenty-first century), a proto-trans sensibility was already in operation.

"The Bay Area has been a curious cross between a backwater and a safe harbor for the arts over the past two decades," Blake wrote in the preface to an exhibition catalog, *Bay Area Conceptualism: Two Generations*, contrasting San Francisco's particular brand of irreverent, material-based conceptual art with their peers' (like Lutz Batcher's and David Cannon Dashiell's) renewed engagement with objects. In 1988 Blake became program coordinator at the important alternative space New Langton Arts. The institution's curatorial remit was anything that did not have a home in commercial galleries: Video, performance art, poetry, and conceptual art abounded in hybrid forms. Blake was responsible for facilitating all aspects of staging these pieces, sometimes stepping forward to contribute critical texts or function as curator. From this intersection an entire alternative art history of the Bay Area materialized, and Blake became increasingly interested in connecting and cross-pollinating the literary, conceptual art, music, film, and gay nightlife scenes—an endeavor that would expand throughout their life.

It was within this multipronged approach that Blake's art practice took shape: tableaux of functional objects—furniture, rugs, metal trolleys, televisions—*détourned* via a haphazard and unexpected selection deployed with surgical precision. Blake took to calling them "props"—not only mobilizing their long-term engagement with artists like Jack Smith but precisely identifying the way each arrangement situates the viewer, imagining one's own body in the increasingly threatening scenarios. Steel tables, chains, and collars are deployed, evoking S&M scenes. In *Work Station #5* (1989), an aluminum-and-glass prep table displays black rubber restraints and meat cleavers swinging from chains below. Far from just objects, these items allude to a scene for which the viewer already knows the script, thanks to countless cultural representations. Implicated, a visitor must acknowledge how their own impulses playact with these props; the experience becomes reflexive, a navigation of that recognition.

In a series of wall-mounted plexiglass boxes Blake began in 1990, each minimalist cube encases mass-market paperbacks: camp diva Beverly Sill's autobiography, *Bubbles* (1976); Xaviera Hollander's sexploitation memoir, *The Happy Hooker* (1971); trash pop biographer Kitty Kelley's biography of Elizabeth Taylor, *The Last Star* (1981); Brooks Stanwood's yuppie horror novel, *The Glow* (1979); and Germaine Greer's feminist manifesto, *The Female Eunuch* (1970); filling the phenomenological emptiness of Donald Judd's cubbies with the detritus of mass cultural unconscious. This mystifying time capsule—its contents all cheaply available from thrift stores—constitutes an ironic disquisition on the self as an accretion of text, the commodification of confession, and the infelicities of taste.

Joining the Bay Area community that prized experimental readings and ad hoc performance art, Blake began composing performance scripts in the vein of their twin influences Acker and Foreman. "Performance Script" (1990) enacts the textual suturing of the kind of paperbacks in the sculptures, juxtaposing excerpts from the memoirs of actress Patty Duke and drag queen Margo Howard-Howard and James Spada's celebrity biography *Judy and Liza* (1983) with their narrative critical examination of William Friedkin's controversial thriller *Cruising* (1980), set in New York's gay leather bars. Other performance scripts form mosaics from disparate sources: Sybil Leek's *Diary of a Witch* (1968), novelizations of the television shows *The Partridge Family* and *Star Trek*, Elizabeth L. Ray's *The Washington*

Fringe Benefit (1976), and Pamela Des Barres's ultimate tell-all, *I'm with the Band: Confessions of a Groupie* (1987). Often these different voices are stitched together with the preface "a fan writes" in which the voice of the devotee/expert moves kaleidoscopically from confession to critique. The authorial *I* of the shifting first-person material, delivered in the same tone, is culturally and psychologically unlocatable, rendered fluid, delimiting a queer subject position.

These collaged performance texts evolved within San Francisco's New Narrative movement, cofounded in the 1970s by writer Robert Glück, referring more to a decidedly queer shared sensibility than to formal connections and uniting writers as different as Kathy Acker, Dennis Cooper, Kevin Killian, and Dodie Bellamy. Glück retrospectively characterized their overlapping attitudes: "We brought gossip and anecdote to our writing because they contain speaker and audience, establish the parameters of community and trumpet their 'unfair' points of view. I hardly ever 'made things up,' a plot still seems exotic, but as a collagist I had an infinite field. I could use the lives we endlessly described to each other as 'found material' which complicates storytelling because the material also exists on the same plane as the reader's life. Found materials have a kind of radiance, the truth of the already-known."[4]

The freedom of these experiments opened the door to short fiction for the first time since Blake's teen years, inspiring them to write a science-fiction parable called "Queer Mysteries" (1993) for the exhibition of the same name by David Cannon Dashiell. The story was a pendant to a speculative fiction by Rebecca Solnit set in the deep past; Blake's contribution envisioned a queer genderless posthuman future. Both texts ran imaginatively parallel to the art rather than explicating it. "The Story of H (Excerpt)," which Blake wrote for their zine *Bunny Butt* (1994) as a parody of Pauline Reage's *Story of O* (1954), describes its protagonist permanently sewn into a bunny costume by a cruel Master, Andre, in a fragment of S&M fantasy: "Once inside the outfit, H had looked into the mirror. Staring back at him was a ludicrous figure, a six-foot-tall rabbit with silly booties and a pair of ears that bobbed with the slightest movement of his head. The suit hung from his shoulders, flaring at the waist and giving the impression of a wide and low-hanging ass that the cottony tail did nothing to dispel."

Picked up on the spur of the moment at a shop on Hollywood Boulevard, the rabbit suit first entered Blake's work as a costume for performing "The Saddest Story I Know." It has become a central surrogate ever since, morphing in scale and function—from custom-made suits to ready-made

Jarrett Earnest

stuffed animals—allowing allusions to slide from the traditional West African trickster to Br'er Rabbit to Bugs Bunny. It entered the repertory of disguises, puppets, toys, props, and restraints that has formed Blake's unique visual grammar since the late 1980s.

In 1991 Blake co-organized the trailblazing exhibition *Situation: Perspectives on Work by Lesbian and Gay Artists* with Los Angeles–based curator Pam Gregg at New Langton Arts. The show included recent work by a diverse group including G. B. Jones, Hunter Reynolds, Martin Wong, Carrie Yamaoka, Catherine Opie, and Rex Ray, among others. Strikingly, in their brief "Curator's Note," Blake introduces an anti-essentialist framework for thinking about queer art: "These artists are willing to adopt any voice, from art historical, to psychoanalytic, to documentary, to pop cultural, in order to make that voice speak queerly. This is a marked departure from previous attempts to essentialize gay voices. These artists do not assume any sort of truly gay way of making work. Instead, they use a position of gayness to skew standard ways of making and reading."[5] This radical proposition blossomed four years later in the exhibition *In a Different Light* at the Berkeley Art Museum. It was one of the most consequential shows in the nascent field of queer art history and an expansive proposal of "queer sensibility" as a lens on making and being. Cocurated with Lawrence Rinder, the exhibition was organized into overlapping constellations, sexual and social as much as aesthetic. In an attempt to map a lineage in which histories and identifications constitute a central concern, Blake writes in their curatorial essay:

> The extremely provisional nature of queer culture is the thing that makes its transmission so fragile. However, this very fragility has encouraged people to seek retroactively its contours in a degree not often found in other groups. Queer people must literally construct the houses they will be born into and adopt their own parents. . . .
>
> From the margins, queers have picked those things that could work for them and recoded them and rewritten their meanings, opening up the possibility of viral reinsertion into the body of general discourse. Denied images of themselves, they have changed the captions on others' family photos. Left without cultural vehicles, they have hijacked somebody else's.

Here we see a theorization and articulation of the procedures that have animated so much of Blake's own output as a writer, sculptor, and performer. They go on to sketch a little parable of history that unsurprisingly aligns with the contours of Blake's intellectual and artistic development, tracing the permissive sign of Duchamp ready-mades through radical film and theater, Fluxus and performance and conceptual art, feminist art, and punk—linking subcultural practices of zines, flyers, street art, and AIDS activism. Nine thematic groupings are proposed, moving from solitary absence and grief in increasing social units, eventually encompassing a holistic visionary social order: void, self, drag, other, couple/family, orgy, world, utopia. This ever-entangled, enlarging vision is not limited to the individual psyche or a set of discrete acts and as such remains the most capacitating conception of queerness. Blake's explication of these sections flashes with ingenious and sometimes provocative interpretations. Take, for instance: "Robert Gober's *Plywood* (1987) is drag in a different key. Gober uses painstaking individual craft to make an object that seems simply mass produced. The plywood is a high-class (unique, handmade) object masquerading as a lower-class one. It also plays on the history of minimal sculpture, evoking the 'humble' materials used by many artists in their efforts to avoid artifice. Gober provides what is in essence a second layer of artifice, making a sculpture that looks like the raw material for the sculpture." This short paragraph, which constitutes one of the great instances of art criticism on its own terms, could have come only from a maker—someone who has thought deeply about the physical and cultural implications of material. It provides an indispensable lens through which to rethink Gober's labor-intensive objects and, beyond that, all the kinds of stuff that populate our lives in the world.

At the essay's conclusion, Blake issues a warning that frames their subsequent relationship with the art world and the work they do as a writer within it: "As it is presently constituted, the mainstream art world is a system for the production, exhibition, valorization, and distribution of the work of heterosexual white men. As long as queer people look to it for their sole source of recognition, they will be disappointed. A few will be picked, as long as they can keep their noses clean, and the rest will be condemned to their 'one-dimensional' life on the sidelines. It is up to queer artists not to wait around for approval but to become agents in the development and support of the work that they value."

In 1996 Nayland Blake left San Francisco and returned to New York City. There they began work on *Hare Follies*, a performance commissioned by the Brooklyn Academy of Music in the third year of their Artists in Action series. Created in collaboration with musician Chris Cochrane and choreographers Patricia Hoffbauer and Ishmael Houston-Jones, it would be

Blake's most ambitious spectacle to date, its script the culmination of the collage methodology Blake had developed over the preceding decade. Taking cues from the history of minstrelsy and turn-of-the-century vaudeville, Blake's script combines stretches of the blaxploitation film *Blacula* (1972) with racist texts such as Dion Boucicault's play *The Octoroon* (1859) and William Luther Price's hate tract *The Turner Diaries* (1978), broken into bits, pulverized into a swirling textual DNA of the racial imaginary. The performance is in dialogue with two works that greatly influenced it: Reza Abdoh's *Tight Right White* (1993)—itself a debauched deconstruction of the film *Mandingo* (1975)—and Darius James's genre-defying fantasia of America's unconscious, *Negrophobia: An Urban Parable* (1992). As a text "Hare Follies" (1997) is the fullest and most complicated examination of Blake's own Blackness, specifically the experience of being a white-passing Black person and the complex system of signification around race and eroticism, violence and sexuality, images and words—the conflicting mythologies that inhabit a self.

Hare Follies marks an important turning point in Blake's trajectory, shifting from the verbally discursive to the materially embodied. Blake's anti-essentialist and provisional definition of queerness was now worked through their own raced, classed, and gendered body, allowing experiences of physical pain or pleasure to guide. This tracks Blake's becoming more deeply involved in kink and S&M communities, where the social-sexual space of the dungeon emerged as the extension of the artist's studio. The video performance *Gorge* (2000) is emblematic; in it, Blake, stripped to the waist and sitting in front of a white wall with a clock, is fed a succession of food and drink—doughnuts, pizza, a hero sandwich, watermelon, and chocolates, punctuated with sparkling water and quantities of milk—by another shirtless, darker-skinned Black man. A mind-numbing loop of the 1950s song "The Bunny Hop" plays in the background. Notably, not a word is said, but the complex communication between them speaks loudly. Exhibited beside the sculpture *Feeder 2* (1998), a life-size three-dimensional gingerbread house with cookie panels held together by steel armature, the video marks a synthesis of Blake's art and kink practices—a kind of coming out as part of the kink scene of gainer/encouragers (eroticizing increasing physical size). Subsequent performances of *Gorge* took place live with the audience feeding the artist in homage to Yoko Ono's *Cut Piece* (1964).

As Blake freed their artistic work from the burden of language, they turned to more straightforward writing for magazines like *Artforum* and museum and exhibition catalogs. In the late 1990s and early 2000s, Blake's brilliant and authoritative essays on Jack Smith, Ray Johnson, Nancy Grossman, and Anthony Friedkin further articulated the alternative histories Blake had advocated for from the beginning. Essays on peers such as James Gobel, Matthew Benedict, Judie Bamber, and Jim Hodges extended the notion of art as an intergenerational knot. These texts stand out within the terrain of art criticism not only for the clarity of purpose—the implicit declaration that all these artists have collaborated in building a world in which Blake themself is more vividly and comfortably recognized—but also for the insights of a mind concerned with larger lineages of making and being.

One of the most striking essays from this time is Blake's complicated engagement with artistic influence and personal friendship, confronting a figure who had loomed so large for so long: Kathy Acker. Written ten years after her death, "Kathy Acker: 'Because I Want to Live Forever in Wonder'" (2006) reflects on their shifting relationship, from fan to collaborator and friend, over a twenty-five-year period. Blake talks about the intensity of their identification with her as an artist, commissioning her to write a text for their first New York show, *Low*, in 1990. In retrospect, Blake's consideration of that piece shifts, but so does their sense of their own intention, a desire to become a character in Acker's art, for a returned fervor.

> It doesn't work that way. Even though queers can choose their tribe, artists can't choose their clan—the clutch of people who will see their work for what it is and value it—any more than one can choose the person who's going to fall in love with you. Artistic communication is more complex than simple identification. My own convictions about the similarities in what we did were no guarantee that she would see it that way. I hadn't reckoned on the one thing that we perhaps had most in common: the highly cultivated narcissism we each used to make our work.

This kind of personal interrogation is also evident in Blake's role as a public lecturer and speaker on queer histories and subcultures. Included here are three representative interviews, from 1993, 2008, and 2018, charting the evolution of Blake's thinking in relation to kink and queer subcultures. A number of Socratic pedagogical texts are also included, such as the workbook for their 2012 show *Free! Love! Tool! Box!* (which includes questions like "What is the best thing about your body?" and "What is your most powerful piece of clothing and why?" for generative self-examination), expanded in the list "100 Assignments: Toward a Curriculum." These kinds of directions are extended in notes for a workshop on "status play" Blake teaches in kink gatherings. Blake advises that an essential aspect of defining one's comfort within the limits of a sexual scene is a commitment to discovering the unconscious structures of desire:

> What are the things they value? Ask them about what they value in others and how others see them.
>
> Who do they believe they are better than? People are trained not to reveal this information directly, so you have to listen carefully for it.
>
> What are their core beliefs about themselves, those things they would hate to lose?

Blake's ambition has always been much larger than objects displayed in a gallery or museum, and their vision has pushed to account for the absences that have produced and that insulate the contemporary art world. On its own terms, it seeks to bring forth another world. A sustaining characteristic of that world is its multivalence—a life practice that interweaves criticism, curating, teaching, art history, queer history, the erotic and marginalized, and the shifting technologies of the body and self that S&M explores. What emerges is an artist who refuses to separate or diminish any part of their life and loves in favor of any other. Their writing is a record of their commitment to an embodied "now" that entails dredging up sometimes thorny figures from the past, which, of course, opens into our shared fantasies. This incredible advocacy, with its philosophical and aesthetic implications, is breezily summed up by Blake's dictum: "Teach it. Promote it. Create it. You are responsible for the continuation of the culture you love. Keep it alive through your actions."[6]

This is a book meant to be read in fits and starts, misread, and remade by what is done with it. It's a self-theorizing primary source for not only queer histories but queerer futures, wherein different kinds of writing are woven together as they appeared, unable to be separated into discrete categories like "performance script," "art review," or "lecture." Many of these pieces are preceded by short, chatty remarks by the artist, helping situate their specific contexts within the unfolding arguments of the book. The cover Blake created for the book is a direct re-creation of and response to the seminal "Polysexuality" issue of *Semiotext(e)*, whose organizational mélange provided the guiding inspiration for the layout. In the introduction of that issue, François Peraldi described the large black-and-white details that unfurl throughout his issue as an artistic and conceptual whole: "Polysexuality is not only a set of texts written by carefully chosen authors and illustrating the plural aspects of sexuality. Polysexuality is a text in itself, the editor of which are the authors. Let's call it a collage or a textual patch-work, if you prefer. It tells what the reality of sex has always been with respect to alienation to 'usurp' and exploitation."[7] With this model in mind, Blake has patched together a visual essay in *My Studio Is a Dungeon Is the Studio*, visually punctuating the texts and fusing them into a wildly textured collage, cutting across forty years, two coasts, and a wide array of histories. The text leads by example; it shows the reader what to do with it. If you don't like its objects or sensibilities, it models how you can do something about it. If you love it, it urges you to do something else with it too. Either way—it's now up to you.

Notes

1. Richard Foreman, "How I Write My (Self: Plays)," in *The Manifestos and Essays* (New York: Theatre Communications Group, 2013) (1977), 99.

2. Kathy Acker, *My Death My Life by Pier Paolo Pasolini*, in *Literal Madness* (New York: Grove Press, 1988), 292.

3. Joanna Russ, "Pornography by Women for Women, with Love," in *The Fan Fiction Studies Reader*, edited by Karen Hellekson and Kristina Busse (Iowa City: University of Iowa Press, 2014), 87.

4. Robert Glück, "Long Note on New Narrative," https://poets.org/text/long-note-new-narrative, accessed January 16, 2025.

5. Nayland Blake, "Curator's Note," in *Situation: Perspectives on Work by Lesbian and Gay Artists* (San Francisco: New Langton Arts, 1991), unpaginated.

6. Nayland Blake, http://www.naylandblake.net/, accessed July 5, 2024.

7. François Peraldi, ed., "Polysexuality," *Semiotext(e)* no. 10 (1981), unpaginated.

THE DIFFICULTIES THAT AFFLICT US IN ART SCHOOL

Previously Unpublished, 1983

This was written in response to the culture I found at CalArts (California Institute of the Arts). At that time visiting artist talks were like a blood sport where someone would present their work, and there was a competition to see which of the students in the audience would take them down first. It was exhausting and horrifying. It extended to class critique, where students spent most of their time coming up with a defensible thesis, regardless of whether or not they were making work. Some stopped making work altogether. It seemed inhumane. So this is my little cri de coeur *about that, addressed to my fellow students: "Stop being so mean." I include it now because so much that's in it continues to ring out to me, particularly the stuff about devaluing the act of making art and hiding within a career ambition, rather than having ambition about everything you could address through the act of making art itself. —NB*

The difficulties that afflict us in the art school are not caused by the preeminence of any particular doctrine or discipline but rather the background against which all approaches are considered. What is lacking is a basic faith in the ability of art practice to produce meaning. From this lack of faith there follows an air of guilt and suspicion, enveloping the people involved in this practice. Guilt—because somehow, by making art, they are getting away with not doing anything real—and suspicion of others for doing the same thing. This atmosphere can only produce division among us.

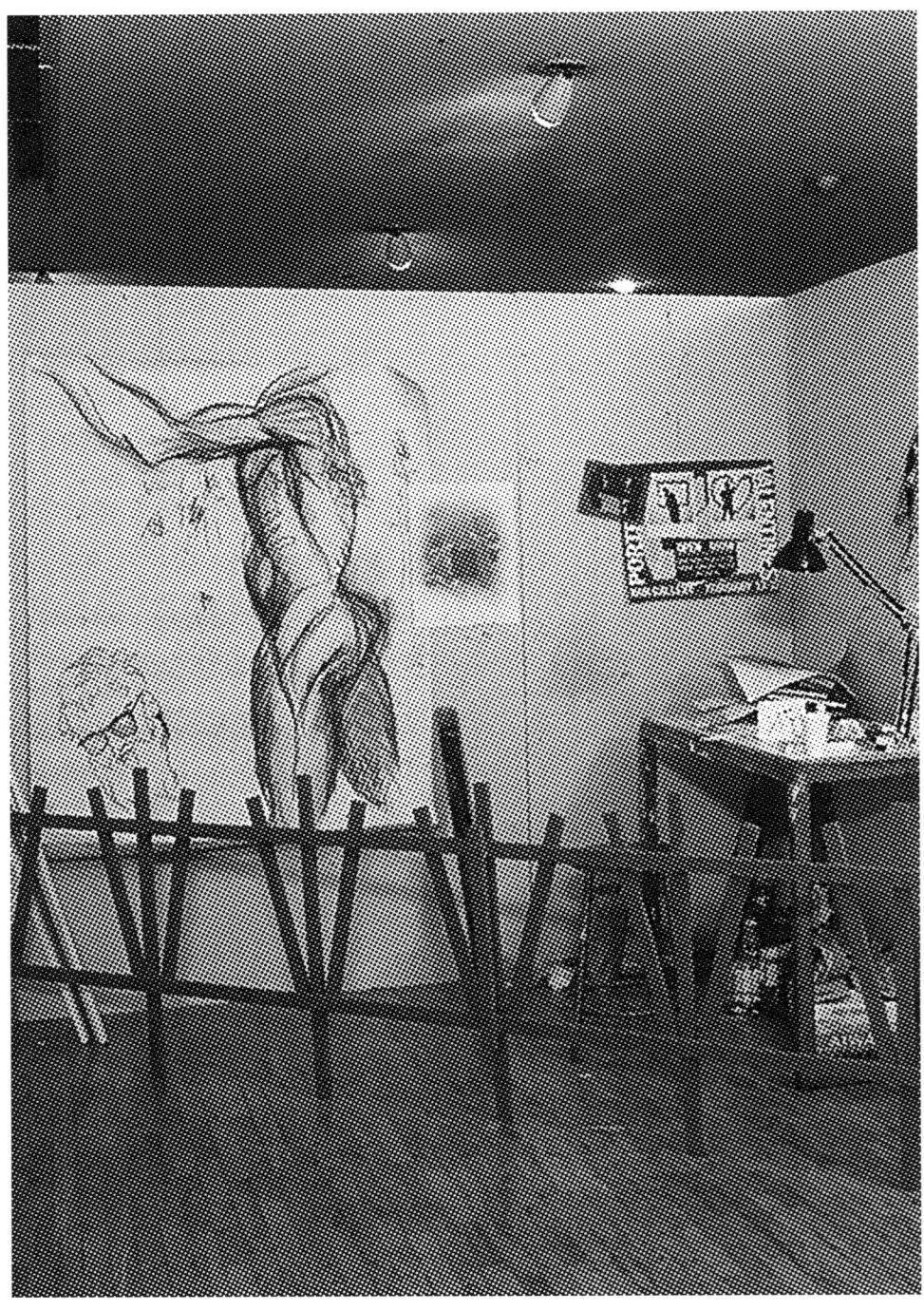

At this point, I am going to introduce the word *respect*. It is both strange and wrong that we refuse to respect each other. I don't mean respecting each other for besting us in an argument, nor do I mean for us to respect each other and revere each other. I am speaking about respecting each other for our willingness to engage in the process of making art. In our negative attitude, we mirror the society we live in. It does not respect the act of making art or the people involved in that act. It attempts to ignore them as much as possible. When it must take notice of them, it is usually to either condemn them as cranks or express a pleased surprise at their ability to make some money. There is no faith in the notion of art to affect anything at all.

We are all in art school for a reason. I like to think that the reason has to do with the fact that we have in some way been touched, excited, engaged, or enraptured by works of art. Given the societal pressures around us, I cannot see much other motivation for choosing art as a discipline, as an approach to life. At some point, we must have a vision of art making as being a good thing, a thing that is more beneficial than stockbroking or striking. What is then awful is the way in which we betray that vision within ourselves by refusing to acknowledge it in others. We produce a language of defense to hide that knowledge from others and a language of attack to deride that knowledge when we find it elsewhere. Against this background of suspicion, differences of approach take on a meaning that they should not have, and people feel critiques are moments that will make or break them—not only personally but professionally. They react by either building immense defenses or removing themselves from the arena entirely. Certain attitudes are shown to withstand assault better than others and are, in an odd way, validated. Thus, the academy looms before us, but it is one we have built out of our own forgetfulness and lack of recognition—forgetfulness of the thing that made us begin to make art in the first place and an unwillingness to recognize that thing in others. It is the walls of that academy that we fidget within now, waiting for release.

Artists are not holy, and they should not be treated as such. Nor is art sacred and beyond comment or reproach: But this willingness to make art a part of one's life is something we should place more value on. It is something no one else will encourage us to do, and it will be better if we learn to encourage each other now.

ASSESSING MY WORK

Previously Unpublished, 1984

I'm the inheritor of a particular method of art making that involves a lot of research and mental processes but results in something physical. I wrote this in grad school as a first attempt to understand that, to speak it to myself. I was still trying to claim space without being pinned down. —NB

In trying to assess my work over the past two years, I have come to a realization about my work habits and the way they are influenced by my patterns of social behavior. While liking work that appears casual or dumb, I am extremely concerned with making it known that I am not dumb or, in some way, incapable. Perhaps this attitude may be summed up thus, "Of course, I can do what you want me to do, but I choose to do this." During my four years at Bard, I had ample time to display my ability for making the formally oriented work that was the encouraged norm there. Having satisfied the faculty's criteria, I could then set about doing what I was interested in doing. In other words, I made sure they knew I was "smart," so that the "dumb" work would get its proper reading.

When I came to CalArts, I carried this mechanism (pattern? neurosis?) along with me. In a less rigidly defined environment, however, the criteria were harder to locate. The attempts to placate authority, whether located in the faculty or my friends, became more attempts to satisfy criteria that I was projecting onto the environment. The work became increasingly divided between works that were calculated to provoke approval or commentary and works that were purely "for me." The process itself became very alienating,

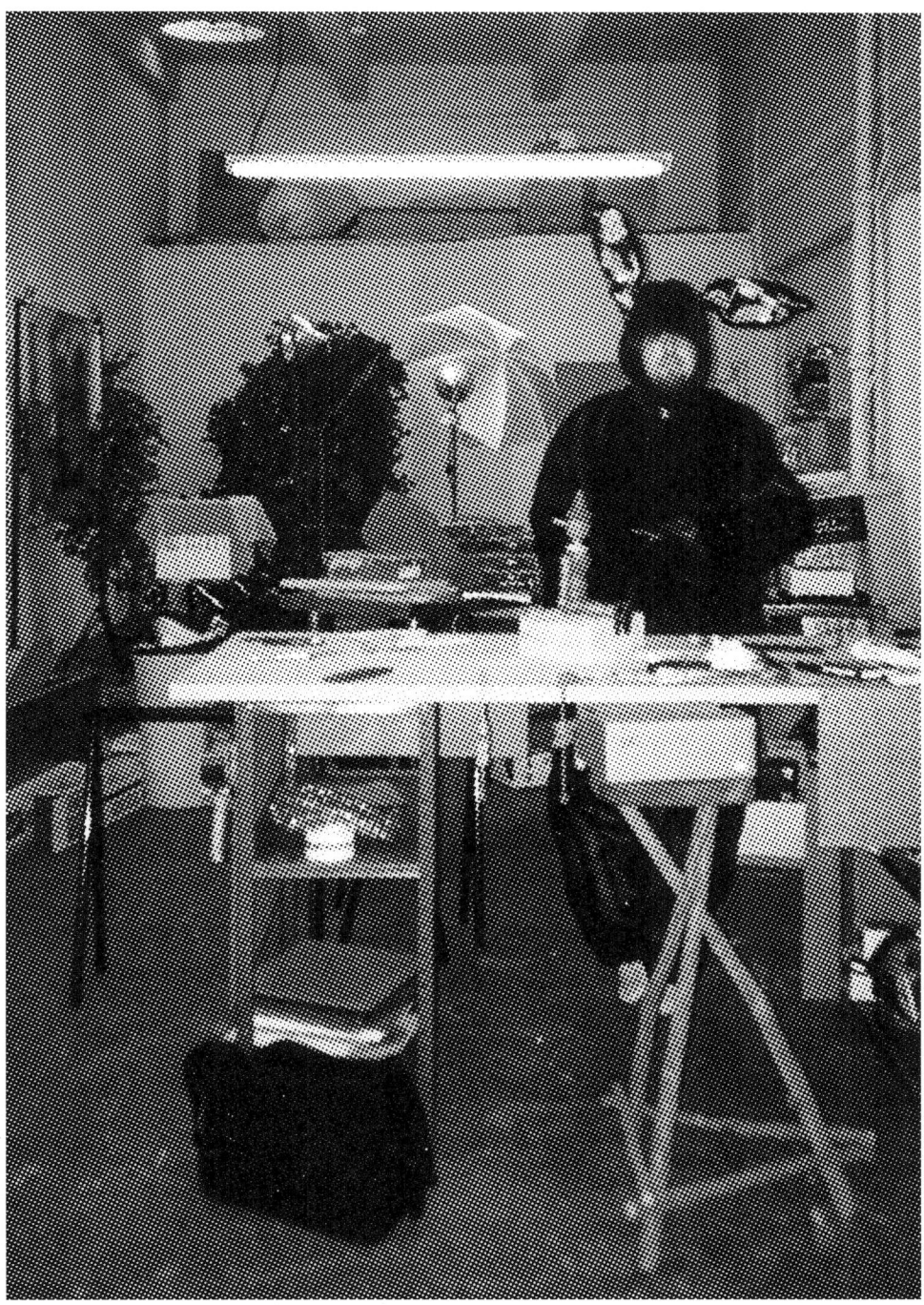

veering as it did between artificialities and emotional outbursts. As I look at the work now, it is difficult to say that it has much value.

In trying to write some sort of summation of my time here, I went back to look at the statement I made upon applying here. The following things strike me: I no longer have the same yearnings to be a folk artist that I did then, and I've been trying to get rid of the faux-naïf touches in my work.

While I wished to avoid the chess game atmosphere of the painting debate, it is the spirit I have found invading my activities here more and more. Some of this is due to an increased awareness of history and theory.

Things that I was able to point to as interests and pleasures have become blurred and difficult to locate. My decrying of signature style has led me to make work that, to me now, looks disconnected and restless. Every work has a story behind it, but the stories do not seem to point to any unified way of seeing.

As the works have become more disparate, it has become harder to edit them together. This has changed my attitude toward installations. For a final piece this semester, I started working on an installation for my studio. After I had finished the planning stages and began building the piece, I realized I was going to have to make all of the components from scratch—something I had neither the time nor the money to do. This was a far cry from the notion of using what I had on hand, and the blockbuster aspects of it struck me as wasteful and excessive.

TOM OF FINLAND:
AN APPRECIATION

OUT/LOOK, 1988

Much of what I was doing at CalArts (California Institute of the Arts) was an attempt to think about "gay identity and presentation" both personally and culturally. Tom of Finland loomed large both as an underground artist and as someone whose work I was aroused and frustrated by. Years later, when I was living in San Francisco, the editors at OUT/LOOK came to me with the assignment to write about and interview Tom. One of the things that I'm proudest about in it is that it adopts multiple viewpoints, doesn't necessarily say that any one of them is conclusive, but also really tries to talk about how the work operates in the world. Throughout my writing I've been trying to argue for the validity and reality of queer expression by talking about the way that I see it operate, not by pleading a case for it in an "art context." Pornography is still not acceptable in an art context because art contexts don't cultivate pleasurable embodiment. And pornography is an aid for us to know our bodies. It is a technology about bodily awareness. That's just always going to be an effect. —NB

Tom of Finland is one of the gay world's few authentic icons. For over thirty years, his drawings have appeared in gay magazines and circulated in pirate editions. His men have entered the fantasy life of thousands, and his vision has influenced such artists as Robert Mapplethorpe, Bruce Weber, and Rainer Werner Fassbinder. Though his popularity has waxed and waned, he has remained modest about his work and committed to the making of it. He was born in Finland, where he worked as an illustrator and art director for an advertising firm. He first came to America in 1978 and now divides his time between Europe and California, where he has established a foundation to promote his work and an archive to preserve and protect it.

Tom's work is diverse. His drawings are at once a system of gay erotics, utopian documents, historical texts, formal puzzles, memories, and love letters. All of this takes place in the context of an effective pornography. This essay is an attempt to present the various ways in which Tom's work might be used to illuminate other areas of sexuality and cultural history. To do this, it is useful to use a model of several "Toms." Each might be understood to exist in separate but overlapping locations and to articulate different vantage points. Each is one-dimensional and, as such, far from any final truth about who Tom is. Taken together, however, they can indicate the diverse nature of Tom's production and the many options available to the person who looks at it.

Tom the Pornographer

Tom's work has been left on the sidelines of any debate about gay sensibility because it is pornography. Pornography remains a taboo: We consume it but will not commit to it. Yet when the history of gay images and representations is written, it will contain a large section on our pornographers. In a milieu that has produced a new connoisseurship of sexual acts, what we arouse ourselves with speaks eloquently about who we are.

Because of the marginalization of pornographic practice, Tom's work has been pirated, his earnings have been stolen by booksellers and art dealers, and his impact as a producer of powerful signs has been ignored by the same gay community he helped to create. It is time to invert the value placed on the production and consumption of pornography and to instead look to it to provide understanding of who we are and how we are.

Tom draws. Most current discussion tends to focus on photographic pornography, treating all other forms as sidelights or subsets of it. But there are important differences between a drawn and a photographic image. Photographic pornography operates as evidence—the documentation that certain acts took place before the camera. Drawings, however, function in a way akin to writing; they provide the props for the viewer to hang a fantasy on rather than a specific person for the viewer to be aroused by. Tom comprehends that his drawings are not renditions of reality. His "men" are machines for fucking—like exotic sofas—and they are constructed accordingly. Unlike the subject of a photograph, their brawn is not the product of endless grooming. Their bodies are not a reproach to our own but an opportunity for luxury.

Tom constructed his ideal gay body on paper. Because of his position as a pornographer, he was able to disseminate his ideas about that body to a sympathetic underground of gay men in Europe and America, to modify and embellish it, and finally to see it celebrated as a central fixture of gay culture.

Tom the Artist

Every work of cultural criticism has its own project. For years, gay cultural critics have been locked into a project of assimilation into the dominant culture. They expect the gay community to produce figures that will stand alongside the masters by satisfying criteria of impact, technique, or seriousness of purpose. We are constantly presented with a parade of gay artists raised to mastery or snatched from the mainstream canon by their critics or publicists. In recent years, we have seen this project attempted with such artists as David Hockney, George Platt Lynes, and Caravaggio. But the urge to "take someone seriously" and confer respectability through placement in art history can easily be a disservice to the artist. Paul Cadmus, for instance, is an artist whose rehabilitation is complete, whose work has been successfully termed both gay and high art.

Cadmus began his career in the 1930s. He was a student of Reginald Marsh and worked on several projects for the Works Progress Administration (WPA). His most famous moment came when he was commissioned to produce a painting for the US Navy and presented them with a portrait of boozy sailors whoring on leave. The resulting scandal thrust him into the mainstream until the schools of postwar abstraction eclipsed his own representational style. In the late 1970s, his reputation was revived by increased interest in the WPA period, and by his lionization in the gay press. But Cadmus's work can only be described as tangential to the entire thrust of modern art. Its overwhelming characteristic is the desire to be taken seriously, to be high art. It attempts to convince us by displaying all the signifiers of mastery: coy allusion to other paintings, meticulous rendering, a tendency to caricature divorced from any real perception, and a slavish devotion to antique craftsmanship (in his case egg tempera—which was supposed to show that the painting took a long time and wasn't easy to make). But the result of such labors is kitsch. Kitsch reassures the bourgeois audience that they are receiving their proper dosage of culture. Progressive politics cannot arise from conservative aesthetics, and to promote Cadmus to a place within the world of museum art is to win a hollow victory for gay politics.

For Cadmus depicts gay people in an ambivalent fashion. In his early work, gay sexuality is slipped in on the sidelines, often with the artist as a knowing spectator winking at the audience. Later, history allowed him the luxury of painting beefcake. Cadmus's paintings are either social commentaries peppered with a series of grotesque homosexual "types" or, in a painting like his *What I Believe*, sentimentalized hymns to a gay middle-brow heaven.

Tom cites Cadmus as an influence, but his work is different in tone and intent. He is skeptical of attempts to classify his work as high art, preferring the terms "fantasy drawings" or "dirty pictures." His images relate to the man in the street far more than to the pantheon of great artists. His work is not an apologia for homosexuality but a direct document of it. With Tom, there are no great themes or high-blown rhetoric but great communication. The fact that his work is utilitarian, that its aim is sexual arousal, means that it cannot make claims to distance or a transhistorical resonance. Tom sacrifices the grand for the immediate. It is his success at this that makes him a much more interesting figure in discussions of gay identity.

Tom the Craftsman

"I wanted to develop a photorealist style." One of the most striking and transgressive features of Tom's drawings is their polish—the obsessive way in which they are rendered. The viewer's attention is shifted away from considering the quality of the line (in the way that we would speak of Henri Matisse's line) to the object or activity that is being depicted. Rendering strives to be seamless, obscuring the process of its own making. In the twentieth century, work that has attempted to hide the process of its making has almost always been allied with extreme aesthetic and political conservatism.

Two examples of this would be Soviet socialist realism and the paintings of Norman Rockwell. They share the same concern as Tom's work does with the fetishized representation of things "as they really are." This last phrase is the most important because it is the project of this work to construct the reality it purports to depict. Such work revives the timeworn metaphor of painting as a mirror to create a fantasy reality and make us believe it as well.

Like Tom, Norman Rockwell worked for years as an illustrator and commercial artist before anyone ever claimed his work was fine art. If you tour the Rockwell Museum in Stockbridge, Massachusetts, you will be treated to endless reminders of how long the paintings took to execute, how exacting

My Studio Is a Dungeon Is the Studio

Rockwell was, and how his models were drawn from the people around him. Not a word will be said about the real agenda of Rockwell's work, which is the construction of a phantom America, where people have disagreements but not differences, where social issues are the occasion for damp sympathy or sly chuckles but not action, and where everything "feels like home." Rockwell supports a type of antihistoricism in the name of American ideals: A bumbling clerk or American soldier looks exactly like his colonial forebears; children commune with the spirit of George Washington; a young man giving a speech bears an uncanny resemblance to Abraham Lincoln. His work achieves its effect by its obsessive rendering (which panders to our wish to see ourselves in the mirror it proffers) without saying it is not our image we see but only its own distorted editorializing.

Socialist realism (the art movement promoted by Joseph Stalin in the early 1930s) has a similar goal. Its aim is the creation, through their depiction, of attitudes proper to the ideal communist state. Its style is a hybrid of nineteenth-century salon painting with the neoclassicism of late art deco. As the official government style, it succeeded in silencing some of the most important art of the twentieth century. Soviet artists moved from the vanguard of ideas in painting, filmmaking, and architecture to become obscure state functionaries. Works that treated the viewer as anything other than a passive receptor for the "correct attitudes" of the propagandists were driven underground. Like Rockwell, the Soviet artists were using arguments of naturalism and realism as a cover for their own political program, and like Rockwell, they relied on the technique of scrupulous depiction to seduce and convince the viewer. It is telling that the works produced under socialist realism began to look like those produced in Nazi Germany.

The burly workers and farmers who stride through socialist realism's paintings and sculptures are not-too-distant relatives of the sailors and cops whose orgies Tom lovingly depicts. Tom, too, is constructing a fantasy world, but with different aims. He is calling into being a world suffused with gay sexuality, using the power of his craft to validate his fantasies.

Tom the Narrator

Tom says, "I wanted to show a world where gays could be freer, not so afraid." He draws an idealized world of sexual courtship and activity that is at once a projection of his own private fantasies about gay behavior and a public articulation of possibilities within the gay community.

The rules of this utopia are spelled out through narrative. Tom uses narrative in two ways. The first is within the individual drawing. We see figures gesture to one another while in the background, a third is enticed toward the scene. A knot of flesh reveals itself to be a series of sexual acts, the individual articulations of which rest like beads on a strand: Here a crotch is being grabbed; here, a neck bitten.

Often, when we feel we have solved this sexual puzzle, there is an unexpected conjunction: A body is given a half twist; a foot is wedged to stroke an asshole. Such moments in the drawings are like turns in the plot. A new erotic site is revealed, and the drawings move from sexual excitement to repletion.

The second use of narrative is the linking up of various drawings into a series. In this, they begin to resemble novels or films more than photographs, displaying the possibilities for sexual conjunction between characters. We anticipate combinations: What if Kake (one of Tom's heroes) fucks this cop who is arriving? Or, if the situation reverses, is that cock sucked later on? The erotic is displaced from an object to a terrain of figures and their possible interactions. Narrative opens up the image; it denies it an authority of hierarchy.

A narrative exists throughout Tom's work as a whole. This is because certain characters have continued to appear in his work for thirty years— not only the heroes Kake and Pekka but the bit players as well. Tom's figures are as generalized in their appearance as they are particularized in their acts. Their similarity makes us feel at home. This is a world we recognize, but it's without the boundaries on our desires.

Tom the Sensualist

Tom is the poet of texture. Notice the characteristics of flesh in his work. Flesh as it is compacted into springy mass, as it pushes from between fingers, as it is ridged during fucking. Tom's men are massive, and it is this sense of the impact of flesh on flesh that provides erotic charge. His bodies are pneumatic and well upholstered—and at the same time pouty.

In Western art, the pout is a potent sexual signifier. It is a fullness (the skin is near to bursting with the flesh that lies beneath it) and at the same time a slackening, a slight droop that connotes a leisure, a gentle lassitude. In Tom, not only the lips but the eyes, the bellies, even the cocks, seem to pout, to be packed with a sexual energy that expresses itself in a slight but significant bulging. It is this flesh that pouts, through clothes and across streets, that produces the heavy air of sex in Tom's world.

Tom is adept at portraying the texture of leather boots and jackets, the starch of uniforms, the tension and give of denim. He admits that it was the

British who first drew his attention to the world of leather, and he is perhaps its most faithful depicter. His leather is shiny and beautifully heavy, draping the men of his drawings with a sort of solemnity. This drapery frames the erotic object; clothing is often retained far into the sex act. The textures and bits of uniform are the variables that allow us to sort out who is who among Tom's generalized figures.

Tom the Voyeur

Most pornography of the image is constructed around the framework of the gaze. The gaze can be understood as the eye as phallus—a powerful and penetrative organ. In most pornography, the object presents itself to the gaze, welcomes its penetration, and is rendered passive by it. In Tom's work, there is surprisingly little of the singular, phallic gaze. Instead, he presents a network of looks. Often, he inserts figures observing the activities into the margins of his drawings. There is a heightened sense of people putting themselves on display.

Two fully clothed men lean against a tree. They look out onto a street where other men cruise and make gestures of sexual enticement. After a while, we realize that the men are fucking. This drawing is not an invitation to us, the viewers, but it is powerfully erotic because of the combination of the men's casual looks and their position as part of an entire world of fucking. Like those of the men, our eyes are invited to roam. This allows for a double current of attraction/participation rather than the single current of gazer/object of the gaze. No longer interested in desire and its implied lack, Tom substitutes a pleasure of looking and being looked at—equating the cruising look with the sexual act.

Tom the Fascist

"Whoever designed the Nazi uniforms had to be gay. Those were the sexiest men I have ever seen in my life."[1] Tom's earliest sexual experiences were with German soldiers during the occupation of Helsinki. He talked about this romantic involvement in an interview with David Reed in *Christopher Street*. His first drawings were attempts to re-create those experiences and fantasies.

The first time I read the above quote, two things came to mind: first, the debate then raging over the meaning of the fashion of leather and uniforms for gay men and, second, the visual similarity between Tom's drawings and the heroic neoclassicism that had been the court style under the fascist regimes of the 1920s through the 1940s.

Can Tom's work be said to provide a direct link between the Übermensch ideals of Nazi Germany and the so-called fascist undercurrents in the gay uniform craze? And by extension, can Tom's work be called fascist?

In Tom's utopian world, roles exist, but power is fluid. He is the keenest depicter of the erotics of lubricious power. Cops may have authority, and a uniformed man may begin to flog his prisoner, but these situations will soon reverse themselves as the cop bends over to be fucked, and the man in the uniform allows himself to be bound. Tom understands that the pleasure of S&M is the successful fulfillment of a role while maintaining the understanding that it is a role. "It is more playful, like acting," he says. There is also a high degree of humor in the drawings, and even when there are scenes of beating or bondage, they are suffused with an avuncular attitude that is difficult to resolve with the notion of fascism.

Some maintain that the symbol itself holds power, that to use it is to invoke all that it has stood for. At the opposite extreme are those who claim that a symbol, like the swastika, is utterly neutral and that it is the viewer's responsibility to get past any negative connotations that it may have had. Both positions contain a certain amount of self-willed naivete. By itself, a symbol is a neutral arrangement of lines, but symbols are never by themselves. Like all signifiers, they are the product of specific historical circumstances.

After the experience of Nazi Germany, it is impossible to claim that its symbols are neutral. However, it is equally wrong to say that once symbols acquire a meaning, that meaning is fixed forever. The meaning of phrases and images does shift depending on who uses them. While Tom's drawings utilize a style of representation popular under fascism, it would be a mistake to say that even those that contain Nazi imagery are fascist in intent or effect.

Tom himself expresses misgivings about drawings he made early in his career. "People saw them in a political way because they had Nazis in them. They thought I was a Nazi. I would not do them today because I do not want people to see them that way—they are my fantasies." Through an understanding of the traumatic effect that they have on people, Tom has removed the drawings that contain Nazi figures from circulation. This is a case in which his private fantasies were not shared by a larger public. Tom also talks about subjects that are too violent for him. "They (people with commissions) asked me to do pictures like of balls being cut off or stomaches [*sic*] opened with all the organs. . . . I could not do them."

A fascist art is one that seeks to silence opposition by means of its own authority, one that uses scale and impersonality to produce power. It renders the viewer mute, denying any voice other than the state. From the first, Tom has been inclusive in his work, incorporating suggestions from others and, through dialogue, coming to an understanding of its various political implications. His art does not glorify power, being all too eager to upset the balance in favor of erotic connection. It is impossible to imagine Kake as some sort of Übermensch. He is too often on the receiving end of Tom's jokes, losing his clothes, or having his cock handcuffed to another man. Tom is too obviously delighted with the possibilities for erotic display to not invite us to join in.

Tom the Sadist

In speaking of sadism, it is important to differentiate between a garden variety of brute and someone whose work is inspired by the Marquis de Sade. Tom is a sadist, not because of any perceived violence in his work, but because he shares similar obsessions with Sade. He is a careful constructor of sexual tableaux. He is concerned with full use of the erotic zones of the body, with saturation. It is important that all orifices be filled, that figures be connected, disrupted, and connected again. In one narrative, a man is pissing in a public toilet. A sailor wanders in and starts fucking him, a blond comes in and starts fucking him, and so on until there are eight people in a row. This is a typical Sadean trope: An asshole is fucked because it is there, and it is important to complete the tableau. The formal demands of sexual positioning overwhelm the ideas of power relationships.

Like Sade's, Tom's work operates by an overlapping and subsequent disruption of codes. In Tom's case, this is the tension between the drawn image and the photograph. His best drawings bounce between the dead-pan style of the camera and the sly exaggerations of his pencil. Without the meticulous rendering, his exaggerations would fail to arouse. There is a sense of outrage with the notion of the painstaking approach to such a low aim—that one should labor so hard to produce images of men fucking.

Sade uses beautifully crafted French prose to describe the most perfidious activities. In our society, the expected result of superlative craft is the sublime. Tom, with his devotion to his fantasy, stands this expectation about high-mindedness and craft on its head. His intense devotion to a pornographic labor is antiestablishment; it is a "waste" of time and talent. It disrupts society's ideas about what pornography is: cheap, thrown together, and without redeeming value.

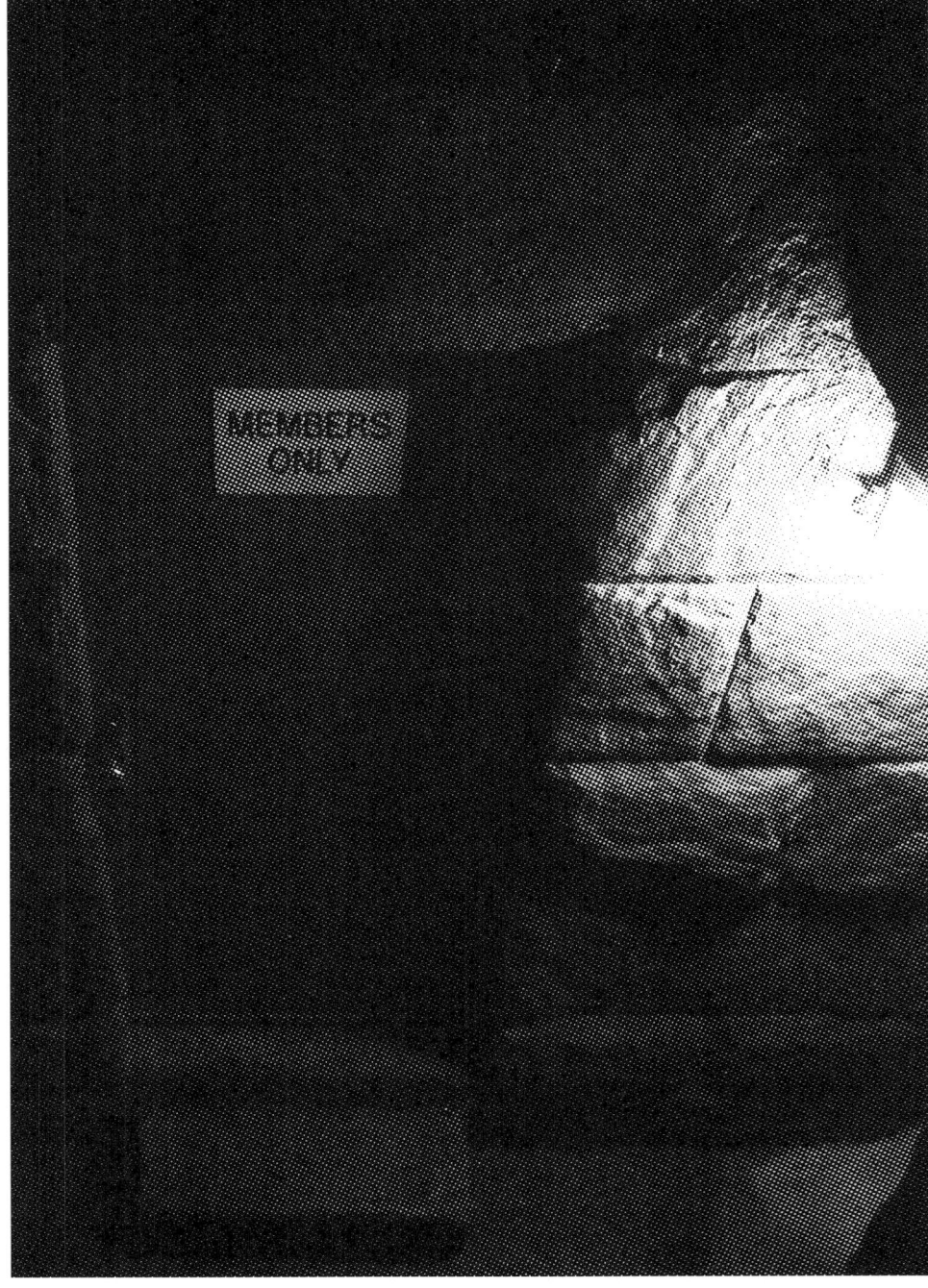

Tom the Physique Artist

Looking at a copy of *Fizeek Art Quarterly*, it is remarkable how Tom's work stands out from the rest of the drawings that surround it—as much for what it doesn't do as for what it does. The majority of early gay pornography is dominated by a desire to return to a mythical past. Images of fauns playing lyres, gladiators, medieval knights and pages, and other never-never lands of gay desire. Tom's drawings, on the other hand, are always of contemporary subjects. Even when they portray cowboys, you know there is a pickup truck or motorcycle lurking around the corner.

This is a world of today, a world of constantly intersecting erotic gazes and gestures, where sexual activity is always a possibility. Over the years, Tom has adopted different styles of dress and hair length to maintain a contemporary look. Tom also abandons the gay figure of the ephebe, the slender hairless teen whose purity and fawn-like bearing presage the sensitive and willowy man. Tom's men are lugs, and the closest he comes to the ephebe are drawings of robust teens who ride around on motorcycles looking to get fucked.

Tom has always drawn images from his own experiences and the world around him, but as his work began to appear in the pages of America's physique magazines, he began to receive suggestions for subject matter and commissions from his publishers and readers. These magazines functioned not only as a source for pinup pictures but also as a ground for the exchange of ideas for fantasies and types of identities. They began to form the image reservoirs from which gay men were able to construct new codes for dress and behavior. They began to constitute a placeless community for gay men before physical communities existed.

The physique magazines should be seen not as cute precursors to today's hardcore porn but as an underground press equal in importance to the first gay political magazines. Tom's drawings passed from the private fantasies of a man in Europe to the underground images that would shape a generation's ideas of how a gay man could look and act. Tom has drawn not only on the paper in front of him but on the consciousness of the men who viewed and continue to view his work.

Note

1. David Reed. "Repression and Exaggeration: The Art of Tom of Finland," *Christopher Street* (April 1980).

THE ABCS OF ART INSTITUTIONS

Previously Unpublished, 1989

This was presented at a conference of nonprofit arts organizations, and so I was addressing fellow artists, administrators, and curator types. I've worked with and within nonprofit arts institutions since 1986 as an artist, a board member, an administrator, and a curator. I wouldn't have a career without them, and I try to train artists to fully inhabit all the roles available to them. I have seen the way that the nonprofit arts were vehicles for self-empowerment for marginalized artists through the 1960s and 1970s. I saw the way that they were attacked, both ideologically and fiscally, in the 1980s. One of the effects of the AIDS crisis was the return to relevance of nonprofit arts organizations. The culture wars are fought through the nonprofits. —NB

Rather than a formal talk, I have tried to list a few of my thoughts on critical writing in general and its current relation to my activities. These thoughts are admittedly skeletal, and I have deliberately tried to make them more open-ended since I always look forward to the question-and-answer section more than the talk part.

1 We are witnessing the collapse of a particular type of critical activity, or rather a usurpation of this activity by the artists who were the previously passive recipients of critical attention.

2 The emergence of a new genre of writing: theory—neither philosophy, history, nor criticism. This genre combines elements of

all three with the added ingredient of glamour and a high price tag. *Art in America* costs $4.50 an issue. *October* costs $7.50. *Semiotext(e)* (when it appears) now costs $15.00. It may be an indication of *Artforum*'s attempt to gain theoretical credibility that its price was recently raised to $6.50. On this scale, it should be clear that the *Bay Guardian*, which is handed out free, is of no theoretical value whatsoever.

3   Where is criticism located? First, in the art magazines—a genre that is becoming increasingly confused with that of fashion magazines. Like any marketing tool, art magazines are seen as delimiting trends and maintaining market value. They function economically as the validation of and distributors of the New York art world—the world that makes up 75 percent of their advertisers. The world that occupies the same three miles of real estate that they do. In books, criticism takes the form of either artist monographs or art history. Both are too often the occasion for expensive reproductions and gushes of laudatory prose. Again, such glossy behemoths come with impressive price tags.

4   It may well be that the art world (that is, the commercial art world) now functions too quickly for art criticism. With dealers attempting to adapt the model of the clothing industry by instituting well-defined seasons with a "look for each season," there is not much time left for the traditional mechanisms of encounter-reflection-elucidation that we associate with classic art criticism. Dealers increasingly dictate the issues that critics engage with. But that engagement is now little more than a hapless chronicling of market strategy. Critics now are more wary than ever of becoming yet another middleman greasing the wheels of the market.

5   In the past two decades, the most important pieces of critical writing have been those that have been linked to issues of cultural difference. This writing is part of the larger project of critiquing twentieth-century Western culture as a whole and has comprised a radical reenvisioning of the history and implications of Western art. This criticism has been, for the most part, the work of women, people of color, and people of varied gender identity and sexual preference. Such a criticism counters the traditional categories of artist biography and historical "art movements" with questions

about the material basis of an artwork's production, its life as a commodity, and the ideological codes that it carries. Such writing begins to constitute a countermemory to Western historicism and opens up new opportunities for community development and social action.

6   What is the point of the artist's writing? For one thing, in an era that understands that knowledge is power, the whimsical naivete of the artist reads like a flight from reality. Artists are not at the mercy of their production. They are not the conduit for the ineffable. As thinking people within the culture, they need to take responsibility not only for the objects they make but for the ideas they support. By entering into the field of critical writing, they begin to formulate community concerns.

7   Artists are producers of signs. They engage in communication. These signs exist with(in) a variety of social fields. In the most broad-reaching sense, we can call these fields *culture*. The culture of a time should be seen as the semiological value of all the activities engaged in by the people of that time. Artists are those who make conscious gestures within that field, whether or not these gestures take place within what we now call *the arts*.

8   Since we are regarding artists as knowing producers of culture, we can call an effective art a knowing intervention in the field of culture that combines progressive intent with appropriate placement. This definition would not, per se, exclude an activity such as painting from the realm of effectiveness, but it would ask: How effective is it for this particular painting to be here? Similar questions could be asked of a manifesto, a piece of graffiti, a critical essay, and so on.

9   It is increasingly important that as artists, we do not cede authority to those structures that are already established for the domestication of our effort. It is important to regard with suspicion rules that say you can be an artist but not an art critic, a curator but not an artist. Such rules are designed to maintain a situation that keeps all cultural producers separate and harmless. We must learn to perform our own cultural archaeologies, construct our own contexts, establish our own dialogues.

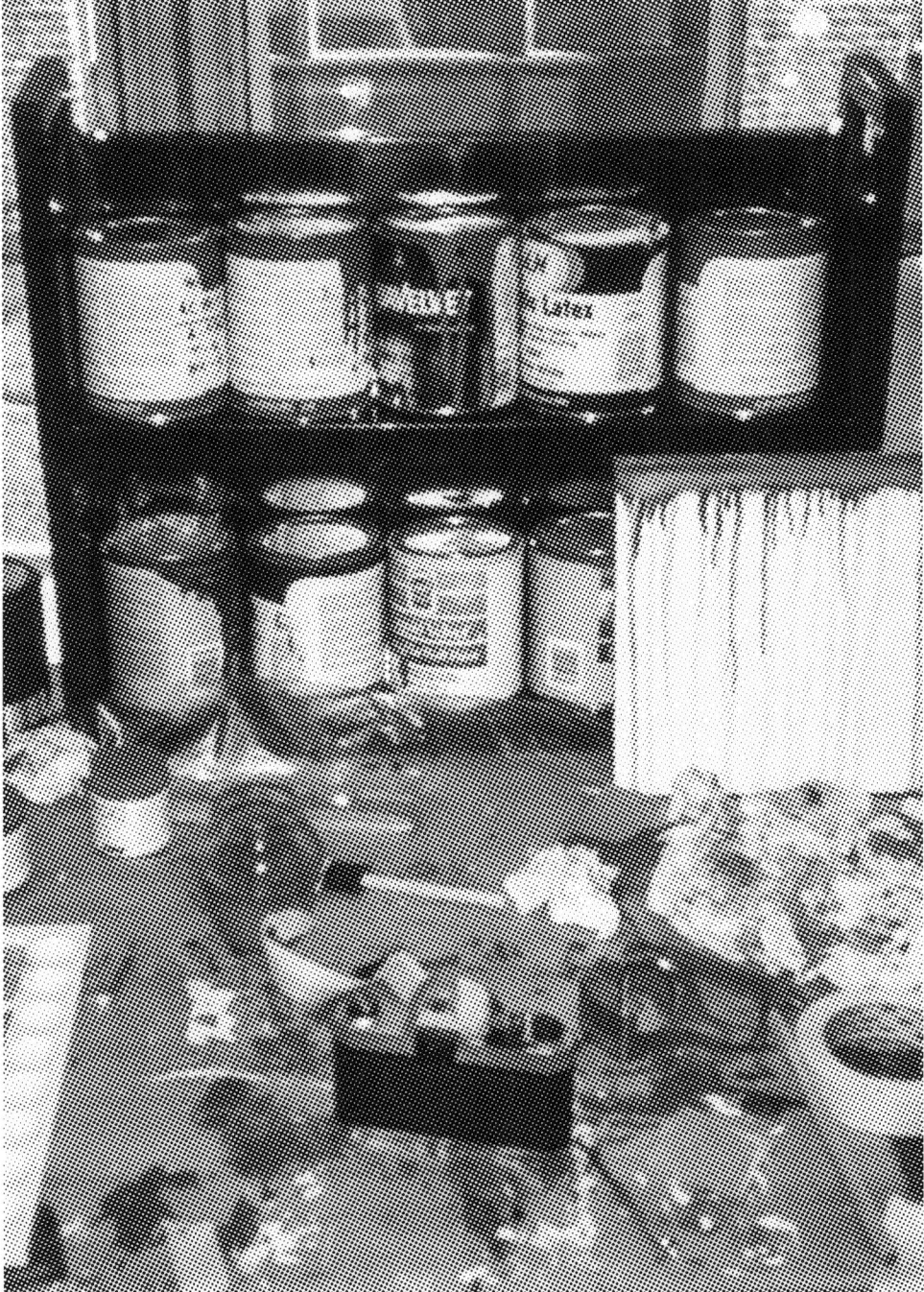

10   It is important for artists to articulate the place that their activity comes from—not in the sense of regionalism but in the sense of a cultural identity. It is, for me, important to produce writings and works that are legible to both the gay community and the art world. I feel that my work is about articulating the tension between my place as an inheritor of Western culture and the particular inter-action I have with it as a gay man. I would like to conclude with a few questions I believe to be important to any discussion of these issues.

How do we, as producers, use critical writing?
Where do we encounter it?
What do its modes of production and distribution mean?

PERFORMANCE SCRIPT

Previously Unpublished, 1990

My performance scripts are like cover songs. They generally were meant to fill up ten minutes at A Different Light bookstore or at some art space. These scripts are found texts cut up with my own writing, in this case about the controversial William Friedkin film Cruising *(1980). —NB*

1   Let us remember that even in this, our most difficult hour, our torments cannot begin to even allude to those undergone almost daily by Liza, Britt, and Candace.

2   To deny power is to deny exchange, to refuse to allow for the action of the self.

3   Let us allow *Cruising* then to be the map of our 1970s intelligence. An incoherent map, as Robin Wood would have it. How can we begin to experience the flavor of that decade except through incoherence?
    Throughout the film, cops are interchangeable with homosexuals. We cannot say interchangeable with gay men because there are barely any in the film. Instead, we are given two types of game pieces to play with: cops and queens.

4   When Pacino enters for his first interview, his leering boss asks him, "Have you ever had your cock sucked by a man before?" We wait breathlessly for this boss to give Pacino a taste of what it feels

like. On-the-job training. What can be made of the interrogation scene, where an enormous Black man in a jockstrap and cowboy hat enters the room and backhands Pacino? This is the fantasy of a straight man about the fantasy of a gay man.

5   The film is a permission for straight men to finally solve the mystery of what gay men do together. The supposed horror of fist-fucking, the amount of equipment carried from place to place.

Let's see. Pacino enters the office of his boss. He gets his name wrong. No one's identity is right here. The murderer is two different people. Pacino's portly boss asks, "Have you ever had your cock sucked by a man?" Pacino says, "No." Will the boss show Pacino what it feels like? Earlier, two cops drive down Christopher Street sneering about scumbags. They haul two drag queen informant hustlers into the black-and-white. The drags say, "I can't afford another bust this month." The cop in the front, who looks like the psycho murderer, says, "Get your ass up here." I want to show you my nightstick. Later, when Pacino wanders into his usual leather bar, instead of the usual fist-fucking, everyone is dressed as cops. One cop queen forces another to go down on his wooden nightstick. Pacino is kicked out of the bar because not only is he an undercover cop, but he is also not dressed as a cop and so is in the wrong drag. When the drag queen informant complains to Pacino's boss that he was forced to go down on a cop in a black-and-white, the boss says, "How do you know they were cops? There are so many guys out there impersonating cops these days." Later, when Pacino is out undercover cruising in a drag bar, he is cruised by one of the cops from the black-and-white. And later still, when the last murder is discovered, this same cop is on duty.

A Fan Writes:

Twenty-

The torch I carried for Harry Falk took a long time dying. Nothing, not even moving into my own apartment in late 1968 and going through the motions of marital settlement agreements, could convince me to give up the ghost. It was impossible to believe that this was happening.

I retaliated by becoming Moby Wife. I tortured the man with phone calls, and I did truly infantile things—real high school antics like sending him pizzas he hadn't ordered. I became more and more manic, even showing up where I knew he'd be, looking my best, and trying to behave in a nonchalant manner. The man would be shooting pool at the Factory or some other private club, and all of a sudden, there I'd be.

I got by during the days. Either I'd spend hours and hours in bed, hungover and calling for takeout food, or else I was able to pull it together enough so that no one noticed what shape I was in, or so I thought. Acquaintances who were concerned about me would try to fix me up with dates or at least invite me to dinner parties. Sometimes I'd go, sometimes I'd say yes and then cancel and stay in bed. I spent a lot of time in bed.

I was hungover most of the day because I drank most of the night. I'd go to various haunts until I met up with some guy who would join us, and both of us would be drunk enough to go back to my apartment. I went home with a lot of men—not on a nightly basis, but compared to my lifestyle before and after, it was a lot. Part of it was simply an escape (somebody anesthetize me). Part of it was my fury at Harry's false accusation. "Okay, you think I screw around? I'll show you screwing around." They were cold acts, full of self-destruction. You don't go to bed with someone you don't know because you like him. It was anger, pure and simple, anger at myself, at men in general, and at Harry in particular. He was all I thought about.

For a while, I dated a young man named Gene Kirkwood. He was a young, good-looking guy, a great dancer with a lot of energy, who really wasn't interested in me at first. We started seeing each other for lunch and developed a nice friendship and rapport.

Gene and I would drive for miles and miles, and he'd tell me his dreams. He wanted to be a movie producer, but his family was in the fish business. They used to keep telling him, "Come home and sell fish! Stop this craziness!" We'd go up to Mulholland Drive, and he'd say, "This is where I'm going to have my house, and it's going to be on this many acres, and it's going to have this and that and the other thing." You could knock him down, you could take his money, you could do anything to him; he was undaunted. He never doubted that his ship would come in.

I became more and more smitten with Gene, and eventually we did go to bed together and became sort of a couple. I even cosigned a car lease for a Firebird for him. Eventually we broke up, and he ended up being one of the producers of the Rocky films. And he forgot all about that car lease. I saw him on television once, going to the Academy Awards, and I said to John Astin, "That's him! That's the guy with the Firebird!"

One night at the Sierra Towers, I wasn't feeling very well, and I thought some soup might do me good. So I dressed in my black pants and my black turtleneck and went across the street to an Italian restaurant called Stefanino's looking very wan and pale, like something out of an Ingmar Bergman movie. Nicky Blair, who ran the place, came over to chat, but I didn't feel like it. I just wanted to have some soup.

The door opened, and in came Frank Sinatra with a group of about sixteen people. They sat down at a long table that'd been specially set up, and when Sinatra—whose date was a tall, statuesque blonde— sat down at the head, he ended up looking directly at me. I was eating my soup and smoking my cigarettes and trying not to feel awkward because I'd noticed that he kept looking at me. There's something about those eyes. I don't know what the hell it is, but they are riveting. I thought to myself, "The next time he looks at me, I'm going to look at him." He did. I did. We both smiled because it seemed so silly, and then we went through the whole thing all over again.

The next thing I knew, he called Nicky Blair over. Nicky nodded, came over to me, and said, "Mr. Sinatra would like you to join his table."

"Oh no, Nicky. I just came from across the street to have some soup. But thank him very much. That's very thoughtful of him."

"I think you'd better join their table."

"No, I really can't. Just tell him how grateful I am for the invitation."

Nicky went away, talked to Sinatra, nodded, came back, and said, "He's not taking no for an answer." I laughed and called to Sinatra, "That's really nice of you, but I'm not dressed, and I'm nursing a cold." And he said, "I insist," stood up, and began to walk over. Now I was really getting nervous. I stood up, met him halfway, and said, "This is very sweet of you." And a place was made for me toward the far end of the table.

After about half an hour, during which he kept really staring at me, Frank got up to go to the men's room. As he passed my end of the table, he leaned over and, without breaking his stride, said, "You are going home with me, aren't you?" and I said, "Yes." It happened just that fast. I thought, "I should be wondering what the hell I'm doing. I'll worry about it tomorrow."

He came back and declared that the party was moving to his place. "Except," he whispered to one of his people, the blonde who was his date. And that was it, the blonde was out, and I was in. He and I drove alone in a white station wagon to his house in Beverly Hills, with every-one else following.

There was a general sort of party hubbub at his place, and then, all of a sudden, as if somebody had pushed a button, people disappeared. Nobody said, "Get out of here." It was just "Shazam," and they were gone. And there I was, saying to myself, "This is insane. What am I going to tell Frank Jr.?" And he said, "Would you like to hear a new record I just made?" What am I going to say? "No, Mr. Sinatra, I really wouldn't." So he put it on, and for the first time, I heard "My Way." Can you imagine? We were sitting next to each other on the couch, drinking the best champagne, and he said, "Come on, let's go to bed."

I suppose I could have said no, but it seemed to me I'd stayed so long, there was no turning back, and I gave it not another thought. He had two bathrooms off his bedroom. He showed me one of them, handed me a robe, opened a drawer, and said, "There's a toothbrush in there if you want it." And indeed, I had my choice of brand-new tooth-brushes in that drawer.

I took a shower and drank a lot more while I was in there, and as soon as I got back to the bedroom, the phone rang. And Frank got very involved in a very serious conversation about his father, who was quite ill at the time. When he hung up, he told me about the surgery his father was going to have. We talked for about two more hours until it was close to dawn, and then we went to sleep. Nothing happened.

When I woke up the next morning, I found my period had started during the night. I was mortified. I wasn't as accepting of life and the human condition as I am now, but he couldn't have cared less; he was much too sophisticated to worry about stuff like that. Also, he was very concerned about his father and soon back on the phone again. I went to the kitchen, and Frank's buddy Jilly Rizzo was there. He offered me aspirin and Coca-Cola for my hangover, which I badly needed.

When Frank came out, he drove me home and said he'd like to see me again. And sure enough, the next day the phone rang, and a voice said, "This is Francis Albert. Do you want to go to Palm Springs?" And I spent a few weeks with him off and on down there. We slept in the same bed, but never was there any sex. Anyone who was around in my life during those few weeks is convinced that I had an affair with Sinatra, and I did, of sorts. Considering my friendship with Frank Jr., however, I was relieved at how things worked out, and I suspect that when it came right down to it, he couldn't do that to his son. Also, he was still troubled about his father, and in fact that's how it ended. There was an emergency call, he left with the jet to pick up his dad, and I never heard from him again. Maybe he didn't want to get involved with someone who was trying to kill herself, especially since she was trying to kill herself over somebody else.

When Sandy Smith returned to Los Angeles, we reestablished our relationship. I'd gotten into the pattern of spending all day in bed and carousing all night, and Sandy tried to extricate me from that. I couldn't bear to be alone, so we'd run around all day doing silly stuff, getting our hair and nails done, and fooling around in Beverly Hills. She'd drop me off at the Sierra Towers, and an hour later I'd call and say, "Come get me. I can't stay here." Finally, she said, "Look, Lucky's never in town. You can come and stay with me." And I did. I was "the lady who came to dinner." I showed up one day and stayed for weeks.

Sandy and I were like a mini-sorority. We had Ovaltine with marshmallows every night. We'd sit around and philosophize until it was time to go to bed. But once she went to sleep, I'd disappear. I was set up on a rollaway in front of Sandy's fireplace, but I had insomnia. Some nights I'd wake her; some nights I'd be too embarrassed. I'd just go out and wend my way back around five or six in the morning.

One night, after Sandy had gone to bed, I decided I had to drive over and see Harry's new house. I knew it was off Laurel Canyon, but I hadn't been there. It was pouring rain—a very dark night, all very dramatic. I went down a lot of steps. His dog, Finn, was barking his head off, and I pounded and pounded on the door. Harry finally opened it; he was naked but pulling on a robe. He was startled to see me, and he started to close the door, but I stuck my foot in the opening.

"Go away," he said.

"Please let me come in. It's raining. Please let me come in."

"No, I can't."

"Please. Please. Just for a minute, and then I promise I'll go."

"No. Go away, Pat. I'll talk to you tomorrow."

"No, I have to talk to you now."

All this time I'd managed to push the door open a little with my foot, enough to get a shoulder and half my body in. Harry didn't want to slam the door on me, yet he did not want me in that house. The staircase to the second floor was directly opposite the door, and while we were talking, down the stairs came Venus, with her flowing blonde hair, wearing a white monogrammed bathrobe I'd given to Harry.

He turned on her viciously and said, "Get the fuck upstairs!" It was the same woman—though I didn't know it then—that the pool man had seen. She just stood there and looked at me. I think I said, "Oh my God," but I'm not sure. I don't know why I was surprised, but I was. And Harry said, "Now will you go?" I don't remember if I said yes or just nodded, but obviously I was going.

I drove back to Sandy's at some insane speed in the rain, screaming, "No! No! No!" all the way; my throat hurt by the time I arrived. I went into her bathroom, and even though she'd tried to hide them, I found a full bottle of tranquilizers. There must have been about forty or fifty in there. I went in the other room and took almost all the pills. I had been careful, however, to take one out and leave it on the counter, because I figured Sandy would be nervous and really need it when she woke up and found me dead!

I don't remember anything more until I regained consciousness after having my stomach pumped, but Sandy has told me the story many times. She got up in the morning and was suspicious about the way I looked; I seemed to be in a deep sleep. She roused me with difficulty, but I insisted I hadn't done anything, that I was just exhausted and needed some. . . .

There are endless psycho homosexual knife murderers. First, the one that does the first killing. This one later cruises Pacino in the park, and Pacino goes with him instead of with the older homosexual. Then there is the boyfriend of the good homosexual who threatens Pacino with a steak knife and who the boss thinks did the last murder. Then there is the busboy at the steak house that Pacino takes to the hotel and gets to tie him up. The one who is bad news. Who gets in fights. Then there is the one who lives near Columbia and kills because his dead father told him to. Then there is Pacino, who stabs the one with the dead father, might have killed the one in the peep show, and probably killed the one with the psycho dancer roommate. The psycho in this world only kills guys who look alike and only kills guys who look like him. So everyone in this world looks alike. Pacino is picked to chase the psycho because he looks like all the victims. But he also looks like all the psychos. Understand that this makes it difficult to sustain continuity through all those panning shots.

A Fan Writes:

Truman and Me

The adventures that involved my various friends and I are countless, yet there is a particular episode that stands out in my mind.

I met Truman Capote in the year of our Lord 1961. It was a fall afternoon, and I was wearing a thin tweed suit, a ranch mink stole, and a charming pillbox hat. Jack Kennedy was putting in his bid for the presidency, and Jacqueline Kennedy was around showing off her wardrobe, and I was lucky enough to share similar tastes. In my hand, I carried a lovely alligator handbag. I wore black leather gloves and black leather shoes. I was feeling quite well that afternoon. In other words, I had just shot a jumbo dose of crystallized meth, which does tend to make one rather hyperactive.

I had just lunched with Mr. Saul Hite. As I strolled down Fifth Avenue, just as I was passing the Hotel Pierre, I noticed, lo and behold, a spectacle ahead that one simply could not miss—a little plump munchkin carrying a cane.

I recognized him immediately as Truman Capote.

Being the kind and gracious lady that I can be at times—besides the bitch that I am the rest of the time—I said, "Mr. Capote, is it?"

"Yes," he replied.

"How do you do?"

"Fine. Do I know you?"

"No, I have not had the distinction of meeting you before, but I've always admired you."

"Thank you," he said. "What is your name?"

"Margo Howard."

"Do I know you?" he asked again. "I know a lot of people. Who's your husband?"

"My husband you wouldn't know."

"Are you sure? You're not in show business, are you?"

"No. I'm not."

He thought, since I was dressed so well, that I was a society lady.

"What can I do for you, dear?"

"It's nothing you can do for me," I stated. "I just wanted to tell you how much I admire you."

"Thank you. You're very kind."

"Oh yes, one of the first books I read was one of your first books, *Other Voices, Other Rooms*, which I was very thrilled with."

"Thank you, thank you. You're so nice."

"Yes, I've always admired you. You're such a great writer. And your new book *Breakfast at Tiffany's* that just came out, it's such an astronomical wonder. You blend reality and fiction, and it's a unique thing for a writer to do. I do a little dabbling myself in writing."

"Oh, that's very nice. Thank you so much. It's so nice to meet you."

"Yes. Now, before you go, I want to tell you something else. I'm like you are."

"You're what?"

"I'm like you are. Gay."

"What?"

"I'm gay."

"Oh. You have a beautiful speaking voice." He seemed confused. "You're a nice lady anyway."

"You're a nice person too. But I'm trying to tell you that I'm like you because I'm gay."

"What does that mean?"

"I will tell you in confidence. Being an admirer of yours—I'm a man like you are. I'm a drag queen."

"What?"

"I'm a drag queen! A man in woman's clothes."

"What? What do you mean?"

"I mean that I'm a queen, like you. I'm a man."

"What do you say?"

"I say what I mean."

He looked at me quizzically, and then his mood turned to annoyance. He said, "It's people like you that make it so very hard for homosexuals in the world. Deceiving and confounding and confusing people. That's why we have as hard a road in America as we do in the rest of the world. You should be dead. You're a disgrace!"

"What are you saying? What are you talking about?"

"I'm saying that you're better off dead. Someone like you has no right to live!"

"You little fag bastard! I'm taking the edge off you. I'll teach you what a real drag queen's like!"

I took my shoes off and stood there in my silk stockings (the chauffeur was still holding the door, as Truman Capote had just about entered the car). I leaned back, my handbag in my hand, and threw a punch like a professional boxer. I knocked him into the car. He turned upside down, his feet flew in the air, and he hit his head on one of the windows.

A gash appeared on his head; he was bleeding all over the place.

"Oh my God," he yelled. "Help, police, help!"

I looked at the chauffeur. "And you, what are you going to do about it? You don't know what I have in this handbag. I might have a gun, a knife, or a bomb."

The chauffeur replied, "I'm not interested, ma'am." (He called me ma'am!) This Irish-American driver said, "I am only here to drive Mr. Capote to the airport. This is a hired limousine service."

I said, "Take that bitch to the hospital first! She's bleeding! She needs stitches."

He said, "It's not my affair. I will take him where I have to take him."

He didn't know what kind of lunatic I was, after all.

I slipped my leather shoes back on and made my way down Fifth Avenue. After a few minutes, I heard the wailing of an ambulance trailing from somewhere behind me.

What I learned from cruising.

1   All cops look like queens.

2   All queens look like cops.

3   Queens are psychos who want to kill other queens because they can never come to terms with the fact that they are men who want to fuck other men.

4   Cops are psychos who bait and kill queens because they are able to fuck men—something that cops can only dream about until they are able to trap queens.

5   Pacino's a cop who has never fucked other men and who becomes a psycho because he is unable to distinguish where he begins and ends in a world where everyone looks alike, acts alike, and is trying to kill each other.

6   Fucking is the same as killing, so what does it matter?

A Fan Writes:

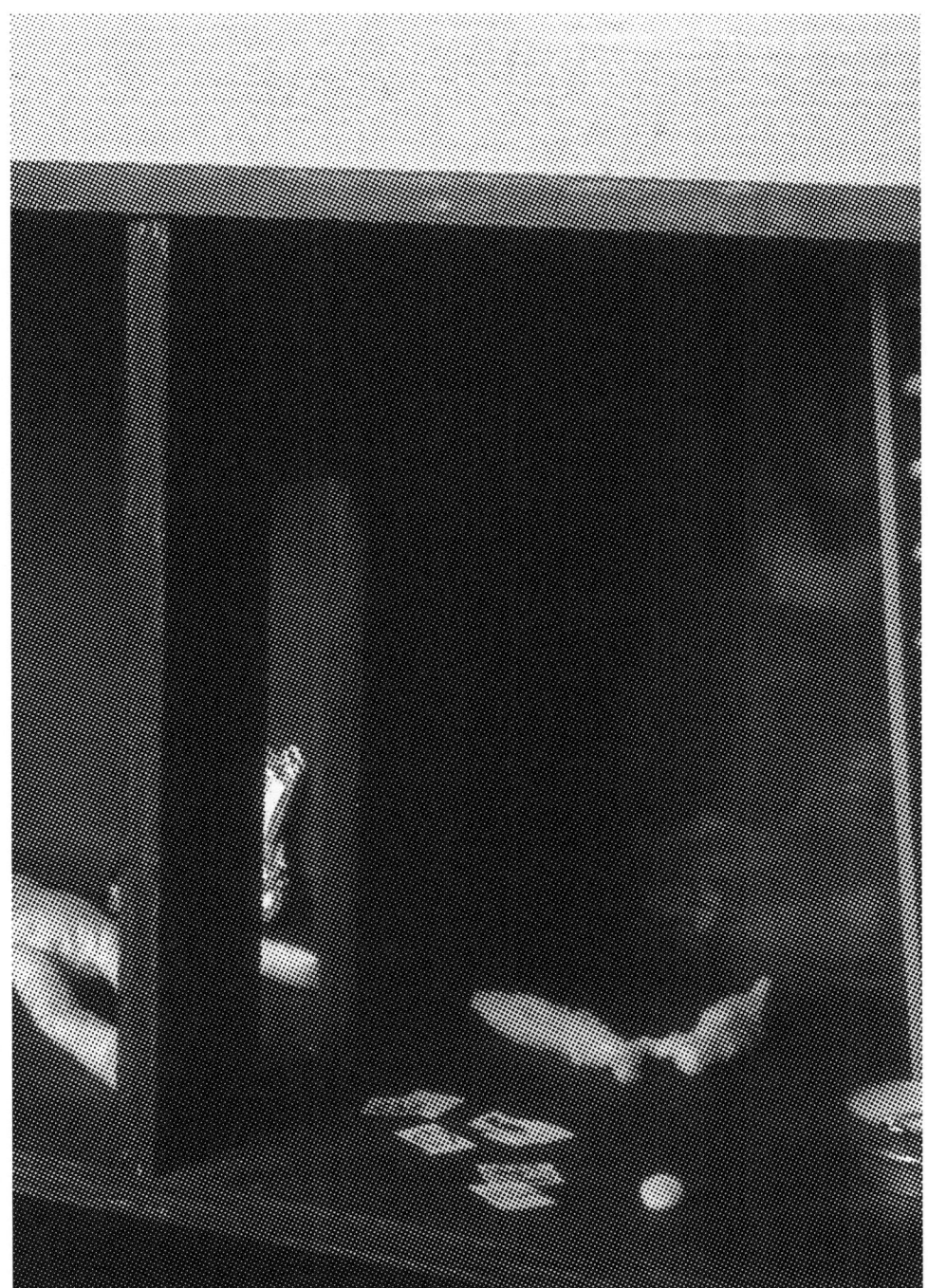

In 1976, the year of the bicentennial, thousands of would-be-debauched lined the walls of New York's Studio 54. On this particular night, Liza with a *Z*—torn between black and blue—had been able, through the careful application of alcohol, Tuinals, and cocaine, to warp her consciousness beyond even its previous limits. Lips ajar, she swirled through the motions of the bus stop and an abbreviated Latin hustle while relentless lights chased the beat provided by Munich's finest disc jockeys. Perhaps it was this Germanic connection, reminding her of her now-a-little-too-long-ago triumph in cabaret, or perhaps it was the now-perceptible swaying of the floor, making her think of her future pairing with the unfortunately homosexual Burt Reynolds in the misnamed film *Lucky Lady* (a piece of cinema awash with oceanic shenanigans). Whatever the cause, the last of Liza's reserve peeled away beneath the torrid strobes. She flung her arms out. Layers of self-doubt, unfinished business, snubs delivered, and snubs received—all of the mind-deadening items that had held her soul in thrall—began to vanish in the clear, unrepentant light of her spirit. Advancing through the forecourts of enlightenment, she danced feet and legs and heart bearing her onward to the plains of flowers washed by rains beyond recognition. As she danced, there appeared on her brow a glowing light licked into stellar brightness by her ever-greater efforts. This was a new one—even on the jaded habitués of America's most bourgeois orgy room. A rapt circle formed around Liza, now America's most talented dervish. Finally, a brave soul dared to yell, "Hey Liza, who you dancin' with?" and from the summit of her rapture Liza screamed back, "I'm dancin' with momma. Can't you see? I'm dancin' with momma!"

THE SADDEST STORY
I KNOW

Previously Unpublished, 1990

My generation is the Liza generation. It's not the Judy generation. The Judy Garland story is the grand tragedy: a diva overflowing with emotion destroyed by an uncaring world. The Liza Minelli story is a tragedy of continuing: a weird, reduced version of Judy that's obsessed with Judy but is also living in the shadow of her. The scripts collected in this book were literally collages, made from fragments of thrift store books and such. This story of collapse and ruin is a description of the postmodern condition. For people who flourished under modernism, its collapse was a tragedy, and a number of artists in the early 1980s made paintings depicting that tragedy. For those who struggled under modernism, the fragmentation of the modernist subject was a kind of freedom to comb the ruins and combine the fragments into new possibilities. Not having a coherent "I" or self is good news if you were only ever going to be punished and ignored for having that self. —NB

Prologue—Me Like a Dog

January 1, 1963

I AM A WITCH.

This is a statement of fact which in this second half of the sophisticated twentieth century still seems to generate mixed emotions throughout the world. I have been called "the most evil woman in the world." But evil, like beauty, is often in the mind and eye of the beholder. Yet many people see me as something of a fairy godmother, a woman who has a secret remedy for all the aches and pains of body and spirit as well as for complex emotional problems. I have also been called "a legend," which seems a rather delightful thing to be.

Of course, popular mythology would have it that we witches are a licentious lot, forever running around half naked under the light of the moon making weird mad-dog noises, with the Devil as a perpetual playmate ready to help us in all sorts of nefarious goings-on. It's nice material for a movie but far removed from the real thing. I have no feelings one way or another about running around naked. People probably clutter themselves up with too many clothes anyway, and witches are really very practical people. In my old home in the New Forest, it would take a tougher character than I to run around naked among all those gorse bushes. I usually wear long, loose, robe-like dresses and see no reason to change when I attend one of our religious meetings, or "Sabbats." I believe there are modern covens these days that prefer to perform their rites in the nude. But then there are many people who join nudist colonies; at least they have the good sense to choose areas with warm climates such as California. As for the Devil, I never met him myself, but I am gregarious enough to be polite to most people. So if I meet a man with little horns on his head and a peculiar taste in footwear, I'm not going to worry. You can't be sure who the Devil is these days. He might be a TV or movie producer in disguise.

Liza put down her pen, closed her diary and softly chuckled.

1. A Double Shot of My Baby's Love

Shortly after Kennedy's assassination, Liza fell ill. Her temperature was dangerously high, and she couldn't get out of bed. A frantic Judy called the doctor, who diagnosed her problem as a kidney stone and put her in the hospital. She spent a painful month there, and just before she was released, her agent (she had signed with Creative Management Associates in September) came to her room and asked if she would like to star in *Carnival*, a successful Broadway show that was being produced in stock. "I grabbed a pen and signed the contract right there."

Judy wasn't happy about Liza leaving for New York to rehearse the show. She wanted Liza with her as an emotional buffer against the depressions that were more and more frequently coming over her. But Liza left and went to work in Mineola, Long Island, where the first *Carnival* production would be presented.

"I shall do everything in my power to stop you," Judy told her, coldly furious.

"Mama went into a rage at my refusal," Liza said later. "I was so frightened. I knew Mama could pull a lot of strings against me—regardless of everything, Mama's power is considerable."

Liza spent every night of the ensuing two weeks crying herself to sleep. "I loved my mother. I wanted to make her happy, but everything went wrong."

Liza went forward with the *Carnival* rehearsals, and Judy continued trying to disrupt her daughter's activities. On opening night, the show had just begun, and Liza was onstage. Bob VanderGriff, *Carnival*'s stage manager, remembers being shocked to hear the backstage telephone ring. "It should not have been ringing," he says, "because it can be heard in the audience."

One of the stagehands picked the phone up quickly. The caller asked to speak to Liza. The stagehand explained that she was in the middle of a performance. The caller asked that a message be left: Judy Garland had just tried to commit suicide.

At that moment Liza was delivering one of *Carousel*'s most touching speeches. Hands clasped in front of her stage gingham, she softly said:

The inner history of the great war between angels and devils which broke out in the Middle Ages has never been fully investigated, but the battlefield itself, the world of mankind, has long been the stamping ground of the historian.

Nevertheless, spiritual stability left much to be desired, for everywhere the people as a whole moved in an atmosphere of devils and ghosts, and only occasionally angels. Even at that late period, they still retained something of the old belief inherited from their savage ancestors that the whole of nature was animated by good and evil entities. The former were now described as angels and the latter as devils, vast armies of whom now sought to destroy mankind.

The producers debated whether to tell Liza immediately or wait until after the performance was over. They decided to wait.

But as Liza was leaving the stage at intermission, the phone rang again, and this time she picked it up. VanderGriff heard her ask into the phone, "Is she going to be okay?" The answer was evidently positive. "Tell her I'll see her after the show," Liza said.

"She went out and gave a terrific second-act performance," Vander-Griff recalls.

February 5

It was because of Aleister Crowley that I wrote my own first poem at the top of the mountain in the evening sun of a late summer evening. Was this my first experience of something else taking over? Was it the magic of Crowley's voice that reached some recess in my mind? I can never be quite sure, but I know I wrote a strange if brief account of an event of history that I had certainly never been taught, and instead of prose sentences, what I had written had a regularity of rhythm. My mother still has this poem, and I'm told it was remarkable for an eight-year-old child. It was about a Scottish character called Alan Breck Stewart. A psychic instant, probably generated by the presence of Crowley, must have occurred.

Crowley told me that words were important in witchcraft but not only for their meaning. It was the sounds that mattered, as each sound set up a vibration. In witchcraft and in the Indian mantras, words are often replaced by strange sounds, which to the uninitiated seem meaningless but undoubtedly help to raise the psychic forces and often induce a state of trance.

One day Crowley cupped my face in his hands and spoke to my grandmother.

"This is the one who will take up where I leave off. She is the one who will survive. She'll live to see occultism almost being understood. That will be the day, won't it, old lady?"

Among other surviving legends of the Wild Hunt is the gruesome anecdote of the onlooker who cried out to the huntsmen as they rode by, "Give us some of your game."

"Take this," said the huntsman, tossing him an ice-cold bundle. When the man opened the bundle, he found inside it his own dead baby.

2. Sniffles

January 8

Dear Sister,

I can't type, I can't file, I can't even answer the telephone.

When Elizabeth Ray came to DC and found work as secretary-receptionist to famous congressmen and lobbyists, she never guessed that her duties would include paying off her bosses' political debts with a little hush-hush hanky-panky.

But Liz warmed quickly to her work—and soon congressmen, senators, lobbyists, and the press out for a quickie, a sneakie, or a "little something on the side" were all sampling Liz's after-hours wares.

NOW IN HER SENSATIONAL NOVEL, SHE BLOWS THE COVER OFF THE STEAMY SECRETS OF WASHINGTON'S MIGHTIEST!

An excerpt follows:

The affection which ghosts continue to retain for the bodies they once occupied is the theme of the tale collected by the folklorist Robert Hunt in the West of England, concerning the curious adventures that befell a woman who discovered a set of teeth sticking out of the earth in a graveyard. Being of an economical turn of mind, she took these home and placed them near her bed. That night, she was awakened by a dreadful howling from outside her bedroom window: "Give me back my teeth. Give me back my teeth." Averting her eyes from whatever it was that lurked outside, the terrified woman hurled the diabolical teeth through the window, where no doubt they were picked up by the toothless specter, which hastily replaced them in its mouth and crept back to its grave in the churchyard.

Bye for now,
Liza

3. Blood and Fire

In 1917 it became psychologically impossible for me to continue studying art. All my life, no matter what befell, I had felt myself an artist. And there I was, left without power to create, imagine, or even think of art.

I turned to dramatic activities. Practicing voice exercises and elocution helped to assuage the irritation and despondency caused by an awareness that I was not doing what had been mapped out for me to do.

Even with all means of sustenance taken away and having to leave the soil, in the steppe of Tambov, where my love of art had taken root, I was still able—glad of heart—to sing scales and do exercises, to concentrate on the sound of my own voice, to work on a theme or on a new shade of intonation for hours or to memorize pages of verse and prose. A burning ambition aided me in doing all this.

But above all loomed puppets, puppet theater, and puppet plays. They took possession of my mind, and it is now twenty years that they have been ensconced there, or rather have been hovering about, absurdly mixed up with nonpuppet thoughts.

If Liza had expected that with Judy's passing, she would be able to become her own woman, she soon realized that she would never be able to erase completely from the public's mind her identification as Judy Garland's daughter. For even as she was becoming a superstar in her own right—developing a strong, trendsetting public image, winning Tonys, an Emmy, and an Oscar, still her mother was never far from her side.

So, too, now in 1972 a global power shift was going on.

Power relationships, when they change, crunch people who have no idea where the crunch and hurt come from, who cannot understand what has made them fat or now drives them from their homes. This was what was happening to Americans in 1972—the world was pressing on them and pressing their politics at home, too, into strange new shapes. The changing world required a concentration of power in the president's hands greater than ever before to negotiate the perilous and delicate passage between two world eras. That concentration of power was changing the office of the presidency at home and abroad.

Like Judy, Liza is surrounded by gay men while seemingly harboring personal disdain for homosexuality and being married to a man rumored to be gay. And, most disturbing, there have been persistent rumors of drug and alcohol problems surrounding Liza, rumors she has consistently denied. In the first several years after Judy's death, Liza's interviews concerning Judy took on the tone of public psychiatric sessions; Liza often appeared to be working out her feelings about her mother as the tape recorder whirled:

One graveyard, in particular, was haunted by a most dramatic ghost. At Teviotdale, a farmer passing the church at night saw to his horror a ghastly white figure gibbering and waving its arms about in front of him. Then with a wild leap, the ghost landed on the back of his horse, grabbed him around the waist with its bony arms, and hung on like grim death while the terrified man rode madly homeward. On reaching his door, the farmer collapsed in a dead faint and was put to bed sick with fear. It later transpired the "ghost" was in fact an imbecile widow who "haunted" the churchyard believing that every passerby was her dead husband.

Epilogue: After Judy

JANUARY 9. . . . I often wonder how I get so carried away, to the extent that I forget what is important, what matters. It took Danny, a Chinese boy in cancer research who danced with me in "Danceland" tonight, to show me where it's at. We got to talking about people; Mick Jagger is made of the same stuff that he is. I'm made out of the exact same stuff as Liz Taylor and Lady Bird Johnson, EVERYone is grand; they're just taking different pathways to ultimately the same goal (even if some aren't aware of it). In the creator's eyes, Jimmy Page is NO BETTER than a skid row bum. NOW we come to my preference, tho' they are no better than lawyers, doctors, engineers, mechanics. . . . I dig musicians. There are girls who dig sailors, you could call them "sailories," and chicks who dig doctors, "doctories." So go ahead, call me a "groupie." It's Jimmy's twenty-seventh birthday today. . . .

I think nobody makes out the statements by listening to a live performance.

> Do I have to talk about her anymore? I don't know what else to say. Can't people accept that? Why do they want me to be the keeper of the flame and the destroyer of the myth at the same time? People are wishing things on me. It never crossed my mind that I would grow up to "be" my mother till people told me so and made me afraid of it. I loved her in so many ways. She was a friend of mine—a trying friend, but a friend. . . . This is what I tell myself: She did everything she ever wanted to do. She never really denied herself anything for me. See, I say, she had a wonderful life—she did what she wanted to do. And I have no right to change her fulfillment into my misery. I'm on my own broom now.

DECEMBER 6. . . . As a matter of extreme principle, I left Altamont an hour before the Stones came on. Scrunge and filth unlimited! I have come to the conclusion that I am spoiled. . . . I just wasn't satisfied to sit in the dirt with half a million smelly, grubby people and wait for the Stones. I really thought that people would be united and brought together in a lovely way . . . but nobody cared about each other. I lasted until the Burritos were over (they were wonderful), and the SLIMY FUCKED-UP Hells Angels started throwing beer on me, and no one around me cared. I started crying and cursing, and we split. I don't have to go through that crap to see MJ in the first place

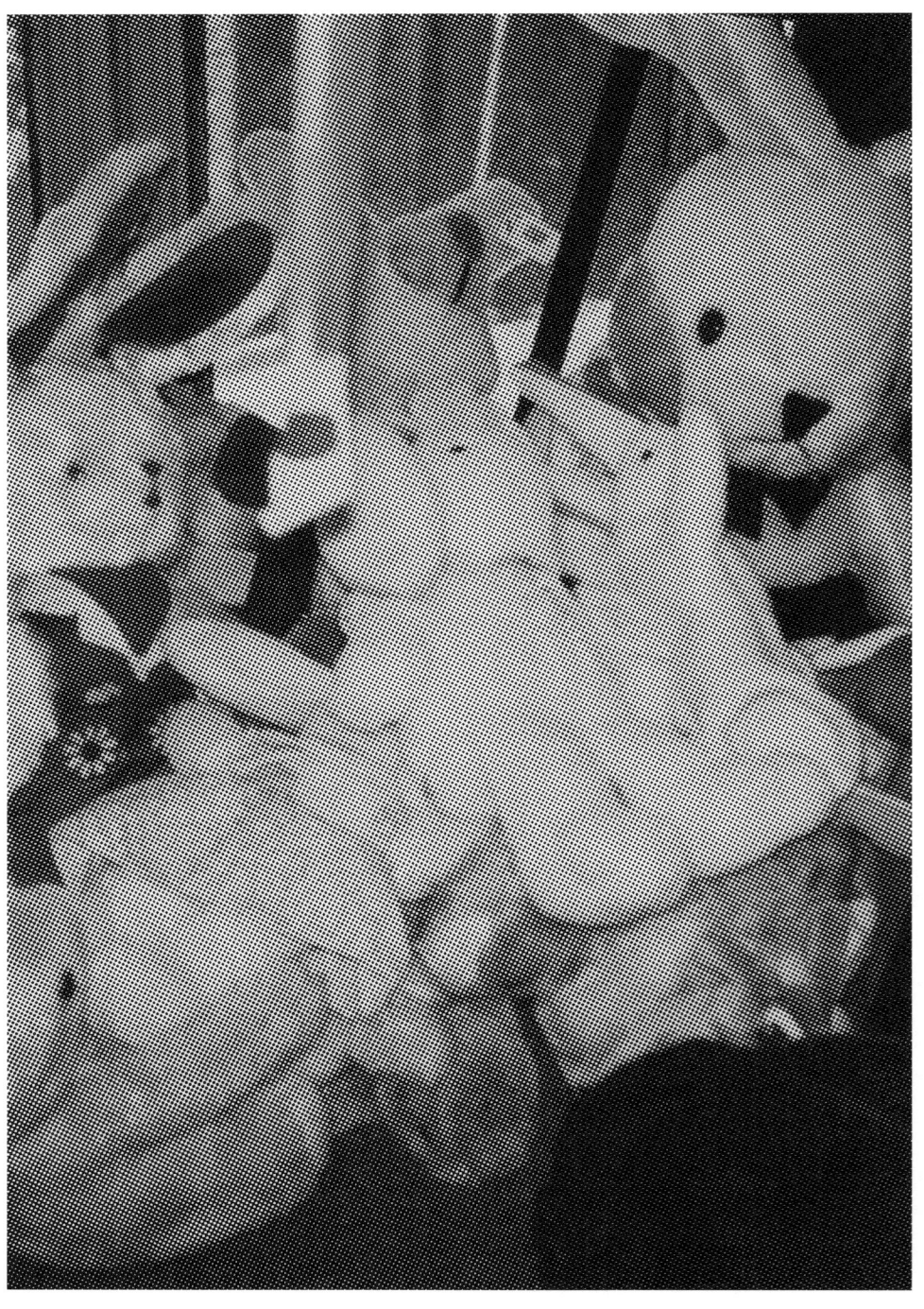

after seeing him so many times. I can close my eyes and see him ANY TIME I PLEASE.

Their pants are tight. Their hair is long. David wears a knobbed red garter around his left black pants leg and glittery clothes. One beautiful boy, his long black hair in a nice hairdo, seconds some of David's lines in his clearer but inaudible voice: He looks David in the eyes and gets his mouth real close to David's. Another, pretty spots of rouge in his cheeks, wishing David a happy birthday, gets something like a faggoty whine into it. But the Dolls are just that—real dolls: nice, pretty, gentle, friendly, clean youngsters. Nothing more (except that David, who is intelligent and a good performer for a public), nothing else. There is no sexual ambiguity here, no faggotry, no decadence, nothing sick.

During the curtain calls, it was reported that Judy pushed Liza off the stage so she could take a bow by herself.

1976

The Hudson is gray and ruffled like the surface of a nickel. Liza stares at Jersey City with filmic unmoving eyes. The falling wing carries the final shreds of Bob Dylan's "Oh, Sister."

SCHREBER, ROUSSEL,
DUCHAMP

Previously Unpublished, 1989

THIS TELEGRAM IS DEAD THAT IS THE ONLY WAY THAT ANYONE CAN UNDERSTAND IT

Jean Cocteau, Les Mariees sur la tour *Eiffel*

I gave this lecture as part of my installation at The Schreber Suite *at the Berkeley Art Museum in 1989. I learned about Daniel Paul Schreber through Guy Hocquenghem and Gilles Deleuze. I wanted to restore the artistic status of Schreber's writing through that installation. Sigmund Freud's use of Schreber in "The Three Case Histories," where he argues for a homosexual basis for paranoia, is highly suspect in retrospect. It's possible to read the book as a memoir of abuse and also as a proto-trans narrative. For me, there is a whole branch of theoretical writing that is incredibly generative and has very much formed my approach to making work. I was thinking about the ways in which texts can engender different kinds of embodiment and bodily possibilities, how we can inhabit them and they can inhabit us. —NB*

In calling this talk "Schreber, Roussel, Duchamp," I wish to point to an approach to material. An approach that does not act as an illustration but that turns the base material into a kind of lens for the viewing of other things. At one point while working on this project, I ran into a sort of impasse. I was caught up in the midst of the various psychoanalytic battles that have been waged over Daniel Paul Schreber's text. I found myself trying to provide illustrations of the various ideas involved in these debates, producing works that could be broken down into counters in various positions, standing in for the argument. I realized that I was too caught up in Schreber as a case history and that my real interest was in Schreber as a text, as a system of possible meanings. In this talk, I have attempted to expand on that idea by bringing Schreber into contact with two other texts. In my mind, they provide a stimulating triad—one that has a strong influence on my work. The other two texts I would like to speak to are the works of Raymond Roussel and the works of Marcel Duchamp. Roussel and Duchamp are already linked historically, and I will not rehearse that linkage here, but I feel that all three figures map similar areas and that their work employs many of the same tropes and terms. Rather than try to cover the subject exhaustively, I've tried to break things up into three general topics, somewhat fecklessly entitled "Glass," "Unmanning," and "Explanation."

Explanation

I would first like to speak briefly of Raymond Roussel's novel *Locus Solus*. Its narrative is relatively simple. A group of acquaintances visit the house of Cantarel, a famous scientist. While there, they are treated to a series of spectacles, each showcasing one of Cantarel's marvelous inventions. As evening falls, they depart.

Roussel's novels embody a peculiar type of structure, a structure that is determined by explanation. Both novels break into two even parts. In the first, activities are described—fantastic occurrences that are both rich and bewildering. In the second, we are supplied with the explanation for these oddities. This is a structure that we can recognize in other writing. For example, it is the structure of the detective story. The detective story asserts the primacy of authority by rehearsing its disappearance and reappearance. Crime is committed—seemingly without explanation—and through a careful examination, the explanation is found, and with it the criminal. Thus, the narrative is resolved, and what seemed to be disruption is instead reassurance. What is odd about Roussel's narratives is not that they refuse to offer the explanation that events seem to demand (which would be the easiest way in which we could imagine a transgressive approach to the detective form) but that in producing the much-needed explanation, they do not resolve the narrative in any valid way. In effect, they are a destruction of the mechanism of explanation itself. They turn explanation hollow. The underlying formal reason that they do this is that the explanations are not based on any rational idea. Instead, they are supplied by linguistic transformations as Roussel explained in an essay called "How I Wrote Certain of My Books." It is this same disruption of the explanation that is experienced in reading Schreber's memoirs. As an aside, I would like to mention that detection provides one of the master narratives often employed by psychoanalysis, particularly in Sigmund Freud's structuring of the case histories. The book again begins with an unusual series of acts, acts that Schreber is painfully aware of having committed. His attempts to provide an explanation for this behavior constitute the body of the work. While Schreber is successful at accounting for his behavior, the account he offers is essentially without meaning. Schreber confounds symptomology with metaphysics. It is as if a detective was suddenly confronted with the explanation that God literally struck down the victim whose murder began the novel.

This refutation of explanation is what has often been discussed as Duchamp's silence. Indeed, much of Duchamp's production seems to be the exegesis of a few central works. He continually produced new versions, groups of notes—in particular, "the boxes." But all of these supposedly secondary texts do not provide any resolution to Duchamp's work. Indeed, they are like an ever-proliferating network of paths and cul-de-sacs leading ever further from any sort of central meaning. As such, all of these works are radically horizontal rather than vertical.

Glass

I would like to consider a number of ideas around glass. Of course, Duchamp is perhaps most famous for *The Large Glass*, a work that he began shortly after seeing a stage production of Roussel's *Impressions of Africa* and seemed, for a long time, unable to finish.

The Large Glass presents a libidinal economy that merges the animal with the mechanical. In it, energy passes from steam to electricity; there is a mimicry of the sexual act in a form that denies contact. The ejaculations of the bachelors, the back-and-forth of the sled, and the emergence and retraction of the bride all take place in a rarefied atmosphere of isolated units and actions. These add up to a perpetual cycle in which energy is neither gained nor lost; the sexual charade continues without resolution; the bride remains a virgin; the bachelors, impotent; the mechanism, active. All of this takes place in a semantically loaded field: glass. Glass is at once barrier and opening; it is the equivalent of the unruptured hymen. Glass is that which allows the pleasure of full disclosure without the fulfillment of tactility. It is pierced only by that most spiritual phallus: light. *Locus Solus* contains a similar closed economy. In chapter 4, the visitors accompany Cantarel to an enormous glass structure that seems to contain a series of stage sets. They witness a bizarre group of pantomimes—tableaux involving a variety of people. Cantarel then provides the explanation. The people on view are actually dead, but Cantarel has discovered a substance named Impervium, which when inserted into the corpse forces the person to reenact the most important moment of their lives. This structure is the large glass in variant. Schreber, too, had his glasses—first, the looking glass that allowed him to follow the stages of his transformation into a woman, but also his "glass of cyanide that is destined for me." Most important, Schreber began to become glass, pierced by the sun, open to all eyes. God's eye was ever upon him. Thus, Schreber's continuing battle with the sun: his defiance of it and his lust for it. He saw the emergence of a second sun and bellowed that the sun was a whore.

Unmanning

Let us now look at two figures. The first sits before its mirror. Colored ribbons decorate the hair—a bit of lace, perhaps. Bared to the waist, it produces "the undeniable impression of a female torso." It sits in the asylum in Sonnenstein. The second wears a cloche hat and fur collar. These frame a face whose contours, softened by the photographer, suggest a bit of the coquette. It graces a bottle of violet-scented water. The first is Schreber, preparing for his impregnation by the upper god Ormudz; the second is Duchamp in his guise as Rrose Sélavy. These two bits of transvestism pose serious questions about meaning and, I believe, can be linked in their intent. Both set themselves in opposition to the phallocentric meanings of their time, opposing a rationalized body with a sexualized one. For both Schreber and Duchamp, the woman becomes a sign for pure sex. Schreber claims that women are almost completely filled with nerves of voluptuousness and that it is the higher concentration of these nerves that is transforming his body into that of a woman. Duchamp gave his female doppelgänger a name that literally means "sex that is life," and he made a comment on the *Mona Lisa's* "secret heat," while providing her with a mustache. I find in this desire to become the woman and, thus, become sex the seeds of a profound critique of the societal structure. In Schreber, one can see the constant battle between the wish to make meaning, use language, and be male and a wish to abandon meaning and redeem the world by simply being—and by being

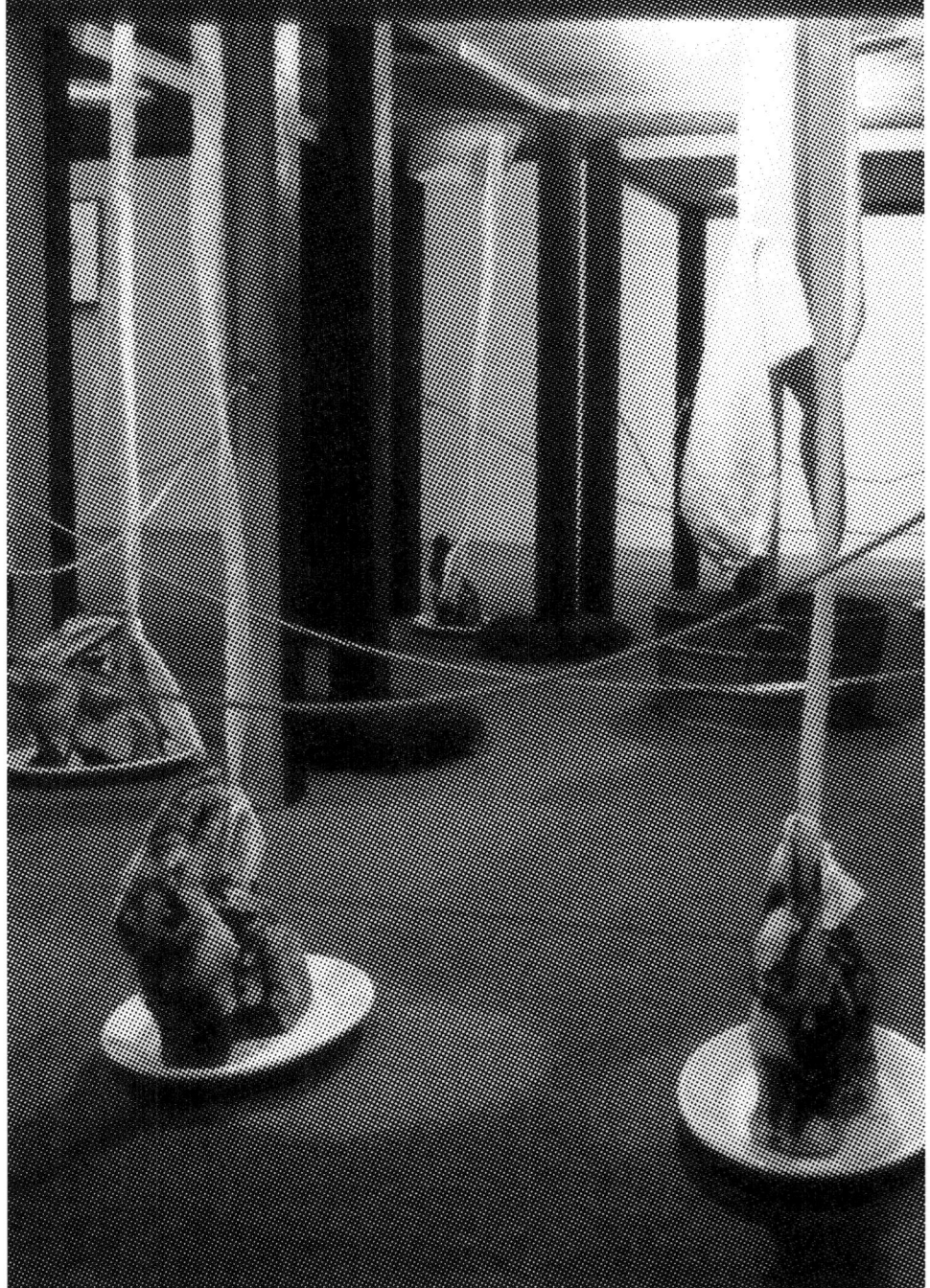

female. In both, female sexuality is both pure and self-sufficient. Schreber is compelled not only to become female but to become a woman engaged in the sexual act with herself, to provide God with the spectacle of a doubled femaleness. Duchamp's women exist without orifices, and their virginity exists as an ironic critique of the phallus. In both senses, these are models of a woman who does not lack. They are not castrated males but truly other. I would like, at this point, to suggest a line of inquiry about homosexuality and meaning. I see in the homosexual, as well, certain aspects of a refusal of the phallus, and I wonder if this refusal can be the genesis for a different type of meaning—one that is aleatory, connective, and diffuse, rather than centralized. It may well be that when conclusion is denied, the way is opened for horizontal reading.

The point I am trying to make is that these structures are not equivalent but are rather variants of the same myth, a myth of potential redemption denied. I have attempted to construct yet another variant of this myth in my work here.

PERFORMANCE SCRIPT

Previously Unpublished, 1991

The Halkan Council was absolutely polite, but its position was rock-hard, and nothing that Kirk, McCoy, Scott, or Uhura could say would alter it. The Federation was not to be allowed to mine dilithium crystals on the planet.

Kirk would have liked to have stayed to argue the question further, but he had already received word from Spock that an ion storm of considerable violence was beginning to blow through the Halkan system—and in fact Kirk could already see evidence of it in the Halkan weather, which was becoming decidedly lowering. To stay longer might risk disruption of transporter transmission, which would strand the landing party for an unknown time. In addition, it was Spock's opinion that the heart of the magnetic storm represented a danger to the *Enterprise* herself.

On this kind of opinion, Kirk would not have argued with Spock for a second; the first officer never erred by a hairline on the wrong side of conservatism. Kirk ordered the landing party beamed up.

That hairline was very nearly split this time. On the first attempt, the transporter got the party only partly materialized aboard the ship when the beam suffered a phase reversal, and all four of them found themselves standing on a bare plateau on the Halkan planet, illuminated only by a barrage of lightning. It was nearly five minutes later before the familiar transporter room sprang fully into being around them.

Kirk stepped quickly from the platform toward Spock. "We may or may not get those power crystals."

And then he stopped, in mid-step as well as mid-sentence. For Spock and the transporter chief were saluting, and a most peculiar salute it was: the arms first folded loosely, then raised stiffly horizontal and squared out.

"At norm," Spock said to the transporter chief, in a voice loaded with savage harshness.

All homosexuality is concerned with anal eroticism, whatever the differentiations and perverse reterritorializations to which the Oedipus complex subsequently subjects it. The anus is not a substitute for the vagina: Women have one as well as men. The phallus's signifying-discerning function is established at the very same moment that the anus-organ breaks away from its imposed privatization, in order to take part in the desire race. To reinvest the anus collectively and libidinally would involve a proportional weakening of the great phallic signifier, which dominates us constantly both in the small-scale hierarchies of the family and in the great social hierarchies. The least acceptable desiring operation (precisely because it is the most desublimating one) is that which is directed at the anus.

This is the generation that must seize the most potent of all weapons: transgression. This generation, Captain, must embrace our transgressive identities. I offer this generation its clarion call to arms: lambada! To digress: Let us here note that the lambada occupies the most powerful nexuses of contemporary discursive formations. The lambada rehearses the subversive strategies whereby the impulse to colonialism is defeated on its own turf: that of the celebration of pillaged third-world cultures in a perverse culture that is in reality an omniculture: a parade of despicable thong bikinis, World Cup soccer stars, and espadrilles. Here the lambada performs a reversal, a *détournement* that abandons French models for one founded in a Santeria-flavored metadiscourse.

As for the lambada's other virtues as a figure of resistance and disruption, two words will suffice: *the body*. What can we say of the body in lambada—this desiring machinery, this aspiring body, this site of hysteria, and tropical fruit juices? This body subjected to the rigors of lessons for the first time since the "bus stop"? This body of rhythms of syncopation, this labyrinth without an Arachne? This body belongs to the preverbal, we cannot speak of it. We can only marvel at this tempest of zouk and jouissance: *La Danse Interdit*: The Forbidden Dance.

Kirk could not answer. He was spared having to, for at that moment Sulu entered the transporter room. His movements, his manner, were cold, arrogant, and hypercompetent, but that was not the worst of it. The symbol on his breast, the galaxy with the dagger through it, had inside it also a clenched fist around the blade of the dagger, from which blood was dripping. It was an extreme parody of something familiar; it showed that the gentle Sulu, the ship's navigator and helmsman, was now her chief security officer.

Sulu did not salute. He barked, "Status of mission, Captain?"

"No change," Kirk said carefully.

"Standard procedure, then?"

Kirk did not know what this question meant under these eerie circumstances, but he doubted that operating by the book—whatever the book might say—would accomplish much more than delaying matters, and time was what he needed. Therefore, he nodded.

Sulu turned to the nearest intercom. "Mr. Chekov."

Let me refresh your memory with a few crucial facts about my life. After years of drifting, I began to realize that it was my duty to become an artist. I would use my considerable expressive gifts to enrich the lives of those around me. I began to practice my craft in a humble way. After a time, I began to receive the attention of those people whose powerful influence would ensure that my vision would be shared by the many who were in desperate need of it. I created a vast work that described the complexities, the injustices, and the pure comedy that make up this thing we call our society. Acclaim was mine, but a doubt gnawed my fevered soul. I knew that even though I had described my entire world, there was still something small about my work.

I searched for a theme whose depth and resonance would finally match the genius that I could bring to it. Oddly enough, at this time, thousands were succumbing to a vast and terrible disease, and while they succumbed, thousands of others joined together to battle the severe social injustices that this crisis created—or, should I say, made evident. Here, at last, was my métier. Here was a mass who needed my transcendent vision and jocular camaraderie. Here was a people whose song I could teach the world to sing. Here were brothers and sisters putting their lives on the line every single day without a way to make sense of their tumultuous experience. Here was something that seemed like a good thing to make work about.

I remember how the whole thing started—with a television appearance and a phone call. It was March 1970. I'd been on *The Merv Griffin Show*. I'd lost weight; my hair was very full and very sexy; I looked quite good. A couple of days later, I got a message from the switchboard at the Sierra Towers that Desi Arnaz Jr. had called. I knew he was Lucille Ball's son, but I'd never met him. I had no idea why he'd called, so I kind of ignored it.

Desi called the next day and sounded different, much more personal. We agreed to have dinner Monday, and it quickly became apparent that records were the furthest thing from his mind. I had to go to New York for a couple of days, and he was very distressed about that. I arrived in the city on St. Patrick's Day, and when I opened my hotel room door, there were green flowers waiting for me and a note that called me his special little Irish leprechaun. I felt a little skip of the heart, and that was it. I called him immediately, and when I got back to LA, we started going everywhere and doing everything together. It was the beginning of the romance. Though I've at times hesitated to say it, the truth is that I loved Desi Arnaz Jr. I loved him very much.

Power/Resistance/Transgression and the Body: An Autopsy

On the bridge, there was a huge duplicate of the galaxy-and-dagger device, and the captain's chair had widely flared arms, almost like a throne. The man who should be Chekov was eyeing Uhura with open, deliberate, speculative interest, his intent unmistakable. Nobody else seemed to find this unusual or even interesting. Kirk went directly to her.

"Any new orders, Lieutenant?"

"No, sir. You are still ordered to annihilate the Halkans unless they comply. No alternative action has been prescribed."

"Thank you." He went to his chair and sank in. It felt downright luxurious. "Report, Mr. Sulu?"

"Phasers locked on Target A, Captain. Approaching optimum range. Shall I commence fire?"

"I want a status report first." He touched the intercom. "Mr. Scott?"

"Scott here, sir."

I have to report that my initial efforts to create beautiful, progressive, sex-positive, and proactive works of art out of the political struggle of my compatriots were met with some reserve on their parts. Indeed, some had expressed the somewhat naive wish that I would appear at more planning meetings rather than clarifying the movement's goal to the cameras at demos. My own professional integrity began to be doubted, and my motives impugned. The final blow came when a local critic (who is a closeted, self-hating queer, I might add) wrote the following: "Just as the political struggles of the nineteenth century French have been cynically recycled into the second act show-stopping barricades scene in *Les Miz*, so are the battles of the activists who confront today's horrifying health crisis being recycled into spectacles of bogus resistance and self-aggrandizement by certain self-serving artists with the same slick aplomb."

I was twenty-four. I'd experienced every trauma on the list, including the separation of my parents and feeling abandoned first by my father and then by my mother.

For myself, I would rather accept this as a condition I have, recognize the tremendous positive change in me, and say to myself, "This is it. For the rest of my life, I take a pill in the morning and a pill at night." Some creative people are especially resistant to lithium; they believe that creativity is born of nuttiness, and if you're insane, you're a genius. In fact, I've found that my creativity has been enhanced by the treatment, that the comfort I now feel with myself allows me to take much bigger risks than I ever would have before. The downside of the drug is so small compared to the release of my power over myself, "Why mess around?"

"Very good, Mr. Scott." In fact, it was very bad, but there was no help for it. As he switched out, Spock came onto the bridge.

We have referred to the notion, today widespread among typical groups of the New Left, that "seizure of power" in the sense of a direct assault on the centers of political control (the state), backed and carried out by mass action under the leadership of centralized mass parties—that such strategy is not, and cannot be, on the agenda in the advanced capitalist countries. The main reasons are (1) the concentration of overwhelming military and police power in the hands of an effectively functioning government and (2) the prevalence of a reformist consciousness among the working classes. Is there a historical alternative?

We recall the pattern of the bourgeois revolution: The attainment of economic power by the bourgeoisie within a feudal society preceded the seizure of political power. To be sure, this pattern cannot simply be passed along to the socialist revolution; but the question arises: Are there any indications that the working class might attain economic though not political power within the capitalist system, and prior to a revolution? This would be the case if the workers would take control in the factories and shops and redirect and reorganize production. But precisely this would be the revolution and would entail political power. Is a gradual change in economic power, turning quantitative into qualitative change through radicalization of workers' demands and successes, conceivable within capitalism?

It is now week 3 into rehearsal, and at 3 p.m., the cast is having its first full nonstop rehearsal. Now everybody will see what they've got. Tension is sweet and high. The entire cast is on one side of the tennis-court-sized

My Studio Is a Dungeon Is the Studio

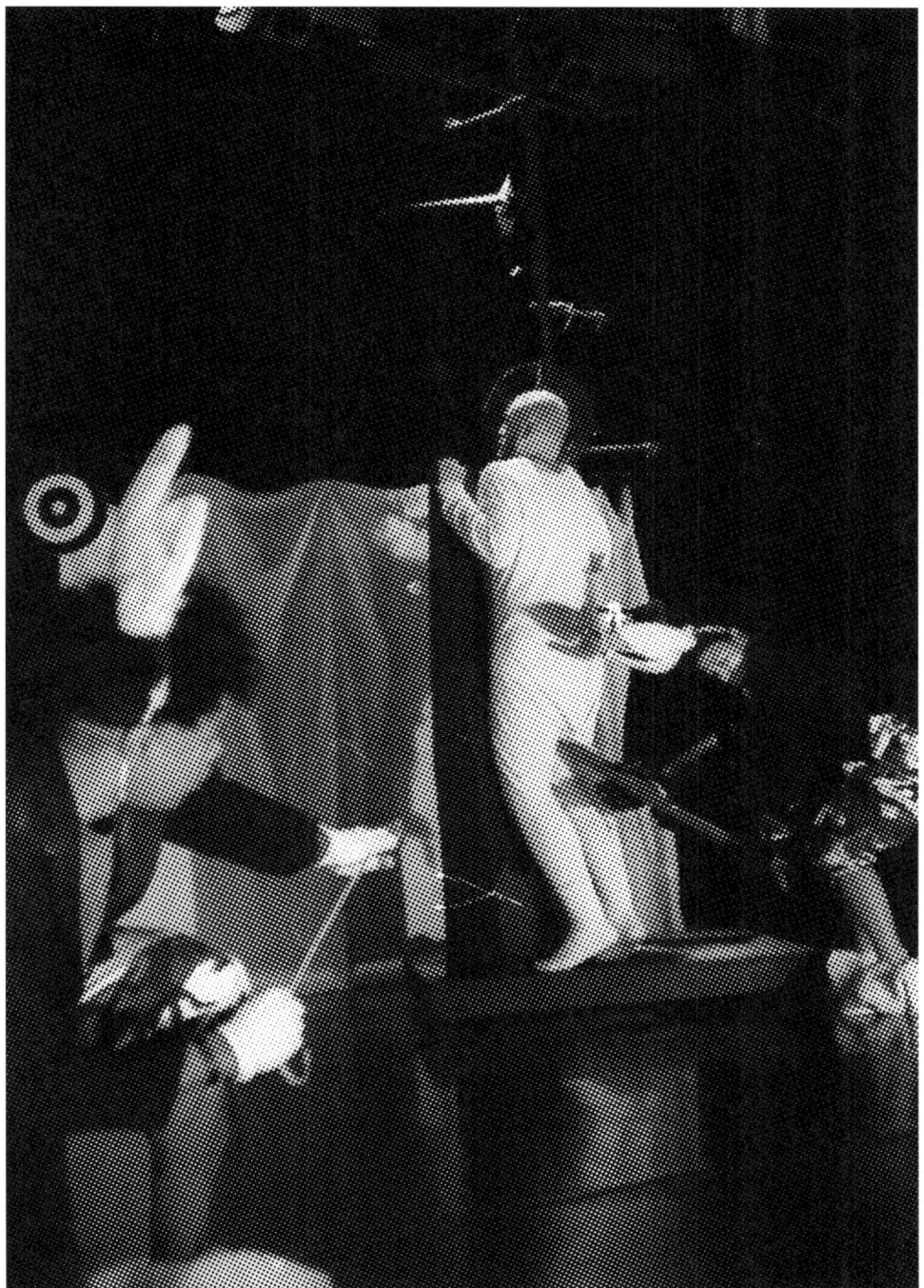

studio looking into the mirror across the floor. The directors, writers, and arrangers sit in chairs in front of the mirror. Act I: Liza goes on.

She is a pile of string, building herself up into a song at one end of the room, unwinding it, and then letting herself go slack into a single line as she moves to the other side of the imaginary apron. It only takes that long for her to divest herself of one set of emotions and call forth another. She builds the string up again, higher and higher, into a new tower of sound, while looking, always with a slight smile on her face, at Mr. Ebb, whose words are coming out of her mouth.

Mr. Ebb, with his chin raised and a rapt expression on his face, holds Ms. Minnelli affectionately in his eyes as if his arms were holding a baby above his head. She beats, belts, shakes, strums. "I live alone; I *like* it!" Da-dum, da-dum, *da-dum*, da! A locomotive of energy is exploding. There is too much power being released in too small a room. Everybody knows it. For the first time, the women in the chorus line realize the obvious: They are working with Liza Minnelli. One by one, without taking their eyes off her, they begin to cry.

In the past, Ms. Minnelli's personal problems have soaked up a lot of tabloid ink. After the rehearsal is over, she is asked how she feels when she is onstage, more or less than herself?

"I feel myself," she answers, "but more purely. Up there, I'm not taunted by people's opinions of me. I am what I do."

THE SECRET SQUARE

Dear World, *1991*

Dear World was a one-shot zine I did with Camille Roy and Wayne Smith. We went to a bunch of our friends and asked them to write a letter that would be prefaced "Dear World." It's a bit astonishing to me now because the contributors are a fucking murderers' row. A wild assortment of people, with contributions by Dorothy Allison, Dodie Bellamy, Gary Indiana, Sarah Schulman, Eileen Myles, Dennis Cooper, Bob Flanagan, Richard Hawkins, Kevin Killian, and Liz Kotz—even one of the first things by David Sedaris. —NB

"Whatever happened, come fire or flood or I don't know what," Shirley Partridge snapped, with more vehemence than anyone in the family could remember, "I'm going to fire Reuben Kincaid if it's the last thing I do! There's no excuse for his not being on time like this! No excuse at all!"

"Now, Mom." Laurie Partridge tried to pacify her, putting her arms around her mother's shoulders. "You're just upset, and you're saying things you don't mean."

"Oh no, I'm not!" Shirley flared angrily, pushing her away, using a burning anger to blot out the almost paralyzing fear that was beginning to fill her mind and soul. "That silly old plane of his! I knew I shouldn't have given in when Keith asked me. I knew it! I'll just bet they ran out of fuel, made a forced landing, somewhere in all that big country, and won't be here for hours!"

She knew she was being extremely silly, knew she was saying outrageous things because she was worried sick and badly frightened, as well as burning mad. But she couldn't help it. The mother in her, the woman who would always see Keith Partridge as a little boy even when he became a head taller than she, just wouldn't stop crying it out. Shirley Partridge, the leader of the Partridge Family, the world-renowned show biz team, was definitely playing second fiddle now. After all, there are limits to a person's patience, even after taking all possibilities into consideration. Especially maternal patience. That was the worst kind. Just ask any mother!

Furious, she stormed into her room and flung herself on the bed. In the nightstand to her right, she found her pen and diary. She wrote as follows:

June 1

Dear You,

I felt as if I had always known him. He did not speak French but read it handily. I asked him a question about his relations with the military. "Oh, me, I'm an agnostic where the military is concerned," he said offhandedly. "I'm neither for nor against on that score."

The conversation quickly took on a bantering tone (and what would my American colleague have thought, "Kissinger is an extraordinarily serious man . . ." etc.), and I asked him what his best and worst memories were.

"Mrs. Partridge," he replied, "if you come into my life again someday, I'll tell you all my memories, but for right now. . . ."

He looked at his watch, asked if I had a few minutes, and called in Tony Lake. Then he said rapidly that he was supposed to speak at the president's news conference, that I could thus see him in action, and had Lake take me up to the floor above the Roosevelt Room. And there I was, suddenly facing a made-up President Nixon, in front of six television cameras, some fifty journalists, and many hand cameras. The heat was overwhelming.

Dressed all in blue (in a blue shirt and a blue tie), heavily powdered, with his deep-set eyes, ski-jump nose, and bulldog jaw, the chin jutting and receding all at once, Nixon looked like a commedia dell'arte character. His immense right hand, monstrous and deformed by far too much handshaking, looked like the hand of a strangler. The whole scene was at the same time phantasmagorical and improvised—like American society.

My Studio Is a Dungeon Is the Studio

That morning the subject was chemical and biological weapons in Vietnam. In front of a velvet drapery (blue, too), Kissinger, who is smaller than the president (though of average stature for a European, Kissinger is smaller than most Americans), with his sloping forehead, aquiline nose, and heavy skeptical chin, looked like a libidinous bird. Yet that rather awkward appearance was lit up by a smile and a tranquility that disturbed me.

Nixon spoke a few words that had been prepared in advance and had already been passed around in handouts, and then Ron Ziegler, his press spokesman, another young man with blue eyes, introduced Kissinger. Suddenly, I realized that Kissinger's skin coloring was yellow, a grayish-ashen kind of yellow, probably from being shut indoors too much. Prisoners have that coloring. Up on the platform, facing the cameras as if he had stepped out of a closet, a self-effacing, modest, chilly Kissinger seemed to be playing the butler in a comedy in which Nixon was the master.

The journalists fired questions at him. Had China signed or had she not signed the Geneva Protocol? Was tear gas being used in Vietnam or not? What was the scientific description of the effects of chemical weapons?

His hands behind him, Kissinger replied in a voice that sounded very sincere. "I'm not an expert on chemical warfare. I don't know the names of all these effects." Before coming into the room, he had whispered to me, "I see journalists often. Generally, they annoy me, but I do this for masochistic reasons."

Personally, I found the press conference macabre. The question of whether it was desirable or not to spread epidemics among the Vietnamese population, and whether the right was to be reserved to use chemical weapons in reprisal, and so on were being discussed as if the subject was distributing powdered milk. None of the newsmen seemed to appreciate the frightening connotations.

When we were back down in Kissinger's office, he asked, expecting a warm reaction, for my impression. I couldn't help saying that it had all seemed rather sinister to me. Astonished, he made no comment. (In his view, the categorical renunciation of chemical and biological weapons, except in cases of reprisal, represented a liberal move intended to satisfy the doves—that is, the antiwar section of American opinion. It was hard for him to understand the lack of unreserved applause for the magnanimity of the decision.)

How European Kissinger seemed in the typically American atmosphere such as that press conference! The appearance, the smile, the sensitivity, and the skepticism—and the vulnerability. He told me he abhorred boring things and boring people. He asked me if I thought he resembled the portrait of him painted by the press. I replied that he seemed younger and not so fat. "Journalists annoy me, but you don't," he said, and I began to find him more and more sympathetic.

June 10

Dear You,

It is commonplace that celebrities obtain their niche by embodying certain allegorical, or as it has often been said, mythic traits. To be a celebrity is to strip away the stuff of individuality to become a conduit for a particular discourse. Liza is perhaps unique in the realm of celebrity because she embodies a discourse that is essentially that of the fan—the discourse of one whose validity is derived from their relation to someone famous. There are famous children, children of famous parents, and children who have finally stepped out from under their parents' shadow, but no other celebrity who for so long has been famous only because her mother was famous. Perhaps the closest corollary is Frank Sinatra Jr., who, like Liza, cannot appear in public without somehow seeming a shabby Xerox of someone else. Liza cannot sing without singing with "momma," and it seems that it will be a terrible, terrible sin if she happens to live longer than her mother did.

There could be a dozen good reasons why Reuben Kincaid and Keith were delayed, any one of which would make good sense. But the mother in Shirley couldn't read anything but dreadful happenings into that fact. She was imagining all sorts of awful things.

Things that wouldn't just go away.

Like, here it was eight o'clock, and the family was comfortably ensconced in one of the best hotels in Lincoln with nothing but a ten-minute limousine ride to the civic auditorium necessary to get them onto the stage with all of their musical equipment to do a show. Shirley and the kids were already dressed in their now-famous red-and-black costumes with the shining brass buttons, and a Mister Shane, who was somebody connected with the local Chamber of Commerce, had come and explained something about how the evening performance had been planned. Shirley had listened politely, nodding her head, made some excuses about Reuben Kincaid and Keith being missing, and then Mister Shane had left the suite of rooms, almost bowing his way out. He was a nice old fellow in a tuxedo and tie with very pleasant manners. Danny Partridge had been very impressed with him and had even managed to exchange some Wall Street chitchat with him. Mister Shane had some oil stock. In Danny's journal, he remembered the events of the following day thus:

June 1

Dear You,

I fucked Nicky last night. It excites me to death to write the word *fuck* concerning Nicky and myself. I've used that word a million times without realizing its meaning. I wish people didn't use it as a swear word. Ahh, I climbed all over him and on him and under him, I clutched at him and moaned. I get weak and lightheaded at the thought. It's such a huge relief to lose every inhibition and lose my mind to my body. When he fell asleep, I could hardly move without choking or reaching into the air for nothing. On the way out, I stopped to kiss his bass. I'm so in love, I don't even realize what I'm doing.

October 2

Dear You,

I came! How do you like that? I phoned Noel (nervous and sweating), and he invited me over "anytime!" I dressed quickly, and Gala split. We got along fantastic, but he must have thought I wanted to be platonic, because after two hours I had to seduce him, and we wound up in his room (fireplace, red lights, etc.). Lovely romance. We played around for a while, and then he made love to me. *Amazing!* I was totally under his control. He put me in a hundred positions and did such stupendous things! It's doubtful that anybody could surpass his prism. It was like being caught in a web, unable to free myself—wanting to get more tangled. What is wrong with Nicky? I don't understand. Noel said, "That, my dear, is what you call a fuck."

I smiled and said, "With this historical shift, capitalism denies its legitimation to rule any longer the life of men and women, to shape nature and society in its own image." Breaking the oppressive rule of material production now shifts the focus from the material to the intellectual sectors of production, from alienated labor to creative work.

Or rather material production, increasingly subjected to technological organization, becomes susceptible to humanization. The weight of dead labor on living labor is reducible through removing progressively living labor from the mechanized and fragmented work process where it is still held by the requirements of capitalist production. The transfer of living labor to 'supervisory' functions would open the possibility of changing the direction and goals of material production itself. Human labor, instead of being a commodity producing commodities in accordance with the law of value, could produce for human needs in accordance with the law of freedom—the needs of a liberated human existence. An alternative appears that would involve the subversion of the material and intellectual culture. The consumer society raises the specter not only of an economic but also of a cultural revolution: a new civilization where culture is no longer a privileged branch in a social division of labor but instead a culture that shapes society in its entirety, in all its branches, including those of material production, and that radically changes prevalent values and aspirations.

"This change is foreshadowed, in an ideological form, by the counterimages and countervalues with which the New Left contradicts the images of the capitalist universe. The exhibition of noncompetitive behavior, the rejection of brutal 'virility,' the debunking of the capitalist productivity of work, the affirmation of the sensibility, sensuality, of the body, the ecological protest, the contempt for the false heroism in outer space and colonial wars, the women's liberation movement (where it does not envisage the liberated woman as merely having an equal share in the repressive features of male prerogatives), the rejection of the anti-erotic, puritan cult of plastic beauty and cleanliness—all these tendencies contribute to the weakening of the Performance Principle. They articulate the deep malaise prevalent among the people at large."

September 1

Dear You,

The Pet Shop Boys have used their position within the entertainment hegemony to examine the specific problem of Liza. Self-professed students of Jean Baudrillard, they have created a cultural intervention in the form of a twelve-inch entitled "Losing My Mind." Their action attempts to construct an archaeology, through the index, of several important points of interaction between gay culture and the music industry.

The first is the primacy of disco. Disco remains the Indigenous folk music of gay men and has proved to be the most resonant development in popular music in the past twenty years. It marked the passage in popular music from the temporal to the architectonic. It is designed to be consumed in public, but for the fascist spectacle of the concert, it substitutes the communal gathering, the dance hall. Over the individual performer, it privileges the organizer, conductor, or DJ, as they are called. It promotes a song type that refuses narrative closure, that is not supposed to end, working instead on rhythmic ebb and flow, or as it is often called, tension and release (as they say, "Can't Stop the Music").

The next phenomenon is what we knew in the 1970s as "going disco." As disco began to dominate the music industry, more and more "old-timers" began to attempt to revive flagging careers with the help of an oompah bass line and imported conga players. It is necessary only to mention the efforts of such music industry flaks as Roxy Music, Barbra Streisand, Rod Stewart, Ethel Merman, and misogynist-former-genderbending-windbags the Rolling Stones. Fans of pathetic rock acts angrily received the news that this or that poseur had "gone disco," while gay men refused to be beguiled by such craven bids for their dollar and remained true to valid divas. With the enormous number of entertainers who "went disco" at this time, it is hard to believe that Liza had not already done so before now, but such is the case.

The next important characteristic of disco is its insatiable appetite for sonic and conceptual matter. The DJ is encouraged to combine elements of many different songs and identities into one mix. Among other things, this idea foreshadows the trend in the entertainment industry, particularly in movies, that is known as *packaging*. Entertainments are devised on the basis of bringing together a number of different celebrities. One memorable example of this is the duet "Enough Is Enough" sung by Barbra Streisand and Donna Summer. The public is increasingly encouraged to envision celebrities as arbitrary elements that can be combined at will. This is in preparation for the future, where celebrities will exist only as information on computer software, along with all scripts, librettos, and settings, allowing you to choose to see Debbie Harry singing *La Bohéme* in Dresden or Drew Barrymore and Danny Bonaduce opposite Walter Brennan in *To Have and Have Not*. Given this, "Losing My Mind" is a package of Liza + the Pet Shop Boys + Stephen Sondheim.

Finally, classic disco evolved the figure of the diva, or rather transposed that figure from that other well of homosexuality: grand opera.

In both forms, the diva's function is fundamentally the same; she is to suffer. This suffering must be expressed in sumptuous terms. Disco also borrowed a trope from gospel by allowing for the concept of redemption. What does it mean that gay men consistently choose to support and produce the image of the fantastic, artificially suffering woman? For a people who have no semiological place in the structure of society, this figure may provide one of the few recognizable images of gay male experience. Sylvester, the only male diva, sings, "When we're out there dancin' on the floor, you make me feel mighty real." This, then, is the idea of redemption through the possibility of becoming actual. Most of the time, we are not real. But what seemed a cherished goal in the 1970s is a pointless pursuit in the 1980s, where finally nothing was real.

Since we can conceive of only one character that Liza lives in relation to, it is abundantly clear she is singing the lyrics of "Losing My Mind" to "The sun comes up, I think about you, the coffee cup, I think about you." This "you" can be only one person in Liza's world. As such, how can we not be moved when she says, "You told me you loved me, or were you just being kind, or am I losing my mind?" In a certain way, Judy Garland is the ultimate diva, and her daughter, the ultimate gay man rapt in his prostration at the clay feet of his goddess.

Shirley had been much too preoccupied and worried to pay much attention to that either. Tracy and Christopher were both playing on the floor with Simone again, and the brown-and-white mascot was barking happily, adding more confusion to the uproar. Shirley began to feel her nerves going very rapidly, something that Laurie Partridge was quick to notice. But nothing really helped. Shirley fidgeted, paced the room, kept casting glances at the door to the suite and at the round gold clock on the wall above the imitation fireplace. But time would not stop. Not even for a mother. It kept getting later and later. Very late.

And soon it was going on eight thirty. Eight thirty! And still no Keith, no Reuben. Only worry and more worry. As if she didn't have enough already.

"Mom," Laurie Partridge said as softly as she could.

Shirley Partridge whirled at the sound of her voice.

"What is it, Laurie?" She sounded shrill, almost hysterical.

"Don't you think we ought to start making tracks to the civic auditorium? If we don't get a move on, we won't even have time to cough before we go into our songs."

"Huh, what . . . ?" Shirley shook her head. "I'm sorry, honey. What did you say, Laurie?" She seemed completely bewildered.

"I said," Laurie declared very firmly, "that it's time we left for the civic auditorium. Or we'll be late."

Shirley Partridge blinked and then passed a slender hand across her forehead. "Uh, yes . . . suppose you're right. Get your coats on, kids. I didn't realize it was so late. . . ."

"Mom," Laurie said with great tenderness, "you've known exactly what time it is—the hour, the minute, the second, since we parked the bus in the hotel garage. Come on, Mom. Stop knocking yourself out. The men will be okay. They're just delayed, that's all. Don't make a federal case out of it. You've got a show to do tonight." Laurie smiled, looking absolutely beautiful. And all-knowing. She rummaged in her purse and pulled out the battered pink notebook she had used as her personal diary since she was eleven. Tossing back her hair, she began to read in her lilting voice:

November 10

Dear You,

Led Zeppelin Live in 1969 was an event unparalleled in musical history. They played longer and harder than any group ever had, totally changing the concept of rock concerts. They flailed around like dervishes, making so much sound that the air was heavy with metal. Two hours after the lights went out, as the band sauntered offstage, the audience was a delirious, parched mass, crawling through the rock and roll desert, thirsting for an encore. Twenty long minutes later, Mighty Zeppelin returned to satiate their famished followers.

The long ride from Santa Barbara was one of those dream experiences that leave you glowing in the dark. From the moment that Jimmy slid his small velvet-clad ass across the seat of the limo, right next to mine, until the door was thrown open in front of the Experience, we cooed and giggled like doves in heat. It was a hundred-mile drive, which gave him plenty of time to come out with "all the lines." He told me he had gotten my number the last time he was in town but was too nervous to use it until the last day, and he called and called but the line was constantly busy. Mm-hmm. He said he wanted to spend time with me *more than anything in the world*. Tell me more. I kissed and slobbered all over the inside crease of his slim white arm until he rolled his head against the plush seat gasping, "Oh Laurie, yes, yes, yes." Yeah, yeah, yeah. He warned me that his previous LA girlfriend would probably be in the club and that I would have to give him the chance to "explain" to her about me. Uh-oh.

He looked hard at me with a tiny smile on his rosebud lips, making me sweat with suspense about the long night to come. He put something into my hand, and it turned out to be a silver ring with twenty little pieces of turquoise embedded in it, and I wondered if I was going steady with the best guitar player in the world. He always messed with his black curls, poofing and fluffing them around his flawless face, and he wore emerald velvet and white chiffon, thin little socks, and the most perfect brooch on his lapel. I couldn't wait to get back to the hotel and take it all off. Our bodies were meant to be together, and he said, "I hope you'll never get rid of me. Please keep me around until you don't want me anymore. . . . I'm not like this, what's happening to me? All I can do is look at your face." I held him so close and told him, "I feel like I've been holding you forever," and he said, "You will be. We'll be together for a long, long time if you want it that way. I've known you for a thousand years. Don't you feel that way?" Yes yes yes Mr. Page. We tried to sleep but woke up every few minutes and kissed. Every time he touched me, he would moan and sigh and call to God. Such a face, so gentle and soft, I'm amazed at his sadistic tendencies; they're such a part of him that I doubt if he'll ever stop. It was really frightening. He changed into another person, but all he did was chew me and slap me a little. We talked about our ages, and he said that five years between couples is perfect. Everything he said drove me nuts. His beautiful gray eyes always there beside me, beneath me, above me. Every time I feel doubtful (which is constantly), I look at his ring, and all I can see is his perfect face.

I saw Jimmy's whips curled up in his suitcase like they were taking a nap and pretended I didn't, looking quickly away as if I had seen someone's private peep show. He came up behind me and put his hands gently around my throat and said, "Don't worry, Miss P., I'll never use those on you. I'll never hurt you like that." Then he sucked on my neck, and when I could feel the bruise being called up out of my bloodstream, he tossed me down on the bed and told me he would throw the whips away to show how much I meant to him. After ripping into my antique lace dress and making raging, blinding love to me, he wrapped the whips 'round and 'round his forearm and slid the leather coils into the flowered plastic wastebasket, where they remained until he left for Somewhere, USA, a week later.

November 5

Dear You,

I finally bought the Liza and the Pet Shop Boys single, and it isn't a disco song at all! I was expecting something along the lines of "It's Raining Men," and instead the orchestration is all synthesizers, and Liza sings the entire song in a stentorian bellow instead of the rapturous disco diva-ing I had envisioned.

November 8

Dear You,

I listened to the song again, this time it kept changing into "Bizarre Love Triangle" by New Order. Now I get it. This single isn't about what would happen if Liza made a disco record; it's about what would happen if Liza was the lead singer in New Order. Now I totally understand her monotone delivery, so like the Sisters of Mercy. It makes perfect sense. I imagine her thinking, "Fuck all of these pouty Brits and their heroin trance music. I've had real pain, real depression, and I've taken more drugs than all of Joy Division put together. Ian Curtis—what a flyweight. I was passing out at Xenon while he was getting blow-dry hairdos and zits. He killed himself, *but I stayed around to suffer*." Liza the grown-up crack baby with the heart of gold. The best part now is when she starts going "losing my mind, losing my mind" over and over again at the end like the Librium is finally starting to kick in.

November 12

Dear You,

What I learned from "Losing My Mind":

1   Disco, in its golden age, pitted highly demanding singing, relentless beat, and orchestral arrangements against each other in an attempt to decenter the self.

2   The 1980s saw gay pop stars in Britain attempting to devise a new aural identity from the fragments of punk. They proposed a model that might best be described as rapturous self-pity and gave voice to a generation.

3   Rather than punk becoming the new disco, disco became the gay punk, as bands like New Order, Human League, and Bronski Beat began to acknowledge their real roots.

4   "Losing My Mind" is not a 1980s song mimicking the heyday of 1970s disco; it is the song that ends the 1980s, by placing Liza Minelli, whose entire life has been spent as a type of meta-homosexual, in front of New Order to sing a song written by the last living composer of Broadway musicals, Stephen Sondheim. In this package, disco, punk, show tunes, psychedelia, emotion, Judy Garland, comebacks, remixes, and interpretation all consume each other in a writhing portrait of contemporary gay consciousness.

5   To make a disco diva song in the late 1980s is to retell the Judy Garland story: loss, redemption, transcendence. But for younger gay men, this story can only have resonance as a museum piece.

6   This story is Liza's story, Liza's and ours, because the horror isn't in self-immolation on the flaming pyre of art; it's in the fact that we got the guy, had the revolution, did the drug, and *nothing changed*. Liza's horror is the horror of continuation, of being awakened every few years, put together with a band, and *going on with the show*.

December 26

Dear You,

You're in Europe. You shouldn't have gone. I told you that you shouldn't have gone.

If you were going to go anyway, you shouldn't have asked me.

Does the reader now understand why the ruling classes decidedly want to bring us to where the guns shoot and the sabers slash? Why they accuse us of cowardice because we do not betake ourselves without more ado into the street, where we are certain of defeat in advance? Why they so earnestly implore us to play for once the part of cannon fodder?

Is the pride of the Partridges doomed to be "Buzzard Bait"?

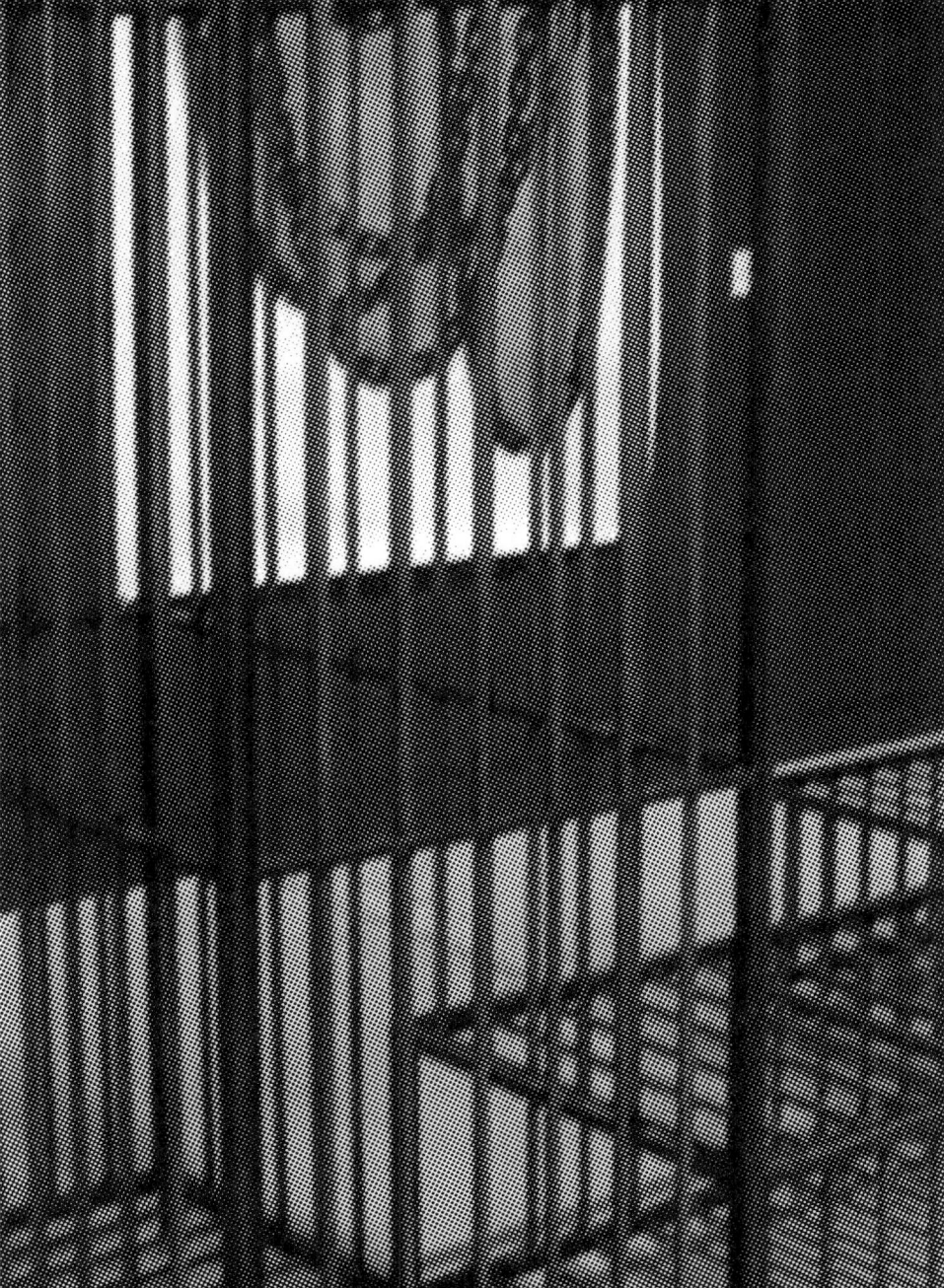

Flying to a concert in Lincoln, Nebraska, Keith Partridge and the Partridges' business manager, Reuben Kincaid, crash in the desert. There, they run afoul of two desperate characters named Big Dog Dawson and Puppy Potter and hear of a fabulous gold mine called Walking Fingers Bonanza. Keith and Reuben are really in for it this time, trying to keep one step ahead of the trap Big Dog and Puppy have set for them. And all the while, there's even more trouble afoot in the haunting figure of an Indian named Lonesome Bear, lurking unnoticed in the background, ghostly and dangerous. . . .

ONE HAND CLAPPING:
PORN REVIEWS

Bay Area Reporter, *1991–1992*

The Bay Area Reporter *was an alternative weekly aimed almost entirely at gay men, and I heard they were looking for a new porn reviewer. I think I submitted the Tom of Finland essay as a writing sample and got the gig. I loved doing it in part because it was great to be able to write about porn in a porn context rather than an art one. What was tricky about it was that it actually was one of the few columns that the publisher really cared about, because that's where a lot of the advertising revenue was coming from. The paper's offices would get batches of VHS tapes from the big porn studios. Sometimes I'd be assigned specific films, and sometimes I could rummage through the pile and pick out the stuff I thought I could have an interesting take on. Most of it was very, very mainstream porn at that point. This was before really the dawn of the alt-porn movement. There were only a handful of studios, with a strict type of model and very formulaic sex. People forget how fringe bears were at the time. Porn stars barely had five-o'clock shadows. After a while, I began running out of things to say. And so it was a tough assignment to find a way into those things. But I loved doing them. —NB*

Out of Doors and in Front of the Tube

September 12, 1991

I've long had a soft spot in my heart for any 1970s porn. There's something endearing about seeing these films made before the industry settled into its ruts. A lot of my first sexual experiences took place in porn houses, and there was something magical about walking into a movie theater and being confronted with the novel (to me, at least) image of a twenty-five-foot-tall rim job.

For a long time, just the fact that there was gay sex on the screen was enough for me. Unfortunately, many producers of the time also looked at it that way. Bijou Video has long been rereleasing these films, the most recent being Brentwood Studio's *Eureka Bound*.

This film is pretty much the standard sort of fare that played in almost every porn theater or booth during my youth, which probably accounts for the little glow I got while watching it. It stars the regular sort of Brentwood guys, who are uncredited, but you've seen them before: kind of built, shading between identifiable gay and hustler types.

I never care much about the plot in porn films, but for those who do, the segments are based loosely around various groups of men going to Eureka, a locale that is presented as some sort of sexual haven. This provides a good excuse for all the sex to take place (shudder) out of doors. Being an urban boy, I've got to admit that all nature and hiking stuff gives me hives, and while I know it's cheaper to shoot out in the godforsaken wilderness, I vote for the studio every time.

One has enough to worry about during sex without having to think about some bug wandering up your butt. The thing that recommends this compilation is that it has one of the best uses of a public domain soundtrack that I've ever come across. Instantly forgettable images of butt-fucking begin to acquire a myriad of strange meanings when they are matched with a soundtrack that's almost as pompous as that of *Airport '79*.

One blond's climax is coupled with symphonic swells of such stately import that you'd think he's just invented penicillin or something equally beneficial to mankind. There are three sequences: Two men pick up a hitchhiker and, oddly enough, end up having sex with him!

The second sequence pits two pumped-up hikers against a snooping farmhand (he's watching the guys with the hitchhiker through binoculars), which is a conceit of delightful originality, but once the clothes came off, I encountered great difficulty in telling the difference between the generic demi-shag haircuts of the models, which made the whole sequence look like "Backstage with the Ramones."

The last sequence has some marine coming home to his boyfriend, provoking a Proustian web of reminiscence on the order of "Remember that time we were walking down the road and I just ripped your pants off and we just got it on right there?"

You then get to see just that happen, which doesn't leave much room for suspense. These two have pedestrian sex, but you wouldn't know it from the music, which, at times, hints that they are about to break into something on the order of the ballet sequence from *An American in Paris*.

EUREKA BOUND

Pluses: Great air of 1970s-ness, righteous soundtrack, driver of truck in first sequence has cute mustache and calves, action is varied.

Minuses: Extremely low on the body hair meter, people frolicking outdoors, bleary and overexposed transfer, all of the guys involved (if that term can be used) seem to be submitting to the demands of art rather than engaging in the spontaneous joie de vivre that true porn demands.

High point: When the hitchhiker says, "Well, it takes all kinds," for the third time and then proceeds to unveil a piece of meat whose girth makes further comment irrelevant.

Released by Bijou Video

Directed by John Travis

Starring: Steven Boyd, Michael, Jack, and Scott

Grade: C

Elusive Prey

Now that I watch porn in my home rather than in movie palaces, I tend to see a lot more of it. With the novelty gone, I find myself looking for personality, the right arrangement of quirks that show that the filmmaker is compelled by something other than the urge for a quick profit. While it's easy to film fucking, "sex" is more elusive prey—basically because it takes place in the mind. The most compelling porn is often that which bears the mark of one person's obsessions, or when it manages to capture people in moments of real abandon.

Rigid Video, Vol. 1 is the sort of affable porn I feel almost compelled to support; it does have the feel of personality and seems very much a product of San Francisco. While it has some problems, all of its basic impulses are right. It's conscientious about safe sex, eager to please, and matter-of-fact in tone. Instead of aloof, abstract "studs," most of the men in it can be easily viewed around the streets of the Castro on any day (which means that you should rent this before you cruise them so you know what you're getting into).

Rigid Video, Vol. 1 also stars its producer, and at least one sequence is shot at his house so that it becomes oddly pitched between a "porn film" and a home video. Like *Eureka Bound*, it's split into a number of episodes, the most successful of which are the ones set in a sex club. This segment starts off with a glory-hole sequence, the tape's best. Greg Roberts and Ricky Johnson move back and forth, feasting on a plethora of dick with an abandon that suggests the delight straight people feel when confronted by the buffet at Sizzler.

Johnson, in chaps and a demure mohawk, shows particular promise in his eagerness to chow down. With a little effort, he could become a cocksucker to rival Richard Locke or Vanessa Del Rio (two of my personal heroes). Roberts seems earnest—perhaps a little too preoccupied with the complexities of filmmaking to fully savor the banquet at hand.

It may be that the stress of being a triple threat clouds his enjoyment. In the next bit, "The Maze," we get to see Johnson wrap his lips around Robert Parks, the only one of the participants to register in the body hair department, while someone named Nick Schrader goes down on Cougar Cash (fabulous name!).

The whole thing ends up with many men cumming on the chest of Roberts in a neat twist of the usual logic of the casting couch. Since Roberts is the focus of so much of the action (he appears in three sequences), it should be mentioned that he is cute, has a groovy tat, and, in his final S&M sequence, really enjoys what he's doing. This doesn't hold true for everyone in the tape, and it should be said that a number of the sequences are marred by perfunctory encounters that drag on too long.

While Tony Angelo (in the "Boyfriends" sequence) shows some initial promise—sporting one of my prime requirements for attraction: sensuous monobrow—once the clothes come off, though, the action between him and Trevor is plodding.

While Roberts seems good at letting us know what he likes, he seems to have a hard time showing us how to like it too.

RIGID VIDEO, VOL. 1

Pluses: Guys that all look like real men rather than bubble-brained models, nice sex club set, tattooed biker-boy top, fly hairstyles, a good mix of vanilla sex and convincing S&M play, proper attention paid to condom use, inspiring oral technique.

Minuses: Lame soundtrack in some sequences, tendency to let scenes go on too long, timid camera use.

All in all, a cool first effort.
Released by Rigid Video
Directed by Greg Roberts
Starring: Greg Roberts, Nick Schrader, Mark Anthony, Cougar Cash, Trevor, Travis, Wolf, Tony Angelo, and Erik Hall
Grade: A–

There Ain't No Cure for the . . .

September 12, 1991

There is nothing so damaging to the libido as this tedious fog that we've been having. The number-one reason I live on the West Coast is that I hate the cold and came here looking forward to years of sunny bliss on the Bay.

All right, hold your snickers. Like so many of life's illusions, this one too swiftly faded, and like everyone else in San Francisco, I learned to grit my teeth and accessorize with sweaters.

But the three hundred days of gray this summer have proved to be the limit. Desperate to feel a little real sizzle, I was forced to flee to the heat box of the East for a week or so. When I returned, I found the following video selections awaiting me, and like the model of diligence I am, I decided to take a second vacation—this one in the torrid kingdom of flesh.

The first tape, Vivid Video's *Summertime Blues*, seemed to promise the greatest evocation of fun in the sun, so after a quick Nestea plunge, I popped it on. The results were disappointing, to say the least. Obviously the product of a factory mentality, *Summertime Blues* goes something like this: Two Young Gay Men are renting a summer place on the beach. One goes off to the store, and the other sunbathes nude. The gardener (a Young Gay Man) comes along and starts giving the sunbather a blow job. We are treated to endless (unprotected) rimming and some unimaginative fucking.

The narrative shifts to the first guy coming back with the groceries. He meets some of his neighbors. To his relief, they are Young Gay Men, and they inform him that their roommate would be overjoyed if he, the shopper, would be willing to let his groceries spoil while he watches the roommate (YGM) have a tedious encounter with some other YGM in a garage.

Watching this clash of the titans proves so arousing for our domestically minded hero that he is compelled to masturbate for a long time. Meanwhile, the neighbors are so excited by the discovery that the summer renters are neither over twenty, hairy, nor people of color that they fuck on a black leather couch—with a lot of commentary (more on this in a minute).

The end of the film finds our two lovers in bed in each other's arms, happy in the knowledge that, for this summer at least, they will not be bothered by that nagging feeling that everyone else is more intelligent and exciting than they are. To celebrate, they fuck each other.

What's the beef?

OK, what's wrong with this picture? All of the settings are fine, the sound isn't horrible, none of the guys are absolute dogs, and no one seems creepy or anything.

So, what's my beef? It is simply that this film is a mind-numbing, jaw-dropping, hard-on-softening product. The whole thing is so rote that watching it feels more like work than anything else.

I have to point out one thing in particular. One of the two neighbors is played by Matt Hammer, and he exhibits one of the most obnoxious ticks in porn. For practically the entire time he is on-screen, he keeps up a running monologue that goes something like, "Eat that big dick. You want that big dick, don't you? You want that big dick. Eat it good. Eat that big dick. Eat it harder. You want it. Don't you want that big dick? Eat it good. I'm gonna fuck your ass. Put that big dick up your ass. You want that. You want that big dick up your ass. You want that. You want that big dick up your ass. Yeah, gonna fuck you good. Come on, eat it. Eat that big dick," etc.

This is supposed to be "hot talk," and to give Matt credit, his dick is big (although, and we can say this together, girls, we've seen bigger). But after twelve minutes of hearing it, I was far from aroused. In fact, I felt like I had tumbled onto the set of Phil Glass's latest opus.

As Matt neared the climax he had been telling us about for five minutes, the camera began a bizarre zoom toward a stack of books in the background. The only readable title was *Native American Architecture*. Was this a subliminal hint that I should be pitching a tent? Distressed, I put on my other tape.

SUMMERTIME BLUES
Released by Vivid Video
Starring: Damian, Alex Thomas, Austin Moore, Matt Hammer, Brad Chase, and Drew Kelly
Grade: C
Fun Fact:

My Studio Is a Dungeon Is the Studio

Q: How many times does Matt Hammer say the phrase big dick *during his thirteen minutes of screen time in* Summertime Blues?

A: Seventy-eight, or once every ten seconds.

My hopes for a tender story about sexual awakening in the summer heat were dashed, however, when the film's opening shot turned out to be a panorama of *Pier 39*. Was this then to be a film about turning tricks with tourists? No, a voice informed me that the film was about "the first time that you actually acted out one of your deepest fantasies."

That use of the word *your* made me nervous. Was this going to be a film of me and that box of Lego? But then the voice went on to give some examples like "having sex with two men at the same time or having a muscle-bound masseur work you over until all of your nerves were on fire." Oh, those deepest fantasies. A quick cut, and we see three Young Gay Men sitting together on a bed:

YGM No. 1: Have you ever had a three-way? (Pause.)
YGM No. 2: (Looks down, then looks up.) Nope. (Pause.)
YGM No. 1: Do you want to do it with us? (Pause.)
YGM No. 2: (Looks down again to where his lines must be written on the bedspread, then looks up.) I want (pause) to be fucked. (Pause.)
YGM No. 1: (Visibly relieved that the exposition is over.) Take off your clothes.

Could Have Been Livelier

Is it quibbling to say that the first time it happened my fantasy was a little livelier? You will be relieved to know that YGM No. 2 is fucked in an acceptable fashion for the next few minutes by his two pals.

After such a walk on the wild side of my fantasy life, I decided to skip ahead to the muscle-bound masseur; my nerves were a little on edge by now, and I was intrigued by the promise of the "enormous dildo" the voice at the opening had promised.

Even this proved to be a bit of a letdown when I was able to note definite stubble on the chest of the masseur and his diffident client.

Why, I ask you, do porn producers feel that every model they use in every film has to look exactly the same? While I am not a hairy fetishist, I do like the men in porn films to look like men and not like characters out of animated kids' shows.

Anyway, the two have gotten back from their full-body waxes just in time to have sex in a tastefully decorated SF apartment. In fact, my prime concern in watching this segment was that the guys might be a little excited and spill the baby oil they were using as lube onto the white carpet they were cavorting on.

I did not need to fear, since even the introduction of the "enormous dildo" did not cause more than a ripple of interest on anyone's part. Another hour of this tedium, and I gave up trying to escape the clammy embrace of a San Francisco summer.

"If you can't beat it, join 'em," I thought glumly. My head must have been still swimming with the aftereffects of the day's viewing, however, because when the waitress at my favorite café said to me, "What do you want?" I was unable to stop myself: "I want that big dick," I said.

THE FIRST TIME
Released by Jocks
Starring: Dean Johnson, Boyer Colt, Johnny Farm, David Grant, Joshua Scott, Tom Walton, Trevor Hanson, and Eric Rieger
Grade: C+

America's Funniest Homo Videos

September 26, 1991

If I seem a little jumpy lately, blame Dom DeLuise. For the past few weeks, every time I settle down to watch *Star Trek: The Next Generation* (Picard is TV's best Daddy after Perry Mason), my erotic musings are brutally interrupted by the sight of DD in Paul Prudhomme's drag—cackling and leering into the camera. "We're out there!" Dom shrieks at me, and I nearly wet myself. "And we're gonna catch you." Is it any wonder I'm scared?

What Dom is promoting is *The New Candid Camera*, the show that is the granddaddy of all of today's home video laff riots. The premise of these shows has always made me nervous, conjuring up, as it does, the spectacle of a society willing to tolerate unlimited amounts of surreptitious surveillance of its citizens in the name of entertainment.

Indeed, the most recent crop of these programs makes the public into willing accomplices by offering them money to follow around their relatives with camcorders in hopes that their pants will fall down. It used to be that you just had to worry about Allen Funt hiding behind something with a bottle of fake ketchup. Now, nobody can be trusted.

What motivates all of these shows is the desire to see behind the facade, to get to what is really going on. This is the same impulse behind much porn. Porn, too, asserts that it will somehow show you the truth of sex, the evidence that sex is occurring, and what sex is like.

That is why so much porn is obsessed with the close-up; we need to see insertion to be sure that things aren't "faked." But of course porn films, like narrative films, are fictions. They, too, set up a facade that we can't see behind. This week's two films both have something to do with that facade.

One Big Queen

In Hand's *Out of Hand Screwing Screw Ups* is the first porn blooper reel. Bloopers have always been about things fucking up, about the gaps between successful and failed illusion. Or rather about reality finally asserting itself—stars lose decorum; lines are flubbed; props don't work. Hand's film has all of these occurrences and, in many ways, shows what is missing from many other films.

First of all, the film is hosted by the delightful Chi Chi LaRue, who is one big queen. Chi Chi keeps things running with a series of double takes, cutaways, and snide commentary that is just like sitting down to some true dish with a good girlfriend.

Chi Chi's presence reminded me of how rarely we get to see queens in porn. I know few gay men who don't have moments of innocent campiness, but somehow this camaraderie is always gone by the time anyone gets in front of the cameras. Porn has a hard time reconciling laughter and arousal, but I think we all know that it is a mighty poor fuck who can't have a couple of laughs while doing the nasty.

One of the nicest things about these clips is that you get to see porn actors with their guard down. Some, however, are possessed of an almost staggering stupidity.

The first group of clips in this tape are taken from the production of *Bat Dude and Throbbin'*, a production that looks like it must have taken a few years off the life of everyone involved. Watching the actors blow line after line, take after take, is to be possessed by a dread that leaves you murmuring, like Kurtz, "the horror."

Others come off a lot better. This tape actually made me warm to Joey Stefano. "The Sneer," as we call him, has always been one to work my nerves with his attitude, but seeing him at ease, he seems, well, sexy. It must be said, however, that as soon as Joey can afford it, he should sue the guy who gave him his tat because that is one sorry item.

There's a lot that's good about this tape, but one of the down points is that the producers felt for some reason that they should include some "hot" footage so that people would also be able to get off. None of this stuff is all that great, and one scene, between two feckless teens on a skimpy pile of fake snow, is just bewildering.

Organ Wrestling

The second tape is *America's Sexiest Home Videos, Volume One*, from Surge Studios. Amateur video is the growth part of "the industry" right now, and the fact that people are out manufacturing their own pornography is great.

Too often, though, that just means that people try to mime the tired conventions of commercial porn. While this tape has got a bit of that, it also has some moments of realness that are riveting.

The first segment, from San Francisco, features what is simply the largest penis that I have ever encountered short of a Japanese woodcut. Large enough to demand separate billing and a percentage of the gross, this organ is attached to a faceless, skinny dude who spends ten minutes patting, wiggling, massaging, and generally tending to the needs of this commanding performer.

I can't even say that this guy is jerking off because what happens on-screen looks a lot more like a wrestling match between unevenly matched contestants. Of course, anything that big barely gets hard (probably not so bad for the performer—if that thing were filled with blood, he would pass out), so I can't say that this is actually sexy, but it is kind of hard to keep your eyes off it.

The next segment is from Chicago, and it's the one that makes the tape worthwhile. Rico, a burly, hairy, stone-cold fox, keeps up a running monologue while he shits, spits, and masturbates, but it's the ferocity of his presence that separates this from most commercial porn.

The segment is a lot like some of the Old Reliable tapes. Rico acts like a commanding top man throughout, but at the point of orgasm, he achieves a kind of transcendent vulnerability that is some of the truest sex I ever viewed. Now, if we could just introduce him to Bob Saget.

AMERICA'S SEXIEST HOME VIDEOS
Released by Serge Studios
Directed and edited by Al Parker
Starring: Al Parker, Grant Lance, Ivan, Rico, Jon Allen, Mark Schatz, and, you, the public
Grade: A–

OUT OF HAND SCREWING SCREW UPS
Released by In Hand Video
Directed by Chi Chi La Rue
Starring: Chi Chi La Rue, Joey Stefano, and a cast of dozens
Grade: B+

Authority Figures

October 26, 1991

Recently, as a friend of mine and I were heading down Castro Street, we stopped in at a bar that has recently converted to a leather and uniform motif. We were intrigued by the attempt to bring South of Market north, but after a desultory hour nursing our Calistogas, we were back on the street, not having seen a single man of authority.

"Girlfriend," my pal sniffed, "the only time there's going to be a man in uniform here is when somebody goes on break from 24-Hour Donuts."

Our appetite for epaulets and polished boots unsated, we turned to the chilly comforts of the video screen, picking up Bijou Video's *Uniformed Fantasies*.

Uniforms and costumes have always abounded in gay porn. Uniforms have an appeal because porn always thrived on generalities, on figures that stand for a set of general attributes rather than specific behaviors.

For the fetishists, the uniform can signify the power that the wearer might have in the outside world. For the wearer, the uniform can allow the person to take on a character and behave sexually in a way that would be otherwise foreign to them.

The most popular uniform fantasies are those that conjure up images of groups of men alone: the military, firemen, and policemen. There is at once the sense of a secret world and a powerful fantasy about sexually possessing the authority figures in our society.

Porn Problems

The problem for porn films, of course, is what happens when the uniform comes off, since people, for the most part, are alike naked. It's a rare actor that can maintain the illusion of "cop-hood" once the uniform slips to the floor. All of these fantasies can easily displace what we know to be true about people's behavior when wearing these uniforms.

I can't deny that I salivate at the sight of sailors, but I was pretty nauseated to find out about the navy shipping them overseas to help them beat the rap for gay bashing. While we may find the category "cops" sexy, specific cops are all too often afflicted with incipient paranoia, various stress-related disorders, and curiously enlarged and flattened butts.

Most of this film is solo jack-off scenes with various types. The camerawork is minimal, as is the sound. This is a method that works well in Old Reliable films, but they always pick men who are full of personality.

In this film most of the men are not that interesting, but there are a few high points. My pick hunk is CHP (as in California Highway Patrolman) Erik, a man who fills out his jodhpurs with class. Eric has to maintain composure while undressing, spitting, masturbating, and manipulating a cigar all at the same time.

Smoking Required

In fact, everyone in *Uniformed Fantasies* smokes cigars, which led me to expect that we might see a sequence starring David Salle, but it was not to be. All of the men in this tape are the kind I go for—substantial, burly guys in their late thirties to forties for the most part.

One person who is not this type is an iffy bodybuilder who is dressed up (unconvincingly) as a leatherman. Watching him masturbate with one hand while waving around a cigar in his other, gloved one, I was forcibly reminded not of Tom of Finland but of Miss Peggy Lee.

One of my favorites, Marine Jake, fingers his asshole with a touching ponderousness. We get to see Erik again in a two-way scene with a younger cop, and he is just as appealing the second time around. This segment shows us just what really goes on between two police officers when nobody's around: cock sucking, light spanking, and JO.

If you want to really see what cops do to unwind, as well as a prime example of what pornography can be, even if it's not hardcore, then check out Palm Drive Video's *Police Wrestling*, shot at the Police Olympics. The tape doesn't have a single bared dick in it but still manages to produce a palpable air of sexual heat.

Batches of cute men warm up, hang around, bullshit, and wrestle, while the camera discreetly watches. Hilarious sequences of men sticking their butts in the air and grunting say more about the barely sublimated homosexual impulses that fill such events than a dozen dime-store analysts.

These men want it. Wrestling, that is. Director Jack Fritscher proves that you don't need a disco soundtrack to get in the mood. All you need is a zoom lens and a vivid imagination. It takes a while to get into the sensibility of this tape, but when you do, it's one of the most satisfying and subversive porn films you'll ever see.

One final word of advice: Just because you get turned on looking at these policemen doesn't mean you should go out and vote for one. Remember: Fuck cops; don't elect them.

Wow! I Could've Had a . . .

November 14, 1991

V-8 is about the surprisingly complicated emotional lives of clean-shaven young white men who run a garage—a profession so stressful that it forces them to have sex a lot. Have I piqued your interest? Then get out your hankies because this plot is murder on the old tear ducts.

Brian and Jim have agreed to become partners in their garage, since they already live together and, as Jim puts it, "both like to work on cars." Jim feels that this is also a good rationale for getting some commitment out of Brian relationship-wise, but Brian nixes that with the old "won't make promises I can't keep" line.

Jim stiff-upper-lips it and leaves for the day. Brian goes to help out a customer (Les Stine), who, it seems, is used to paying for his bodywork on all fours. Brian demurs but is quickly swayed when Les clamps the lip-lock on to his meat. Meanwhile, the garage's one employee, Nick Manetti, is out "buying parts" when he spies Jim drowning his sorrows over Brian in the butt of a complete stranger (Tanner Marshall).

Manetti is delectable, but his taste is all in his mouth because while the sight of Jim and Tanner provokes nothing in the audience but prodigious yawns, it's enough to make him drop his drawers for a quick waist-high Braille lesson.

After this interlude, he returns to the shop to find Brian contrite and ready to get flowers for Jim but manages to blow that by diplomatically spilling the beans about Jim and whomever. Brian is bummed and splits, leaving Nick to close the garage and have sex with some unexplained guy who's hanging around the garage in a state of undress.

Honeyed Words

Brian heads home, where he confronts Jim and uses honeyed words to express his true devotion, to wit, "Now give me some of that head you were giving that other guy today" (clearly there was a relationship counselor on retainer for this part). True love, or perhaps the realization that this is probably as good as he's going to get, suffuses Jim's features, and he burrows into Brian's crotch as we head for the fade.

The one standout in this film is Nick Manetti, a yummy little buzz-head with a furry butt and juicy balls. Manetti gave me a full-on critical chubby by dropping trow and playing with his ass, which is worthy of a film of its own. The other decent part of the film was the fact that, from certain angles, customer Les Stine looks like Michael Keaton, a notion that made for some entertaining moments while he was being plugged. I couldn't develop a scintilla of empathy for either of the two stars, who seemed to me to deserve each other given the pedestrian nature of their lovemaking.

V-8
Released by Vivid Video
Directed by Jim Steel
Starring: Jim Montana, Brian Yates, Les Stine, Nick Manetti, and Tanner Marshal
Grade: B–

Score 10 has a decent cast, adequate lighting, and a forgettable story about a bunch of college football players who are interested only in goofing off and sniffing jockstraps. If you like well-scrubbed young men having fairly pedestrian sex, you should probably check this out. The only man who looks remotely grown-up is the math teacher, but right at the moment that you are hoping for some intellectual bear bondage action, he manages to doze off in the middle of class, thereby missing the shocking spectacle of his charges cheating on his exam and fantasizing about sex in all-terrain vehicles.

I must register a bit of ire here about the implication that the only thing you have to do to get by in college is to go down on the coach (in my day, you had to go down on the dean as well). Ryan Idol appears as a cocky football player/fantasy object and acquits himself professionally. Chris Stone is the standout here. He has a butt that can only be described as "bubbleiscious." The coach (Craig Slater) evidently thinks so too, since he spends a fair amount of time probing its charming depths with his tongue, under the pretense of giving Stone a massage.

Having never been a jock, I cannot testify that this is a standard gym procedure, but it seems to have the desired relaxing effect. Director Matt Sterling makes the film look good on the whole, and I particularly liked the recurring motif of jock sniffing. In fact, Chad Knight has a charming scene where he raids the lockers for underwear and then avidly samples the fragrances they contain. I found myself wishing for Smell-O-Vision, thinking that it would not be all that hard to produce a scratch 'n' sniff package for porn films. After being drenched with Giorgio every time I open *Cosmo* (purely for the horoscope), I would welcome the chance to fill my nostrils with the heavenly essence of Ryan Idol's athletic supporter.

Much of the rest of *Score 10* is okay sexual encounters among mostly forgettable men, with the exception of Mike Henson, who is beguiling as the guy who gets fucked on top of a bunch of jerseys.

SCORE 10
Released by Video 10
Directed by Matt Sterling
Starring: Ryan Idol, Craig Slater, Chad Knight, Chris Stone, Mike Henson, and Dolph Knight
Grade: B+

Blast from the Past

January 2, 1992

If you're like me (not that there's any reason you should be), you sometimes find yourself frustrated with the sameness of contemporary pornography. In the past, people have accused me of not liking porn at all, but this is hardly the case. I just don't like run-of-the-mill porn—the kind of porn that doesn't offer the viewer a variety of bodies, positions, and attitudes. Too many porn films show the same things in the same ways.

Like anything else you might see too often on TV (Maury Povich, Kirstie Alley), explicit fucking can become tired, tired, tired. That's why I was glad to see that Jerico Video has collected a bunch of films from AMG and other studios and released them as *Gay Erotica from the Past*.

There's nothing more exhilarating than a dive into the gay image bank of the 1940s, 1950s, and 1960s. These films have been reviewed in this paper earlier (several were part of the Days of the Greek Gods program at the SF gay film festival a few years back) for their historical and aesthetic merits, so I will endeavor to apply this column's standard criterion to them—namely, can you beat off to them?

The answer would have to be yes, with qualifications. Time has definitely passed since these films were made, and it may be difficult to reconcile your expectations of pornography with what goes on in them. What does go on is for the most part metaphorical: You see wrestling but not a hard-on and much less penetration.

Contemporary Look

On the other hand, the costumes, hairstyles, and body types actually look a lot more contemporary than what one sees in most of today's porn. Guys who hang out at Underworld will appreciate the loving attention paid to cotton briefs in these movies, and fans of avant-garde film will be quick to detect their influence on such classics as *Fireworks*, *Hold Me While I'm Naked*, and *Querelle*.

I think the best way to view these tapes is to watch them all the way through at first and immerse yourself in the mood. Then you can start to see how individual moments can become very hot given the context. After seeing a number of films with models' members always shrouded by posing straps, by the time (in volume 1) you reach *Cell Mates*, the nakedness creates a real frisson that is topped by the tender embrace the actors go into at the fade.

The point seems to be that these films are aids to the erotic imagination in much the same way porn books are: You get all the basic components for a fantasy, and the resolution is up to you.

This isn't to say that some of these films aren't hotter than others. For my money, the posing films are for the most part bores, particularly in the second volume, where sequences of naked guys doing calisthenics had me reaching for the scan button. The best moments in these tapes are the extravaganzas like volume 1's two toga epics, *Two Slaves* and *Ben Hurry*.

The latter purports to be backstage antics on the set of some Hollywood gladiator pic, and since I spent much of my adolescence wanting to wrap my butt around the mighty meat of Hercules, I was overjoyed to watch three humpsters whip off their togas and frolic in the pool until some assistant director yells at them to get back to work. It's a scene one imagines went on all the time with Sir Larry on the set of *Spartacus*.

Yummy John

Other high points are John Novak, the sexy galoot who stars in *No Rest for the Wicked* (volume 2), a man so yummy even his bedclothes refuse to cover him up; the entire cast of *The Beach Bar Nightmare* (also released as *Vice Badge* and a number of other titles, I'm told); a smorgasbord of proto-daddy types including some leathermen in complicated underwear; and *Strangers at Play*, a film that looks like it could have been made yesterday since it's mostly a wrestling match between two lads in goatees.

Some warnings: The talking head at the beginning of the first volume and the packaging are slightly misleading. Both talk about films from the 1930s, and, at least in the two volumes I viewed, there seems to be no material shot earlier than 1949. The introduction also talks about the films reflecting the new assertiveness of women in the 1950s. I can only think that it is referring to the topless woman leading a pie fight in *Fanny's Hill*. She's the only woman I could find in either tape.

They claim to have added music of the period, but they must mean the lunch period because the soundtrack is nothing but present-day Muzak. If you want something really of the time, I suggest that you turn the volume down on your TV and go to your record collection. Start with some Bob Willis, then go on to anything by Maria Callas, and finish up with The Ventures.

Special mention must be made of the wonderfully dippy contributions of Pat Rocco, whose films are both proudly titled *Made in Hollywood U.S.A.* and who has the best moment of both anthologies. It occurs in *Three's a Crowd*, the film that ends volume 2. Two campers sleep through the crash landing of a spaceship, but they're in for a surprise the next morning when they run into its occupant (the queen of outer space, obviously).

The alien, in a much more convincing costume than the one in *Hideous Sun Demon*, piteously asks for help but is rewarded with a hail of stones from the cruel hunks. Pissed, she (he? it?) whips out a ray gun that allows her to freeze the earthlings long enough to rip their pants off and make them do the frug in the altogether. If that idea doesn't give you a chubby, you just don't know what sexy is.

BAY AREA CONCEPTUALISM: TWO GENERATIONS

Bay Area Conceptualism: Two Generations, *New Langton Arts, 1992*

Despite the neat formulation of this exhibition's title, the history of conceptual practice in the Bay Area has been rich and nearly continuous for twenty years. Developing out of "happenings" and avant-garde ideas in literature, film, and video, Bay Area conceptualism assumed a form that has been, at once, less rhetorical and more direct than that of New York. Since the early 1970s, the Bay Area has been home to a number of artists who have consistently worked to expand the parameters of art making and to blend the various tendencies prevalent in the community. For the most complete documentation of the dozens of artists who worked in this field during this period, the reader is referred to Suzanne Foley's accompanying text for the exhibition *Space, Time, Sound*, held at the San Francisco Museum of Modern Art in 1981.

The Bay Area has been a curious cross between a backwater and a safe harbor for the arts over the past two decades. The various schools of abstract and figurative painting have ceased to dominate. In addition, there has been a marked increase in the number of alternative art spaces and artists' organizations. For the most part, these have served to foster a vigorous environment for experimentation in the field, particularly in video, installation, and performance. Indeed, many of the artists mentioned below have worked, at one time or another, in all of these areas. While this was seen as a dated holdover at the beginning of the decade, it now makes clearer the affinities between artists working in the Bay Area and those in western Europe. The lack of market scrutiny for both communities has actually made it possible to expand the issues addressed within the conceptual tradition, as well as to incorporate the discourses of contemporary theory. Now that the art world is reexamining the terrain of conceptualism, it is clear that its attention will have to turn to one of its most prolific sources: the West.

This exhibition was conceived as a way of commemorating two moments: the first, at the beginning of the 1970s, and the second, beginning in 1985. While most of the artists in this exhibition have produced bodies of work that span the past two decades, there have been certain points at which their work has reached critical mass—when their varied practices have come together to enter into discourse and to have an impact beyond their immediate environment. While the five artists discussed here may not share chronology, they share an approach. They participate in the reformulation and expansion of the parameters of the legacy of conceptual artistic practice. This strategic sensibility is a direct result of the dissemination, in the late 1970s, of a variety of theories engaging issues of textuality, sexual politics, and psychology.

It can be argued that there existed a sort of "feedback effect," since the most progressive aesthetic of the period was conceived in relation to conceptual art itself. Certainly, the arguments surrounding the nature of the art object as commodity and the problematic place of painting, in particular, would not have been conceivable without the example of "idea art." By the early 1980s, however, the art object was wrapped in the glow of its new place as the investment of choice. As a result, there was a stampede to introduce the new painting as the international glamour product par excellence. In the San Francisco Bay Area, this meant two things: an influx of work from New York and elsewhere, exacerbated by an intensive search for local versions of whichever painting style held sway at the moment.

During this time, however, conceptually oriented artists continued their practice within the network of alternative spaces and programs. Successive generations, newly arrived from art schools and other cities, continued to stimulate dialogue and contention by forming new organizations. While many of these venues were short-lived, by mid-decade, the Bay Area boasted fifteen artist-run, nonprofit arts organizations. Concurrently, a number of artists began to open commercial spaces that functioned to bring much of the new work to the attention of a wider and more receptive audience. As a result of these trends, recent years have seen an increased interest in the work of younger conceptualists, as well as a rediscovery of many of their now-mature predecessors.

What does it mean to term *conceptual* artists with a decided investment in objects? It is here that the generational split alluded to in the title of this exhibition becomes most apparent. The original aim of conceptual art was the elimination of the object—an aim that was derived from a combination of the progressive politics of the 1960s and the concerted distrust of and disdain for formalist aesthetics. The art experience was conceived as reducible to a set of conditions that could be reproduced independently of their armature: the object. The exhibition of artworks meant either the presentation of diagrams from or residues of the meeting of those conditions. The medium of choice became words.

While formalist theory pushed the object into language, poststructuralist theory pulled language into objecthood. Laying bare the networks of discourse that informed such activities as government, architecture, design, and forms of representation in general, it became possible to speak of the object in ways that acknowledged its sociopolitical history, and thus fostered a critique of that history from various viewpoints (e.g., through feminist, gay, and transcultural experience). It is this new language-saturated object that is examined by the younger generation represented in this exhibition—an endeavor they share with many in America and Europe.

Both Lutz Bacher and David Dashiell have been working in the Bay Area since the mid-1970s. Bacher has used a variety of media, including in her work as a magazine editor, to examine issues of gender, sexuality, and representation. Bacher's work explicitly addresses the question of what it means for women to represent, to act as producers of images. She depicts a highly mediated subject, examining by turns famous celebrities and anonymous individuals, all of whom find their existence through various media tags. In her series *Jokes* (1987), figures such as Joe Namath, Henry Kissinger, Bella Abzug, and Jane Fonda give utterance to what would seem to be highly personal, often obscene, phrases. Bacher makes the blatancy of the jokes function doubly to disrupt the popular public image of her subjects but also to forestall our own expectations of a "good joke." She elicits from us nervous giggles rather than warm chuckles. In contrast, Bacher's *Spectacle* (1988) reverses this view. Consisting of a series of black-framed color photographs of televised images of women watching Geraldine Ferraro speak at the 1984 Democratic Convention, a complex interplay is set up as these women watch a woman become history. They gain in stature by participating in a moment that is ostensibly about them. But the participation of these women is that of audience and emblem, appearing on the screen as tokens of women who are made into history rather than making it. Bacher's work in this exhibition, *Big Uterus* (1989), presents the most extreme conjunction of these two themes, producing a body that exists at once on the most visceral level and the most attenuated. Her installation, which includes videotaped footage of an experimental surgical procedure, threatens to actually take us inside the body. The audio element of this work combines new-age homilies on experience and subjective reality that counter these disturbingly direct images. In tandem, both create the body as spectacle, evoking the image of the operating theater and the extremes of earlier body art.

The human body is at once present and absent as well in *Seven Deadly Sins* (1989), David Dashiell's series of allegorical fun-house mirrors included in this exhibition. Dashiell has long been concerned with systems, an interest usually associated with "high conceptualism," particularly its romance with numbers theory, linguistics, and phenomenology. However, Dashiell does not seek to ally his practice with science or mathematics; he is more concerned with the arbitrary groupings familiar to allegory, looking to systems that seek to describe attributes rather than objective reality. It is the precariousness of the truth claims posited by these inexact sciences that are the focus of Dashiell's work. His recent installation, *Invert, Oracle* (1988), utilized the tarot as a basis for a sly examination of bodily hysteria and memory. The title of this work refers both to the notion of the homosexual as invert and to the transmutation that Dashiell has worked on the system of the tarot itself. Instead of an impersonal system that can be used to read the future, the tarot is recast as a system for sorting personal memories. *Invert, Oracle* confounds the "flaccid iconographies of fortune telling and confessional autobiography."

Dashiell's work included here juxtaposes two iconographic systems: the Christian prescription of the seven deadly sins against seven diseases (i.e., cancer, mental retardation, AIDS, etc.) that function as popular icons of shame, marginalization, and spectacle. These are presented in the form of allegorical figures that are then painted beneath mirrored surfaces. Mapping his signifiers onto the body of the viewer, Dashiell deliberately overloads them, forcing images and ideas to do double and triple time. Preventing their passage into the poetic realm of metaphor, the resulting tension enforced by the work produces a dynamic that is at once calculated and arbitrary, slicing the viewer into vertical indexes to engender possible meanings. It is through this conflation of charged signs and images that Dashiell hopes to resurrect true allegory, pure shapes of meaning, direct and dangerous.

Jon Winet and Margaret Crane create an effect that might be described as a rapture of the known. They detonate the visual and verbal clichés predominating in contemporary American culture, combining phrases and images that seem frozen in strata of ossified media. These nuggets, at first, present themselves as palatable, but soon become indigestible, remaining awkwardly present. Winter and Crane construct a counterdiscourse of authority, commerce and government out of the same instrumental master discourses which act to insure the privileged position of dominating class interests. In this way they act as "anti-spin doctors," tinkering with the torrent of language and image that constitute modern politics. Their cool approach allows for a far greater implication of the viewer than those that overwhelm through liberal bombast. While much first-generation conceptual work gathered facts and dispensed information, Winet and Crane acknowledge a societal condition in which fact has vanished into an obscene manipulation, where ecstatic flow of information threatens to destroy us. This is profoundly portrayed in *TIME* (1986) where oddly cropped bits of *Time Magazine* compete with each other to foretell the greatest doom.

Recently, Winter and Crane have looked to installation to further implicate the viewer in this dilemma. For example, *The Big Chill* (1989) included here posits the viewer as a political candidate forced to perform the debased ritual of addressing a crowd. This is a demolition of generations of tedious "interactive art" that claimed to put the viewer in the driver's seat. Winter and Crane understand that there is no untainted space for political address, that the public conspires to perpetuate its own oppression by refusing to abandon its belief in political "double-think."

Dawn Frying has been at work over the past two years assembling an eccentric vocabulary of objects and materials which she has managed to render surprisingly discursive. Rarely including text, her resonant use of materials manages to bridge the gap between formalist sculpture and conceptual textuality. In her numbers individual works, installations and performances, Frying interprets the object as icon and the exhibition as tableau. *Seven Marks* (1988) uses overcoats as both arbitrary units of marriage and subtle irritants. Unlike much object centered work of the last few years, Fryling's objects are neither the hydras of overwhelming commodity nor engaged in a mystification of detritus. These objects are stubborn in their mundanity, their matter-of-factness; in their collision with the viewer's gaze they spring suddenly to life. For instance, Fryling uses flour in a manner that evinces its formal as well as associative properties. Her "flour shelves" point to the dispersive, unsupported nature of flour as a material,

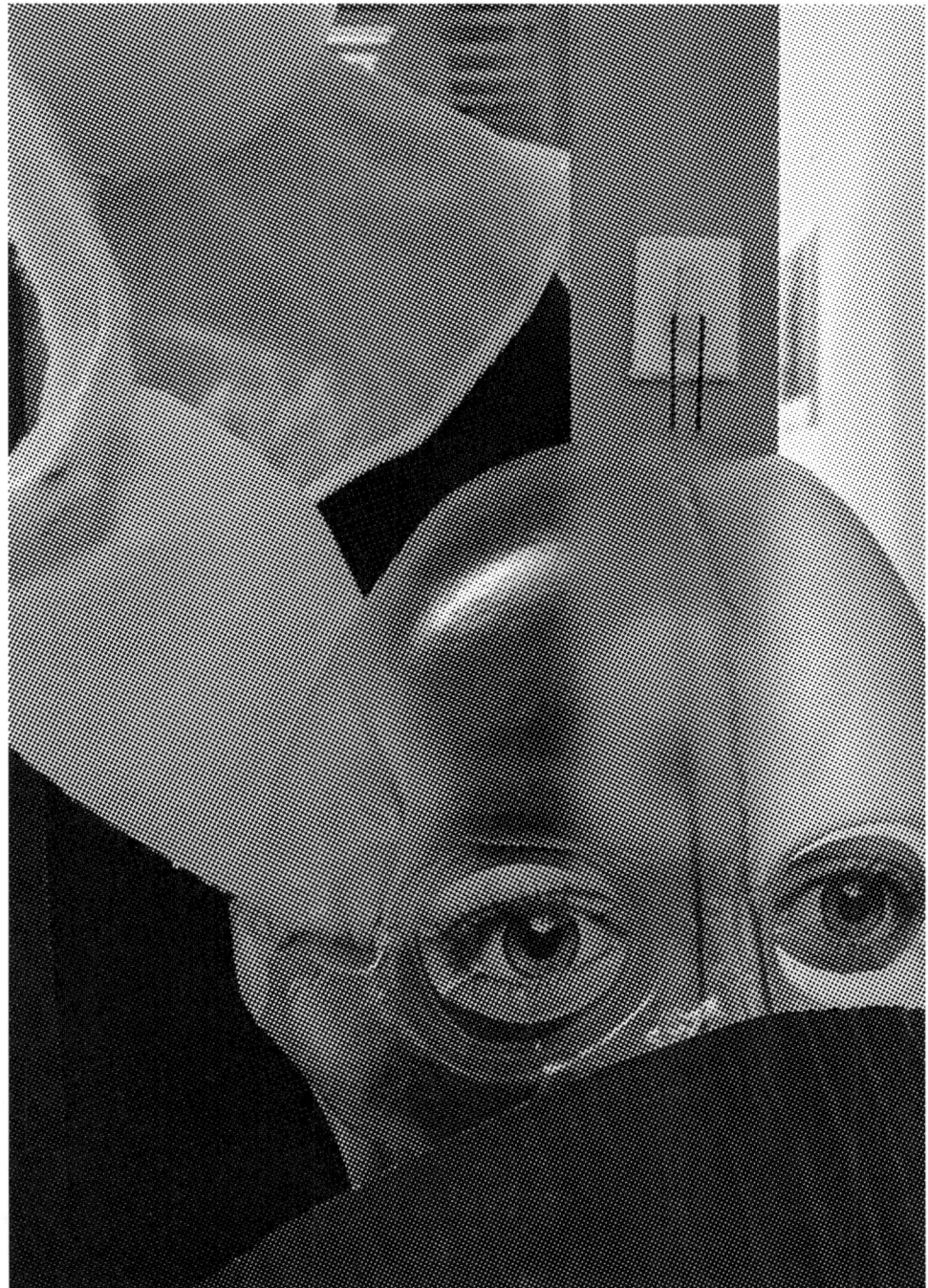

but also to an extremely equivocal relationship to mark making and the commons of flour itself. These works contain often surprisingly low levels of visual interest, instead resonating in an area of the mind that can find them beautiful without needing to see them.

Temporarily Untitled (1989) in this exhibition, presents materials that are more worked, although they retain the same equivocal distance from the realm of the object that Fryling establishes in other works. The casts are somehow portrait busts, giant queen chess pieces offering themselves as tenuous representations of "femaleness." Like *Seven Marks*, the positioning of the busts within the exhibition space designates them again as markers, arbitrary units placed in a line. Yet they continue to generate additional associations, an understated surplus of significations that allows them to remain vivid in their quietude. As signposts, each holds equal emphasis for the territories to which they direct the viewer—each destination being a distinct thought site.

The exhibition of the work of this later generation of conceptual artists in the San Francisco Bay Area only points the way to a more serious examination of the history and sustained dialogue in conceptual issues in artistic practice. Rather than an exhaustive look at the personalities that have made important contributions to the region, it is hoped that this will serve as an intriguing glimpse, a fragment that will spur others to investigate work in this region and its impact on and relationship to similar work being produced throughout the United States.

QUEER MYSTERIES

David Cannon Dashiell: Queer Mysteries, *San Francisco Art Institute, 1993*

David Dashiell was one of the Bay Area's most interesting and underap-
preciated artists. David was an early supporter of my work and also just
a really interesting thinker. One of his most fully realized projects was an
installation at the San Francisco Art Institute called Queer Mysteries, *his*
take on the Villa of the Mysteries in Pompeii, depicting a queer initiatory
ceremony. Rebecca Solnit and I were commissioned to write pieces for the
catalog. Since David's take on the villa was twofold—an archaeological
past and then a science-fiction future with visors and ray guns—it was
decided that Rebecca would do the past-looking essay, and I would do the
sci-fi one. What it tries to imagine is a sort of incorporeal genderless intel-
ligence that discovers David's installation as a ruin far in the future. The
way that this intelligence comes to understanding or generates knowledge
is through orgies. And so the thinking and the orgy are things that happen
simultaneously in an entity that can choose to have multiple bodies but
has moved past gender. What if the way that you got to know something
was fucking around it? I finally got to write my sci-fi/porn story, and this
is like the first iteration of my dream body. —NB

Bleary from her subrem, iell amped the 'face with her work prog and entered
archeosite #12098377389, known to her and her team as "oz." In accordance
with their current hypotheses and the info being relayed back by several
hundred thousand insectoid scanners, simulation was a concrete, bunkerish
structure, whose walls were composed of a varicolored petrochemical layer.

In earlier manifestations, it had been pitch-black in oz until iell had realized that some of the site's artifacts were a system for producing light. Lately, she had been spending some of her off time tinkering with various ideas about the light's dispersal, and now she felt a mild pleasure as she surveyed the effect. Despite the illumination, iell couldn't shake the unease that always accompanied her visits to the site. The notion of walls, the prime characteristic of architecture pre-'face, always made her tense. There was even a pre-'face word for it: *claustrophobia*—the fear of contained spaces. It was a fear that was even more insistent for someone who had lost a coherent notion of what space was. iell found it difficult to comprehend the ease with which the p'fers had delineated inside and outside—the "me" and "not me" and their obsession with division, inclusion, exclusion, and boundaries. It had even structured their entire sexual life, down to dividing each other up according to gender, race, species, or age. Worse, the fact that the divisions seemed to be linked to some kind of value judgment. . . . It was one of the aspects of p'fers' life iell still couldn't understand.

Other members of the team winked into the sim, inspecting various updates, flashing approval for iell's lumen manipulation. Finally, iell felt avid, the team's chief lens, clearing her thought, and focusing the team in anticipation of the inflomating.

avid was manifesting herself as a pool of water in the middle of the sim, and iell watched as she rippled disapprovingly at ashi, the team's play lenser. Lately, ashi had taken to manifesting as a p'fer image from an earlier site: curling brown hair, dimpled body, wings, winking sex—a cherub.

"ashi, must you be so . . . corporeal? it's inflo-restrictive for your orifices to be so specific." To illustrate her point, avid turned stagnant and inert. ashi laughed and plucked a rush from avid's surface: "We're 98 percent on the structure, right? So, that means we're mating about use, and who better to figure out how to use this thing but one of the owners?" The rush faded in the chubby fist, and ashi made it into a bluebottle fly. avid sighed. It was ashi's job to introduce nonlinear method, surprise, difficulty. She let the fly settle on her surface and drowned it. "All right, so long as your manifestation isn't meant to convince us this place was heaven, or an aerie." She turned her attention back to the rest of the team and cleared. A few flashes appeared in her depths as the team's thought began to 'face. A hush fell, and iell could sense within it the team's quickening need. ashi obediently joined the mating by wading into avid's shallow end. for all of her dread of oz's enclosing walls, iell still felt the hunger to know its truth—a hunger that had brought her together with the rest of this team into a grouping that the p'fers would probably describe as a family, or a symposium, or an orgy.

Around the team, the sim began to slide in and out of definition as the group's thought tried to fill in the missing bits in oz's continuum. iell thought of oz, of the actual site. It was an eroded pit filled with silt and sunk for an eon beneath the sea of another globe. For a decade now, the team had pondered it, probed it with their army of symbiotic crawlers, burrowers, peepers. In the first years, they wondered on the cataclysm that had placed it there. At last, they decided that it was simply the cataclysm of time. Then they sought its contours, its particulars. The sim had sprouted lines, surfaces, walls. Its looming shapes had flickered with color while the team debated the chemical composition of its various coatings. It was idda, their most accomplished historian, who had brought them to the pleasurable theory that the colored groupings were a two-dimensional system of representation. iell could still remember the blush of orgasm that had accompanied their comprehension of the word *outline*. How they had floed! On another level, though, the word troubled her. It was more evidence of the alien nature of pre-'face thought, another example of their insistence on the discrete natures of within and without. How could the p'fers think that when borders between the two were being crossed all the time, even without 'face?

They imagined the boundary kept one thing in and something else out. But iell knew from other teams that even at the time of oz's beginning, the infant 'face was making its presence felt as communications systems, waterways, drugs, pheromones, ESP, viruses. With all the evidence of this dissolution, what had maintained their faith in separation?

Upon learning its shape, the team had thought then on oz's maker. For a while, portions of it had seemed to be similar in organization to some earlier obscure cosmologies, even with a handbook on love, a quaint reminder of the time when pleasure was regarded as separate from other existence. But the connections were too vague, or somehow the team could not come to a satisfying conclusion about them. That had led them to their current ruminations. If they knew what oz was for, perhaps they could decide who had made it.

The team sought its pleasure in earnest now, and as its thoughts floed together, the sim displayed the myriad of oz's possible uses. Blackened ivy wriggled over the walls. Herds of cattle lowed in confusion while they felt the floor crack under them. A mist rose. Two men pried off chunks of concrete and sold them to each other over and over again. Bats infested the ceiling and ate flies that they had lured with a purplish excretion. Fires burned on the stairs. A murder was committed. White sheets were riven and used to

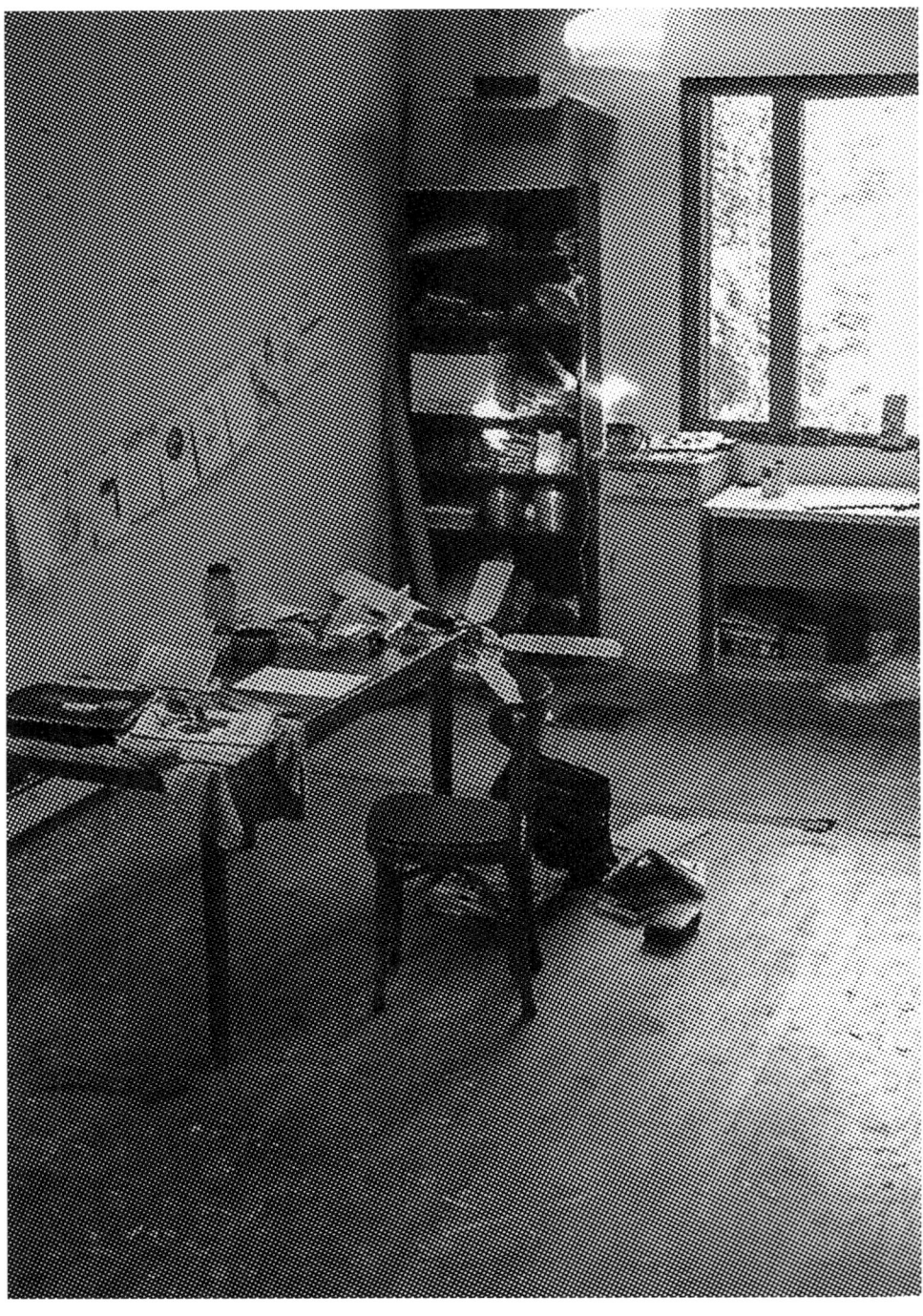

blot out the sunlight. Five infants made slow circuits of the room, licking and receiving nourishment from the sockets. A cat was disassembled and reassembled. Through it all, the team searched for the ideas that would increase the pleasure that was beginning to suffuse their 'face. The word *initiation* rolled amongst them, and they began to luxuriate in its truth. To initiate, to begin. Was oz then some sort of place of beginning? iell began to wish for the conclusion she felt building within all of them. Her thoughts ripened in the depths of avid's focus. She could feel them brushing against ashi's limbs as the cherub swam to and fro. She longed for them to burst.

A group of worshippers trouped into the sim. Slowly they began to acknowledge each other, speaking in lowered voices, sharing cups of wine. Around them, the flat images of the things they might be kept watch—impassive before the halting dance of the initiates. A table was laid. Food was presented, and the sacrificial amount was left for the images, the true inhabitants of the place. Time went past. Few of the worshippers were left now. They wandered, fearfully gazing into the bright faces that beckoned them into their new lives as . . . what? iell felt doubts like coppery chills. They gnawed the team, fraying the voluptuous interchange that seconds ago had bound them all. Questions threatened a dispersal of their ecstasy. If these walls kept something in, what was being kept out? If this body has an edge, how can it know another? What was oz the image of? What was it the beginning of? Why would anyone make a picture of themselves that was not themselves? Or are all pictures their makers because they represent all that the makers can know about picture making? Who is being initiated here? In the service of what god?

iell felt brackish, connected to the team by cords of muck. A light flashed on one of the walls, niggling counterpoint to their disappointment. The flickering turned into ashi's laugh as the cherub gasped and pointed and giggled and said over and over, "look! look! ah what fools these mortals be! can't you see what it is?" iell looked where ashi pointed, looked at the patterning, looked where the light had isolated a single portion of the scene. And iell saw the figure, the figure laid forever into the wall, the figure wearing the garb of the initiate, the figure surrounded by the attentions of others, the mouth agape, orifices open, receptors active, the figure who was ascending into knowledge and the rapture knowledge brings.

the figure of herself.

ashi's excitement was an irresistible tickling, a stroking, a luscious pounding, "the 'face . . . the 'face! don't you see—oz is showing the beginning of the 'face!" And with ashi's voice came understanding, and with understanding came their bliss, which came and came and came again.

INTERVIEW BY JOHN GANGE
AND STEPHEN JOHNSTONE

New Formations, *1993*

If there's one gift I would give to artists, it is this: Don't wait; don't wait to find career security and then come out with your weirdness. Come out at the start because it doesn't get any easier. And so in this interview I'm talking probably more from an aspirational position than a lived position. In the interim I got to do the living. I called forth the person I dreamed of being. —NB

Nayland Blake is known in this country primarily for their *Workstation* and *Restraint* sculptures. Variously described as fantasized bondage and torture devices, imaginary instruments of restraint, or sinister-looking tableaux that suggest sadomasochistic activities, the pieces that Blake made zin the late 1980s developed an absurdist, but clinically disquieting, strain of S&M paraphernalia. Made from aluminum, rubber, leather, and stainless steel, the *Workstations* explicitly refer to the possibility of the body in sexual bondage while at the same time mimicking the functionality of the operating theater, the laboratory, and the site of torture.

Whereas a British audience will have only seen the *Workstations* in isolation as illustrations in the art press, in exhibitions in the United States they have been shown as part of a much wider and ambitious project in which Blake, as they put it, "makes a case for a different definition of a gay sensibility." In installations such as *The Schreber Suite* (a rereading of Sigmund Freud's *Psychoanalytic Notes on a Case of Autobiographical Paranoia*, in which Freud analyses the homosexuality of Judge Daniel Paul Schreber), *The*

Philosopher's Suite (a conglomeration of materials for a marionette production of the Marquis de Sade's *Philosophy in the Bedroom*), and *Punch Agonistes* (in which the *Workstations* were juxtaposed with mock Victorian ornaments and portraits of Punch), Blake attempts to produce an "archaeology of contemporary homosexuality apart from the idea of homosexual desire." During the course of the interview that follows, Blake talks about this archaeology in terms of a refusal of the phallus and an investment in anality, suggesting that a silent and unacknowledged pervert sits at the base of modernism.

At the same time, Blake's most recent installation *Bleep*, shown at the Milch Gallery in London during May 1992, betrayed, at first sight at least, a rather disarming, not to say confusing, fascination with the "perversion" of serial murder. "Named after Dennis Nilsen's pet dog, *Bleep* also denotes the high-pitched sound which American Television channels use to delete anything embarrassing or outspoken. Treating their space as a three-dimensional equivalent of such a hiatus, Blake brings poetic logic to bear on current patterns of behavior and habits of the mind: murder, prejudice, dependency, and consumption in its broadest sense."[1]

Blake distances themself from the current (American) fascination with the serial killer by suggesting that his interest in Nilsen, and in mass killer Jeffrey Dahmer, has more to do with questions of race and extrapolations of formal or art historical concerns than with the sensational and the shocking. Such a reading of *Bleep* was supported by reviews: "The installation addresses a cluster of related issues around sex, race, and violence: questions of appropriate and deviant behavior and the means by which social norms are arrived at and enforced. As a gay man who looks white—fair skinned and blue-eyed—but is officially Black (because of his father), Blake has a keen interest in the negotiable gray areas concerning status and legality."[2]

Concomitantly, however, Blake admits to "binges of reading true crime stories" and a desire to "understand" Nilsen both as "an iconographic figure and as a state of mind." This ambiguity was certainly present in the installation at Milch, and it is an ambiguity we attempted to address in the following interview. We begin by asking Blake about their concern to reread Freud's analysis of Schreber and what this means for a psychoanalytic theorization of homosexuality, perversion, and paranoia.

John Gange Schreber seems to have become an exemplary or idealized pervert. How is such a figure employed to generate art?

Nayland Blake For me, the initial reason I turned to Schreber was because the text was extremely compelling and quite beautiful. There is much in Schreber's book that almost word for word could be writing by someone like Raymond Roussel, and after looking at that text and seeing what has happened to it historically, I saw that installation as an attempt to reposition that text. This is where I would say that the notion of the perverse comes in quite specifically.

The entire installation was conceived of for a museum in the university I was at in Berkeley and consisted of pieces that I had constructed, reconstructions and repositioning of pieces from other parts of the gallery and the museum, and a selection of contemporaneous works from their permanent collection. Everything in the show had wall labels, which were all bits of Schreber's texts. So, basically, it took the form of a sort of didactic exhibition with artifacts from the period as well as artifacts I had constructed. The first time I heard about Schreber was through Gilles Deleuze and Félix Guattari and Guy Hocquenghem's book *Homosexual Desire*, and through that, I went back and read the Freud case and then from that read Schreber's text. There are the beginnings of a Schreber scholarship going on right now, taking another look at the text itself and his life, and I found, in going back to the text, how selective Freud's reading had been, particularly given the consequences of his essay, which positions homosexuality and homosexual desire at the basis of paranoia and was particularly important in the pathological reading of homosexuality.

Two aspects that will prove decisive in Schreber's case: first, his *body* as the favored object of his imaginings (at first in a mostly negative sense: he claims to suffer from a softening of the brain, to feel himself to be dead, to have begun to decay, to be plague-stricken, to have had his penis twisted off, and so on); and second, the aspect of language, in the form of verbal hallucinations ("God spoke openly to him"). The homosexual aspect also appears ("he thinks he is a woman"), and this is connected both with fantasies of castration and with illusions of persecutions (that he had to repulse the "homosexual love of certain persons")—a complex that Freud places at the very centre of his interpretation.[3]

Stephen Johnstone In Freud's papers The Case of Paranoia Running Counter to the Psychoanalytic Theory of the Disease and Some

Neurotic Mechanisms in Jealousy, Paranoia, and Homosexuality, it would seem that the Schreber case is the foundation of that trajectory; homosexuality is theorized as the result of a different object choice on the one hand and, on the other, a paranoid mechanism.

Gange And so you could reverse that formulation, so that paranoia is the base of homosexuality.

Blake One of the things that is revealing is that if you go back to Schreber's actual life, for example, central to his paranoia was the idea that his doctor was attempting to transform him into a woman in order to bear the children of God; and Freud's whole formulation is that his own desire for the doctor and, in actuality, for a homosexual relationship with his father is then transformed into the father figure's desire for Schreber himself and is then further displaced into a hatred or an antagonistic relationship.

In fact, Schreber's doctor, Flechsig, ran a psychological institute and had on several occasions prescribed castration as a form of dealing with manic depression. There is some evidence from the Freud archives that Freud knew that this was the case. Flechsig was a very important doctor to the psychological community, and Freud repressed that evidence in favor of his very convoluted reading—a highly selective reading of the facts and all of the evidence, which I was trying to address in the work. I see Schreber's book as opening up certain possibilities for an examination of a type of gay sensibility that exists at the base of modernism—and, particularly, to look at that work in relation to the work of [Marcel] Duchamp and what that might possibly mean for a reanalysis, a rereading of what gay sensibility could be imagined to be.

Johnstone Do you think that your work is, then, counterhegemonic in that sense? Do you think that the psychoanalytic formulations of homosexuality and the perverse have always been highly ambivalent and have tended to counterpose the perverse to some kind of norm?

Blake I think that what these discourses have relied on has been a "silent pervert" who lies at their base, silent and discounted. At the moment that you go to the speech on the pervert, you are confronted with something that is counterhegemonic because the hegemony only exists through the continued silence of those margins and because of the margins.

Johnstone What do you think counts as perversion here, is there a sense in which you have a boundary to perversion? In other words, are there acceptable and unacceptable or recoupable and irrecoupable perverts? In the current installation, *Bleep*, for instance, there is an obvious reference to Dennis Nilsen. Is Nilsen perverse in some way, and do you think it is helpful to talk about Nilsen as perverse, as press coverage was keen to diagnose him at the time?

Blake I think that if we say that Dennis Nilsen is perverse, period, then we don't say much, we basically state what we already know.

I think that the thing that is valuable and compelling about Freud is the formulation of polymorphous perversity, which is a notion that is immediately backed away from on every front because of its implications for established moralities. It is certainly why I am interested in someone like de Sade.

I think that in the case of Nilsen, making this work is an attempt for me to come to some sort of understanding about him, both in terms of an iconographic figure but also as a state of mind.

The severed heads of men killed by Nilsen and Jeffrey Dahmer; the contrast between highbrow racism and down-home minstrel show; the poster that hung in Dahmer's apartment; visual equivalents of a castration-complex and various forms of dependency and coercion. . . . See it all at MILCH.[4]

Blake I think we are continually in dialogue with the possibility of death. It is one of the first things that children understand. Certainly, in the case of Nilsen, the notion is that death is the way, paradoxically, that one stops from disappearing, and it is better to have someone around and dead than to have someone be alive and leave you. One of the other things that is going on in the show is an attempt to start to talk about issues of race in relation to that. The initial impulse for making these bronze heads was seeing a group of bronze grotesques in the V&A, which are men's heads on bases, some of them are cast birds' feet, and they are little oil lamps, sixteenth-century Italian indoor decorative bronzes. On the cases, they are all labeled as "grotesque man's head," but in actuality all the features are black, and that brought to mind the blackamoor in decoration supporting a lamp. I think that embedded within decoration is the notion of ownership. You have a permanent version of something to demonstrate that you could, theoretically, possess the living version.

Gange This relates to the whole questions of the primitive in modern art and the valorization of the Black body around a notion of transgression.

Blake To me, there is a continuing dialogue in the history of sculpture between two poles within Greek sculpture: What we assume to be the public, sacred pole of the carved white marble statue, which comes from the earth. The dross is chipped away, and we have this pure form underneath—the dialogue between that and molded, domestic, sacrificial bronzes and lamps and interiors that are dark, that are fecal, that are earthbound in a way, that are not transcendent. I see a kind of racial duality in that, but we now know that Greek sculpture was not pure and white, that it was painted, and that it was made by a race of dark-skinned people to represent them. I have always been more interested in the domestic—the commonplace—object rather than the large-scale public object.

Gange In the catalog for the *Mind over Matter* show at the Whitney last year, the introductory essay states, "The specter of AIDS hovers around most of [Blake's] sculpture, adding to its ineffable feeling of absence and loss."[5] Do you think that the work of any gay artists currently working, particularly in the United States, will automatically be read in relation to AIDS?

Blake I think that the fact of AIDS has completely reorganized the way in which gay artists have represented themselves, and I think that certainly in the United States, it is hard to conceive of a work of art at this point that doesn't have some relationship to AIDS.

Johnstone Looking at the reviews of your work over the past five years, the question of AIDS seems to come up immediately, but in the reviews, it is left at "This work is concerned with AIDS," and a critical sense of how the work might consider or interrogate questions of AIDS and representation never really develops.

Gange AIDS has come to represent that which you can't not speak about, but at the same time, it's not spoken about.

Blake Exactly.

The lessons Blake offers can be read as a direct and graceful reaction to the AIDS crisis. Life has its unusual implements to assist the population in existence and extinction. Blake's impulse is to mix the ornate with the contemporary. He contrasts Poe's gothic obsession with death with his own sterilized assemblages of disaster. The result is a compelling fetishized circle.[6]

Gange It becomes the perverse.

Blake If one can speak about the aesthetic consequences of AIDS. . . . I chart a specific transformation in the notion of gay sensibility; prior to AIDS the only thing that a gay man could speak about, the only way in which a work of art was legible as gay, is that it presented a mechanism of a male gaze but with a male rather than a female object. Clearly, it was possible to read the work of David Hockney as being encoded as gay because of that. I think that, as a result of AIDS, the iconographic position of the homosexual became much more complicated, and you also started to have a generation of gay artists who were saying, "If the art world at large is going to pay attention to us—because we are supposed to take on the mourning function for the culture in regard to AIDS—that's not enough. If you're going to ask our opinion about that, you're also going to have to hear our opinion about x, y, and z." And I think that it's precisely because there has been a shift in meaning that there is a greater sense of urgency in the work of gay men and lesbian women.

Johnstone I saw your work in the group exhibition *How It Is Organized* earlier this year in New York. That show, and an exhibition like Ralph Rugoff's *Just Pathetic*, seemed to be a curatorial attempt to capture a specific contemporary moment, and I was really not sure what that moment might be. An awful lot of very different work was thrown together as if in merely juxtaposing it within the gallery space a zeitgeist or. . . .

Blake . . . something would appear. I would not say these large group shows have outlived their function, but their function needs to be rethought extensively.

I think that one of the things that has happened with the generation of artists that came up in the 1980s is that their work has continually been bracketed within itself. We see a lot of curating that consists of lists of names, and everyone within the art world is so conversant with the supposed discourses that those names embody that the show is just seen as an indexing of the relative position of those discourses.

Johnstone To return to the current show, *Bleep*. I wondered: Did you know about Nilsen when you were in the States, or did you "discover" him when you came over here?

Blake I did know about Nilsen. I had heard about Nilsen for a long time. One of the people I have done some work with and whose work is very important to me, and I admire, is Dennis Cooper. I had seen Dennis's copy of *Killing for Company*, and I bought a copy.

Johnstone Mike Kelley has a show coming up at the ICA [Institute of Contemporary Art] and apparently, the curators of the exhibition have been searching for a British counterpart for Kelley's *Pay for Your Pleasure* installation. In this piece, as you know, Kelley hangs banners featuring writers and artists such as André Breton, Victor Hugo, and Michel Foucault—all of whom are quoted celebrating the artist as a cultural pervert or outsider who willingly embraces criminality, madness, or deviance. In among these banners, Kelley places a vitrine with a painting of Pogo the Clown painted by the mass killer John Wayne Gacy. At the exit of the installation, Kelley then places a collection box for victim support schemes. If, on the one hand, Kelley plays with the moral ambiguity of the artist as transgressor and the role of art in therapy, on the other, his use of Gacy's *Pogo the Clown* (an image all the more disturbing in the light of our knowledge of Gacy's crimes) fits all too easily into what appears to be the contemporary American fascination with, if not glamorization of, the serial killer.

Blake In the cultural scene in LA and among people that I know, there has been a lot of fascination with serial murder and a lot of speculation on it, and we have all gone through binges of reading true crime stories. I see much of this piece as an outgrowth of my pieces with puppets. This is the first time that I have really addressed the notion of these serial killers explicitly.

Johnstone Could you say something about your frequent return to the figure of Punch in this context? The press release for *Bleep* suggests that you view Punch as the "despotic anti-hero of popular culture." Why does Punch turn up in this installation?

Blake Punch is a popular entertainment based on the notion of serial murder. I have talked a little bit about the idea of Punch as a kind of Sadean figure. One of the things in this show is the notion of a sort of castrated Punch. It is why there are so many images of decapitation as a metaphor for castration and for impotence. Essentially, I do not believe that there is some kind of transcendence within the notion of serial killing.

One of the things about Jeffrey Dahmer keeping skulls around is that he particularly preyed on Black and Asian men, and the skulls were kept around as trophies.

Primarily, the show is concerned with the figure of Bleep. Reading *Killing for Company*, it seems Bleep is really the thing that Nilsen cares for. Bleep is continually being put outside to miss out on the horror—shielded from it. Then at the moment Nilsen goes into prison and it is clear that he is not going to be bailed out, Bleep is killed—primarily, to my mind, because of the fact that the state does not require immediate revenge. Myra Hindley's dog was killed in the same circumstances, you know—completely innocent animals. It is not like they were accomplices.

Johnstone It is as if these pets had witnessed something and could not be allowed to live with the knowledge. What is strange is that Nilsen invests Bleep with innocence, and so he puts him out while the killing goes on while, at the same time, the state would seem to invest Bleep with the knowledge of those crimes.

Gange Returning to John Wayne Gacy: There is a certain fashionableness about owning artworks by serial killers.

Johnstone For instance, I understand the filmmaker John Waters owns at least one of Gacy's works.

Blake It is not hard to get hold of Gacy's paintings. For me, the images of these guys have come up more through thinking about race and as extensions of extrapolations of art historical or formal concerns, rather than the notion of sensationalism, because I think that there is a real danger in the sort of feckless acceptance of criminals for their own sake—or, basically, because it is cool.

Johnstone Richard Linklater's cult film *Slacker* is interesting in this context because, in a film concerned with mapping a certain kind of postadolescent, twenty-something apathy, one of the few moments of excitement in the film is when one of the characters talks about serial murder. Looking at that film from England, it is almost as if the serial killer in contemporary American culture is represented as the last, albeit psychotic, frontiersperson. It is as if the serial killer is fantasized as the last person who can act.

Gange Is this serial killing as the end point of fashionable transgression?

Blake Yes, but the community in which I live, for instance, is so quick to adopt transgression that things very quickly cease to be transgressive. Believe me, everybody has something pierced in San Francisco! And what we learn from that is that notions of piercing per se are not transgressive.

Johnstone What happens to the notion of the perverse then?

Blake My formulation is that perversions are those areas that are lacunae within the norm, and they do not exist in any absolute sense at all. That norm can shift immediately. To go back to Foucault, one could almost formulate that to be perverse in our time means not to speak of sex. We continually interrogate sex as some limit, as some territory. It is remarkable in Britain because you have a state that has been much more willing to prescribe the notion of the norm for the individual, to a much greater extent than has been allowed in the United States.

Johnstone Operation Spanner being an example.

Blake Exactly, but that is a situation extremely specific to this culture.

Johnstone You could not imagine that happening in Los Angeles or New York?

Blake No—partially because there is a Bill of Rights. There is a much clearer delineation between the public and the private. The thing that is remarkable about Spanner is that even if the people involved in the activity wanted to be involved, the state is given the final sanction on that activity.

Johnstone In this sense, Spanner might be an index of a particularly English relationship between individual behavior and the gaze of the state. What is extraordinary about the Spanner prosecutions is the need to find someone who has been hurt.

Blake And posthumously that is what is remarkable. Because, in general, the state always attempts to find or to formulate a victim. If you have a crime, you have to have a victim. Victimless crimes do not exist very long because eventually somebody finds a victim from them—one way or the other. Finally, this produces an extremely abstracted form of victim.

Johnstone Do you think the "victim" in the Operation Spanner case might be the public?

Blake Yes, which is an extremely abstracted notion because the state basically admits that the public does not reside in any of the people who participate in the activity of the people who know about the activity. So somewhere is this phantom public that is victimized.

Gange Alternatively, it is the symbolic, in the Lacanian sense, which is often constituted as perverse—[Jacques] Lacan's "perversion."

In the *Mind over Matter* catalog text, you refer to being interested in "a type of refusal of the phallus." Could you expand on this remark?

Blake This goes back to this notion of what could be a different type of homosexual mode within the history of modernism. It has to do, for me, with a notion of seeing one's own work as a number of activities within a field at the same time as describing this field; progressing through the notion of the fragment as opposed to the linear progression of masterpiece after masterpiece, which is the traditional notion of mastery, of what a successful artist is. It is why I would really point to someone like Duchamp as an example of what I would call a gay sensibility within modernism.

I think it is a [Maurice] Blanchot quote that is something like, "The concern of the Modern artist is the reconstruction of the universe; the method of the Modern artist is the fragment," and I think that, to me, that is a kind of refusal of the phallus. To talk of fragmented meaning and a nonlinear progression in terms of the way that work emerges and activates the things around it—that, to me, would be nonphallic.

Gange But you seem to be relating, or not adjuncting, the possible relation between phallus and the male body.

Blake Well, I do agree with Hocquenghem when he talks about the crucial point of difference between what you might call a gay and straight sensibility as the investing of value in the anus or in anality, and I think that that produces a very different perspective, which does lead us back to this notion of the perverse. To attempt to conceive of the artist as being involved in a type of anal pleasure rather than a phallic pleasure or phallic desire, I think implies a different type of practice.

Johnstone Is that only a certain kind of artist, or are you talking about the artist in general?

Blake I would say that it is only a certain type of artist who might be engaged in that, and I would also say, very specifically, that to talk about this homosexual sensibility does not mean to immediately link it to some sort of sexual behavior. I think it has, basically, to do with one's relationships toward meaning structures, and it is quite possible for a person to be a homosexual and still have a relationship to their work that is very traditional.

Gange Would you extend this as far as, in reference to Duchamp and the idea of the found object, a Freudian notion of retention and collection around anality?

Blake Yes, I think so. There is also, in Duchamp, a continual interrogation of void, of empty and full, all of the Wedge pieces, the castings, a lot of notions around transformations along the lines of gender, that seem to me to be very gay ideas. Also, Duchamp's work is very campy; the *Green Box* is a very campy object in its notion of being like a purse that you sort of tote around and that has everything you need in it.

Gange The vessel has featured a lot in your own work.

Blake Yes, and that has come not only through the notion of the medicalization of the gay body but also through a distancing or bracketing effect that those things impart—again, going back to this notion of the natural history museum.

Johnstone This brings us to the *Workstation* pieces. While the most obvious referent here is the paraphernalia of S&M and bondage practices, the workstations also clearly have some relationship to the machinery on which the body is interrogated by medical knowledge. In addition, there is also the hint of torture and the extraction of truth. How are these referents connected?

Restraint 6 (ankle, shelf, mirror) looks like a straightforward sado-masochistic sex device. A sheet of polished steel is bolted to the wall. At the bottom, protrudes a shelf, and dangling from the shelf, 24 inches apart, are two leather ankle straps. At the top is a thick bar with three shower rings. Although the use is unspecified, the message is clear.[7]

Blake I would like to add to that the Bauhaus notion of functionality. One of the things that all of the artifacts from those three fields—the S&M, the medical, and torture—have in common is that they tend to reveal their function through one's perception of them, and that is a trait that they share with exemplary modernist designs. One of my constant concerns has been: How does an object embody narrative; how can you express narrative through an object? All of those objects immediately implicate the viewer in a particular type of narrative and are, in some ways, the invitation to a possible narrative.

Johnstone One of the workstations contains a polished sheet of metal that acts as a mirror, and attached to it are manacles. The suggestion is that the participant is chained into looking at his mirror image.

Blake Right. The *Workstations* provide a possibility of examination. But one of the things that I would point to, specifically, is the notion of sexual bondage rather than S&M, because, to me, S&M is about theater. It is about a successful theatrical interaction between two actors, who script, direct, stage, and watch the scene, and sexual pleasure is derived from that play between enacting a scene and introducing variation into it. But also through the sense of being inside and outside of one's body at once. The pain that is involved in S&M, for the bottom, can be a particular grounding that supposedly obliterates boundaries but at the same time reinforces boundaries because it is always the bottom who really controls the scene and always sets the limit.

Johnstone In the past, you have talked about the role of the tableau in bondage.

Blake Well, that to me is what bondage is about. Bondage is about an erotic relationship to the pose, toward being posed. I think that for the bottom in bondage, there is an erotic relation or realization to not having to move, not having to act, being secured in a position. I suppose that one could make an almost trite connection to one's relationship as a child to being able to be still, to not having to move, and being satisfied in that position vis-à-vis the mother.

Gange To me, it seems that S&M sexuality, in general, is where the "sexual act" becomes secondary to the hypersigns of sexuality in its extremity.

Mapplethorpe's photography is perverse, not just in content but in attitude. No doubt the notion of perversion is suspect these enlightened days, but it is nonetheless legitimate and visible. "Perversion exists," as Robert Stoller says. "Perversion is the result of an essential interplay between hostility and sexual desire, hostility that is manifest in the connotations on the term." There is a sense of latent, impacted hostility patiently waiting to make itself known and become operational—hostility knowing that it will sooner or later be called into play. This is transparent in the explicitly sadomasochistic bondage pictures, especially *Brian Ridley and Lyle Heeter* (1979). The proudly posing couple, dressed for violent sexual action, are no doubt waiting for the photographer to leave to lovingly inflict themselves on one another. (Such great effort—the dressing up in exotic garb, the elaborate staging of the copulation—almost resembles a forced march to pleasure. The ritualization of the event, in part intended to prevent it from becoming a routine, has itself become routine, as their posing in a luxurious, haute bourgeois context suggests.)[8]

Blake Much of what we associate with or assume to be the core aspects of the sexual act may not even be present in something like bondage or S&M. I think that if we want to talk about perversion, we might talk about something like foot fetishism, for example, which could be imagined as a powerfully perverse reading of contemporary culture. From the point of view of the foot fetishist, much of what is construed as sexual would not even show up on the map of "normal" sexuality.

Johnstone What about the way that S&M imagery and the icons of S&M and bondage have gone overground? Your work has consistently been reviewed as concerned with the interface between certain forms of homosexual practice and the ways in which these practices have been represented in popular culture.

More pointed is *Workstation # 5*, a metal clothes rack with meat cleavers hanging from it by chains. Lying on the rack are a piece of black rubber hose and black leather (or rubber) leggings. This work is loaded with sadomasochistic associations that touch on the rarely explored semantic exchange between gay and mainstream culture. Sadomasochism, once considered the darkest of sexual predilections, has since crossed over—in its outward accouterments, anyhow—to the mainstream television, film, advertising, popular music, and, not least, clothing industries, all of which dip into the fantasies of domination and submission upon which it is based.[9]

Blake Well, I would say about the referencing of S&M: I believe really firmly that if you want to talk about an issue, do not come up with a high-art interpretation of that issue; if you want to talk about issues of immobilizing the body, or constraining the body, or leathering the body, it is much more interesting to look at the people who are actually invested in that and doing that.

To go back to the issue of AIDS in relation to the medical dissection and scrutiny of the body, women and gay men are the two groups that have been at the forefront of the medical invasion of the body. To me, it is much more important to look at what is happening from that viewpoint, rather than through layers of abstraction.

To go back to the notion of an extended gay sensibility in the practice of someone like Duchamp, here is a situation where objects and items from the outside culture are bracketed, represented, and repositioned in terms of their signification. And that is an exact model of how gay male culture has proceeded in, at least, the nineteenth and twentieth centuries. Because there has not been a place where autonomous gay culture could be made, gay men are continually in the position of having to take items from the outside world and make them gay, make them speak clearly, and sometimes that takes the form of a sort of camp take on them; sometimes it takes the form of a revised sexual reading of them. In that way, one can say that gay male culture has been in advance of postmodern culture. It has been, sort of, the model for postmodern culture.

Johnstone Recently, a number of newspapers, including the *Independent* and the *Guardian*, have run articles exploring a range of "subcultural activities" like attending Kinky Gelinky, cross-dressing, and body piercing. It is as if these newspapers draw on the iconography in order to legitimize certain forms of fantasy within straight culture, now that there is a generalized worry about simple notions of penetrative sex.

Blake Yes. I would say, right now, and I can see it more clearly in the States than here—partially because of the notions of what has happened vis-à-vis the NEA [National Endowment for the Arts] and other things in the States—that gay sexuality has come to represent sexuality, period.

Heterosexual iconography is so pervasive—and particularly with the need that it continually up the ante in terms of its explicitness—explicit heterosexual imagery is now so commonplace that it no longer carries the weight of sexuality. What you are starting to see in the case of someone like Marky Mark, say, is a straight person positioning themselves with all the significations of gay sexuality in order to make themselves read as sexual.

It is exactly the same thing that Madonna has done, and I think you are going to start to see it in the work of many artists. I think it is becoming an increasing trend in the culture, where a certain degree of homoerotic content or homoerotic signification does not necessarily signify any homosexual orientation. I think it is the fact that right now heterosexual sex is not legible as sex, so gay sex has started to take over that function.

Gange It has seemed to me for some time that as female sexuality and gay sexuality have become theorized as discourses, then it almost seems that there is no straight male sexuality anymore. Straight men still have sex, but they do not have a sexuality.

Blake One thing that I would point to as being very important and revealing about gay culture is that gay men and women have the notion of coming out, which essentially is an announcement to themselves, more than anything else, that they are a sexual being. There is no parallel mechanism for straight people; there is never any particular point in your life that you have to acknowledge the fact that you have a sexuality, that you are sexual in that way. I think that coming out is one of the most particularly positive notions, because I think that the announcement and understanding of that as a point in one's life gives you a type of knowledge of its, not necessarily artifice, but of it as a construct and a ritual.

Gange Part of the possible move for straight men is to rethink passivity, which links back to that question of questioning the phallus, as [Julia] Kristeva implies, of modernity relinquishing the phallus. Possibly, the fetishist is a good example of someone staking a claim on passivity. I would suggest that [Georges] Bataille, for example, is in that space.

Blake The next thing that I am working on will hopefully be on [Leopold von] Sacher-Masoch. One of the things that I am thinking about in terms of masochism is that it seems like a sort of corruption of the Romantic sublime, where the notions of terror, transcendence, and disruption that the Romantic sublime invests in the outside world instead become localized in the form of a person. The masochist is a person who experiences all of the sublime emotions, but they are all located within another person, which makes it extremely different from a notion of inverse sadism.

Gange Again, to refer to the catalog article, you say, "I'm concerned with the idea of pleasure, as opposed to desire." Could you detail what you understand by this dialectic?

Blake I think that we have had drilled into us the notion of desire as a kind of fuel. To me, the work of many of the so-called Simulationist artists of the mid-1980s was about this notion of desire and the way that desire basically empties us, and the commodity is the demon commodity and how it serves to maintain our alienation, and desire is the spring to all of that. I agree with all of that, but my feeling is that we understand that now, and that desire itself is actually quite generic.

Our society trains us to all have the same desires because that is what capitalism needs. Where someone takes their pleasure is highly individual, and it is where people separate themselves out, and it is much more interesting to me. You can see where an artist's pleasure lies or if there is pleasure in what they do. To me, it is the thing that makes Roland Barthes a much more interesting writer and thinker than Jean Baudrillard—because of that attempt to interrogate pleasure.

Johnstone Returning to what you implied earlier about scale and modernity, would it be fair to précis this observation in the following way?

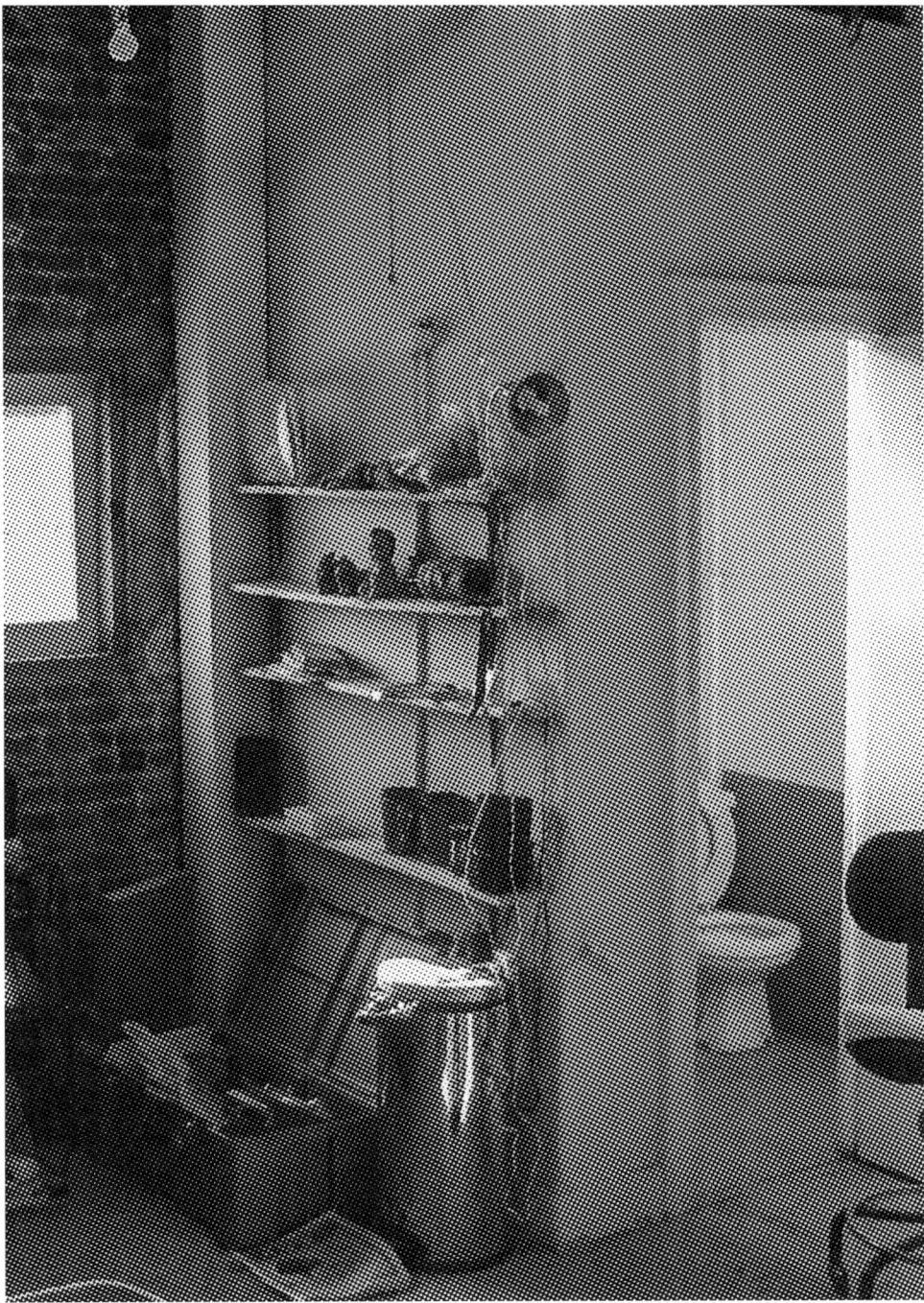

Desire equates with the ideal of the general, and pleasure with the fragment or the detail.

Blake Yes.

Notes

1. From press release on Nayland Blake's *Bleep*, Milch Gallery, London, May 16–July 11, 1992.

2. Sarah Kent, review of *Bleep*, *Time Out*, June 1992.

3. Samuel M. Weber, introduction to *Memoirs of My Nervous Illness*, by Daniel Paul Schreber (1903), translated and edited by Ida Macalpine and Richard A. Hunter (Cambridge, MA: Harvard University Press, 1988), which quotes from Sigmund Freud's "Psycho-Analytic Notes on an Autobiographical Account of a Case of Paranoia *(Dementia Paranoides),*" xxii.

4. From press release on Nayland Blake's *Bleep*.

5. Richard Armstrong, "Mind over Matter," in *Mind over Matter: Concept and Object* (New York: Whitney Museum of American Art, 1990), 13. This exhibition at Whitney Museum of American Art from, October 1990–January 1991, featured Ashley Bickerton, Nayland Blake, Tishan Hsu, Ronald Jones, Liz Larner, and Annette Lemieux.

6. Benjamin Weissman, review of "Punch Agonistes" at Richard Khulenschmidt in Los Angeles, *Artforum*, September 1989, 154.

7. Weissman, review, 154.

8. Donald Kuspit, "Robert Mapplethorpe—Aestheticising the Perverse," *Artscribe*, November/December 1988, 68. As Blake implies above, this reading of Mapplethorpe's *Brian Ridley and Lyle Heeter* entirely misrepresents the "scene" or "tableau" of bondage and fundamentally ignores the participants' erotic relationship to the pose.

9. Gay Morris, "Exhibition Reviews: San Francisco, Nayland Blake at Mincher/Wilcox," *Art in America*, March 1990, 209.

CITY OF HARES:
A PROPOSAL

Previously Unpublished, 1994

It's rare that I produce proposals this detailed for exhibitions, but by the mid-1990s, I had started making installations that were also occasions for me to make work on-site in the museum, combining the space of work with the space of display. Many of the ideas presented in this proposal found their way into later pieces, especially the performance of Hare Follies *in 1997. —NB*

City of Hares is an installation comprising three stations: the Grotto, the Workshop, and the Gallows. These represent three moments in the life of the central character—an allegorical hero to be portrayed by the artist in a rabbit suit. In sequence, the three stations represent a passage from the underground to the air, reflecting the rabbit's identity as an animal that moves from above the earth to below, an animal that appears and disappears.

The Grotto is represented by a Victorian stage set mounted on scaffolding. The set is freestanding and surrounded by shallow troughs of tar, a substance that captures animals and that is black and reflective and is formed by decayed organic matter. The tar is also suggestive of Br'er Rabbit's struggles with the Tar Baby—a silent, passive adversary. The Grotto is the Hare's place of reflection, hibernation, rebirth.

The Workshop comprises several of the artist's workstations, where the Hare will perform various tasks during the exhibition, such as casting dark and white chocolate rabbits in a mold, embroidering rabbit banners, coating

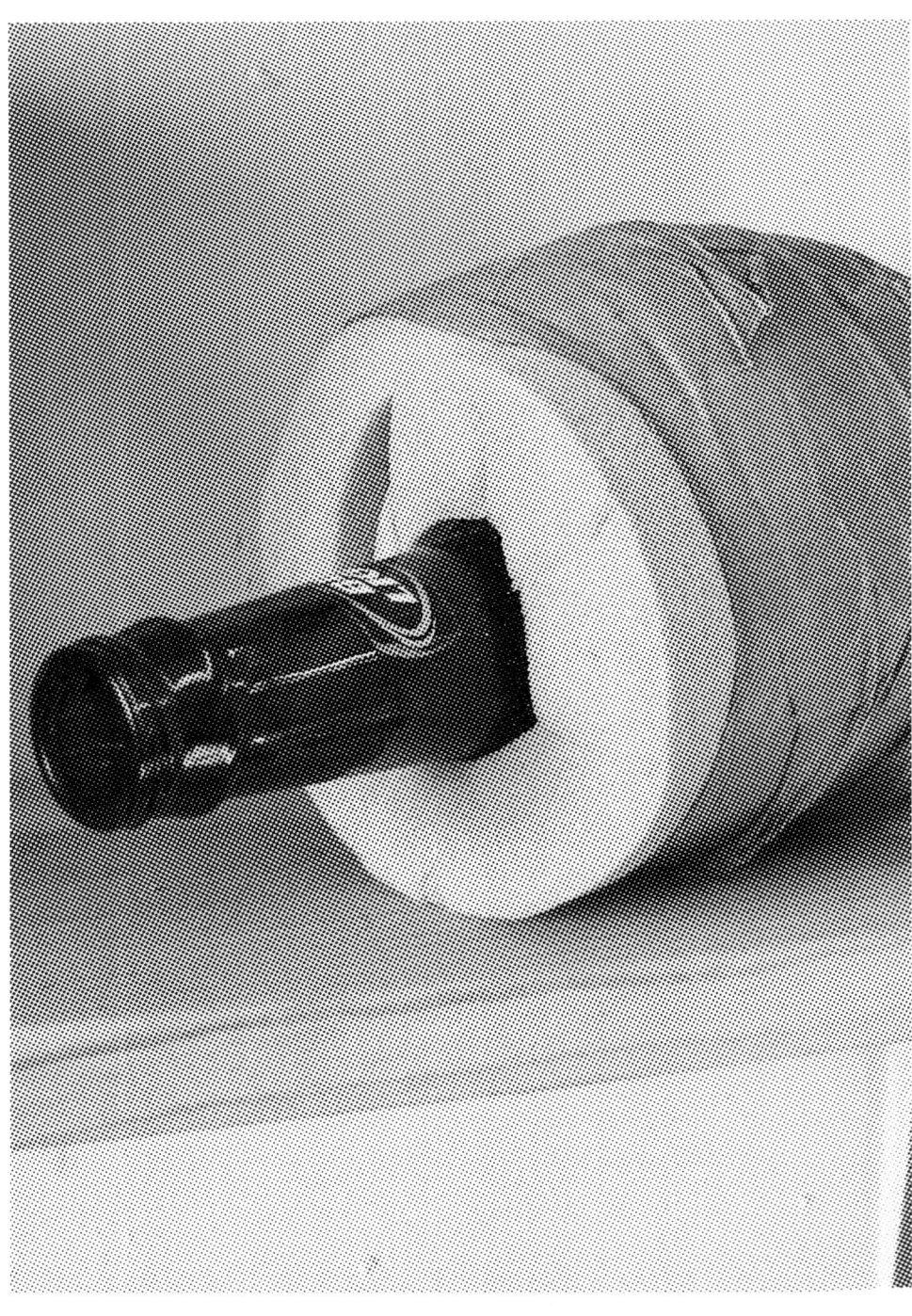

ropes for the gallows station, and carving and printing wood blocks. The results of these labors will be on display around the Workshop.

The Gallows will consist of a functioning, self-triggered gallows and a large number of coils of rope coated with rubber. The rubber is another sticky insulating substance suggestive of skin and tar. The Gallows evokes both Southern lynching and autoerotic asphyxiation. It is a tree, producing sap, like rubber. As the Hare reaches for the sky, it can do so only at the cost of its life.

Where appropriate, the components of the installation will be fabricated ahead of time and assembled on-site.

CURATING "IN A DIFFERENT LIGHT"

In a Different Light: Visual Culture, Sexual Identity, Queer Practice, *1995*

"In a Different Light," cocurated with Lawrence Rinder for the Berkeley Art Museum, was the culmination of a decade of curatorial thinking on my part. Larry was incredibly generous in extending the museum's resources and expertise to the creation of a show that was extremely eccentric in conception and execution. At the time we hoped that it would be the first in a series of shows, but it took at least another decade before other curators began to take on the ideas and approaches in the show. —NB

In 1991 I organized an exhibition with Pam Gregg for San Francisco's New Langton Arts called *Situation*. It was a gathering of works by over thirty young gay and lesbian artists. For the most part, these were artists whom I regarded as my peers, and the exhibition was conceived of as the third in a series of exhibitions—the Bay Area's contribution to a discussion that had included *Against Nature* in Los Angeles and *Erotophobia* in New York. When *Situation* was installed and had its opening, I felt a sense of disappointment—not with the selection of artists or with the individual works but with the entire emotional tone of the event. *Situation* felt more like an ending than a beginning. The two previous exhibitions had opened people's eyes to a new type of activity. *Situation* documented the fact that that activity had established itself in the art world and had found its voice. While that was good news, it was difficult to see where to go next, in terms of both a gay and lesbian dialogue and my own curatorial practice. Thus, when Larry Rinder approached me about this exhibition, I reacted to the idea with a low level of interest, if not outright hostility. It seemed pointless to rehash the ideas presented in *Situation*. I became interested only after Larry and I had a discussion of some of the things that we might do differently. Over the course of several conversations, we developed several requirements the show would have to fulfill in order to be a genuine step forward.

First, it would have to be multigenerational. For almost fifteen years, museums have been unable or unwilling to bring together the work of successive generations of artists. Instead, artists are continually grouped within their own generation, leading to the continual reinforcement of whatever critical discourse has surrounded that period. We are thus encouraged to believe that we already know the truth about a particular group of artists and that nothing more remains to be said. Artists themselves do not impose such neat distinctions on their influences. I know I don't.

Second, the show should have both queer and straight artists in it. In the same way that artists are not simply responding to the work of people of the same age, they are not only looking at works by those who share their sexual preference. Indeed, much of what queer artists are doing these days is questioning the value of identity politics.

In light of that concern, my third requirement was that the exhibition should not have the words *gay*, *lesbian*, or *queer* in its title. The title is the doorway through which the viewer enters the exhibition. If we essentialize the work of these artists in the title, we limit the viewers' chances of being able to find new information and connections among the works. The artists would be once again ghettoized. It also seemed important not to mislead the public. Given the limited time and space resources of the museum, we were not going to be able to present an exhibition that might fully document the enormous historical and artistic achievements of gay and lesbian people. It seemed important to let people know up front that they were viewing a different type of exhibition.

Finally, I hoped to make the show responsive to the ways in which artists operate in the world, as distinct from the way curators or art historians might imagine them operating. This exhibition began, like many others, in response to a type of energy and activity around a community of artists. What, then, is it like for artists to be around that energy, that excitement? What are artists doing? In working on this show, I have thought about those times when being in the world as an artist has meant the most to me—those times when I could feel a presence, a looming joy in the works around me. The early 1990s were such a time in the queer community in San Francisco; notions that had been circulating began to come together in new constellations. The world seemed full of fresh messages—truths perhaps addressed to us alone but connecting us to other initiates. These group epiphanies are the calls we respond to when we make work. Sometimes, it is the work of an individual artist that can call forth our own voices; at other times, it is the conjunction of previously separated works of art. These realizations happen for different artists at different times, but when they happen for enough people at one time, new moments are born. We say that "history is being made," but it would be more accurate to say that "life is being lived." In various ways, the works in this show are records of that life being lived and how that chain of flowerings has led us to where we are today. In working on this exhibition, it is my hope that it will also lead to the next one of those flowerings and not simply document this one's passing.

Larry and I wanted to make an exhibition that might, in some way, be true to the sense of energy we had experienced around this queer art. We began our journey by throwing away our maps. Our methods were intuitive rather than linear. In this project, we have endeavored to move away from the identification of *queer* as a noun or adjective and toward using it as a verb. Previous attempts to discuss the relationship between sexual prefer- ence and art making have asked the question, "What does gay art look like?" We decided to ask the question, "What do queer artists do?" Rather than assume that we knew what gay sensibility was, and looking for works that fit that definition, we began by assuming that we did not know the shape of the terrain beforehand. We gave ourselves a few arbitrary parameters: We would restrict our exploration to the United States and to the twentieth century. For the most part, we have honored those borders. We placed works we found compelling as markers within that terrain. Connections were con- jured, examined, discarded. At all times, we tried to let the works we were examining provide the guide for our future peregrinations.

The works in this exhibition form a new map that is the result of that wandering. This is a map of a queer practice in the visual arts over the past thirty years. It is, like our journey, incomplete and personal. This very process of mapping, or remapping, is one of the most important compo- nents of the particular practice we are trying to document. Many of the artists included in this show have been involved, either individually or in groups, with the project of creating and discovering queer territory. These mappings have proceeded across either the physical terrain of cities, the ideological space of the art world, or history. In many ways, this process has been the same for other marginalized groups, and the ability of artists today to queer the reading of various signs owes much to the previous efforts of those groups. Those on the outside have to struggle to find their face in the distorting mirror of mainstream discourse. This struggle has a deeper meaning for queers since they do not have recourse to the usual alternative repositories of meaning: religious, ethnic, or familial heritages.

Queer people are the only minority whose culture is not transmitted within the family. Indeed, the assertion of one's queer identity often is made as a form of contradiction to familial identity. Thus, for queer people, all of the words that serve as touchstones for cultural identification (family, home, people, neighborhood, heritage) must be recognized as constructions for and by the individual members of that community. The extremely provisional nature of queer culture is the thing that makes its transmission so fragile. However, this very fragility has encouraged people to seek retroactively its contours in a degree not often found in other groups. Queer people must literally construct the houses they will be born into and adopt their own parents. The idea that identity and culture are nonorganic constructs is also one of the most important characteristics of postmodernism. It should be noted that many of the theoreticians of the postmodern— the generation of critics and philosophers that came of age in the late 1960s—were gay and lesbian. In certain ways, the discourse of the postmodern is the queer experience rewritten to describe the experience of the whole world.

From the margins, queers have picked those things that could work for them and recoded them and rewritten their meanings, opening up the possibility of viral reinsertion into the body of general discourse. Denied images of themselves, they have changed the captions on others' family photos. Left without cultural vehicles, they have hijacked somebody else's. They have been forced to trespass and poach. To be queer is to cobble together identity, to fashion provisional tactics at will, to pollute and deflate all discourses. Historically, this activity has been a possibility for either the upper class, whose privilege is utilized to exercise in power, or the lower class, whose reworkings of high culture have often served as a form of social resistance. At various times queer practice has been associated with both upper- and lower-class positions. Because queers do not share a set of physical characteristics, we have also had to have greater recourse to semiotic means to express our tribal affiliations. We resort to dress codes, colors, earrings, and references to telltale cultural interests—whether Judy Garland or Joan Jett. In histories and biographies, we scan for words like *companion* and *spinster*. Or we read the obituaries looking for men who die before their fifties of a lingering illness.

Queers are a minority because of what we do, not what we are. As such, we continue to pose a dilemma for a society that can only believe in equality if it is linked to biology. What used to be true only of queer culture, though, has now become true of all culture. All artists today are confronted with a culture that is no longer unified or even divided into the convenient binary of high and low. Postmodern culture is an ever-mutating system of signs and meanings. Value is fluid. Artists have developed a number of strategies for negotiating this circumstance—strategies that bear a marked resemblance to those employed by queers in relation to the heterosexual world. How then do those strategies differ for queer artists? In my view, part of the answer lies in the family tree that has suggested itself to me as a result of the process of working on this show. I want to present the lineage that I have conjured up for these queer artists. I think that their fates might allow us to guess at the answer to that question.

I do not present the following genealogy as part of some positivistic historical progression that will lead us through the high points of artistic production inevitably to the glory of queer art. Rather, the activity that we are calling *queer*—the works and ideas that interested us for this exhibition in the first place—is similar in its intention, organization, and tactics to several other previous activities. In the past, those activities have been organized around other group identifications and other social concerns. But by placing queerness within this progression, I hope both to show what is different about the work of queer people from that of previous generations of lesbian and gay artists and to retroactively claim space for queer activities in previous situations not associated with queerness. I'll move from this chronological mapping to a spatial mapping of the specific groups of works within the show.

During many of the attempts to articulate what a queer practice might be, I have found myself drawn back to the work of Marcel Duchamp. Duchamp's practice challenged assumptions about the ways in which things are classified as works of art and also the roles of those individual works within the artist's "body" of work. Laconic, fragmentary, and condensed, Duchamp's work pointed the way to an artistic production based in ellipsis rather than mastery. While his ready-mades provided much fodder for discussions of the nature of the art object, more important is the way that Duchamp's work derived meaning from its internal cross-referencing and dialectic between gesture and silence. Much of the meaning in Duchamp is made between: between lines, between pieces, between periods. This proved inspiring for many artists—not only the famous group of Cage, Cunningham,

Johns, and Rauschenberg (although their adoption of Duchamp as a parent of their work is a clear example of the mapping process I have discussed). It is not my purpose here to argue that Duchamp is the progenitor of queer art but rather to point out that his practice, more than that of any other artist, opened a space for queers to formulate points of resistance to the monolithic structure of "culture." By stepping to one side of aesthetic culture, Duchamp managed to produce works that prefigured many of the experiences and strategies of queers when confronted with straight culture. His works play with gender, twist language into arch double entendres, and (in the form of the *3 Standard Stoppages*) question the notion of straightness as the measure of all things. Duchamp's work has acted like a call, a series of ironic questions (What does an artist do? What is a work of art? When is a work complete?) spoken into the canyon of history; successive generations have struggled to formulate their answers. Not all of the work in this exhibition derives from Duchamp, but Duchamp's work is the place where many of the strategies for contradicting the homilies of modernism were formed.

A number of American artists used Duchamp as one of the ways to move beyond the ideological strictures of mid-century abstraction and found what was later called *pop art*. This generation had grown up in a country where to self-identify as gay was to invite, at best, dismissal and, at worst, incarceration and shock therapy. At the end of the 1940s, the nation attempted to make explicit links between patriotism and heterosexuality. The House Un-American Activities Committee investigated two things: communists and homosexuals. In the art world, abstraction had become America's ticket to the big time, its chance to bask in art history's spotlight. As much as critics delved into the tortured psyches of the abstract expressionists, they drew the line at sexual deviance. It was impossible to be both a serious American artist and a gay artist. Thus, much of the work made by gay artists in response to this situation either proceeds by veiled allusion or avoids discussion of sexual matters altogether. Bohemia provided a haven for queers to live lives exempt from constant persecution, but it effectively eliminated the possibilities for any real impact as well. Artists enjoyed success only insofar as they were able to remain closeted.

The first rumblings of what we could call a queer practice began to be heard in places where there was already no chance of real acceptance, where queers had nothing to lose: independent film and theater. Made far afield from the attention and financial clout of the culture industries, and playing to minuscule audiences of like-minded outsiders, the films, plays, and spectacles of Kenneth Anger, Jack Smith, Ronald Tavel, and Charles Ludlam conjured a new world of glamour and terror out of the city's rubbish. As desperate leaps of faith, these down-at-heels extravaganzas pointed the way for a series of new challenges to the cultural mainstream.

One of the first of these was Fluxus, founded in the late 1950s by a loose confederation of artists, composers, and poets in an attempt to dissolve the boundaries of the art world. By exploding form, confusing authorship, and relying on the multiple rather than the unique, Fluxus answered Duchamp's call with a questioning of the very formulation of art movements. While drawing inspiration from many of the twentieth century's avant-gardes, Fluxus always managed to elude easy definition. It was the aggregation of individuals—a "movement" that could barely be charted and that, by some accounts, has not yet ended. If the Cage group attempted to take Duchamp's practice as a lesson on the individual level, Fluxus used it as the blueprint for collective experiment. Ultimately, many of the artists around Cage moved through the mainstream art world without difficulty, their formal innovations finally posing little problem for the art world. By contrast, much of Fluxus remains unassimilated. Fluxus also spawned a host of corollary movements—performance and conceptual art, mail art, and body art—that have continued to thrive on the margins of the commercial art world and have acted as a conduit for Fluxus's spirit over the past thirty years.

It is important to see Fluxus also as another one of the many discourses of freedom that flowered throughout Europe and the United States in the late 1950s and early 1960s. It was very much part of the nascent counterculture, an event like many others that combined a pointed questioning of received knowledge with a giddy celebration of unexpected possibilities. Against a centralized art world bound to the notion of a historical progression of unique masters and their great works, Fluxus deployed a blizzard of incidental objects, bottles, scrawled notes, tiny books, stamps—squeaks and stumbles that refused to play the part of masterpieces. In Fluxus, people were demonstrating their exuberance in overturning boundaries between disciplines (painting, sculpture, music, sports, theater, dance), identities (composer, performer, audience), and values (uniqueness, authenticity, permanence). It acted in some ways as the universal solvent of artistic hierarchy, and its economics of generosity and democracy were and still are a challenge to the closed economy of the mainstream art world.

While Fluxus could posit many types of freedoms, it still retained many of the blind spots of the culture it tried to revolutionize. The most important one of these was that of gender. While many women produced and participated in Fluxus works, their place within the Fluxus culture was often the

My Studio Is a Dungeon Is the Studio

same as that of women throughout the art world—wife, muse, or objecti-fied body. In this, as in many other things, Fluxus was a product of its time. Women were beginning to find that much of the counterculture of the 1960s could not or would not listen to them or provide opportunities for them to exercise agency. The civil rights, Black Power, and student movements of the later 1960s—all attempts to make real the rhetorics of freedom that had energized the early part of the decade—provided much of the blue-print for the women's liberation movement. In the art world, this has come to be known as the *women's art movement*. The movement is often dated from 1972, when a protest of the Corcoran Biennial's exclusion of women led to a national conference of women artists, organizers, and critics. At the conference many artists had their first large-scale exposure to the work of their peers around the country. The groundwork was laid for an explosion of activity by women throughout the United States.

For many of the women involved in transforming the structure of their practice in those years, the experience of making community has been as important as that of making art. Their efforts were designed not only to showcase the works of individual artists but also to call a community into being. This community transformed many of the collective, anticapitalist strains of 1960s culture into much of what we now call the *nonprofit art world*. But these structures differed from later bursts of independent en-trepreneurial activity. This was not a group of young dealers bursting onto the marketplace. The places these artists created were part gallery, part school, part theater, part archive, part counseling center. All of the vari-ous activities that activated these spaces were important, and they reflect in their diversity a series of new possibilities in the way artists could see themselves. These were also products of necessity: Women had only limited access to the places of power in the society. As such, they had to construct their support system from the ground up.

One of the major achievements of the women's art movement, and one of particular importance here, was the invention and promulgation of a gendered reading of form. The argument that certain formal choices within works reflected the gender of the work's maker allowed for the first sub-stantive discussions of the differences in men's and women's approaches to abstraction. It also made possible a gendered critique of the assumptions of a (supposedly) universal and neutral modernist abstraction. Like many aesthetic theories, this critique eventually became a way of setting up and policing borders rather than a way of talking about and understanding the practice of artists. Unfortunately, it also became, in some cases, an instrument with which to exclude artists whose work was somehow not female enough, using an essentializing approach as a way of trying to sort out the "true" practitioners from the false. The women's art movement also sparked an enormous project of historical research. Women artists began to sift through art history to resurrect the vanished voices of their forebears. They began to question the way that value had been bestowed on the artists of the past and labored to construct institutions that would allow them to take control of the way that their own work would be valued. Artists began to take on the roles of curator, critic, and historian. Their efforts have provided the model for every outsider practice since.

If Fluxus valued the ephemeral, the trivial, the modest, and low forms shunned by modernism, the women's art movement was quick to point out that many of these forms were regarded as inconsequential specifically because they were forms traditionally used by women. The early 1970s saw another flowering of formal and conceptual experimentation as women artists reclaimed materials and approaches from crafts, the domestic sphere, and previous avant-gardes in an attempt to produce a visual language more suited to the expression of women's experience. While many of the artists involved identified as lesbians, there was not a consistent examination of the place of lesbian identity in the art of the time. On one hand, there were attempts to posit a continuum between feminism and lesbian consciousness; on the other, there was the homophobic purge of lesbians from the women's movement. Even within the context of an alternative art system, there were many who were uninterested in or hostile to the voices of lesbians.

The innovations of both Fluxus and the women's art movement suffered the same fate once they entered the mainstream art world. In both cases, the formal innovations were separated from the political components, diluted, and adopted. This segmentation and absorption mirrored the society at large's reaction to the challenge posed by the various countercultures. In the 1970s, America transformed a call for radical change into a blueprint for consumer hedonism. Token members of disenfranchised groups were bought off with the promise of inclusion and affluence. In the art world, this meant marginally better careers for some women artists and a diversification of formal strictures, but only under a depoliticized banner of pluralism. Abstraction and distancing techniques were used to eliminate the social dimensions of the work. Thus, many of the artists of the period produced images of themselves in various types of drag but in a fashion that divorced the image from any questioning of the sexual preference of the person depicted. Pattern and decoration were related to formal considerations of grid and pictorial flatness, rather than to effeminacy. The questions raised by Fluxus (Why do we need galleries? What is the value of professionalism?) and the women's movement went ignored or unanswered.

By the mid-1970s, much of the momentum of social liberation movements of the 1960s had been lost or derailed into increasingly limited lifestyle choices. Popular culture embraced escapist nostalgias instead of engaging with social issues. The 1950s became a sign of lost innocence—the last time America felt good about itself. The 1970s also saw the maturation of the Stonewall generation into gay male ghetto clones. Gay liberation was replaced by gay power, often imagined in terms of economic self-determination and institution building. Gay men and lesbians both began to operate businesses, open their own bars, establish neighborhoods. To some extent, this form of community building reflected a continuing commitment to creating a separate space of tolerance and diversity, but often it reflected an aspiration to join in with the class assumptions and blind commercialism of the straight world.

The decade's strongest attack on those assumptions came in the form of punk. Punk can perhaps best be characterized as a pair of mutually reinforcing explosions of musical activity based initially in New York and London in the late 1970s. It drew its name from prisoners' slang term for faggot. Punk is rarely talked about as a queer movement, but much of its history and many of its poses and strategies are tied to queerness. In New York the punk scene traced its roots back through glam rock to the Velvet Underground and Andy Warhol's Factory. In London punk was dreamed up by a group of ex–art students as an attempt to recapture the social upheaval of the 1968 Paris student revolts through the construction of self-contradictory consumer artifacts. Vivienne Westwood and Malcolm McLaren's shop, SEX, became the launching pad for a series of provocations in the form of clothing, posters, and finally the Sex Pistols. From the start, SEX's clientele was a mix of gay fetishists and bored teens. (One of the earliest items in the SEX line was a T-shirt bearing the image of a pair of half naked, Tom-of-Finland-esque cowboys talking about their boredom with the same old scene.)

More important, punk was the beginning of a critique of the stultifying cultural quietism that followed the flirtation with progressive social change in the 1960s. Punk overturned the notion that everything was all right by demonstrating that there were needs that consumerism hadn't filled. It fragmented consumer culture and expanded the pieces into obscene horror shows. While much of punk's imagery was sexual, it deployed that imagery to demonstrate the impossibility of any redemption through sex. In punk the body assumed presence only through a demonstration of its extreme alienation. Punk parodied capitalism's annexation of romance and sexual desire to commodity fetishism by portraying sex itself only through fetishism. It turned the private language of fetish wear into street style. Punk refashioned the street into a place of excitement, danger, and longing. It also created an enormous groundswell of cultural producers— thousands and thousands of people who found in punk the permission to wrench culture into their own meaning. Many punk graphics, band posters, record sleeves, and zines communicate the sense that new codes and new possibilities are shining out from the fragments of shattered signs. Punk was negation turned into a raucous noise of refusal. Like Fluxus, punk is a movement of fragments—a deliberate lack of mastery, of abjection. Like queers, punks are on the bottom of the cultural transaction, but punk rewrote the terms so that the bottom becomes the escape point—an escape into fury and blankness that demolishes the top.

Punk spread its message through flyers, records, and self-published magazines. The networks of zine distribution that grew up as a result of punk have had a crucial impact on the formation of new queer culture. The magazine has always occupied a vital place in the lives of gay men and lesbians. In the 1950s, magazines were the medium of gay and lesbian culture to people outside urban centers—magazines such as *The Ladder*, the *Mattachine Newsletter*, and *Physique Art Pictorial*. Queer zines are inheritors of this tradition, as well as that of artist-published magazines like *File* that were outgrowths of the international mail art movement. They have served as forums for sexual debate, as well as a way of identifying like-minded people outside the gay and lesbian mainstream.

Punk was not the only attempt to produce and distribute alternative music in the 1970s. Part of the explosion of women's culture at the time was the women's music movement. Women's music became one of the most successful lesbian cultural expressions, not only generating a new roster of lesbian stars but also providing through concerts and festivals new possibilities for women to meet each other and forge communities. Both punk and the women's music movement were attempts to confront social problems via cultural strategies. Yet, while their forms might be similar, their underlying ideologies were obviously vastly different. While punk was profoundly antihumanist, women's music was strongly informed by the humanist ideals of social activism (an attitude shared by many women in the visual arts at the time). While strongly critiquing patriarchy, many of the women involved

My Studio Is a Dungeon Is the Studio

had a positive attitude toward libertarian notions of self-determination and social dignity. The artists involved were attempting to redeem culture by positing the positive, unifying potential of a culture made by and for women. The belief in essentialism allowed women to create the most visible lesbian culture in the history of the United States. That culture came under attack, however, by a younger generation of women who were highly skeptical of both essentialism and humanism.

Both lesbian and gay culture of the 1970s should be understood as first-generation: valuing integrity and identity and searching for heritage. Those communities attempted to create cultural structures alongside and as good as straight culture. Much of what was understood as gay and lesbian art of the time was concerned with depicting the realities of lesbian and gay life. This is a community striving to recognize itself, and in striving to do so, it relied on simplistic, if not retrograde, aesthetic strategies. It was, thus, at odds with the prevailing forms of the time but in a way that could not constitute a true critique.

The 1980s began on a promising note in the art world: The scene that had given birth to the punk movement was mutating into a visual art scene of surprising generosity. On the Lower East Side of New York, musicians and artists were trading places as arbiters of hip. In the summer of 1980, the Times Square show opened—a sprawling and varied mix of artists and styles crammed into four stories of an abandoned massage parlor in Midtown. The sheer energy and democracy of the installation signaled new possibilities for the making and viewing of art. Because the names of the artists were listed only on a map available on the first floor, it was possible to see the whole exhibition without ever knowing who had made what. At the same time, the streets of New York were blooming with new sets of signs, left in Magic Marker, wheat-pasted flyers, and spray-painted stencils. Later we found out who had made these marks, but our first encounters with them made us realize that we didn't need to know. These new markings reterritorialized the city for us in ways very similar to when we recognized and were recognized by the first punks. Once again, energy was there; anything was possible. Within one season, however, that energy was transmuted into a new roster of white, male art stars. What had been an urban style compounded of graffiti color, rewritten pop culture, and fucked-up image making was elevated into neo-Expressionism—a parade of high-culture angst with pretensions to internationalism. In response to yet another challenge, the art world consolidated and tried to confuse the excitement of making culture with the excitement of making money. (Later this was turned into the excitement of watching other people spend money, once auction fever set in.) As neo-Expressionism progressed into various postmodernisms, the 1980s began to be characterized as a time when an exquisite refinement of art theories was coupled with an art of massive bad faith. The first (and still most lucrative) wave of postmodernism was an art that used the fragments of postmodernism to both rehearse its death and mourn its loss. The loss was mourned because, for the most part, this art was being made by people who had most benefited from the rhetorics of modernism. But as the decade progressed, gay men were encountering death but not on an ideological level. Many artists found their voices in response to the massive indifference displayed by the straight world to the deaths of their lovers, teachers, coworkers, and neighbors.

The AIDS epidemic became the catalyst for the first viable social protest movements since the feminist heyday of the mid-1970s. For a generation of gay men who had previously indulged themselves in assimilationist fantasies, it provided the undeniable evidence of America's profound homophobia. Many became activists for the first time; many of them became artists. In combating the hatred and disdain of straight society, these new activists drew on the techniques of the movements that had come before them. The response also varied greatly from place to place. In New York artists and activists countered gay invisibility by forging a new street art of arresting immediacy. Once again, the streets teemed with new information, on T-shirts, posters, and stickers. The city was remapped as an infected zone. Artists began producing works for the gallery context that explored the loss they experienced. These elegiac works had profound implications for queer artists. Specifically for gay men, they marked the first time that there was recognized gay content that was not simply representations of gay desire. Ironically, gay artists were exploring issues of mortality at precisely the time that the rest of the art world was abandoning personal content in favor of highly theoretical discussions of simulation and spectacle. The art world was recognizing gay artists' right to speak on a crucial issue. But there was little interest in hearing about anything else. AIDS had provided the wedge, however, and increasing numbers of artists insisted on being heard. Many younger artists explored explicit identifications as queer only after a period of social activism. The experience of opening up a place for queer identity on the street then provided the model for doing so in the context of the gallery. The traditional model of cultural progress posits that ideas surface first in avant-garde elites and are then dispersed into the general culture. In the case of this new queer content, the model was reversed.

The AIDS epidemic occurred at a crucial juncture for gay and lesbian communities. I have referred to this social activism and community building of the 1970s as first-generation activities. By the early 1980s, gay and lesbian communities, however tenuous, were facts of life. There was a new generation entering the picture. These people, in their late teens to early twenties, had been children at the time of Stonewall and had not participated in the construction of any of the community structures that had occupied the previous generation. It was not a given that they would have an investment in the continuation of these structures. In one sense, they grew up in a world that was much easier to come out into, but they also had a tenuous relationship to the values of essentialism and identity politics that had informed their predecessors. The tension between these generations was making itself felt in the early 1980s but was subsumed in the midst of the AIDS struggle. As the 1980s came to a close, the split began to reassert itself. It has assumed many forms, but one of the most persistent has been the conflict over the use of the term *queer*. The controversial attempt to reclaim a previously negative term has become the symbol of the emerging generation gap in the gay world. *Queer* has come to mean an attitude that is aggressive and anti-assimilationist. The term is supposed to be gender neutral, and thus indicative of the idea that queer men and women may have more in common with each other than they do with older homosexuals.

The work that I am characterizing as *queer* is the inheritor of all this history. It derives much of its aesthetic strategy from Fluxus and punk, producing ephemeral, funky objects that seem thrown together. It also embraces the gendered reading of form promulgated by the women's art movement. Many of its forms are skewed, floppy, and tenuously made. At those points where it has recourse to rigorous craft, it often does so as a sort of drag, wearing the mantle of authority as a way of deflating the power of that authority. Often the artists involved in this work are operating in a variety of formats and employing several different distribution strategies. Many of these artists not only show work in galleries but also work as activists or caregivers. They make up the staff and boards of nonprofit arts organizations. They are educators. They publish zines, write stories, perform. These roles are important because they demonstrate queer artists coming to consciousness at many different levels of the art complex.

Much of this work looks back to the 1970s. Many of the male artists are re-creating working methods that originated in the women's art movement. They are employing a premodern rhetoric of sentiment. Many of the women are using 1970s gay male culture as a template for expressions of sexual exploration and community. They are exploring drag, S&M technologies, and flaneurism as a way of moving lesbian identification beyond the feel-good homilies of essentialism. As such, there is an interesting crossover in this work. The issues of representation and abstraction have different meanings for men and women at this point, but the willingness of individual artists to move back and forth between them is the thing that separates out this generation from the previous ones. Also pertinent is that these artists are actually finding this energy secondhand. Much of this work draws on conceptualism and postminimalism. Both of these movements were, in a sense, the official versions of artists' activities that were tied to structures that had far greater implications for the mainstream art world. But we have seen how the gallery/museum system has been unable and unwilling to engage those implications. Instead, it has chopped the Fluxus and women's art movements down to a size that it could digest. It has consistently seen social challenges as simple permutations in either form or content and has recognized those aspects of artists' work. Thus, much innovative work has disappeared from the visual memory of the art world. Young artists are often reinventing the wheel, much to the consternation of those who have been around long enough to remember the first version. But often, by following the energy refracted through these official versions, queer artists have found their way to that energy's true source in the discarded history. Identification as queer has helped many of these artists recognize their connections and debt to their peers in other mediums. Many of these artists are looking at drag but as part of a larger community-wide debate over the meanings and uses of gender. Both women and men have resurrected punk—this time, with the sexual charge intact. Punk is informing both the anger and abjection in much of this work, but it is also providing much of the energy and democracy. Much of this work continues the queer strategy of treating straight culture as a series of ready-mades, available for appropriation, manipulation, and *détournement*. In this way, it looks back to Duchamp.

Works in *In a Different Light*

Void

This group of works is built around images of blankness, absence, and loss. In some cases, this is loss directly related to the AIDS epidemic, but the way in which that loss has been expressed owes much to previous formal experiments. Judy Chicago's drawing from the *Rejection Quintet* documents a moment of personal and professional loss. She uses her trademark central-ized composition and floral, vaginal imagery as a vehicle for expressing grief and distress rather than the wholeness and celebration her work is usually known for. Chicago's work speaks the formal language of its time with its solid frontality, underlying grid structure, and cool execution; but it is also reaching out historically to evoke the work of other artists—notably Georgia O'Keeffe and Frida Kahlo. Grief is thus connected, via a formal device, with the struggles of other women. Chicago's work, in some ways, has come to be emblematic of much of the women's art movement. The associative chain of center-vagina-flower has been echoed in the work of many gay male artists who have replaced the vagina with the anus. In this context, Brett Reich-man's painting *Blind Spot* confronts the viewer with multiple readings—its imagery shifting through the registers of sunburst, flower, mirror, anus. The anus shines seductively like the sun, a floral mirror that reflects, that offers the viewers themselves. But this mirror is blank; the viewer has been erased. Reichman refers to Chicago to make the point: The anus is the va-gina for gay men—their "flower"—but one that harbors the possibility of annihilation rather than birth. This ambivalent reaction to the anus as both source of pleasure (and in Reichman's case, a certain form of gay male iden-tity) and source of disease, death, and loss has colored much of our society's reaction to the AIDS epidemic. It is also echoed in the work of John J. Priola and Peter Nagy. Nagy's work *Internal Erotic* is from 1983, nine years after Chicago's and ten years before Reichman's. While its title seems to refer to the sexuality referred to above, it actually addresses illness as part of a critique of consumer society. Nagy produces an image of viral malignancy by fusing corporate logos into flowers of evil: a swirling, malignant mass of confused information and desires. Nagy's work is profoundly skeptical of the ability of any imagery to operate sincerely.

Ree Morton's *Fading Flowers* shares with Judy Chicago's work the aim of recovering a lost mode of address. Morton uses the nineteenth-century language of sentiment. Her work's tone is deliberately conversational, dis-arming in its modesty, but earnest about evoking sensations of passage and death. Morton consistently worked this edge, making pieces that revealed the serious undercurrents of funky domestic decoration and feminine activ-ity. This recuperation of emotional affect was part of women's attempt to forge an art out of postminimalism that spoke more directly to their lives and their work in terms parallel to gay men's attempts to find a language appropriate to describing mournful emptiness left in the wake of AIDS. Ross Bleckner's work since the mid-1980s has been the most dramatic example of this. Bleckner's inky heavens, flickering birds, and funerary urns have caught the emotional devastation of the epidemic. His urn paintings were some of the first to refer explicitly to the enormous numbers of those lost. Like Bleckner, both Judie Bamber and Michael Jenkins have developed personal iconographies to describe emotional states. Jenkins's white felt dots refer both to snow and to Kaposi's sarcoma lesions. They form a freezing blizzard of infection in contrast to the woolen blankets they rest on. Judie Bamber dispassionately isolates individual objects on grounds of seductive color. Her works might seem at first glance to be firmly in the Chicago tradition, but the fierceness of Bamber's regard for these objects strips them of sentimentality.

The void is not only the result of loss, however. It is also the state preceding existence. In this sense, both Scott Burton's work and David Tudor's *Reconstructed Score from John Cage's 4 Minutes and 33 Seconds* present voids that are liberating: situations where anything can happen. By focusing on the void, we become alert to the possibilities of the moment. Cage's is perhaps the most powerful example of this truth to have come to us in the twentieth century. Burton's stage furniture awaits our inhabitation rather than our attention. But the void can also rebuff us. Zoe Leonard's aerial photograph of Washington, DC, is like Reichman's mirror: It refuses to reflect back ourselves, to make a place for us. Leonard's photographs often play on the profoundly threatening inertness of the captured image. This is a Capitol that we can see but that we cannot find a place within. Its surface complication hides a profound blankness.

Self

The first of these works explores the self as a physical entity before the formation of identity. If, in a primal void, we begin to sense ourselves, how do we picture those selves? Often these artists are operating through synecdoche, using one portion of the anatomy to stand for the entire body. Harmony Hammond's *Flesh Journals* and Eva Hesse's *Test Piece* both treat latex as a stand-in for human skin. Hesse is searching within form for gender, but her alert manipulations also evoke the body in its various activities. Hammond is more directly concerned with skin as a surface, a page that can be inscribed by experience. This inscription takes place literally in the artist's skin, as seen in Catherine Opie's *Self-Portrait*. Opie's wounding is also seen as part of a tribal identification since the lines on her back describe a fantasy scene of lesbian suburban bliss. The wounded self can also construct armor, whether of attitude or surface, as in the works of Nancy

Grossman and Scott Hewicker. Hewicker's mute polyester bundle is the flip side of Grossman's elegantly defended *Head*. Both works evoke the shadow of abuse with differing strategies for coping with it. This wounding can be deliberate, self-imposed, and symbolic, as in Frida Kahlo's *Self-Portrait with Cropped Hair*. Kahlo, with her insistent interminglings of the mundane and the fantastic, as well as her transformation of personal tragedy and limitation into a position of aesthetic power, has proved to be one of the most influential artists of the past thirty years, providing the inspiration and emotional tone for much feminist, diary, and body art. In this painting Kahlo's defiant inhabiting of Diego Rivera's suit and her strewn hair point to the notion of gender as a self-proclaimed reality. Many artists in this show use hair and its lack or abundance as the signifier of gender, and the ease with which it can be adopted or discarded becomes an indicator of a queer destabilization of gender constructs.

The questioning of gender is one of the things about queerness that provokes anxiety on the part of the straight world. Another is the notion of the queer as somehow self-pleasuring and self-sufficient. Both Laura Aguilar's *In Sandy's Room* and Robert Mapplethorpe's *Self-Portrait with Whip* are images of queers that are powerfully self-contained. By being self-sufficient, by not needing "the opposite," the people in these photographs exhibit a sexuality that escapes the functionalized libidinal economy. It is only at the moment of leisure that the possibility of resistance can come into being. Thus, modern society strives to regulate leisure, making it yet another type of work. Sex has not escaped from this regulation. Straight sex is functional sex. (Needless to say, all heterosexual sex is not necessarily straight sex.) This is one of the places where gay men and lesbians share a common place of resistance. They both demonstrate the fact that sex is not simply a type of work, geared to the perpetuation of the species and the social norm. This nonproductive queer sex that can exist in leisure, without being put to work, that is satisfied with itself, points up the constructed, regulated nature of "straight" sex. This is what Aguilar's and Mapplethorpe's works share. Neither of them needs the viewer. They do not make a place for us in the way that we expect sexual images to.

Drag

There are two types of drag in this section. The first is drag as travesty, where the artist is using a sort of exaggerated gender costuming in order to play with the possibilities of switching identity. In many cases, the fluidity of gender identification is staged for the camera. Photography is still so insistently associated with the real that one of our first impulses seems to be to trick it. But while many artists in the late 1960s and early 1970s did pieces incorporating the methodologies of drag, they were using those methodologies to question identity, not sexual preference. Often this cross-dressing is presented in such a way that it demonstrates the impossibility of really changing genders. Vito Acconci's *Conversations Part III* (1971) is a case in point. Like many of his other works from this time, the piece hinges on our ability to see Acconci's actions as sincere attempts but also as failures. Whether he is attempting to sing a blues song "just like the record," make himself into a woman, or construct a masturbatory fantasy about the viewer, Acconci is presenting gaps that can never be bridged, no matter how much they can be narrowed. For a generation of artists just beginning to come to grips with an all-pervasive popular culture that leveled differences, it is possible that the drag queen's willful embrace of constructed identity seemed a tantalizing strategy for survival. Again, queer methodologies were anticipating the postmodern condition.

Younger artists have shifted from using drag as a subject matter (depictions of people in drag) to drag as a method. In this sense, they are turning the making of certain objects into a type of drag. While the earlier approach to drag deals with it as a type of parody of gender norms and emphasizes drag's artificiality, this new approach often involves artists taking on each other's personas and voices and is, thus, based on the notion of drag "realness": the ability to pass. Much of the feminist approach to appropriation is this type of drag. Sherrie Levine's representations of the works of photographers like Alexander Rodchenko, and in this show Walker Evans, serve to foreground the assumptions of male privilege inherent in the photographer's ability to take, produce, and circulate images. Levine's disruption of authorship operates almost subliminally to induce the disquiet that makes us look again. Deb Kass's reinvention of the works of Andy Warhol brings that disquiet to another level. Kass no longer remakes famous Warhol works but rather has inhabited Warhol's method, like Drag King Elvis Herselvis. Kass takes Warhol's starstruck outsider manner and uses it to point up new areas of marginality. Warhol's gay Catholic veneration for Jackie Onassis gets replayed as Jewish veneration of and lesbian desire for Barbra Streisand. Kass brings the edginess of Warhol back into focus by showing that while history may have made a place for him, it still has not made a place for all outsiders. Amy Adler makes this point again, by referencing not only Edward Weston's but Sherrie Levine's appropriation of him.

Robert Gober's *Plywood* (1987) is drag in a different key. Gober uses painstaking individual craft to make an object that seems simply mass produced. The plywood is a high-class (unique, handmade) object masquerading as a lower-class one. It also plays on the history of minimal sculpture, evoking the "humble" materials used by many artists in their efforts to avoid artifice. Gober provides what is in essence a second layer of artifice, making a sculpture that looks like the raw material for the sculpture.

Other

This section deals with artists stepping outside of themselves to engage with another. Often this is the beloved, the object of desire, or the object of worship. Some of these works try to cast light on the dilemmas of "otherness" itself. In a trio of works, this otherness is examined as a series of permutations of the image of the bride. In Duchamp's *The Bride Stripped Bare by Her Bachelors, Even* (represented in this show by a catalog illustration), the bride occupies the upper realms—a machine whose presence excites the sexual advances of the bachelors below, but who ultimately remains aloof, impenetrable, and self-enclosed. The bride is an apt example of Sigmund Freud's fetishized female. A flattened object of desire for the bachelors clustered below her, the bride is oblivious to their fetishizing essence. This impenetrable object is the phallic woman, a figure both authoritarian and immaculate, a male fantasy of the uncastrated mother. In 1972 Kathy Huberland offered the female riposte to this fetish as part of the landmark installation *Womanhouse* in Los Angeles. Perched at the top of *Womanhouse*'s staircase, the bride was a store mannequin wearing a standard-issue white lace gown. As the gown's long train descended the staircase, it became dirtier and dirtier until it arrived soiled and dingy at the house's kitchen. Here again, is the phallic woman: an impenetrable dummy clad in blank white and standing on high. Her self-containment is now seen as an impossibility: a straitjacket offered to women. The female experience of this fetish is about the discrepancy between "me" and "the bride." This disjunction becomes clear in the frozen immobility of the mannequin. One can only be a bride at the time of a wedding: For a brief moment, I am the bride, and then I lapse into being myself again. As time goes on, I descend from the pedestal and become "worn" and "soiled." The *Womanhouse* piece points up the cruel toll Duchamp's libidinal economy exerts on real women, perennially punished for not being abstractions. The third variant in this tale is from 1992. It is a stack of newspapers, bound, perhaps, for recycling. The top section is folded, opened to an ad out of which a bride wistfully gazes;

above her head is the slogan "Having It All." The bride's image is at the top of the heap as well as above the fold—crucial placement in newspaper cosmology. On closer examination, we can see something odd about the model, and indeed, she is, in actuality, the artist Robert Gober, whose drag displacement reawakens the gender anxiety in Duchamp's original. Our attention is directed below the fold, to the mystery of what lies beneath the bride's white skirts. This bride is also self-sufficient since she "has it all." The image of the bride has then shifted through three registers: fetishized and desired other, alienating fetish figure, and fetished self.

The desire, anticipation, and sometimes fear we encounter when we imagine the other is powerfully evoked in the works in this section by Romaine Brooks, Zoe Leonard, Millie Wilson, and Joel Otterson. Brooks's *Peter, a Young English Girl* is an image of unalloyed glamour, a painting whose silvery palette and sinuous lines produce a portrait of a young woman who combines coolness and swagger. Looking at her now, we could easily see her as a rock 'n' roll or film star: Brooks seems clearly smitten. Joel Otterson and Millie Wilson both use inanimate objects to make their figures of desire. Both of their pieces are columnar, but Wilson's oversized wig becomes a zoftig, working-class caryatid, while Otterson's assemblage is an example of overdetermined phallicism that revels in its own excess. Both of them are images of the other tinged with danger and humor.

Connie Samaras's photo portrait of an alien "visitor" makes explicit the ways that queer desire for the other can assume proportions that extend beyond gender itself. In many ways, the lesbian and gay fascination with science fiction and alien life is part of the desire for a third term, neither male nor female. This utopian wish for something else also sees in the representations of alienness the possibilities for queer identification. For much of his career, David Bowie presented himself as this dually sexed alien—an identification that allowed him to play queer whether or not he was playing gay. The world of science fiction continues to prove hospitable to images of "other" couplings, thus allowing a space for queer interpretations.

Couple/Family

These works are about the experience of trying to evoke queer social structures, often in the face of societal indifference or hostility. These structures range anywhere from couples to depictions of the gay and lesbian community as a whole. In some cases, these works are signals sent out to call a community into being—potential tribal markers, flags to rally around. Others are documents of an existing group or of a time when a group finally did come into being. As queers are forced to construct their own families, the forms that these families can take are endlessly varied. Both Carrie Moyer and Charles LeDray examine the tensions, erotic and/or violent, that can occur within the biological family. In other cases, the gay community is linked to a "family of man," as in the case of the Gay Liberation Front poster designed by Peter Hujar. Others reach back to claim figures from the past as members of the family.

Diane Arbus, Nan Goldin, and Kate Millett present three distinct images of lesbian couples. While Arbus's photograph is set at home and is sympathetic in tone, it remains the view of an outsider. Nan Goldin's *Siobhan and I: sex (black bra), NYC*, an image of great tenderness, is an insider's view, a personal revelation of intimacy. Millett's work is almost diaristic, a record of the vicissitudes that plague all relationships set forth plainly in brush and ink.

Over the past thirty years, there have also been a number of figurations of the male couple, not all of them by gay artists. Some of these couples have operated as collaborative teams, who then depict their relationship as benign and cooperative, as in the work of Gilbert & George, or violent and contestatory, as in the work of the Kipper Kids. Pruitt-Early present themselves as collectible souvenir dolls, equal in their banality and cuddliness.

Geoffrey Hendricks represents both the dissolution of one couple and the union of another. His *Flux Divorce Box* documents the process by which he and his wife ended their marriage by bisecting all of their possessions. Hendricks's divided wedding album stands in poignant contrast to his bound-together chair, made as part of Jill Johnston's Fluxus marriage to her lover. Both objects are examples of the ways that Fluxus artists could take very literal ideas and use them to invent new ceremonies of surprising resonance.

Suzanne Lacy's *One Woman Shows* was a similar type of experiment in creating family by creating new structures for making family possible. Lacy's work has always been explicitly concerned with finding new ways for women to come together, often in situations that emphasize the connection between emotional and physical territory. This piece's branching form, made up of participants picking others to participate, mimics the family tree's structure, as well as dispersing the power among all of the performers. This is a community that forms itself, with the artist as a guide rather than as an autocrat.

A similar interplay between individual and group is evident in Harmony Hammond's *Presences* and Kate Delos's quartet of symbolic paintings.

Both posit families of tranquility, a tranquility that slips into self-parody in General Idea's *Baby Makes 3*, an image of the bliss of a new nuclear family with their heads in the clouds. The image ended up on the cover of *File*, General Idea's inversion of *Life* magazine, and there is something of *Life*'s flattened worldview in this retouched image of the three artists with their demonic putti faces.

Thomas Lanigan-Schmidt's cellophane and tinfoil drag queens are similarly poised between angel and demon. Lanigan-Schmidt was one of the first artists to resurrect extravagant decoration and ephemeral materials in the late 1960s. The avatar of this style was Jack Smith, whose performances, tableaux, and films transformed the work of innumerable artists in the New York scene. Smith's devotion to the secret alchemy of debris, his resolutely outsider position, and his baroque imagination left their mark on artists ranging from Andy Warhol to Karen Kilimnik. Smith's *Beautiful Book* is a collection of photographs that, like his film *Flaming Creatures*, documents and constructs a variety of queer scenarios. Smith's work is always oddly timeless: his poses orgiastic and yet somehow strangely frozen.

While many of the posters and magazines presented in this exhibition stress the upbeat image of community, McDermott & McGough's painting *A Friend of Dorothy, 1943* shows a gay community constituted in a history of invective. Vincent Fecteau turns a jaundiced eye on the queer "family."

Orgy

As people come together, there are different possibilities for pleasure. These works explore the pleasures of connection, of excess, of overflowing boundaries. Often this is expressed in formal terms in works that are knotted together, works that flow into each other. In many cases, these are artists who celebrate the democratic experience of urban life. Several of them seem to want to remake the entire world in their image.

Nicole Eisenman's installations are composed of hundreds of drawings that endlessly shuffle styles and voices. Eisenman's work can run from starstruck mooning to raunch to mythologizing to pungent self-mockery, sometimes in the same drawing. She borrows visual stylings from 1920s neoclassicism, underground comics, and clip art. Her work documents a new kind of queer subjectivity: angry, horny, raucous, and smart. Donna Han shares Eisenman's capacity for output, but her work charts a different geography. While the majority of Eisenman's work is based in the image,

Han achieves her effects through patterning and exuberant color. Her sensibility touches on both Sanrio and psychedelia. Otherworldly characters float through her pieced-together fabric works.

Jerome Caja's paintings, with their snickering, crystalline figures and scenarios of copulation and doom, evoke the worldviews of both Jack Smith and Thomas Lanigan-Schmidt. It is also possible to catch glimpses of Kahlo in Caja's autobiographical wrestlings with selfhood, existential pain, and oppressive Catholicism. Like Han and Eisenman, however, Caja deals with serious issues by flipping them into parody.

Cary Leibowitz describes the queer experience in the world with an unending supply of self-mockery and black humor. Leibowitz's objects can't even believe in themselves, much less anything else. He depicts himself in his works as a perennial loser unworthy of love or even regard. His works are rescued from obnoxious self-pity by the misplaced enthusiasm with which his downer sentiments are expressed (GO SADNESS! on a sports pennant).

In *Orgy*, we've tried to stress works that have broken away from previous formal assumptions. Claes Oldenburg's *Soft Drum Set* exhibits a yielding sexuality that retains its charge even in its detumescence. Its forms are interlaced, collapsing on each other. Its hardness made soft is contrasted with Steve Wolfe's *The Andy Warhol Diaries*, where the softness of the paperback book is made hard by turning it into silkscreen on wood. Wolfe is quoting Warhol when he turns *The Diaries* into a variant of the Brillo boxes, but he is adding something as well. We are reminded of Warhol's uncanny ability to turn almost any form to his use. Wolfe's amendment encourages us to see *The Diaries* as one of Warhol's best pieces, albeit a posthumous one. While in form it is not orgiastic, the book's endless detailing of social commerce, petty squabbling, drug excess, and relentless voyeurism could hardly be more so. Both the sealed diaries and the flaccid drum set refer to raucous sounds that are now silenced. Oldenburg's soft sculptures were part of the earliest explorations of new materials for sculpture. As the 1960s progressed, that exploration was joined by a great many artists, and the formal innovations of those artists have proved to be one of the greatest influences on the younger generation. Jim Hodges and Richard Hawkins are both artists strongly influenced by the earlier work of Eva Hesse, Barry Le Va, and Alan Saret, and Hawkins uses flimsy and pathetic materials to present a formalism of the fop. He combines starstruck fascination with a dandy's fastidiousness, alternatively venerating and attacking the porn stars and rockers that populate his assemblages, ultimately lifting them to the status of beautiful trash.

David Hockney's *The Hitchhiker* and Tee A. Corinne's *Photographs #27* and *#42* (from *Yantras for Womanlove*), all from 1982, use combined and overlapping imagery to represent the nature of consciousness. In Hockney, this consciousness is shifting, fractured from moment to moment, while Corinne employs similar techniques to imply integration and wholeness. Her orgy is peaceful and fulfilling, a utopia of pleasure forged out of community.

World

If the previous sections have dealt with the ways in which queer artists have striven to understand first themselves and then their tribe, this section deals with their attempts to envision the interaction, abrasive and otherwise, of that tribe with the society at large. It also looks to the work of artists who attempt to engage the public and forces beyond the art world.

In New York, in the late 1970s and early 1980s, a number of artists began to use the city's surfaces as a platform. Jenny Holzer's *Truisms* articulated an unrelenting urban paranoia all the more chilling for its anonymity. It was impossible to tell if they were warnings, jokes, or some bizarre ad campaign. The *Truisms* are an outgrowth of almost two decades of "idea art" experimentation, but they also owe a great debt to the blank anger and low-budget means of punk graphics. At the same time, Keith Haring began amending street and subway ads by adding in drawings of dogs, UFOs, and his soon-to-be-trademark babies. Haring's drawings migrated to blacked-out posters in the subways, where they began to tell increasingly bizarre stories of alien abduction, social strife, and communication with dolphins. Haring's work has always been valued more on the streets than in the gallery—much of it genuinely democratic in spirit, a trait that Haring shared with Warhol. Despite all of the hoopla about art in the 1980s, Haring and Barbara Kruger are the only artists from that decade whose work has had any impact on the visual sensibility of the society as a whole. As early as 1982, Haring's characters and lines were already being pirated for use on low-budget T-shirts and skirts on Fourteenth Street. Haring's enormous acceptance on the street has stopped almost any serious discussion of his work in the art world; but in a certain sense, it is possible to see Haring's retail outlet, the Pop Shop, as the inheritor of several generation's desires for an art that was direct and anti-elitist. Haring's buttons, radios, and inflatable babies have more to do with Fluxus boxes and stamps than with classy prints or even objects in Oldenburg's *Store*.

A sense of unease and confrontation fills Marlene McCarty's match-book piece, *Crossfire*. The double-edged slogan "Lick Me I'm Sick" invites the viewer to literally play with fire, while the matches' arrangement on the floor suggests a freshly turned grave. AIDS, sex, and danger come together on this bed of fire. McCarty was a member of Gran Fury, one of the first art-ist collectives to take on the AIDS crisis, and her work retains much of the rage and direction of that experience.

AIDS activism brought a vast number of artists onto the streets. Gran Fury, Boy with Arms Akimbo/Girls with Arms Akimbo, and Dyke Action Machine! use the street as the place to promote queer visibility, confront health issues, and counter straight media's phobic depictions of lesbians and gay men. These projects have also become places for queer artists to meet one another and examine issues that have had a profound impact on their work in galleries as well. In many of these gallery works, the confrontation between the queer and straight worlds can take a more intimate, ambiva-lent tone.

Utopia

Beyond the vicissitudes of this world lie the infinite possibilities of another. These works embody artists' visions of the final outcome, visions of loca-tions and futures hopeful and not. Roni Horn's photographic explorations of Iceland's natural hot springs and works from Catherine Opie's freeway series are attempts to reinvent the frontier from a lesbian perspective. If Zoe Leonard's image of Washington, DC, shows us a space that refuses to make room for us, Horn and Opie both attempt to find the space that will. Opie's photographs record a wistful flaneurism on and around Southern California freeways. The overpasses and concrete vistas assume an odd majesty, sum-moning us to the road. These images speak with ease and reflection. Horn, on the other hand, is more guarded in her approach. Her suites of photo-graphs show Iceland both as a place of great natural beauty and power and as a place where that power has been trivialized by human incursion. Horn's work, both photographic and sculptural, has consistently grappled with the question, "What does it mean to occupy space?" Her installations have answered that question with discretion, elegance, and intelligence, employing objects that strive, through their design and finish, to achieve a prelapsarian state of perfection. These photographs ask whether Iceland might be the place that contains such perfection.

If perfection is not a possibility, perhaps transformation is Siobhan Lid-dell's and Tony Feher's attempt to turn the barest of possibilities into the greatest of triumphs. Liddell's materials are so slight that they barely exist, yet her sculptures share with Roni Horn's an enormous capacity for both beauty and rectitude. If this is a lesbian art, it is one that draws its inspiration from Gertrude Stein, finding poetic power in the simplest of means, severe and generous at once. Tony Feher has more in common with the lushly transformative gifts of Joseph Cornell. Feher's sculptures are always a little askew, but their humility is laced with a joyous vision. That joy also fills *Banana Pudding*, a joy that may seem a little silly to us at first but one that we desperately need in our lives. Sally Elesby shares with Feher some formal concerns, but her works are built around an unalloyed visual and tactile pleasure. Elesby's beads, pipe cleaners, and ribbons enact an elaborate dance of beauty and bliss.

If this show is going to be not an ending but a beginning, what can we look forward to? A look at the fate of previous moments of outsider energy should prepare us for the inevitable time when this energy is converted into style and pushed through the art world's intestinal tract. We are already seeing versions of this, in the way that the art world views anal sexuality or drag or working with fabric or medical surveillance or decoration as fascinating and important only as long as it is explored by a straight man. This should not surprise us. As it is presently constituted, the mainstream art world is a system for the production, exhibition, valorization, and distribution of the work of heterosexual white men. As long as queer people look to it for their sole source of recognition, they will be disappointed. A few will be picked, as long as they can keep their noses clean, and the rest will be condemned to their "one-dimensional" life on the sidelines. It is up to queer artists not to wait around for approval but to become agents in the development and support of the work that they value. *In a Different Light* records the views of eight curators of queer exhibitions in the United States over the past fifteen years. Not one of those shows was initiated by a straight artist or curator, however much support straight people may have given them. Straight people should have a stake in dismantling the labels and distinctions that keep us from seeing ourselves and each other as we really are: No sex is as "straight" as bigots wish it might be, and there is no art that is untouched by the experience, innovation, and vision of lesbians and gay men. A queer sensibility has roots far back in modernism, and queer methodologies continue to proliferate. Simply because this show is appearing in a museum, the art world should not think that it has done "queer," and queers should not think they are done with the art world. Rather than submitting ourselves to another cycle of marginalization and cultural amnesia, we should

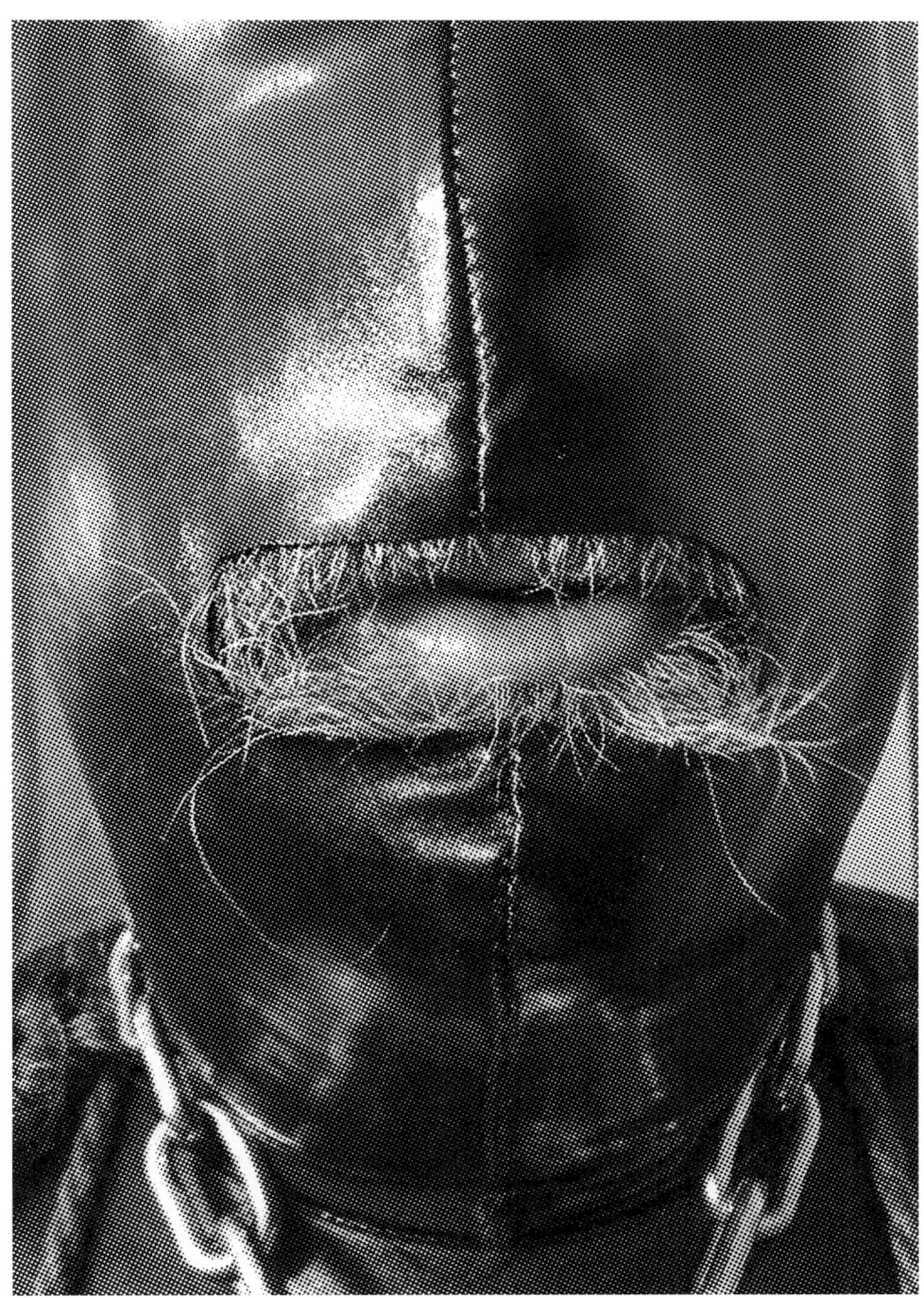

continue to learn from the past and keep queering the discourse. I hope that this exhibition can be a catalyst, a launching pad for a new discourse—a new flowering for artists to respond to.

If you love this exhibition or if you hate it, go out and organize another one. We've all got a lot more to say.

THE STORY OF H
(EXCERPT)

Bunny Butt, *1994*

A quick parody of the novel Story of O, *by Pauline Reage.* Bunny Butt *was a little zine I made critiquing consumerist gay identity in the wake of AIDS. —NB*

The suit itched. H had thought it was a joke when his lover Elwood rolled out of bed after a long evening of mutual frottage, rummaged in the closet, and pulled out a bulky box splashed with lurid color. "Open it," Elwood had said, and H heard the steely tone that meant no argument would be tolerated. Inside the box was a mass of white artificial fur, pale pink satin, and wire that finally resolved itself into a bulky one-piece suit, a hood with tapering pink ears, and mittens. H fumbled self-consciously with the zipper, and Elwood hissed, "Get it on," his gray eyes blank with impatience.

Once inside the outfit, H had looked into the mirror. Staring back at him was a ludicrous figure, a six-foot-tall rabbit with silly booties and a pair of ears that bobbed with the slightest movement of his head. The suit hung from his shoulders, flaring at the waist and giving the impression of a wide and low-hanging ass that the cottony tail did nothing to dispel. The outfit radiated a cheeriness that contrasted sharply with H's mood.

Elwood had pulled an elegant robe on over his customary harness and was now puffing on a short, pungent cigar. His contempt for H was evident in every gesture, and H found himself standing in awkward silence, his normal lassitude deepening into a frozen panic.

"You're an idiot, H. You think that by putting up with my simple demands you know something about me or about your body's life. You smugly offer a tiny piece of yourself and think that it is enough to buy off fate. It isn't enough, and I'm sick of having my intelligence insulted by your pretensions. You know nothing about what I want; indeed, you know nothing about just about everything. I'm letting you know that from this point forward, I'm not standing for it. From now on I will decide what you do, when you do it, and what it means. You will make yourself available in any manner and at any time. And to anyone—since I sincerely believe that it would take much more than you have to offer for me to make use of your banal body again. I intend to devote myself to demonstrating to you what your truer nature is, has been, and always will be. To foreground your essence as it were. I now think of you as a pile of scrap, a wreck from which some minimally useful bits may be salvaged. If, at the end of this training, I can look at you and see an assortment of available holes with something less than a catastrophe connecting them, then I will consider myself a miracle worker."

"And now for the rules that will govern your existence from this day forward. First, you will never be taking off the suit. In fact. . . ." At this point Elwood rang, and Mme. Sophia, the elderly transvestite who acted as their concierge, entered with her sewing box. "Sophia's needle will serve to put the seal of finality on your new station. Next will be constant silence on your part, since I don't want anything coming out of your cake hole that I didn't first stuff in there myself. This collar and leash will remind you of your status as a stupid and tedious pet. Finally, I don't want to hear even the vaguest rumor that you have stirred from this pile of wood shavings without my saying so. You will receive notes from me from time to time concerning your duties, should you somehow evolve the capacity to be capable of them. Other than that, anything I have to say to you will be said with the whip, the irons, and spittle. That's all."

Elwood blew onto the cigar's end to make its tip glow. Then, with a sigh, he mashed the burning end into H's nose, turned on his heel, and strode from the room.

H stood in silence as Sophia's pudgy fingers forced the needle back and forth through the stiff polyester fur of the suit. Warring emotions battered his heart. H's great love for Elwood caused nearly invisible shudders to run the length of his body. In contrast, the end of his nose was a minor fugue of pain, bringing tears to the eyes too often described as doe-like. He didn't dare raise his mittens to brush them away. Other than that, he felt only the

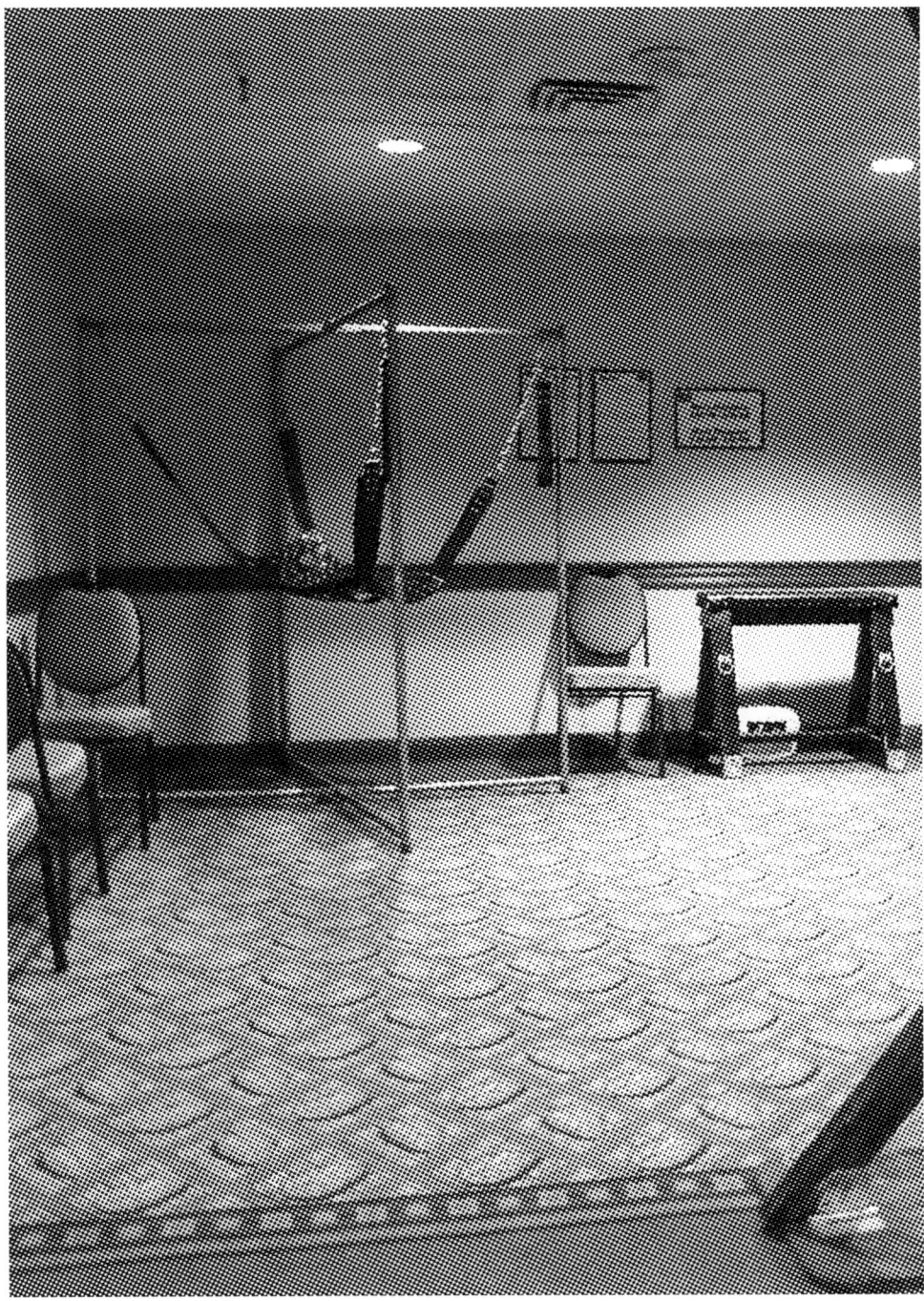

gaping emptiness that welcomed him whenever he looked for his own personality. Perhaps Elwood was right, he did seem . . .

"Another pointless reverie?" Sophia sniggered. "I expect you won't have much more time for them once *he* gets going, and I say good riddance." As she straightened up, H noted with hurt that she had abandoned the "monsieur" that had previously filled her address to him. It was true, then; he was going to be made low. How low he could only guess. Wasn't life strange, one minute you . . .

"Cut that out, you cipher," Elwood's voice cracked across the room. "Madame, that is sufficient. Call us a cab, we're going out."

To be continued . . .

HARE FOLLIES

Previously Unpublished, 1997

I returned to New York from the Bay Area in 1996, and a year later, the Brooklyn Academy of Music (BAM) commissioned Hare Follies, *an hour-long performance. I collaborated with the musician Chris Cochrane and the choreographers and dancers Ishmael Houston-Jones and Patricia Hoffbauer. I wrote the script, made the sets, and directed. The piece is an attempt to delineate the discourses that produce internalized racism. It's a fragmentary and elliptical script, but the story is essentially about two trickster rabbit figures played by people of color in whiteface abusing and tricking me and calling me on my shit. It's very inward as a thing. I basically got the resources to stage my own psychodrama at BAM. After that experience, I got more involved in the kink scene in New York, and my performances shifted away from heavily scripted texts and more toward embodied actions. When performed at BAM lines in this script marked "N" were performed by Nayland Blake, "I" were Ismael Houston-Jones, "P" were Patricia Hoffbauer, and "C" were Chris Cochrane—NB*

Opening

c. (*Sung.*)
Bathe me in between
Select or refuse it
Confess or remain
My ears render my body

Muddy through my vice,
My ears listen when you call it
Call my name
I follow once you ask me
Flea-bitten often sleeping
Make a wish on a rewind
Can't stop this magic

Lost my name
And left it behind
The loose remains

The noose remains

1. Trees

I. Professor!

P. Talk.

N. I.

P. Talk.

N. My.

P. Lord.

I. Tarzan.

P. Is the king.

I. Of the jungle Tarzan—Speak.

P. Speak.

N. My Lord/given th-this place—gives—Lord first I was given a—Lord—

P. The Lord watches.

N. Over me.

P. I will tell you what the procedure will be, while your family and others are being seated.

I. Jungle.

P. Bunny.

I. Isakingadajungle.

P. A jungle is undifferentiated space, unmapped, indifferent space.

I. A so-called dark.

P. A shadow continent.

I. A rabbit threads through tangled space.

P. A line from tree to tree. . . . Look—a rabbit is born and bred in a briar patch; your back-door man.

I. Look, look at this diagram.

N. My Lord.

I. It speaks!

P. Mud below.

I. Mud, crap, tar, you should know it by now—speak, speak slavish words of love to me.

P. Look—Lord.

I. The thought comes to me that all mud peoples are incapable of speech and that they are an offense to the eyes.

P. But fairness means doing our best to understand, no matter what we do or do not believe.

I. The land is the horizon is the arm of the cross is the limb of the tree.

P. The rabbit hole is the light/line through the cross—the upright, the path of resurrection.

I. What hangs from a tree?

P. The fruit of knowledge.

I. What clings to a gate?

N. But that is old! I don't have to listen to this! I've got a date with a man upstairs, I've got a white eye, it sees all lines, got a blank tongue, licks every pot and kettle clean. You won't find no ravelin' strings on me, my toes don't dig the dust, and my ears, my. . . .

I. Gentlemen, be seated! Drag a shadow . . . let order come into hearing.

(*Transition.*)

P. Judge, certain subjects are simply irrelevant to the issue of hares meant, namely, the private conduct out of the workplace relationships, and intimate lives and practices of Judge Tar, Professor Dark, and any other witness that comes before us. Later we will introduce the flickers of celluloid that will unmask this blank, subterranean clan.

N. Well, I remember two occasions.

P. C'mon, man, I'm dangling.

N. These incidents occurred at lunch in the cafeteria.

P. Do you remember which of those two incidents were at lunch, professor?

N. The—Good morning.

P. Thus, perhaps fourteen men sitting here today cannot understand these things fully. I called on the strength that helped me get here from Pin Point, and it was all sapped out of me.

N. I have never, in all my life, felt such hurt, such pain, such agony.

I. Can't be helped.

P. People are bloody, ignorant apes.

I. You spoke about acts that you had seen in pornographic films involving such matters as men having sex with animals, and films showing group sex or rape scenes. You've gotten me through the days since September 25th and you are my judge?

P. We could kill ourselves.

I. This is a person I have helped at every turn in the road, since we met—as did virtually all of the members.

I. I have complied with the rules.

I and P. I have never, in all my life, felt such hurt, such pain, such agony.

P. My family and I have been done a grave and irreparable injustice. During the past two weeks, I lost the belief that if I did my best all would work out.

N. Calls all over the country specifically requesting dirt.

P. There is nothing this committee, this body, or this country can do to give me my good name back, nothing.

I. His conversations were very vivid. I notice there are a number of people sitting behind you. Are any of them your family members you would like to introduce? I might ask, Is everyone who is sitting behind you necessary to sit behind you and maybe they could stand and let your family sit behind you? Look, look at this hole, maybe rabbits live here like in a warren.

N. Well, actually my family members have not arrived yet. Yes, they have. They are outside the door; they were not here for my statement. It is a very large family. They live. . . .

P. Coal digger! Dun bunny!

N. They've been deballed—in those days there was no shame about public delousing—STOP-housing. Please I want to look, look, I think at them.

P. At the experiment?

N. Yes. They were very ugly. They were very dirty. They were disgusting. Senator, excuse me for interrupting, but some of my members on this end cannot hear.

P. I would assume the reason why—to make it clear—the reason why your family is not here at the moment is that you did not anticipate coming.

N. Excuse me?

I. Gentlemen, be speakered up!

P. Can you pull that closer? I raised or reared its ugly head.

I. I know that makes it cumbersome. I have tried that carefully to avoid that.

P. Well, it worked.

N. I was very passive in the conversation.

P. Yesterday, I called my mother. She was confined to her bed, unable to work and unable to stop crying.

N. Excuse me?

P. Bleached out—gray like an old beach house just . . . filthy.

I. I was very passive in the conversation. They are just wrong? The latter part is certainly wrong.

P. With the physical characteristic of—

I. The large breasts/ears.

N. I have been misunderstood. It wasn't the physical characteristic of having large breasts. I really cannot say that.

P. Where is your family? We will make room for your family to be able to sit. Perhaps you can all swing from that same tree.

I. Dunk the clown.

P. Shoot the moon.

I. Bean the nigger.

P. Plug the hole and confess.

I. In the hedges, shoot the rabbit.

P. Cross the line.

I. Pull the rope.

P. Chop the tree.

I. Learn the choke hold.

P. Break on through to the other side.

I. Help me, Rhonda.

I and P. Help me, how can I rise if you don't fall?

(*Transition.*)

I. You don't know your ass from a hole in the ground. (*Show target.*)

N. My ass . . . muddy, wants that hole.

I. Ass . . . you mean mule . . . his words, not yours, don't fake your outrage please . . . if you can't see the back of the room, that's fine . . . concentrate on the circle I'm showing you.

P. Give your hole to the Lord.

N. White . . . all around and cold like flour in the grave.

P. Snow queen—snowshoe hare—Snow White—I'd like to get you—on a showboat to Africa—your black star . . . well, we can all integrate our record collection.

I. Look at this record; it's black.

P. Look at this record; it's a mirror.

C. (*Sung.*)
In a long, long log cabin
and along white Cadillac
I found a little roll
I put the log in the roll, the jelly jelly roll,
move me through the roll the jelly jelly roll
from frank to hole the jelly jelly roll
Hoppin' down the jelly trail
the other one was under the trail. . . . I was perhaps mistaken in my
　　speech

P. And don't you have a skill to show me? Something to do with filing? Your tree looks spotty from this rabbit's hole. Kinda dark around the roots . . . And the tar baby, she don't say nothin'. *E agora senhoras e senhores urn vores o maior show do mundi— "Vamos escovega urn mulatinho!"*

I. Let me proceed by illustration. Look that! D'ye see that tree? It's called a live oak, and it's a native here: Beside it grows a creeper: Year after year that creeper twines its long arms round and round that tree suckin' the earth dry about all its roots, living on its life, overrunning its branches, until, at last, the live oak withers and dies out . . . do you know what niggers around here call that sight? They call it the Yankee hugging the Creole.

P. Should take care of that shit.

I. You're the shit—she's the shit.

P. You're the big shit. Give us our daily something. Kneel down to the Lord—

I. Clarify.

P. Sanctify.

I. Expiate.

P. Sermonize.

I. Commune.

I. My Lord, you have no community (little white prince, thinks his shit doesn't stink).

P. Come up to the big house. I'll show you something. My lethal plantation is . . . what do you call it? My mind.

N. An image of a house—a head hardly worthwhile.

I. Turn that into an affirmation. I love this little house head! Every two to four hundred years of genocide has a silver lining. Like now you've got a God you can go to in your time of guilty need.

N. Up high like a treehouse.

P. Then my ass is the basement, home to an invisible man.

I. If you sit like a baby but tilt your ass up and invert the social order, we'se all gonna be massas afta the revolution.

P. The earth will be one big briar patch after the commission.

I. The low shall be made high after the restitution.

P. This is your fourth confirmation, is that not right?

N. I will not provide the rope for my own lynching or for further humiliation.

P. Don't take a rope as a badge of pride.

I. Sniff a library John and call that your integration, your crusty brown loaf.

P. The mucky shred of a rope above a hole, a shack, strings of it hang from your rump.

(*Transition.*)

I. Professor, what do you call a rabbit that lives in a tree?

N. A rat?

I. Bite back and try again. What do you call a tree that drops a rotten fruit?

N. Father?

I. What do you call a nest full of tar?

N. Our Lord who art in. . . .

I. Filth? Who calls all around this country specifically requesting dusty white dirt? Who looks down and feeds you his paste and asks you to be his mule? You'll never make your head like that.

P. If you want to go high? You got to get low.

N. Jerusalem, on my back I looked up to see the palms at the crossroads.

I. There's all kinds of being ridden, but a mule is only half a horse. Tell—tell about your family, the characteristics of the large ears, the bulging eyes, the abomination, the acts of sex with animals, the side-show rabbit man, the flaming crossroads, tell it or admit you can't hit the target.

N. I have compiled the rules, I came out, I asked upstairs for a pair of words, but the braided voices elude my ears, shut out by flat stark pictures thrown on a wall. I want my hearing . . .

P. If there is not absolute order and decorum in here, we will recess the hearing, and those who engage in any outburst at all will be asked to leave the committee room. . . . You'll get your chance to recite . . . know there are many people watching today who suspect we never will understand, but opinions are like assholes; everyone came out of one.

N. Spanish moss, swamp gas, jungle drums, and hunted night; there's no dark interior, just shadows made by someone else's leftover flame. Tell me how to cast them out.

I. Families are like assholes; they're both full of shit. You got some story cloggin' your pipes? Tough. Speak your little speech, dance your little dance, and get the fuck out of my jungle.

N. Come down, all of you, my head is clean, my house is empty; I won't talk, I won't look, only listen. Help me papa Lord legba who I don't believe in, make my branches ears all spread, open and waiting.

I. Did you want the carrot . . . or the stick?

N. What Fassbinder film is it? The one where a man walks into a pet shop and says what flower expresses: A pressure builds up behind your eyes, you live life as a nonrepresentation, you see spots, your tongue is ashen, you scramble up a class, a ladder on the backs of people who don't even know you are betraying them, days go by endlessly, they can't even see your lie when you offer them a paltry collection of jerry-rigged plagiarisms to make up for a lifetime of stealing and bloodsucking? And the florist says: white rabbit.

(*Transition.*)

2. Blood

NARRATOR.
White he's
omega
Man, he's still
white he's
omega.
Man, he's still
full of fight.
Transylvania
White

1780, Castle
White
Dracula

Count. It is the ineffaceable curse of Cain, of the blood that feeds my heart, one drop in eight is black—bright red as the rest may be, that one drop poisons all the flood: Those seven bright drops give me love like yours—hope like yours, ambition like yours—life hung with passions like dewdrops on the morning flowers: But the one black drop gives me despair for I'm an unclean thing—forbidden by the laws—I'm an Octoroon!

(*Rewind.*)

Count I've never before had the opportunity of entertaining a personage from the, uh, dark continent. I hope the reception was not boring for you.

Prince Quite the contrary, Count Dracula. The evening was a delight, and we found your guests to be most impressive. I liked particularly your Doctor Duvalier.

Count It was you who impressed him?

Luba Mamuwalde is the crystallization of our people's pride.

Prince My Luba, she does me too much credit, but notwithstanding, my people are eager to bring our ancient culture into the community of nations.

Count That may take a good deal of time.

Prince It will at least be time well spent as opposed to an exchange of banalities with dilettantes and pseudo-intellectuals.

Count Charming.

Prince What with dignitaries of your stature lending the weight of your statesmanship to the fulfillment of our objective, I believe we will succeed—Luba?

Count To totally cease the slave trade? Isn't that unrealistic? Slavery has merit, I believe.

Prince Merit? You find merit in barbarity?

Count Barbarous from the viewpoint of the slave perhaps. Intriguing and delightful from mine. I would willingly pay for such a beautiful addition to my household as your delicious wife, for example.

Prince Sir, are you ill?

Count Oh, I meant no insult, prince. It is a compliment for a man of my station to look with desire on one of your color.

Prince Sir, I suddenly find your cognac as distasteful as your manner. You're behaving like some sort of animal.

Count Really?

Prince Really.

Count Let us not forget, sir. It is you who comes from the jungle.

Prince Our evening is finished! I beg you to tell your coachmen we are leaving!

Count I do not think so.

Prince How dare you? Let me go.

Count Heheheh.

(*Fight.*)

Luba Look out!

Count You shall pay, Black prince. I shall place a curse of suffering on you that will doom you to a living hell, a hunger, a wild, gnawing, animal hunger will grow in you. A hunger for human blood; here you will starve for an eternity, torn by an unquenchable lust I curse you with my name—you shall be Blacula vampire, imprisoned, a living fiend. You will be doomed never to know that sweet blood that will become your only desire. (*To audience.*)

(*Rewind.*)

Count Give me your blood, I'll give you your name.

Prince Single-drop rule but no more—the truth in the appearance. Here's my letter—do you know when to abandon a book that won't give you what you want?

Count The colonized come to talk of equality . . . ! See your equality . . . isn't it that we both bleed? But not for just anybody.

Prince I think you control your women like we control our appetites and can thus give them away.

Count But you can't control your appetites. Isn't that the problem?

Prince A problem I'm willing to share with you and that . . . hat.

Count Share it in the theater? The theater of beautiful deaths? Revolution? Revolution—you can't even plan brunch! Let's make a bargain, shall we? I'll answer you if you'll tell me where you hope to destroy Count Dracula.

Prince No.

Count Too bad, my lover. It would be an experiment in thought transference. He can read my mind, you know, as I can read his.

Prince Hey, I want that hat. It's got something in it. (*Luba emerges from the hat.*)

Luba Farewell, and good luck to you. Decent girl that I am, I hope all goes well for you. As for us, we've lived a long time. We're now going to rest at last. (*Makes a gesture of impatience.*) We're going, we're going, but keep in mind that we shall lie torpid in the earth like larvae or moles and if some day . . . ten thousand years hence . . . Mamuwallboard, you bleed.

Prince A trifle.

Luba He does not bleed.

Count Here at plantation Dracula, we will give the name of pride to a savage king the name of Blacula! Not in the photo, not in the mirror, love the end, the end of coloration as the end of the not-representable. There is truth in sanguinity, not in opticality.

Prince How well you hate! How I have loved! And now, I die—I must confess—choked by my desire for a big black buck. Buck nakedness, thou hast conquered me! For two nights I called your name, begged you to release me from that solitary cell, and you never answered. Your promises to me were lies, all lies! Listen, you said if I hid in massa's room, you said I'd be rewarded, that I would have my first taste of human blood, a saturnalia of blood, he called it! But you lied! Not a drop—not one tiny drop!

Count Shit smells like garlic

It clarifies my blood
Dark vine—blood in yer stool like
Ropes from a window
Smells like a curse in a breeze
You will hunger
Bite the master you will never taste.

Prince I did not betray you, master! I didn't say where it was hidden! They know nothing! I am your slave! I worship you! Master . . . ? Master, answer me!!!

(*Rewind.*)

Count So then these two fag antique dealers show up three hundred years later and they're an interracial couple so um they want to buy the mirrors and stuff especially the mirrors and sell them to their fag friends or use them to suck up the social ladder by decorating the homes of Jewish faded film matrons in Bel Air so these bloodsuckers er cocksuckers pillage the castle Dracula like midwestern crackers adopting babies from Romania or Cabrini-Green when they don't even know the fuckin' language.

Prince Where we come from, the legend of Dracula, I mean, it's the crème de la crème of camp!

Count My blood is weak.

Prince My neck is sensitive.

Count How big are you?

Prince I'm party sized.

Count What are you into?

Prince I go anywhere. I don't do anything.

Count That's cool—hips or lips?

Prince So, Europe infects Africa, sticks Africa underground, and fags bring it to America so it can be resurrected.

Count Their ass is grass.

Prince Hmm, indeed. Go on, I'm sympathetic. These interracial fags, or fags race, peddle the debris of Europe to other deracinated stooges.

Count So, then it's later, and this Black doctor or coroner, he works for the cops, so, inotherwords, for whiteness, he's got a white-ass pal, but he's no fag, just got a big white friend like a white invisible rabbit. He works for whitey the bunny, looking at corpses, and he starts to see that Blacula is killing Black folks or rather the whiteness of Dracula's blood or lack of blood is making for some weird shit out there in Watts, and shit, oh, please, this can't go on. Hey, watch me pull a rabbit out of my hat.

Prince But that trick never works!

Count This time for sure! (*Luba emerges from the hat.*)

Luba Don't look in his eyes! He'll enslave you.

Count White left means what? I can't remember, cum eater? Hips or lips? You will be called Dragula, Dragella, Dragzilla, Bunnicula, Darkula (*Bite.*)—Don't shake your fatuous head at me—I didn't kill him.

Luba But you will kill unless we save you.

Count Go where your blood beats blood calls to blood.

Prince Blood. . . . I wanted a hat, a black hat to turn white on me to keep the sun out of my eyes.

Count White people turn Black, Black people turn white, he's omega man, he's still full of—(*To audience.*) You think to baffle me, you—with your pale faces all in a row like sheep at a butcher's. But you shall be sorry yet, each one of you! You think you have left me without a place to rest, but I have more! My revenge has just begun! I spread it out over centuries, and time is on my side!

3. Magic

(*Monologue by a rabbit puppet.*)

c. As many of you probably know, tonight we were going to unfold a program which we felt would be beneficial to the struggle of our people in this country, but because of events which are beyond our control, we feel that it is best to postpone unfolding the program that we had in mind until a later date. You have asked me to give a history of the motives which induced me to undertake the late insurrection, as you call it. To do so, I must go back to the days of my infancy and even before. Thirty-seven years ago, I was born the property of Benjamin Turner of this county. From the age of three, I was blessed with the knowledge of things that happened before my birth. My mother and others said in my hearing that I would be a prophet, as the Lord had shown me things that had happened before I was born.

From the very beginning, charges were leveled against me from the shadows—charges of drug abuse, anti-Semitism, wife beating, drug use by family members, that I was a quota appointment, confirmation conversion, and much, much more. And now this. But from the first to the last, I was made perfect, and the holy ghost was with me and said, "Behold me as I stand in the heavens," and I looked and saw the forms of men in different attitudes, embracing, licking and vomiting; and I saw the lights of the savior's hands stretched forth from east to west, even as they were extended on the cross at Calvary for the redemption of sinners, and shortly afterward while laboring in the field, I discovered drops of blood on the corn as though it were dew from heaven, and I found on the leaves in the woods hieroglyphic characters and numbers with the forms of men in different attitudes portrayed in blood and representing the figures I had seen before me in the heavens. I started to walk down the street, and I heard a voice saying, "Good evening." I turned, and there was this great white rabbit leaning against a lamppost. He talked about pornographic materials depicting individuals with large penises or large breasts involved in various sex acts. He told me graphically of his own sexual prowess. Because I was extremely uncomfortable talking about sex with him at all, at this point I began to feel severe stress on the job. I also recall engaging in discussions about politics and current events. I told these things to a white man on whom it had a wonderful effect—he ceased from his wickedness and was attacked immediately by a cutaneous eruption, and the blood oozed from the pores of his skin. After praying and fasting for nine days, he was healed. On the appearance of this sign, I heard a spirit, and it laid out a plan: that I should arise and prepare myself and slay my enemies with their own weapons. Armed with a hatchet, and accompanied by my God, I entered my master's room. It was observed that I must spill the first blood. The hatchet glanced off his head; he sprang from his bed and called for his wife. It was his last word. I laid him dead with one blow and then his wife as she lay in bed. The murder of this family, five in number, was the work of a moment; their slumber joined with that of the dead. There was an infant, sleeping in a cradle, that was forgotten until we had left the house and gone some distance, whereupon we remembered it and returned to kill it. It was the day of the rope—a grim and bloody day but an unavoidable one. Today all is quiet, but the night is filled with silent horrors: From tens of thousands of lampposts, power poles, and trees throughout the city, silent forms hang. At practically every street corner I passed this evening, there was a dangling corpse, four at every intersection. Hanging from a single overpass a mile from here is a group of about thirty, each with an identical placard around its neck bearing the printed legend "I betrayed my race." There are thousands of hanging corpses like that in the city tonight, all wearing identical placards that proclaim, "I defiled my race" around their necks. They are the white women who were married to or living with Blacks, with Jews, or with other nonwhite males. Those wearing the "I betrayed my race" placards are the politicians, the lawyers, the businessmen, the TV newscasters, the newspaper reporters and editors, the judges, the teachers, the school officials, the civic leaders, the bureaucrats, the preachers, and all the others who, for reason of career or status or votes or whatever, helped promote or implement the system's racial program. The system has already paid them their thirty pieces of silver—today we paid them in the coin of their own blood.

Essentially, what we are doing with our program of strategic sabotage is hastening along the natural decay of America. The Turner revolt may not have ended slavery, but its role can be summed up with the one word: *accelerator*. The strength of the vampire is that people will not believe in him. It has been true all through history that only small portions of a population are either good or evil—a great bulk are incapable of distinguishing right from wrong, and they take their cue from whoever is on top at the moment. Thus, there is no point in killing them all. Their moral weakness will have to be bred out of the race over hundreds of generations. For now, it is sufficient for us to eliminate the consciously evil portion of our population, plus a few hundred thousand of our morally crippled "good citizens" across the country as an example to the rest. All our program aims to do is find the taint, find the blot, find the criminal, find the bigot, and cut it down.

(*N. puts down puppet and delivers the rest.*)

N. So, I feel responsible for having played a major role in the development of a criminal organization. It was not a criminal organization at the outset. It was an organization that had the power, the spiritual power, to reform the criminal. And this is what you have to understand. I prayed for enlightenment, but I prayed to a God with a face like plaster dust. It was time to slay my enemies, but which of these hands had held the whip, which had tossed the rope over the waiting branch, which had laid the hatchet against the skull? What hunk of my flesh should I chop out to purify myself? You move stuff around and hope for the best. I know that's not much to offer. I may have used poor judgment early on in my relationship with this issue. Perhaps I should have taken angry or even militant steps, but if there's a cure for this, I don't want it. I don't want to be owned—even by an idea. So, Brother James, is everything all set? Yes, we're going to have a—those lights are something else—we're going to have a collection period right now.

C. (*Sung.*)
My name is
My name is
Gone not cold

Here alone well
Here alone well
Plans are made so
I can't
Home dry alone

My name is dry
My name is dry

Gone not cold
Here alone well
Here alone well
Plans are made so
I can't

Dry home alone

I. I was late for work.

P. You got a job? That's a surprise. Where are you working?

I. At the Market Street Cleaners and Dyers.

P. What do you do there?

I. I dye.

P. You what?

I. I dye for a living. If I don't dye, I can't live.

P. Are you sick?

I. No, you don't have to be sick to dye.

P. You don't?

I. In fact, if you're sick, you can't dye.

P. How long have you been dyeing?

I. All my life, since I was a kid.

P. How did you get started dyeing?

I. My family—they all dye. My father dyed ten years before I was born.

P. Must have been hard on your mother.

I. Not at all—in fact, she went ahead and dyed the very next day.

P. Well, if you're dyeing, what are you doing here?

I. I took a day off. You can't dye every day, you know, it wears you out.

P. It must.

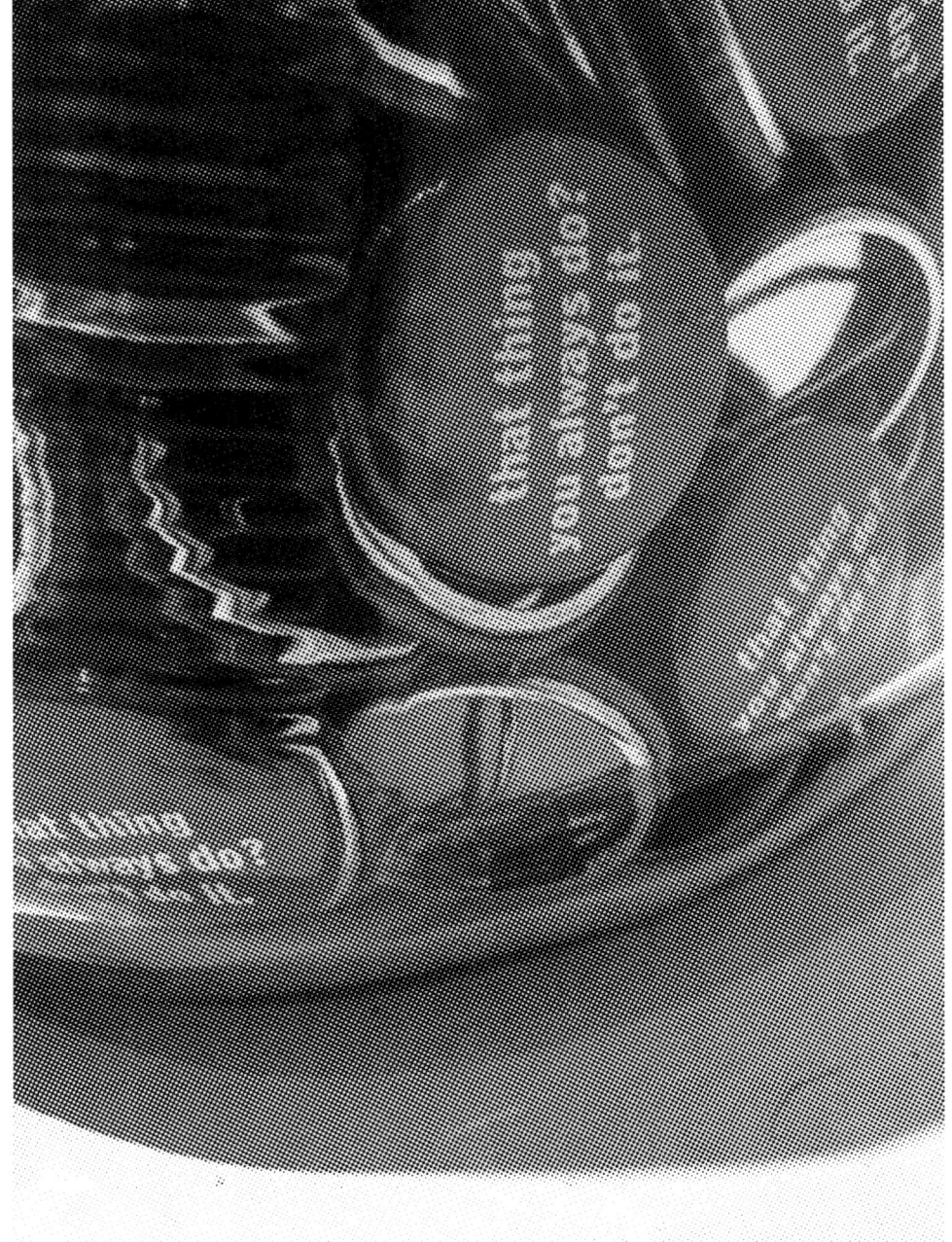

I. But now I have it figured out. I don't do it all at once. I dye by degrees.

P. Are the hours good?

I. Well, you've got to get up early. Each dawn, I dye. And every time we say goodbye, I dye a little.

P. So, you didn't feel like dyeing today?

I. No, you see, I'm not dyeing for myself.

P. You're dyeing for somebody else?

I. Yup.

P. Well, why doesn't this other guy dye for himself?

I. Oh, he used to dye, but now he doesn't have to. He's the boss. Others dye for him.

P. Others?

P. Oh yeah, he's got fourteen, fifteen guys dyeing for him right now.

P. Hey, this dyeing sounds like a good racket. Maybe I should get in on it. Can you make some real money doin' it?

P. Well, you know what they say—it's a living.

(*Curtain.*)

JACK SMITH: THE MESSAGE FROM ATLANTIS

Flaming Creature: The Life and Times of Jack Smith, Artist Performer, Exotic Consultant, *1997*

One of the things that started to happen at this point is that because of In a Different Light, *people became more comfortable with thinking about me as a writer. I got approached: "We're doing this catalog; would you be interested in writing an essay?" And about artists I admired, like Ray Johnson or Nancy Grossman, or people I knew, like Jim Hodges and Judie Bamber. It was a dream for me to write about Jack Smith. It was also frightening to write about an artist I will never have the guts to be. We've been talking about criticism as a species of loving, and I love Jack, but it also feels like a dishonor. I'm too bourgeois for my love to mean anything. —NB*

Jack Smith's work was like a powerful essence dispersed during his lifetime throughout the worlds of theater, film, writing, and art; a time bomb that continues to explode; a submerged continent whose artifacts—gifts from nearly forgotten gods—wash up on our mundane shores. The effects of his work appear everywhere today, and yet most people in the arts—practitioners and spectators alike—have little, if any, knowledge of the man who originated them. As Smith's work enters into history, the danger is that his essential difference will be lost, that he will be made to fit into the polite parody pantheon that American culture reserves for those it posthumously defangs.

How does one do honor to the achievements of past artists without also enacting a kind of violence on their memory? Our use of the past ultimately says more about us than it does about the past. We queers, especially, are always constructing our forebears in retrospect, feeding on a distortion of the dead, granting ourselves permission to move forward by reading (and, often, misreading) the works of those who went before us. Even the resurrection of the recent past can produce archaeological aberrations, distortions that betray their subject more often than not. Both Smith's life and work were, and are, difficult—demanding in the best sense of the word. It is important to understand and preserve that difficulty as we try to unravel the legacy of that life and work.

As it was for many people, my own path to Jack Smith was circuitous. I grew up in Manhattan during the 1960s and by my early teens had become an art nerd—a social misfit who, along with a group of friends, used a glue of science fiction, free jazz, avant-garde art, and film to cement a "superior" outsider status. I had also become a homo, which meant that I spent the mid-1970s doing things like bluffing my way into the Adonis Theater to watch porn movies and to give and receive furtive hand jobs, leafing secretly through issues of *Michael's Thing* at out-of-the-way newsstands, and wandering around Christopher Street looking at clones and feeling like a freak. Gay culture was coming into being in the West Village, and I was desperately looking for something that corresponded to my interior emotional experience. But there was something mismatched—a discrepancy between the bourgeois consumerism of the emerging gay market and the iconoclastic aestheticism I valued. I didn't know then that there was more than one way of being gay, and I felt irrevocably split.

Those two sides of my life—the art nerd and the homo—came together in 1976, when, at the age of sixteen, I first saw Jack Smith's *Flaming Creatures* and *Scotch Tape* at the Anthology Film Archives. My friends and I had been seeing whatever was being shown there: Robert Breer animations, Paul Sharits flickers, Maya Deren, Stan Brakhage—all of which fed our sense of superiority, of being in the know. But *Flaming Creatures* was an entirely different order of experience. For the first time, I saw art that spoke to both halves of me. What was on the screen was at once intimate, ludicrous, and ravishingly beautiful: a bunch of queers cavorting in front of a barely discernible painting of a vase of flowers, mincing drag queens putting on lipstick as if it were a sacrament, a vampire and a Spanish dancer flickering in and out of existence through the veils of flaring, overexposed film. Something peculiar was animating these elements, something that was faggoty, smart, and fun; something that left its mark on me—a message from Atlantis. I knew then that Christopher Street was not the whole story of gay life.

In the summer of 1980, I read an article in the *Village Voice* called "The First Radical Art Show of the Eighties." It described *The Times Square Show*, an exhibition of the work of dozens of artists installed in an abandoned massage parlor not far from where I lived. I saw that Jack Smith was billed to perform at the show one Saturday at midnight. I showed up and waited with a bunch of other devotees for about an hour. Having had no previous experience with Jack's audience "winnowing," I finally gave up, baffled, and went home. *The Times Square Show* changed my ambitions for my work. Just as I had seen that I didn't need to settle for the middle-brow aesthetic of the gay mainstream, I also saw that my work didn't have to fit in with the sterile white boxes in SoHo or in stiff, distant museums.

In 1984, after art school, I moved to San Francisco. While it was filled with gay people, San Francisco's cultural universe had no overlap between the art world and the gay community. Paradoxically, I was reliving my adolescent split between identifying as a gay man on one hand and as a post-structurally theorized artist on the other. I was casting about for another way of working, another sort of paradigm. Luckily, I came across Stefan Brecht's book *Queer Theatre*, with its sympathetic descriptions of Jack's performances in the 1960s. I remembered *Flaming Creatures*, heard that Jack was showing up at the San Francisco Cinematheque to screen it, and off I went. Of course, he didn't show. But I began thinking about Jack and remembering what my experience of his films had been. I reread Brecht's book often in the years that followed. I recalled my surprise and delight in the sexuality and buffoonery and drop-dead glamour of *Flaming Creatures*. I understood that that spirit was what was missing from my work. I also understood that it was what was missing from both the gay and art worlds of my time.

For much of my artistic life, I had fumbled toward queerness, toward "queer art," and my fumblings kept leading me back to Jack Smith. Even his no-shows were calculated statements of value and elusiveness. My points of connection/nonconnection with Jack and his work are exemplary of the ways artistic influence works. We imagine that artist X sees the work of artist Y, or studies with, or works for, them, becoming the bearer of a seed of influence that germinates and is passed on successively. But often influence proceeds fitfully and piecemeal. Often, all we have to lead us on as artists is our hunger for a type of experience or information or our own dissatisfaction. Part of us senses that we don't know what we need to know, and we fumble for it. Sometimes we are left with secondary texts, apocrypha, or only absences.

What are the lessons and qualities of Smith's art? Smith asserted that seriousness and dedication—not production value—created artistic worth. In all mediums, his art is one of fragmentation and transformation, often conducted at an incremental pace. He favored compositions that were over-wrought, knotted together, difficult to decipher. In his images, we are always looking through something—veils, bodies, encrusted junk. These allover compositions are then contrasted with eccentric details that leap out at us. There is mess and occlusion, and then there is a flash of naked insight. Disarray and hierarchy battle each other, illustrating how commonplace it has become in the twentieth century to see art in the arrangement of objects as well as in their creation. Smith believed this so deeply that many of his performances were little more than opportunities for the audience to watch him arrange things. His impromptu deflated the twinned pomposi-ties of performer and spectator.

Smith reveled in images of decay, death, humidity. In his work, rot is often presented as a desirable state, a condition in which boundaries break down and rebirth becomes possible. Rot is contrasted in Smith's work with encrus-tation, a process that he continually derides, linking it to plaster, falseness, icing, sugar. The wet and crumbling fecundity that brings forth orchids is set against the dry, powdery scabbed crust, the "black roachcrust" that covers over our everyday lives. Smith's villains are creatures with exoskeletons, lobsters, roaches, crabs, scorpions—animals covered with crusts.

Rot and decay are the result of death, of course, and Smith, like many artists, was haunted by images of death. But for him death and decay exist as the positive pole opposed to undeath—vampirism and zombification. Smith exploited this dynamic in film, which, like all photographic mediums, is inherently vampiric: It freezes its subjects in time on the screen while the actors and audience continue to age. The moving picture image thus mocks the body's frailty. Stories of resurrection, death, and vampirism have always sprung from cinema's dark heart. Sharing in this thematic bloodline, *Flam-ing Creatures* contains a literal vampire story. The film seems haunted by the ghosts of film's earliest images. Mario Montez's charming dance under-neath a lamp could have been lifted from an experiment by Thomas Edison or a Georges Méliès magic film. It seems to contain some irreducible nug-get of pure cinema-ism.

In addition to its formal and thematic complexity, Smith's work is also politically challenging. But when Smith is talked about at all, it is rarely as a political artist. His political ideas are treated as ludicrous and secondary, but in fact they are the crux of his work. Smith's politics were the only kind of politics that matters—utterly utopian, visionary, and grounded in his everyday experience, something he shared with many artists of his generation. But Smith also shares in the scorn that is now heaped on the political ambitions of that generation.

His work rests on two aesthetic assertions: first, that art is being made around us all the time—every time we arrange something—and that everyone is acting all the time; and, second, that the organizations supposedly dedicated to presenting, preserving, and fostering art are actually engaged in endless attempts to stamp it out and bury it beneath layers of plaster and crust. It thus becomes essential for artists to refuse to make art in the old-fashioned manner and to refute and resist the art establishment, even in its most benign forms. Smith's cancellations and no-shows underlined the point that while art may be all around us, it is not at our disposal, not something to be picked up like a Kleenex and airily disposed of. Art has to be worked for, even if that work is of a highly eccentric nature.

Smith's activities also included a sustained and spirited attack on the injustice of capitalism, an injustice exemplified in the notion of rent. Smith continually pointed out the fundamental absurdity of rent, the idea of paying over and over again for what one already owns (obviously, this was not an opinion that endeared him to his various landlords). This view extended into his criticism of the nascent underground film scene as well. Smith's endless embittered attacks on Jonas Mekas pointed out how, the moment we begin to codify our experience of art and to manage it, we become yet another museum, another landlord. Unlike the pageantry, the queerness, and the play in Smith's work, this uncomfortable assertion is hard to digest. It is Smith's version of the leftist political rhetoric that was floating through the art world in the late 1950s and early 1960s.

His assertions about social issues seem fresh today because they are grounded in the experience of capitalism's everyday boredoms and frustrations. Smith's politics were those of the downtrodden as opposed to the academic; he hated rent because he was a hapless renter; he distrusted critics, curators, and academics because he saw them as continually prospering at the expense of artists. All of Smith's work, in one way or another, pointed to the real purpose of the art establishment. The domestication and trivialization of art itself, as part of capitalism's relentless trampling of the humane.

It is difficult to place Smith in relation to other artists. Certainly, there are points of overlap between his work and the work of people around him (for example, the relationship between Smith's settings and the elaborate interiors of Allan Kaprow's *Happenings* or the chaotic environment of Claes Oldenburg's store). But these similarities do little to illuminate what was, and remains, important about Smith and his work today. His connection to other artists is less one of visual similarity than it is of type. Smith was a visionary, an outsider artist. Even though he functioned at the center of a sophisticated art scene, the tone of his work was closer to folk art than contemporary art.

More particularly, Smith's work has much in common with that of religious visionaries like James Hampton and Georgia's St. EOM (Eddie Owens Martin). Hampton is the constructor of the *Throne of the Third Heaven of the Nation's Millennium General Assembly*, a work composed of 180 objects (chairs, cabinets, frames, and other bric-a-brac) covered in foil and purple paper and dedicated to the Second Coming of Christ. He began working on the piece around 1950 when he was in his late forties, and he continued for over twenty years, eventually filling the obscure garage he had rented to house it. The throne is at once an elaborate altar, a physicalization of scriptural teaching, and a model of an earthly paradise. Like much modern art, the *Throne* is a transfiguration of mundane materials into glittering powerful objects, but this metamorphosis is the result of Hampton's prophetic vision of himself as the herald of Christ, not the result of a rhetorical point about high and low culture.

St. EOM's major work was the *Land of Pasaquan*, a house and sculpture garden that celebrated his spiritual awakening. EOM had been a gay hustler, a drug runner, and a fortune teller in New York in the 1920s. He eventually developed his own elaborate religion and returned to his home in rural Georgia to build a sacred temple to it. *Pasaquan* ended up being more than a temple, however. It grew into a compound of stucco-and-adobe pagodas, linked with brightly decorated walls. The garden is punctuated with totemic columns depicting faces of the enlightened. The constant use of bright color, scalloped edging, and ziggurat shapes evokes Mayan pyramids and Bavarian gingerbread, all at once. The walls are covered with murals of landscapes, erotically entwined figures, and religious geometry, derived from EOM's attempts to achieve a spiritual synthesis—a depiction of utopia and an evocation of the lost cultures of Atlantis and Mu.

One major difference between Smith and other visionary artists is that he talked back to the art establishment. For the most part, visionary and folk artists are relegated to the role of idiot savant and assumed to be unable or unwilling to defend or explicate their work. Smith, on the other hand, was eloquent, if elliptical, in his statements about his work and its place in the world. His knowledge, coupled with his unwillingness to play any of the roles laid out for artists by the art world, doomed him to an unjust obscurity.

In both its forms and its politics, Smith's work was difficult, if not impossible, for the critical establishment to manage. Like much of history, art history is written by the victors, and current attempts to reassess the art of the 1960s betray this. Those figures most opposed to the workings of art history have been conveniently "disappeared" by art historians. Perhaps it is fairer to say that they have successfully escaped the system they opposed, but the price of escape has been eventual anonymity. Today we are left with secondary sources, with traces sometimes thrice removed. The disappearance of the political dimension of much 1960s art is certainly part of the larger cultural tendency to jettison historical veracity in favor of academia's overreaching interest in historical style. Smith's activities left him in the paradoxical position of exerting great influence on a cultural scene that he was largely written out of; he was both insider and outsider.

Another artist who had a similar insider/outsider relationship to the mainstream art world and who could be called a spiritual father to Smith was Joseph Cornell. Like Smith, Cornell had little formal art education. Both were eccentric visual stylists who were entranced by the abundance of New York's streets and cobbled together the detritus of the city into fantastic worlds of their own invention. Cornell clipped and filed obsessively, compiling extensive dossiers on his favorite stars. Smith built an altar to Maria Montez in his apartment.

While many other artists are drawn to the look of their pieces (what Jack would call the icing), few plumb their spirit.

Both Smith and Cornell were artists of arrangement, rather than invention. They worked with existing materials and forms, creating something new from their juxtapositions. This montage method is obviously filmic, and both artists loved silent film. Cornell's *Rose Hobart* is a reedited silent one-reeler that turns a few moments from a hokey jungle adventure into an aching meditation on dreams and longing. Its wistful romance is a far cry from *Flaming Creatures*' disorienting frenzy, but Smith was clearly influenced by it. He and his collaborator Ken Jacobs screened a print of *Rose Hobart* over and over when Jacobs worked as an assistant to Cornell. *Flaming Creatures* occupies a temporally suspended place in film history that is analogous to the sense of timelessness of Cornell's boxes, which look as though they could have been made in the mid-nineteenth century.

More than an individual artist, Smith was an emblematic cultural figure. In this sense, he resembled another cultural trickster and genius: jazz musician Sun Ra. Starting in the late 1950s, Sun Ra forged an identity as a bandleader, pianist, and bricoleur that has inspired artists like George Clinton and David Hammons. Sun Ra's stage shows combined big band jazz with modern dance, loopy tribalism, psychedelia, group singalongs, Egyptology, and science fiction. He claimed to be a descendant of Egyptian gods who were visiting Earth from his home planet, Saturn. Previous leaders might have asserted that the future of Black people was in Africa; Sun Ra asserted that it was in outer space. His musical sets ranged from the bop arrangements he had grown up playing to extended improvisations that evoked European composers like Karlheinz Stockhausen and Iannis Xenakis. He dressed his band in elaborate, glittery costumes and strange plastic turbans of obscure religious significance.

Like Smith, Sun Ra took ordinary artistic rules and roles and utterly transformed them, combining artistry and travesty. A quick glance at the Sun Ra discography yields albums with titles such as *Holiday for Soul Dance*, *Outer Space Incorporated*, *Pathways to Unknown Worlds*, *Cosmo Omnibus Imaginable Illusion: Live at Pit Inn*, *Cosmic Tones for Mental Therapy*, and *Other Planets of There*. His records are miracles of the unexpected, veering from extended percussion jams into soapy renditions of gay chestnuts like "Over the Rainbow." Both Smith and Sun Ra queered the traditions they grew out of. Both used the metaphor of the lost continent of Atlantis as a place of escape, a location for their projections of utopian fantasies. Both invented lost continents at a time when their culture was extremely homophobic and racist, constructing fantastic worlds as defenses against the intolerable conditions around them.

Visionaries do not have heirs; they have disciples. While much of today's art world seems influenced by Smith's innovations, he cannot be said to have founded a school. Echoes of his work are evident, however, in the art of Jessica Stockholder, Mike Kelley, Nicole Eisenman, Cindy Sherman, Jerome Caja, Judy Pfaff, Cady Noland, Lucas Samaras, Vincent Fecteau, the performance artist Collette, and Ethyl Eichelberger, to name but a few.

Certainly, Mike Kelley, an artist omnivorous in his use of devalued icons of working-class culture, uses many of the same visual and performative devices as Smith. His references to scatology, the pathetic, and queer culture bring him further into Smith's orbit. Before Kelley worked seriously as an object maker, he was a performer who combined props, images, autobiography, and theoretical musings into vaudevillian tableaux. His best objects, like brilliant pop songs, retain that performative spirit. Kelley's *Arena* series presents pairs of thrift store stuffed animals confronting each other on blankets and afghans. Within the confines of these simplified "stages," the animals appear to be acting out mock philosophical dialogues that play on audiotapes. These pieces contain many parallels to Smith's *Secret of Rented Island*—from the stuffed animals, as surrogate actors, to Kelley's attenuated, overstylized voices on the tapes. But the guiding principle of Kelley's work has always been a kind of morphology—particularly evident in his performances—where the narrative thread is preserved by one object or statement of a transformative nature. Kelley seems to be continually saying, "This is like this—" a statement quite different from the obscure and more magical transformation in Smith's work.

Karen Kilimnik also echoes Smith's work in her seemingly haphazard arrangements and installations. Since the late 1980s, Kilimnik has used everything from flour to pop songs to live horses in her sculptures, which are often moody meditations on media figures or loving evocations of romantic pasts. Kilimnik's works seem barely organized, recalling Smith's tenuous settings, but they are underlaid with a punkish anger that surfaces in surprising ways. Her 1995 exhibition at the Jack Hanley Gallery in San Francisco brought together Smith's method and some of his subject matter. In a space filled with sepulchral, reddish light, the viewer found a dozen tiny, flimsy cardboard coffins, covered in felt and cheap plush, surrounded by framed photographs of the interior of burial vaults and pencil drawings of fashion models. Inside some of the coffins were candles in the shape of cherubs, cosmetics, and a Barbie doll made into a dual bride/vampire figure. With a sense of self-parody, Kilimnik melded expressions of her lesbian sexuality with notions of social, sexual, and psychic vampirism.

In 1993 Cindy Sherman produced a body of work that evokes the elegant rot of Smith's cosmos. Sherman photographed the contents of a bag of festering garbage over a period of months, using saturated colored lighting and extreme close-ups. The resulting images are postapocalyptic landscapes, seductive and nauseating in their moistness. The original forms of the individual components are impossible to make out. Instead, the heaps of trash merge in a spectacle of decay. While some of Sherman's earlier work may remind one of the careful posing and seduction of Smith's *The Beautiful Book*, this series of pictures possesses the deepest affinity with Smith's orchestrated piles of refuse.

The differences between Jack Smith's work and that of young artists today are striking. The political, disruptive dimension of Smith's work—its

My Studio Is a Dungeon Is the Studio

utopian ambitions—is often absent from today's work, much of which is predicated on an assumption of inadequacy and failure. The use of pathetic materials and the slipshod, provisional gestures all point to an inability to imagine a single way in which this unredeemed world might be different. Contemporary artists cluster around garbage cans in New York, hoping to find something thrown out by real people so that its new utilization might reinvigorate the dying twitches of the commercial art world. Thus, much of today's funky, slim art trades on the energy of previous innovations.

The good thing about today's ephemera is that it falls apart so fast that in ten years you can try the same thing again and it looks fresh. On the surface, this seems to be part of Smith's legacy, but in actuality his work was concerned with success. Smith's hesitations, dislocations, and dysfunctions are not images of inability but the breaking through of an entirely new order of thinking into the self-congratulatory world of American culture. His romance of rot, for example, denounces the banalities of capitalism and attacks the American consciousness, much as the extremes of butoh were an attack on the postwar Japanese consciousness. Smith realized that when art has been converted into another sideshow of the rented lagoon, the most powerful thing it can do is to *not show up*. Slack they may be, but today's artists (God save us) are punctual. The show opens; the audience gets what it came for—all is made easy.

This earnestness and punctuality reinforce the assumption that pervades today's art practice, namely, that artists, dealers, critics, collectors, and the public are all on the same side. This illusion gained currency in the 1980s as the art world grew increasingly fascinated by the spectacle of its own success. These various constituencies, which coincidentally circulate around art objects and events, came to see themselves as slightly varied parts of the same system, each with its own place and function. To question this notion is to risk accusations of foot-dragging, sour grapes, or naivete, but such shallow, soporific coziness immediately raised Smith's indignation and scorn. That anger underlies the demands he placed on his audience and his friends—an anger that looks as quaint to today's art milieu as pilgrim probity or medieval chivalry.

The thing that finally sets Jack apart is the time he lived in, a time when it was still possible to conceive of a past. Today we are continually haunted by the husks of our trends and fads, as our culture presents the past as a parade of styles offered to us on a dessert tray. Today's artists also have had their expertise made easy for them; the undead past swirls around in our heads all the time. Want to get into baroque art? Fluxus? Dixieland?

Japanese manga? Santeria? *The Mary Tyler Moore Show*? Just turn on the tap. Maria Montez's films are more available than ever before. PS1's exhibition and publication almost ensure that Smith's films will finally find their place in the marketplace of ideas. The expansion and development of information storage and transmission technologies like the VCR and the PC in the 1980s have produced an enormous content shortage, a gap that is now being filled with everything from music and movies from around the world to enormous compilations of previous material. In the late 1950s and early 1960s, just seeing movies from the 1930s and 1940s required a surprising amount of diligence. The underground, at that time, was not a foyer. It was, like most ghettos, part prison and part refuge—but definitely not what it is today: a term designating a market niche.

Irony has become the crucial methodology for getting young people to buy old stuff; nostalgia is the selling point for old consumers. Combined with a cynical collapse of belief in a viable future, this phenomenon has spelled the end of the past as past. Contemporary art functions in the same fashion as other sectors of the retail market. Young artists peddle various retreads of work from thirty years ago, which helps their profile and reopens areas of profitability in the secondary market. We see the soulless transformation of trash into art, and the outside visionary turn into the insider huckster, so often that we can't imagine a situation where it wouldn't happen.

Instant access to data destroys the uniqueness of events just as modern architecture, urban planning, and commercial development have conspired to destroy the uniqueness of place. Insofar as revolutions are events, the death of the event means that for artists today, the revolutionary dimension of artistic practice has become even more elusive; indeed, the "revolutionary" has simply been co-opted as yet another style. Society at large has become, in fact, more vehement in its assertion that the revolutionary dimension doesn't even exist, that it is impossible to transform the essential conditions of one's existence. From now until eternity, there is only rent: the endless paying out for things one already owns.

Given today's context of ubiquitous, commerce-driven information, difference is quickly subsumed by the marketplace. Communities, which come together through shared oppression, struggle for self-definition in the face of dissolving identities and trivialized meanings. Queer art runs the risk of becoming just another channel for viewers to flip past.

The queer contribution to cultural discourse is often discussed in terms of camp. Contemporary culture is seen to be pervaded by camp attitudes, and camp itself is portrayed as an outsider's action of cultural resistance.

Camp is a thorny subject, a cultural gesture that both subverts and reinforces convention, but one thing is true: Camp has become an impossibility today. Camp, as Jack Smith practiced it, is an attitude of profound seriousness and connoisseurship directed at an inappropriate subject. Thus, it parodies notions of scholarship and cultural value. The subjects of camp are not fit for the type of study and veneration applied to them. By indulging in recondite social fetishisms, camp carves out a place of cultural refuge, if not resistance. The crucial component of this formulation is the seriousness and scrupulousness that underlies camp, an attitude of mind that has wholly escaped us as a culture, only to be replaced by a defanged, ubiquitous irony. This is presented in some circles as evidence of a widespread queer sensibility, but the difference is that irony, requiring no work, never presents a challenge to its practitioner, nor does it provide the possibility of cultural resistance. Unlike irony, true camp is not waiting to tear aside the mask and agree that we are all on the same side after all. But to practice camp, one must be in earnest. In the arts, the era of the late 1950s and early 1960s was one of great public play, but it was play conducted with steely determination. For queer artists, camp was a prime tool in that play.

In 1963 and 1964, in anticipation of its role as host for the world's fair, New York began to clean up the ragged fringe of its brilliant tapestry. The city closed gay bars, cracked down on prostitution, began to use health and obscenity laws to harass the artistic avant-garde, and grouped the left; queers and artists were considered equally dangerous. The underground of the early 1960s was indeed a mélange of people who identified with groups that put their own spins on what it might mean to be queer, leftist, or an artist.

For homosexuals, the rash of obscenity prosecutions provoked a class split, driving the aesthetically advanced queer world further underground and clearing the way for the bourgeois gay movement to become the dominant voice. The West Village triumphed over the East. The gay culture that grew up after Stonewall aspired to assimilate, leaving little room for those freaks who, like Jack, were beyond the pale and could never conceive of— much less hope for—assimilation. The aesthetic sense of this group was bounded on the left by socialist realism (affirmative images of gay people) and on the right by beefcake (affirmative images of dick). This may go some distance in explaining the emergence and subsequent popularity of Robert Mapplethorpe. By the mid-1970s, porn theaters were showing gay sex infinitely more prurient and explicit than anything that had been made by underground filmmakers (whose legal travails had done much to ease censorship). Indeed, it was not the explicit sexual acts but the art itself that had troubled the authorities. The early 1960s also marked the point at which the art world began to distance itself from queer content and identity, moving from a garrulous, ambisexual representation toward an increasingly formalist abstraction. As the avant-garde art scene began to repress its queerness, the gay scene began to repress its avant-garde-ness.

If one were to view Jack Smith's work as a precursor to today's explosion of drag performance and mass media drag images, it would not only be a gross oversimplification of his work but a misreading of the genealogy of contemporary drag. For Jack's drag was about neither passing nor clowning: It was an evocation of travesty, of the carnivalesque. His costumes do not play on gender roles but subsume gender into a fetishistic celebration of societal confusion. While *Flaming Creatures'* cast appears to be composed mainly of drag queens, many of the actors are simply heavily made-up women. And in Smith's later works, extravagant costuming replaces crossdressing almost entirely. The drag in his work, consequently, is far from the legacy that has given us today's battalions of RuPauls and Lypsinkas. Much of the performing tradition of today's drag is derived from vaudeville and, ultimately, from minstrelsy: working-class forms of gender and racial anxiety. In the same way that donning blackface allowed whites to illustrate both their desire for and difference from Black bodies and Black cultural expression, most drag allows men the luxury of playing at female identification without losing phallic power. Thus, drag is a sanctioned, temporary crossing of boundaries, rather than an elimination of those boundaries. Indeed, in the 1990s drag queens have been trotted out as happy-go-lucky window dressing on the periphery of modern life, as outrageous-looking (is there a more boring emotion than outrage?) men who still care about straight folks—papas and mamas and kinder on the inside—and as fairies who, like the fairies in Disney's world, just want folks to love and tolerate each other. In the gay community, drag has become so accepted that notions of its transgression scarcely ever occur.

Mainstream artists are obsessively searching for the true outsider spirit that used to exist within the hidden margins of American society. But they search for that spirit only to make it perform tricks of a special effects dummy (RIP, Ed Wood). They want a past whose revival has no consequences for the present. The marginal has ceased to exist as a real cultural category; it has been replaced by the underdeveloped. Official culture has always had a vampiric relationship to real vision, transforming primal power into undead commodity. The excitement we experience in relation to true

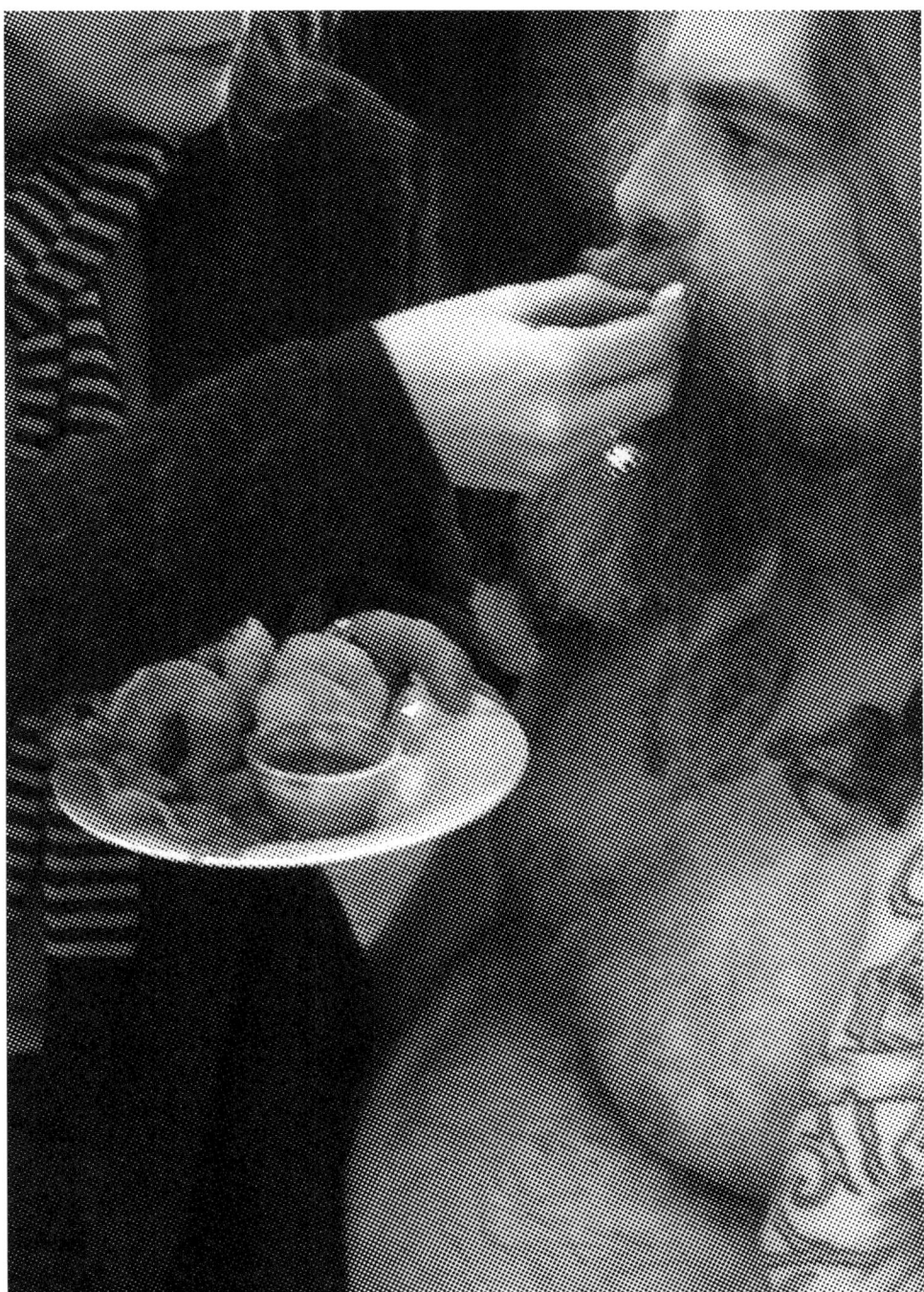

works of art is the knowledge that anything can happen, that we don't know where a narrative line or note is taking us. In works like *Jurassic Park*, the notion is dangled in front of us, only to be replaced by the deadening certainty of knowing exactly what will happen. The knowledge of infinite possibility is perhaps the only thing that art can teach us and the only thing it need teach us. The brilliance of Jack Smith's work is that it constantly proceeds in unexpected directions, making unexpected connections, startling us with its newness.

Like hired-gun scientists in *Jurassic Park*, I have been trying, as an artist, to reconstruct a dead titan. And like them, I've used secondary sources, blood from a mosquito trapped in amber, a written description of a performance, a funerary reminiscence. Like every other artist, I take my nourishment from past efforts, a fly on the corpse. But how can we sustain ourselves without betraying those who came before? How do we honor a body of work without destroying its spirit? This exhibition and book are ways of honoring Jack Smith. But it is a half measure at best, one that treads perilously close to the institutions that Smith so mistrusted.

Why Jack Smith today? What is the importance of looking at his work? Perhaps, because we need it so much. As we look around, it is clear that we have given so much up that we have forgotten that we even had the right to ask for things that previous generations demanded without qualm, like the utter transformation of the conditions of our existence. To understand the true genius of Smith's work, we must take it whole, not chop it up into highlights and masterpieces. Much of Smith's interaction with the public was characterized by deep dissatisfaction, scorn, and frustration on both sides. It's important not to lose sight of that fact. It may well be that the legacy of prophetic artists is to give us, not specific ways of doing something, but, by their example, the permission to be fearless in our own search for a way to do something. Viewed in that spirit, Smith's vision is far from understood but still enormously potent in its potential to change our lives.

RAY JOHNSON:
CORRESPONDENCES

Artforum, *1999*

Despite the fact that his career spanned nearly fifty years—much of it spent in New York and in contact with the most important artists of his day—Ray Johnson has long been famous for being famously unknown. If at times he resented this contradiction, it was also something he relished, refusing to behave in regular-artist ways. He turned down shows, declined interviews, and refused sales. And even though he produced a few trademark images and techniques (his Ignatz-like bunny heads, his clunky yet precise calligraphy, his rubber stamps), none of his works has passed into the common image bank like those of so many of his peers.

More often than not, Johnson's obscurity was deliberately and lovingly cultivated, and his hermetic systems, running gags, and visual twists and turns can be off-putting at first encounter. When this motley group of oddball items is seen as a group, the logic of his aesthetic begins to make much more sense. Organized by Donna De Salvo (curator at large of the Wexner Center for the Arts, where the show will travel), the Whitney's retrospective—the first comprehensive look at the artist's multifaceted output since his death in 1995—offers a valuable opportunity to glimpse the scope of Johnson's project. Yet it also seems clear that, for Johnson, meaning resided in his practice, in the circulation of his work. This aspect of his art is nearly impossible to capture in a museum exhibition, and in some ways, this show doesn't even make the attempt. It strives to present Johnson as a fit object of study—a serious artist. It's clear that he was that, but also much more.

On one level, walking through the Whitney's show makes for a revealing recap of the concerns and formal approaches common to artists of the 1950s and early 1960s. Like Jasper Johns, Robert Rauschenberg, and Andy Warhol, Johnson belonged to a generation that found a way out of abstract expressionism through a democracy of content and artistic influences as well as styles of working that, for all their playfulness, were deliberate and controlled. This generation had no qualms about looking at comic strips or experimenting in graphic design. Johnson attended Black Mountain College and claimed to have studied "mostly with Josef Albers." Once he arrived in New York, he developed friendships with Warhol and Joseph Cornell. This unlikely triumvirate seems to have served as his most important set of influences. But Johnson's work is interesting less for the ways in which he honored Albers, Warhol, and Cornell than for how he disrupted every artistic idea he dealt with. His formalism is laced with in-jokes and cartoony imagery; his pop is personal and intimate; his surrealist tendencies are pursued at such a glacial pace that they end up having very little to do with the unconscious. He took the Zen-derived notions of acceptance and impermanence that John Cage pursued and stood them on their head. He delighted in mistakes—slips of the tongue or pen—yet maintained a tight control over everything that subsequently happened to his work.

Shortly after moving to New York in 1948, Johnson abandoned painting, destroyed many of his previous works, and focused his talents on collage. He continued to explore this medium for the rest of his life, developing a highly idiosyncratic approach to both his content and materials. Early on, in works he dubbed *moticos*, Johnson worked directly, cutting and pasting images from magazines and newspapers. As time went on, however, each gesture became more considered and distanced from the source material. He would draw a squiggle and then photocopy the drawing, paste the result onto board, and sand the image until it nearly disappeared. This procedure would be repeated over and over until the gesture and the chronology of the piece became impossible to disentangle. Johnson would work and rework his collages, which ultimately left many of them airless in their intricacy. These pieces were his official art, the stuff he showed and sold. It was clear that Johnson wanted his talent recognized by the art world at large, but he chafed at the closed nature of the gallery system and developed a way out through his mailings. This split is quite marked in the Whitney show, where the early rooms, dominated by the collages, feel pious and a little dull. The show picks up energy once it moves into the early 1960s, where a series of vitrines filled with Johnson's correspondence make the energy of the entire show jump a few notches.

Johnson had been sending things to friends and acquaintances for years, but by the late 1950s, this activity began to take on new dimensions in his work. The messages in individual pieces became more complex and allusive, and more people were let in on the game. He regulated his mailing activities by having one person send mail to another. Dubbed the "New York Correspondence School" (NYCS) by one of its participants, the roundabout method of distribution became a way for Johnson to include admirers or banish detractors, as well as dole out gifts. Bits of imagery, reviews, and other people's letters all found their way into Johnson's mailings in ways that highlighted the unique that lurked below the mundane. He collected stories of bizarre deaths (one collage includes an item about a girl who choked to death on a peanut butter sandwich) and celebrated the draftsmanship of comic artists like Ernie Bushmiller. (Johnson shared this taste for the tabloid with Warhol, yet their treatment of similar subjects could hardly be more different. Where Warhol enlarges, Johnson reduces.) The correspondence school stands in opposition to the traditional art world; perhaps its closest analogue (in the sense that it challenges the usual ways art is made, distributed, and consumed) is Warhol's Factory.

In many ways, the NYCS was a performance: an elaborate three-and-a-half-decade dance choreographed by Johnson. He used it to weave together his past and present, to entertain friends, to construct an encyclopedia whose definitions were the resistance to definition. The NYCS was also redubbed *dubs* or *fan clubs* (as in the "Shelley Duvall Fan Club"), pointing up Johnson's enthusiasm for both the obscure and the mundane. Rather than an artist struggling with weighty ideas, he became a fan among fans. The fan clubs also allowed him to be picky. His Pablo Picasso fan club included nearly everyone in Picasso's circle but Picasso. A similar tension charges his thinking about Marcel Duchamp. One collage, entitled *Untitled (Mona Lisa with Coil)* (1966–81), consists of a reproduction of the *Mona Lisa*, the figure sprouting rabbit ears, her face obscured by a spiral coil of string. Tucked to the side is a newspaper story of a man with a five-foot mustache; his photo shows the mustache curled into the same spiral, a shape that echoes Johnson's potato-masher drawings as much as *L.H.O.O.Q.* One mailing includes a picture of a young man at the doctor's. The speech balloon above the man reads, "Oh doctor I detest being told i have that con-ceputalism," while the doctor replies, "Mr Andre, you seem to have a slight case of concept-ualism"; the whole absurd piece is titled the *Marcel Duchamp Club* (note the missing

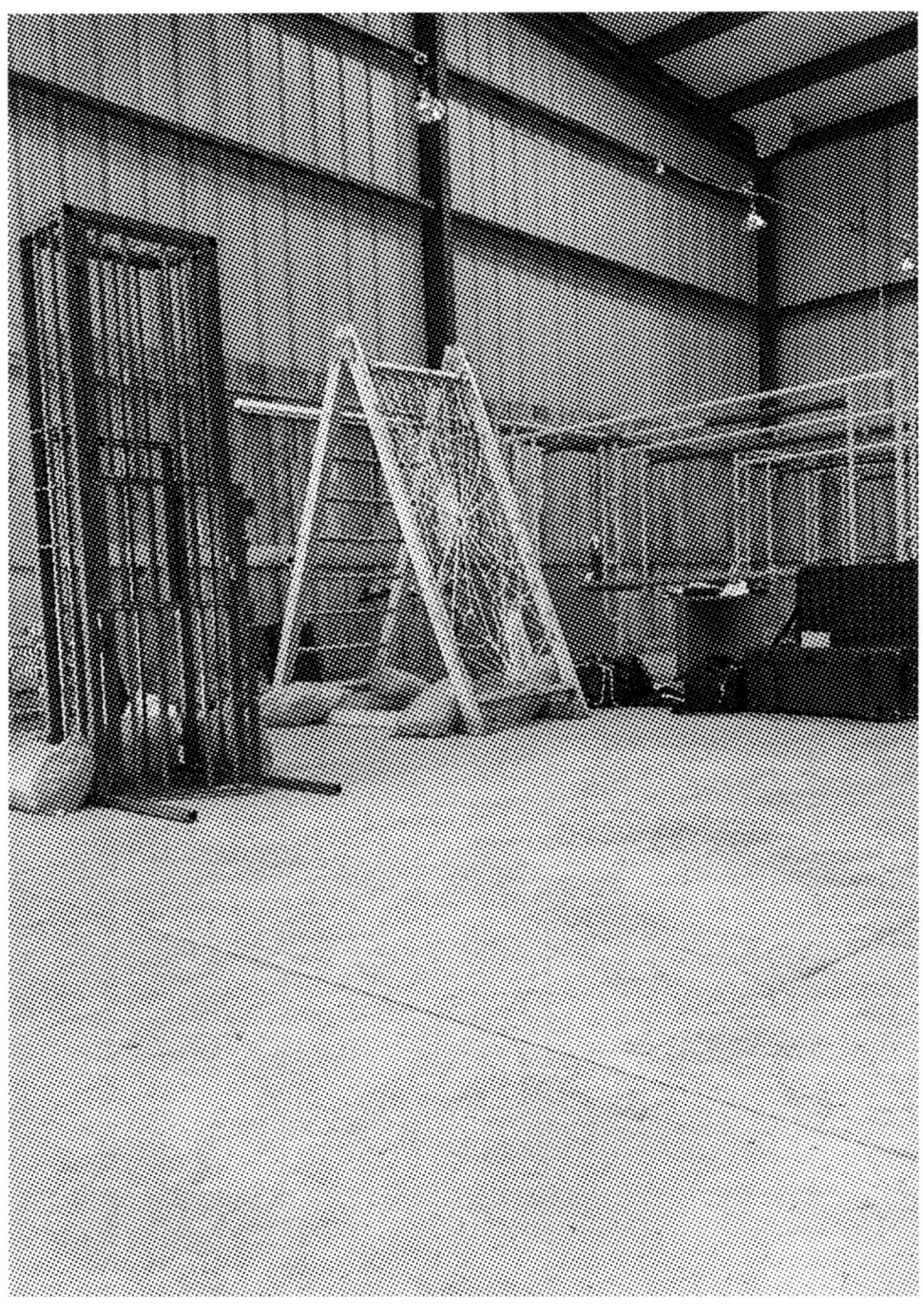

fan). For all his Duchamp references, it seems Johnson had little use for those who claimed to be continuing Duchamp's work.

By contrast, Johnson seemed eager to embrace Gertrude Stein. Her image appears in several collages in the show, notably as a stand-in for Jackson Pollock in Johnson's portrait of the painter. Stein was, of course, another ringleader, the doyenne of an avant-garde circle, but her influence on Johnson also extends to the language in his collages, his use of repetition and variation. Like Stein, he strings his words together with equal stress and uses the device of naming and misnaming as a method of description. In *René Magritte*, 1971, the one recognizable face is also the one "misnamed": Montgomery Clift substitutes for Magritte while in the background are an array of Johnson's signature fetus-like figures, each bearing different names: Charlie Chaplin, Greta Garbo, John Gunther, Erich von Stroheim, Charles Boyer, and so on.

It's a shame that the freewheeling spirit that pervades this work isn't more apparent in the Whitney's presentation. *Ray Johnson: Correspondences* perhaps inadvertently emphasizes the chilly formal side of Johnson's production, and in this light, the gambols of the New York Correspondance School seem an awful lot like homework. Some of this is inherent in the limitations of the material. It is difficult to exhibit many pages of the correspondence and still maintain visual interest. But some of the problem is that the meaning of much of Johnson's art was in how he did things, not what he did. Did Johnson ultimately outsmart himself? He left behind a body of work so complex that enormous amounts of it need to be seen in order for it to be understood. The same strategies Johnson used to dodge the art world also close him off from the recognition he craved. This show takes up the admirable task of trying to sift and shape the sprawl. It also makes evident the difficulty of bringing it all back together again.

TOP TEN

Artforum, *2000*

1. Kaz, *Underworld*

Kaz is the only cartoonist left who can actually write a four-panel strip that's funny—milk-through-your-nose funny—instead of rotten with whimsy and chuckles. *Underworld* is populated by perverts, drug users, and chumps of every stripe, just as every great metropolis should be—except sometimes the comic's set in an enchanted forest or in hillbilly country. You can tell from the drawing that Kaz has studied everyone from Jaime Hernandez to E. C. Segar to Philip Guston, blending their influences into a vision of broken boards and barf depicted with elegant clarity.

2. Rick Steiner and Tank Abbott Team Up (World Championship Wrestling)

This tag team was too good to last, but while it was going strong, it was the best reason to watch WCW. Abbott is a lug, an escapee from ultimate fighting, who can't wrestle and can't talk. His big move is to stand in one spot and whack the opponent with his deadly right hand. He's the most appealing piece of manflesh on television, with squinty blue eyes, a dusting of bristly hair, and a ZZ Top goatee. Steiner, the Dog-Faced Gremlin, a veteran who's still nursing a grudge against his brother Scott (aka Big Poppa Pump), has a body that's gone to seed in a way that makes my mouth water. Together they were a devastating pair.

3. Creation, "How Does It Feel?" (1968)

It all starts with a thudding, plodding kick drum. Then the guitars come in—the sort of shrieking slides you play when you don't really know what you're doing but know you have to make a lot of noise. The rest is a lurching, thrilling onslaught that leaves the singer moaning, "How does it feeeeeeeel to feeeeeeel? How does it feeeeeel to feeeeeel?" How indeed?

4. *Leprechaun 5: In the 'Hood* (Dir. Rob Spera, 2000)

Needless to say, all the *Leprechaun* movies are worth watching, but this one contains a line of dialogue I would give a limb to have written: "From the depths of Hell, I summon thee. ME ZOMBIE FLYGIRLS!" Ice-T must need a paycheck pretty bad these days since he consented to star. Contains the most frightening thing ever committed to film: leprechaun rap.

5. *Sock Monkey* (Dark Horse Comics, 1999–)

Tony Millionaire is another brilliant cartoonist, and *Sock Monkey* is his comic book, which depicts a universe tangential to the one explored in *Maakies*, his syndicated strip. The hero here is a stuffed sock, a creature of elegant locution and feckless optimism. Set vaguely at the turn of the century, *Sock Monkey* weaves courtliness and sudden savagery seamlessly together in a manner at times evocative of Edgar Allan Poe.

6. Sludgemaster

Ostensibly porn for those who like it sloppy, these tapes (available via Sludgemaster.com) should be viewed by every graduate art student in America. Here, men explore their relationship to mud, sewage, canned pudding, space-born toxic waste, worms, puke—you get the idea—all under the camera's devoted gaze. This is what pornography used to be: an aesthetic form that allowed for any contingency, so long as it's in the service of pleasure. The result? Thrilling narrative unpredictability. In many a *Sludgemaster* scene, you couldn't begin to guess what might happen next—and you're left bewildered by your capacity to get off on it. Pure jouissance. This is why Jesse Helms hates homosexuality. (And that's why we hate him.)

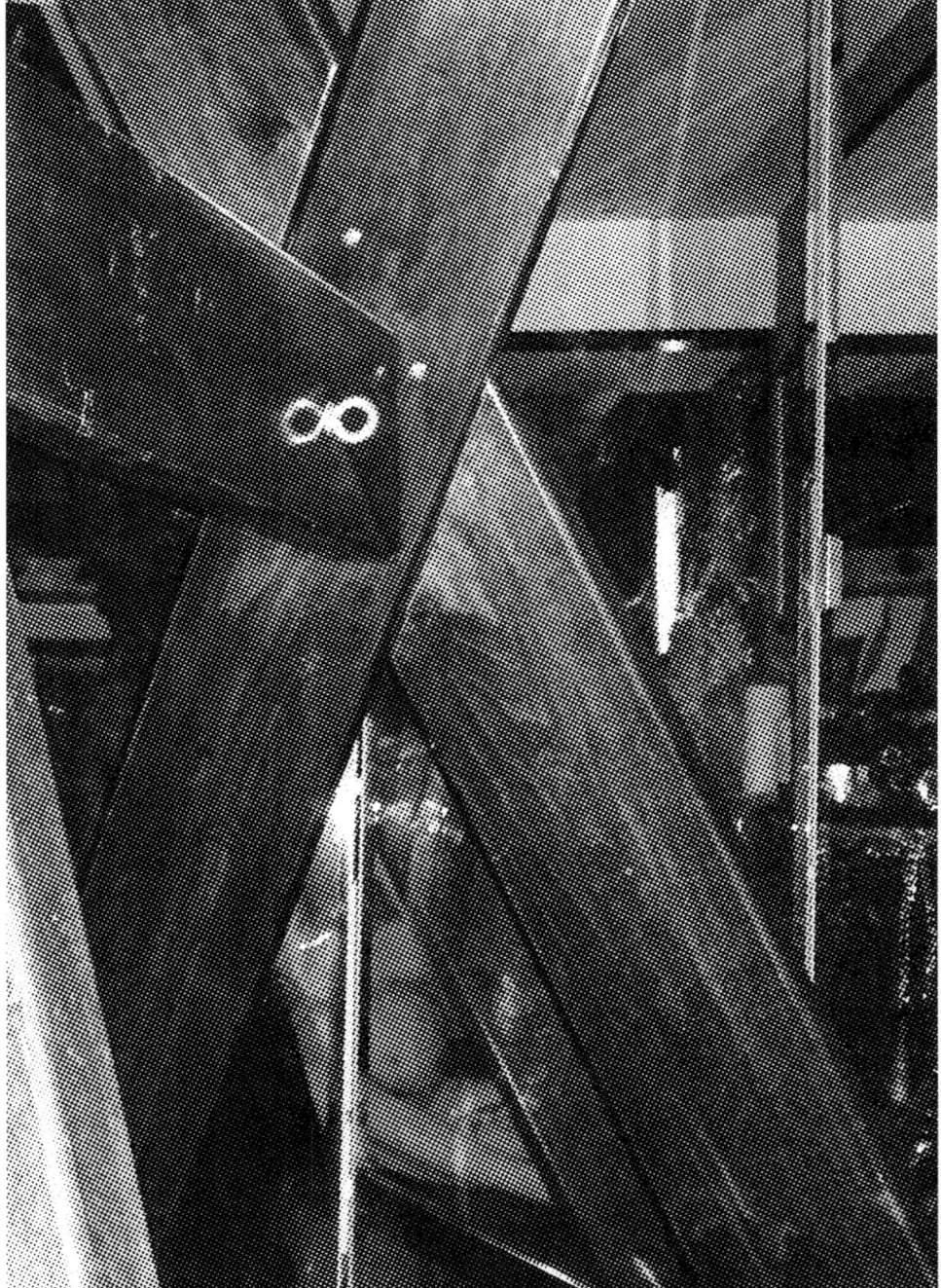

7. Him of the *Powerpuff Girls*

With his Santa Claus jacket and fishnet hose, his finicky facial hair and lobster-claw hands, and a voice that ranges from unctuous ululation to stentorian bellow, Him makes me think that one of the *Powerpuff* animators took a long, loving look at the work of Jack Smith. The symbol of ultimate evil, He doesn't indulge in the usual rock 'em sock 'em capers typical of the other villains on the show. No, His crimes are all psychological (making the citizens of Townsville hate the show's heroines, for example), which makes Him the only genuinely creepy villain on kids' TV.

8. Bill Traylor (1854–1949)

Some of the finest drawings made in America in the twentieth century, by a man who was treated with a reverence that could never fully mask the condescension behind it. Traylor's pared shapes and aching symmetries drain the fake jollity out of "folk art" and replace it with ecstasy.

9. Phase Four (Cambridge, MA)

Every good record I bought this year came from this shop. A labor of love, this is the kind of place you walk into and get an education. They don't have much floor space, so the stock of used CDs, vinyl, and Atari video games has been carefully culled. Nine times out of ten, I buy whatever happens to be playing when I stop in—and I end up listening to it for months after.

10. Terry Andrews, *The Story of Harold* (Holt, Rinehart and Winston, 1974)

A friend lent me this book, and it's a revelation: a novel that recasts Scheherazade as an envenomed children's author who flings himself from fuck to fuck all the while beguiling us with anecdotes on the way to his impending suicide. First published in 1974, it's the missing link between Gore Vidal's *Myron* and Kathy Acker's *The Childlike Life of the Black Tarantula by the Black Tarantula*. Is this the first American novel to use fisting as a motif?

JAMES GOBEL

Hammer Museum brochure, 2000

I feel fat today, and I'm glad. James Gobel's pictures make me feel glad, make me want to live in the world they present, a world of smiling fat men, shown singly or in pairs, at home, in bars, and outdoors. Meticulously constructed of yarn and felt, Gobel's pictures are at once warm and blank, homey, and oddly unsettling in their single-mindedness. At first, they seem to be pictures of "regular guys"—truckers, repairmen, working-class buds for the most part. They wear flannel shirts and facial hair and hang out in bars or cellars. They might all be members of the same extended family. As I look at them longer, I notice the details that lurk around the corners of the images—the logo on a T-shirt, a particular tattoo—which clue me in to the fact that something else is going on with these guys.

Like most young artists, James Gobel was able to discover what he needed to do only by first collecting a bunch of stuff he wanted to look at. That stuff turned out to be pinup magazines featuring large men: *Bear, Bulk Male, Heavy Duty, American Bear, American Grizzly, Husky,* the *Big Ad.* We can make a picture of what we love, we can make ourselves into what we love, or we can love ourselves. In 1995 Gobel deliberately made himself bigger, gaining thirty-five pounds in a month. In documenting his weight gain, he referred to *Carving: A Traditional Sculpture* (1973), a work in which conceptual artist Eleanor Antin documented her own weight loss. Antin was one of many women artists active in the early 1970s whose work reinvigorated contemporary art by foregrounding issues of gender and physicality. *Carving* makes clear the ways in which art helps to frame our ideas about which bodies are acceptable and which are not. Many gay artists of Gobel's generation have used the works of feminist artists like Antin as templates for their own attempts to articulate a queer position in opposition to the orthodoxies of today.

Gobel went on to produce a series of works in which piles of objects stood in for the added thirty-five pounds. A group of paintings followed in a variety of materials and styles: Things that initially looked like monochromatic abstractions proved to have words like *chubby* and *bear* worked into their impastoed surfaces; the walls of a suburban interior held faux thrift store paintings of depressed, chunky boys. Although it may seem that Gobel's work has moved in a contradictory trajectory, from more "difficult" conceptual work to more "traditional" paintings, this should alert us to the more difficult ideas that lurk in these seemingly traditional objects. Any artist struggles to find that place where idea and method finally work in concert. In his most recent works, Gobel has found that place.

Starting with photographs, either posed or found, Gobel proceeds to make drawings, first in pencil and then in yarn, and then, finally, composes a mosaic of felt pieces. Once a piece of felt is in place, he's committed. Any mistake means having to start over. This technique makes all of the parts of the picture equally important; he has to lavish as much attention on a stone in a fireplace as on a nipple. These objects take a casual, conventional moment (the snapshot) and make it the occasion for an extraordinary act of devotion. The materials and careful crafting of these objects, the quiet planning, the piecing together of fabric, evoke traditionally feminine pursuits such as quilting, yet their imagery would most readily be called masculine.

I use the word *objects* advisedly since these things only seem to be paintings. Gobel's works are certainly not the "magic windows" that we traditionally think of representational paintings as being. They do everything to insist on the impurity of their origin, the visual impenetrability of their surfaces. Their materials are not those we associate with high art. Rather, they come from the world of home craft, the feminine world of dried-flower wreaths and hot-glue guns. But felt also has a history in contemporary art, linked to Joseph Beuys, who used it to represent insulation and warmth. Beuys is also famous for his use of fat as a sculptural material. In Gobel's work, fat and felt are also the things that simultaneously protect and separate us from the outside world. Both his materials and his imagery combine masculine and feminine associations.

Homey in their conception, extravagant in their execution, Gobel's pictures remind us of the eager hobbyist. They appear to be more at home in someone's bedroom than in an art gallery—just like their subjects, or us. Thus, Gobel's practice has come to parallel his concerns.

While Gobel starts with photographs of specific people, his images are ultimately hybrids, portraying types rather than individuals. He is not concerned with the psychology of the sitter as such. This mirrors in some ways the mindset of the men he depicts, who present themselves as both individuals and "bears" or "chubs." How do we know these men are gay? And what kind of gay men might they be?

In the late 1980s, various types of gay men began to identify themselves in a new way, as "bears." They adopted some styles from straight culture— notably, work clothes—and rejected what was then the gay physical ideal: youthful, muscular, and without body hair. Bears think of themselves as more real, earthier, less hung up on appearance, more accepting of a diversity of ages and body types. A subculture in the process of inventing itself needs signs and a medium to transmit them. For bears, the mediums of choice have been independent magazines and, in the past ten years, the internet. These forums have been the places where men separated by age, distance, language, and class have created an elaborate set of styles, behaviors, and signals that have come to characterize an international community, one that is richly inflected but that remains largely invisible to outsiders. Gobel's work draws on the imagery of this community, notably the personal ads that fill the back pages of various magazines. The personal ad makes us the advertiser, consumer, and product advertised; indeed, it is an ad for our wish to consume and be consumed. But if Gobel is changing these images, if the men in his pictures don't really exist, then what are these images ads for?

Gobel's project is utopian. He believes that chubby guys have been relegated to the margins of gay life. So he places them in marginal spaces: the rec room, the basement, the rest stop, the barn, the bar, the backwoods. He is trying to make visible something previously unseen: fat gay men acting normal—that is, not out of control, not jolly, not pathetic. One of the dilemmas is that fat, by its very presence on our bodies, is wildly significant. The men in these pictures recline like odalisques, flaunting their curves. They stare directly out of the picture at the camera, at us.

Gobel's subjects know they're being photographed, but it doesn't bother them. He says that he likes showing fat men who are comfortable with themselves, and his men are not lumpy or unmanageable. Instead, they are sleek, with the promise of abundance that the word *zaftig* implies. They stand close together. Their fat doesn't separate them; it brings them together. In the most ambitious piece here, two men lounge on a bed, perhaps in a

My Studio Is a Dungeon Is the Studio

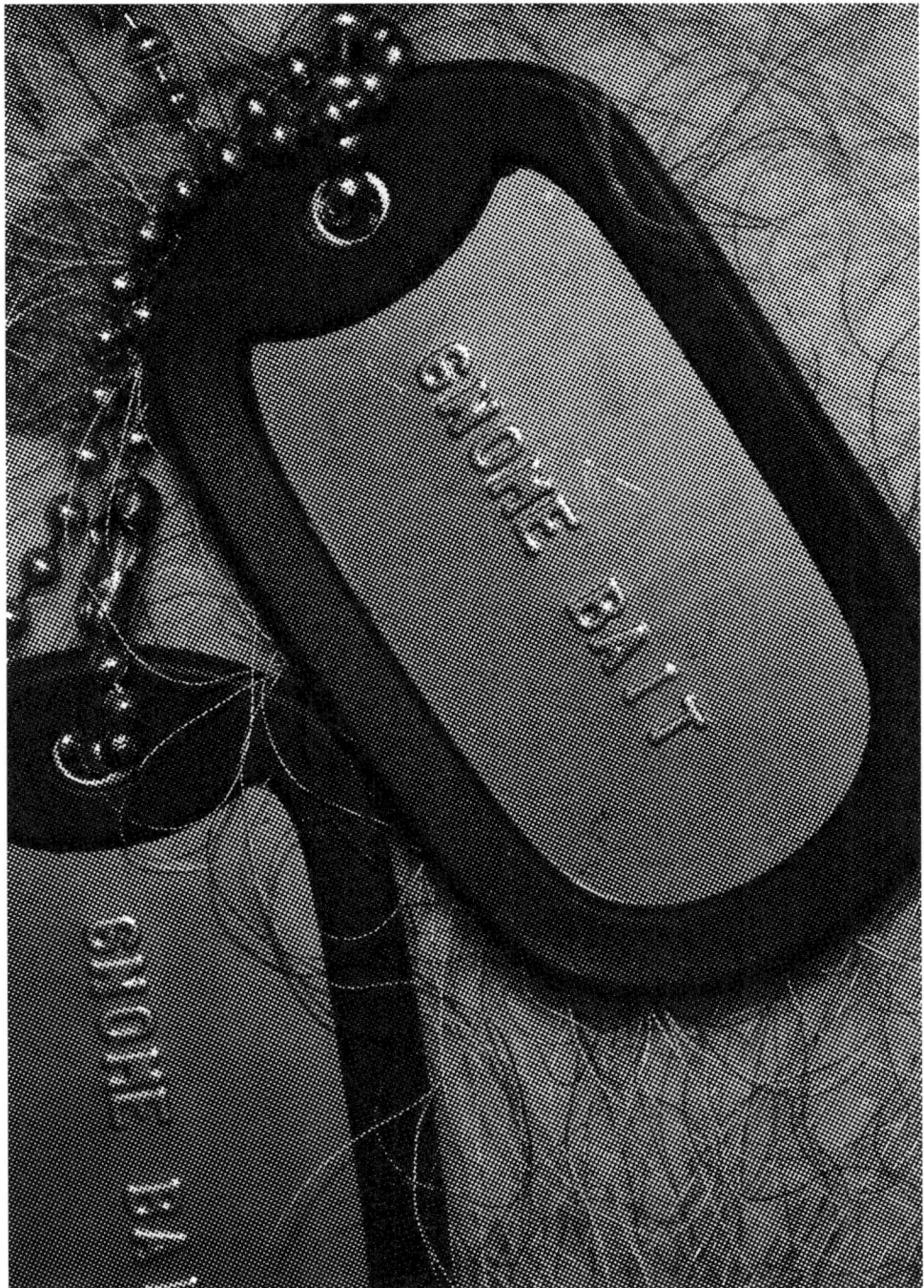

hotel room. Their eyes don't quite converge on us, and this pair of flattened, oblique gazes brings to mind another artist whose paintings examined the place where specific depiction collapses into type: Alex Katz. Gobel's works share with Katz's a sense of leisure, an elusive psychology, and a tension between inflected and uninflected pictorial space.

Gobel says that his latest pictures are about vacations, and there is something profoundly hopeful in the way that his subjects have moved out of doors, staking a greater claim to visibility. The place where we can be ourselves in all our complexity and love freely, isn't that utopia?

MATTHEW BENEDICT:
SHROUD OF TRURO

Artforum, *2001*

THAT PROFOUND SILENCE, THAT ONLY VOICE OF OUR GOD, WHICH I BEFORE
SPOKE OF; FROM THAT DIVINE THING WITHOUT A NAME, THOSE IMPOSTOR
PHILOSOPHERS PRETEND SOMEHOW TO HAVE GOT AN ANSWER; WHICH IS AS
ABSURD, AS THOUGH THEY SHOULD SAY THEY HAD GOT WATER OUT OF STONE;
FOR HOW CAN A MAN GET A VOICE OUT OF SILENCE?

Herman Melville, *Pierre; or, The Ambiguities*

In 1998 the American Museum of Natural History hosted an exhibition
called *Sacred Arts of Haitian Vodou*. In the final section of the show, one
came across several elaborately reconstructed altars, including one for the
Haitian secret society known as the Bizango. There, amid carved phallic
canes, shrouded machetes, and beaded bottles, was a jarring representation
of Bawon Samdi, the Vodou lord of the dead: a twelve-inch figurine of Darth
Vader. Samdi is usually shown in funereal black clothing, with a skull for a
face and carrying a sword. The Bizango's easy grasp of Vader's underlying
attributes was a case of the dry, seminar-room concept of syncretism col-
liding with the reality of a living, breathing practice. With his phallic flared
helmet and implacable menace, Vader fit in easily and pointed up the ways
that Vodou is a living religion, still incorporating images and narratives
from the world around it. Popular culture has become yet another source
for the faithful, taking its place alongside African gods, Catholic saints,
and Masonic symbols.

If a branch of Vodou had sprouted up in turn-of-the-century New England, its artifacts might look something like the work of the thirty-two-year-old, New York–based Matthew Benedict. In form, Benedict's art is kaleidoscopic, incorporating embroidery, printmaking, painting, and found objects, but underlying these varied impulses is a constant sense of swooning, skeptical melancholy. At first glance, his pieces look like odd finds from a Cape Cod antique shop stocked with ephemera from the period between, say, the Civil War and World War I, an era marked by a Yankee faith in progress crossed with an obsession with the supernatural, a time of textile mills and spirit mediums. The odd admixture was forcefully imagined by Herman Melville, one of Benedict's favorite authors of the period, who was capable of creating a character as eighteenth century as Billy Budd and one as twentieth century as the Confidence-Man. It was the heyday of a protomodernism that still dared to imagine a human dimension. World War I brought an end to all that, brutally introducing rampant national-ism wedded to advanced technology and producing in its wake a cynicism that destroyed the vestiges of nineteenth-century humanism. In turn, the war created a cult for the soldiers maimed and killed in its trenches, dead youths who would become poster boys for movements across the political and aesthetic spectrum.

Benedict's work savors this moment of lost innocence while question-ing the extent to which we can ever truly understand the past we venerate. His objects often seem like fragments from a parallel universe where the allegorical practices of the Renaissance never disappeared. This is fitting, given Benedict's concern with the occult and its eruptions into the mundane. In his work, desire, especially gay desire, is seen as the entrance to another realm, a secret society filled with coded imagery. Several of his pieces are bits from extended narratives. A painting and sculpture in a recent show at Alexander and Bonin in New York depicted episodes from the life of a cer-tain Officer Fellows, a 1920s motorcycle policeman whom Benedict portrays on a desolate nocturnal highway, racing past the beacon of a northeastern lighthouse. The works offer a romantic meditation across the gulf of time on a man Benedict could know only in the most glancing way: Happening on some of the officer's equipment in an antique shop, he imagined the details of Officer Fellows's life. The very act of faith involved in their construction is a melancholy, quietly moving gesture. Benedict seems possessed by his possessions, the medium for the voice of a departed spirit. The emotional resonance at the heart of Benedict's paintings and sculptures is hard to rec-oncile with the work's physical reality. His carefully made pieces often have their origins in the most inert or puerile materials. *Looking Glass*, 2000, is a fogged mirror with splintered plastic models of schooners glued around its frame. Nothing has been done to glamorize these little shards; they are simply covered with a unifying coat of off-white paint. At first, the item looks old and dear, but even a cursory examination makes clear that these things are wood and plastic and inexpensive. Still, the longer one views the work, the more one is struck by the emotional power of the mirror wreathed in maritime disaster, a disaster rendered even more poignant by our awareness of its artifice.

Other sculptures contrast this world of nostalgia and shadows with the fantastic, aggressively optimistic physiques of action figures. *The Trumps* (1998–2000), is a parade of the Major Arcana (in a simplified sense, the face cards) of the tarot marching across a long, narrow table. The twenty-two cards making up the Major Arcana are the most emblematic of the deck and supposedly the oldest. They constitute a system of archetypes that can be seen as descriptive of the entire universe. In Benedict's version, each figure is made of a conglomeration of various toys, plastic-doll wrestlers, comic-book heroes, crib ornaments, and so on, following the description of the cards. The tower, for example, is depicted by a souvenir ceramic lighthouse, broken at the tip, with an army man spilling out the top. The artist has tied the disparate elements together by painting them a creamy white and numbering each tableau, retaining the cards' classic order. There is a delightful inventiveness in the way that he has remained faithful to the cards while pillaging Toys "R" Us.

Though Benedict's objects are not antiques, they approximate the look of vintage goods; then, they turn around and draw attention to the approximation. No one would be fooled into believing that *Lucifer* (2000), a bowling ball on a base with a toy attached, is a black patinated bronze. *Rude Screen* (2000), is clearly a row of crutches with plastic figures glued to it. And yet, for a moment, these pieces hover convincingly in the realm of elegance, even piety. Christianity, in particular, turns on the passage between the mundane and the divine, and on some level, all of the artist's work is a wish for transubstantiation. In an earlier series depicting Catholic saints, he takes pains to couple each saint with his or her proper emblem while introducing distancing mechanisms to make sure we remain in the here and now.

Benedict approaches painting in much the same way he does sculpture. With their palette of luscious putties and blue grays that call to mind turn-of-the-century commercial and decorative artists—particularly J. C. Leyendecker, an illustrator best known for his 1920s Arrow shirt advertisements—Benedict's paintings evoke the homosocial world of period magazines filled with tales of manly adventure among the Rough Riders or the Dough Boys. His yearning for the milieu of his subjects is palpable, but his distancing devices prevent our immersion in that universe. Several recent works pile faux on faux, mimicking trompe l'oeil conventions only to give the lie to them the next moment. In *Baking Bread for the Boys* (2000), for example, Benedict has painted a ragged edge along the top of the image that at first seems baffling.

Anyone wishing us to believe we were looking at a "real" painting from the time would have actually torn the edge of the canvas or rendered the painted tear more exactingly. Benedict must be pointing to something else. Like the other clearly contemporary elements in his works, these insistent indications are a second level of secret sign. Benedict is laying bare the fact that every imagination of the past is a fiction, but a fiction that gains its power through our enactment of it. As in a Masonic ritual serving to remind its participants of abstract meanings through a supposedly ancient ceremony, the understanding that the symbol is a symbol doesn't negate its capacity to move us. Indeed, occult practices depend on that understanding for their power to amplify our response. The seeming inconsistencies in Benedict's work make us all adepts, decoders of a clandestine language of modern image and historical misstep.

For all Benedict's admiration of Melville, his work veers closer to that of another New Englander: horror writer H. P. Lovecraft. Melville's generation believed in the possibility of a new mythology appropriate to the New World and equal in power to that of Europe; for Lovecraft, the mythical has become a dimension of terror, and the isolated woods of New England harbor the fragmentary knowledge of old gods, alien and vengeful. Benedict's imagery—founding fathers engaged in Masonic ritual, samplers embroidered with magical symbols—seems haunted by a similar sense of debasement. Conceived in devotion, these pieces flirt with paranoia and can seem mournful in their figuring of desire awoken and then knowingly renounced. But can devotion to a moving, emotionally charged image actually redeem us?

At its source, Benedict's work tackles the mystery of faith, of devotion to a set of venerated images, by pursuing it in all its permutations and approaching it through the lens of desire. His is a peculiar idolatry, but it is heartening that he tries to look seriously at what many artists would never consider. Faith remains the hardest nut for contemporary artists to crack. After the severe jolts of the past century, the replacement of the human by

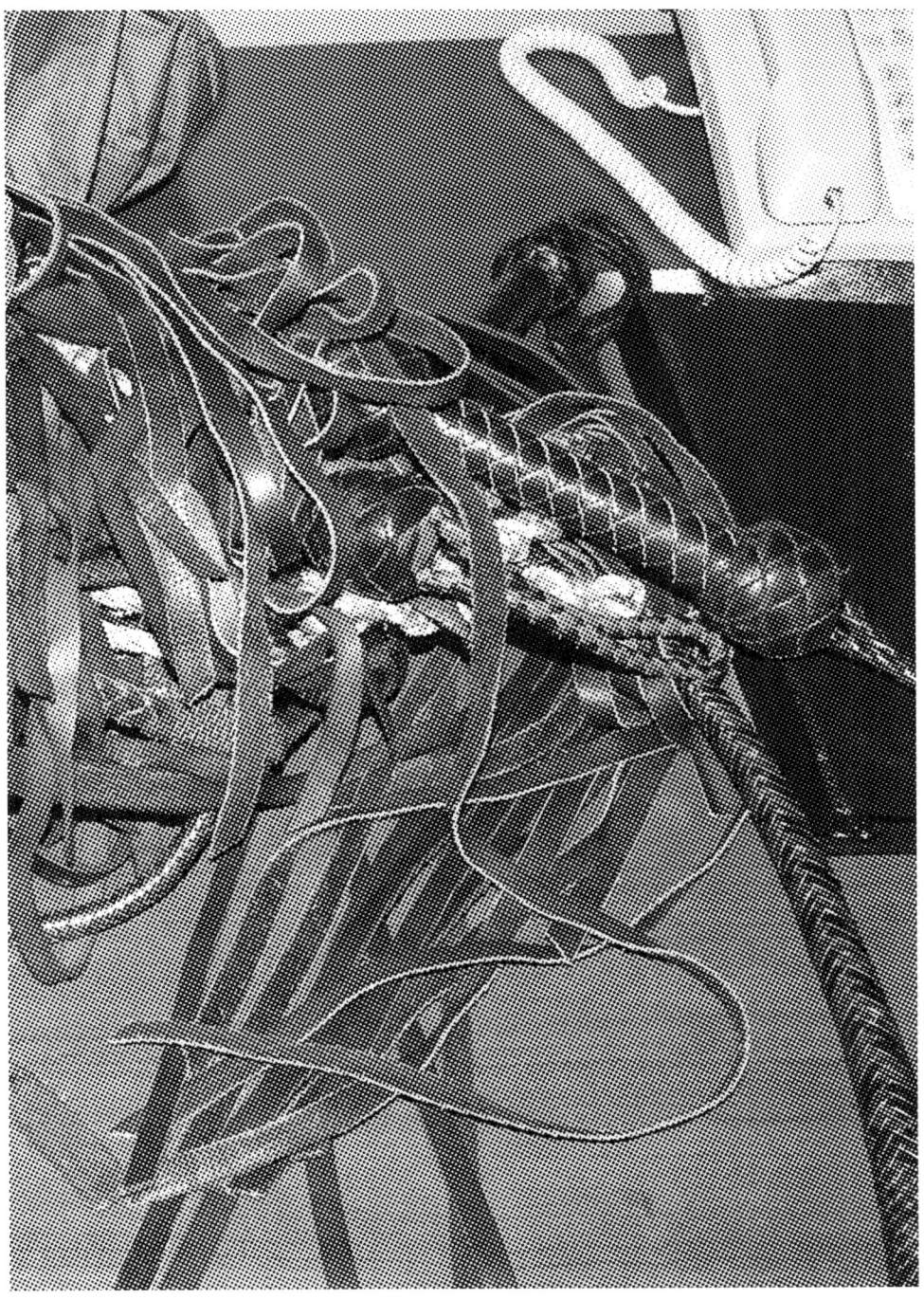

the machine, and the machine by information, it is easier for an artist to profess an interest in, even an obsession with, an idea, image, or activity than to profess a faith in the power of an image, to give himself or herself over to its peculiar charge. Benedict may have located the one place where genuine feeling is still available to us: that place where, fully conscious of the compromised nature of this world, we still dare to imagine and inhabit another one.

JUDIE BAMBER: FURTHER HORIZONS

Pomona College brochure, 2004

Our first idea of the horizon is as a line where the sky meets the earth. The horizon is a line that we look at every day, yet it always recedes from us—a place of aspiration and finitude. In Judie Bamber's new paintings, the horizon exists as motif and thematic lodestone. It anchors the compositions and also provides the metaphor. The physical truth of the horizon is that it is always a plane, not a line, a plane where two membranes engage and whose actual edge is elusive and mutable: a plane like a painting.

We think that to make a painting requires sight, but in fact painting is a species of touching, of enriching the fickle perceptions of the eye with the action of the fingers, arm, and wrist. When we paint something, we touch it, by proxy. Vision prompts action, a series of strokings, whose characteristics become known as the painter's hand. And when we look at paintings, part of us is tracing the history of that hand, noting the agitation of the stroke, the flight or drag of the brush. As we are inventorying those passages of tactility, we are experiencing the syntax of the painting: the pace at which the ideas in the work are being presented, and the order of their presentation.

We experience vision as overall and instantaneous. Touch, however, unfolds through time, and even the glossiest surface provides us with the sensation of rapid movement across and through it, a movement that is a different order of experience from vision's immediacy.

Every painting contains these two kinds of time coiled within it: the flash of vision and the trail of touch. Canny painters know how to make the two agitate and enrich each other.

In these paintings, looking, touching, time, and remembrance are in intimate conjunction.

The quality of Bamber's painting practice has been evident in the ease with which she has grasped the medium's truths and the changes she has rung on them. One of her earliest paintings contained a pair of Masonite cutouts, painted in the style of mid-century commercial illustration and mounted in a box. When the attached tab was slid back and forth, you could make the figures' hands touch and separate, join and part: Emotional connection and distance played out in a toy theater. Later she painted scrupulous still lifes in which single objects (canned fruits; a dead infant bird) were isolated in the midst of monochromatic fields. The diminutive objects were painted at a one-to-one scale, which lent them a surprising grandeur. Single entities took their stand against an indifferent, moody universe. The titling of these paintings usually took the form of emotionally charged phrases. The intimacy of address in the titles disrupted the cool affect of the images; again, distances were mingled, both in the paintings' making and in our encounter with them. Of this group, there is one that stands out as an early emblem of tactility and evanescence: a bruise, rendered with the coolness of Jean Siméon Chardin. Here was an instance of touch and its emotional aftermath fused with minimal chic, to unsettling effect.

These were followed by a series of remarkable images of vaginas also painted at one-to-one scale on chunky wooden panels. These portraits provoked an even greater experience of bodily engagement with the work, not only through their subject matter but also in the proximity they demanded of the viewer. To see them properly, one had to move to a distance that was roughly analogous to that of the painter. This intimacy of viewing hearkened back to the intimacy of making and, through it, to the vulnerability of personal encounter. To paint something is to provide yourself with the permission to look at it, of course, but it is also a way to take ownership of it.

At the root of representational painting is the desire to possess something through its depiction. The painter makes a thing that is not a thing, an image that gains in value because of the care of its making, its rarity. Dutch still lifes, with their hybrid, evanescent flowers, their rare shells and glasses, provided an index of possession designed to withstand the vicissitudes of time, amplified by artistry. The possessions are fleeting; the artist has transfixed them by making them into an image. And yet our act of possessing that image visually is even more fleeting. In this light how can one possess the horizon, even as a view?

Throughout both of these series, Bamber used photographs as aids in the painting. Her next paintings moved photographic reproduction and its many confusions to center stage. She began making watercolors of family photographs, focusing on those that contained images of her father. At this point, she abandoned the one-to-one scale and abstract passages of the earlier paintings. At first puzzling, this strategy makes sense when we try to think about size in relation to the photograph. In the previous paintings, there was a correlation between the physical object depicted and the resulting image. This relationship allowed for a kind of embodiment on the part of the viewer, bringing us back to the solid ground of our daily existence. But photographs are rarely ever the size of what they depict. They almost always rely on reduction or expansion, and even in our hands, they invite us to plunge in, to enter a wonderland of detail that is divorced from our physicality. Bamber's paintings from this time existed, in part, as an excavation of this disembodiment and a rebuke to it.

More than any other material, watercolor requires that the artist cultivate the virtues of patience, control, and grace. The concentration demanded to practice watercolor painting successfully is the polar opposite of the mindset one has while taking a snapshot. There is something poignant and unsettling about using this delicate and rigorous medium to investigate images that were made in moments of supreme casualness.

The photograph is made in an instant and purports to be the record of an instant; the painting takes months. And yet the snapshot's offhandedness can result in documents that retain an enormous power to determine the ways in which we read the narratives of our lives. For Bamber, the early loss of her father and his subsequent presence in her life solely as an image marked a kind of terminus, a place of emotional collapse. Her paintings of these images, then, are an exorcism. The snapshot is remade, and the experience of making it recasts the experience of viewing it. The image's power is confronted and worked through, by being turned into material. In the arc of Bamber's practice, these are her history paintings, in which the action of recalling the past is made complex and haunting, not by the easy palaver of nostalgia, but by the scrupulous translation of image into deft maneuvers of hand and brush, alchemies of pigment and water.

Bamber's paintings have moved from genre to genre: still life, portrait, history painting—and have come now to perch in landscape or more accurately seascape. For the past few years, she has been painting the Pacific shore near Southern California, first in watercolor and then in oil.

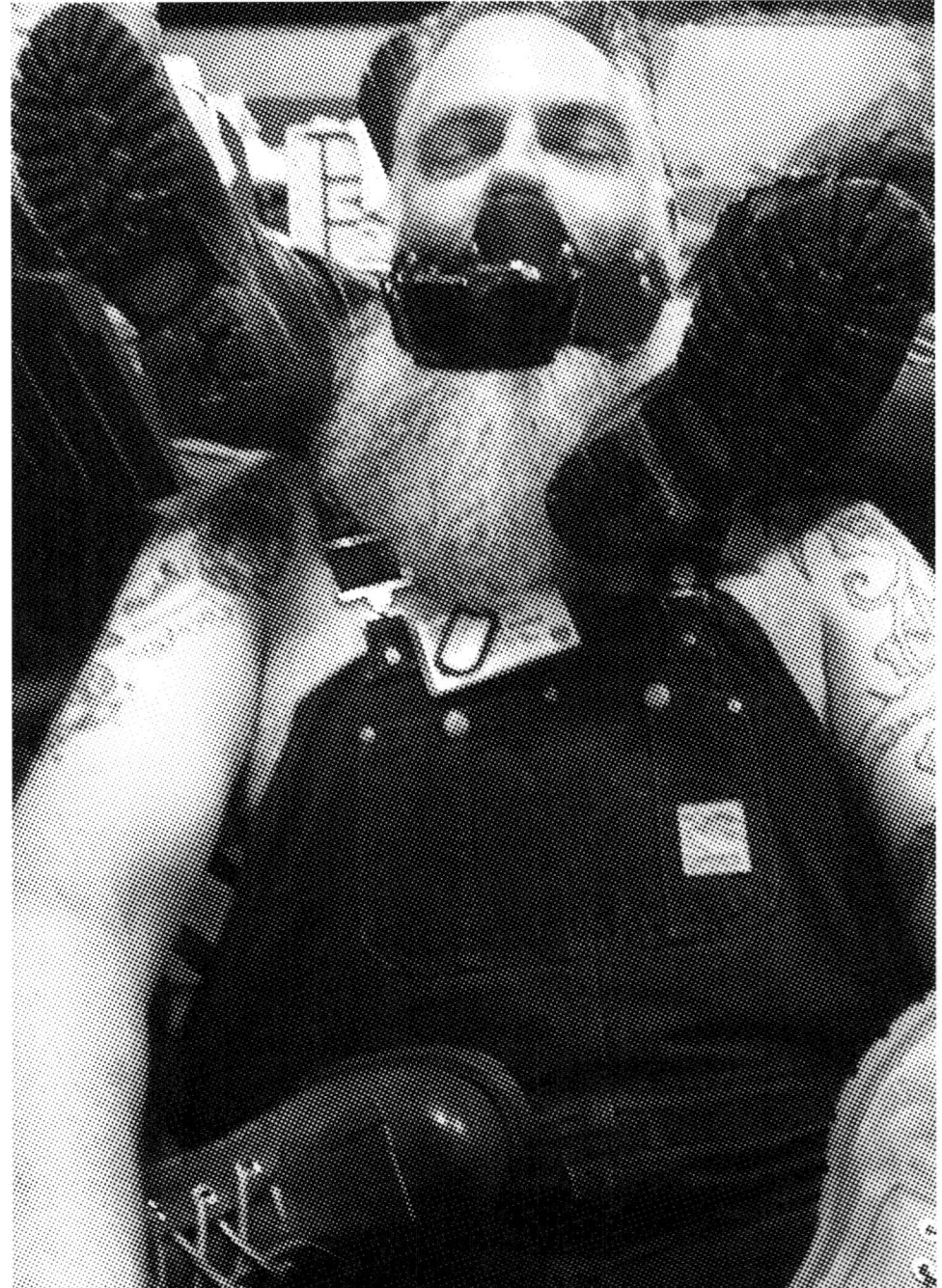

As records of an image, the paintings look like one thing; as records of a sensory experience, they look like something else entirely. In the first place, they represent a glance, the sea and sky fused in an instant. And yet, when it is time to consider the act of their creation, we can see these paintings as the unfolding of hours of looking and moving. They are the representation of a moment but the literal embodiment of much greater amounts of time. As one looks at them, they pass rapidly between these two states: seemingly graspable, slyly baffling. Their subtlety in orchestrating the confusion of those boundaries echoes the subtlety of the passage from water to sky in the image, the way in which we are unable to say exactly when we have shifted from looking at one to looking at the other.

These paintings make it clear that there is a world of difference between the deployment of ambiguity from cowardice and the investigation of the indeterminate as a tool for thought. Our search for the edge, as it moves from our desire to resolve the image, to our understanding of the impossibility of doing so, is an experiential re-creation of the moment the paintings depict. That point in time is captured in all of its complexity. These paintings reproduce the way in which abstract thought is an ordering principle of vision. When we are in the moment, we are in a place of the concrete and the abstract simultaneously.

It is important that these are paintings of the Pacific—the terminating point of American westward expansion. From a place of completion, we gaze into a haze of potential that arrests our gaze and yet offers us back nothing that could orient us. We have come to the end and are released, ultimately into ourselves. From a moment of ending and regret, the paintings wrest an injunction to action, to movement and continuance.

SEVEN QUICK NOTES ON WRITING AN ARTIST'S STATEMENT

Previously Unpublished, 2004

1   Tell the truth. Describe your work and your life as it is, not as you think someone wants to hear it to be. Don't anticipate your reader's biases.

2   Write often. Get into the habit of writing about what you do on a regular basis. It will give you much more material to pick from when the time comes for you to make a formal statement.

3   Rewrite often. It's much easier to edit and rewrite an existing piece than it is to generate something new on deadline. Revising allows you to sharpen ideas and cut out redundancies. Allow yourself to make messy first drafts and then go back into them.

4   Use specific examples. Watch out for generalities about your work. If you want to make a point about how an idea functions for you, show how it functions in a specific piece. Don't feel like what you have to say has to be equally true of everything you make. Practice describing pieces as if your audience were sightless.

5   Use history sparingly. Don't assume that everyone will know what you mean when you refer to the work of other artists or artistic movements; their ideas may well be antithetical to yours, and your point may be lost.

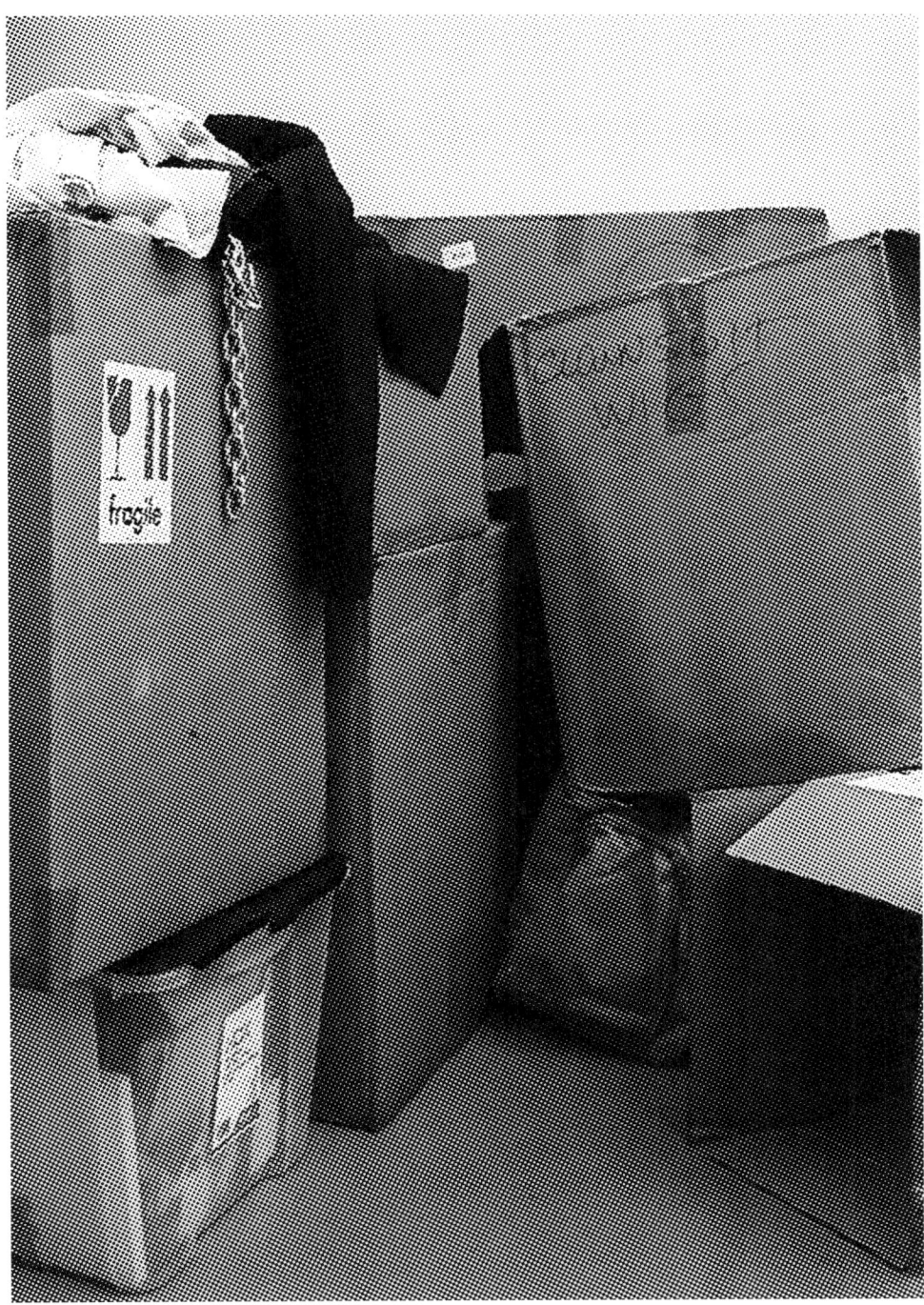

6   Big words do not make your work look better or make it any more meaningful.

7   Phrases to watch out for:

   A   *As a* . . . is often used to sneak in biographical information and as justification for the work, for example, "As a veteran, my work is concerned with the ideologies of bodily distress . . . ," "As a volcano survivor, I want my pieces to have a certain vibrancy . . ." Find another way to tell people who you are and why you do what you do.

   B   *The viewer is invited* . . . or any of its variations. Often, folks use this to try to force people into a specific experience of the work. It begs the questions of "how" and "why" the viewer is invited.

   C   *Interest, interesting, interests* . . . Try writing about your enthusiasms rather than your interests.

   D   *The body* . . . Resist the temptation to make an idea sound more theoretical by sticking the word *the* in front of it. Always ask yourself, "Which body?" or "Whose body?"

Finally, imagine that you are writing in sand, not carving in stone. Your artist's statement is not a contract made for all eternity; it is a snapshot of your thinking about your practice at a specific moment.

KATHY ACKER: "BECAUSE I WANT TO LIVE FOREVER IN WONDER"

Lust for Life: On the Writings of Kathy Acker, *2006*

1. Dates

I'm listening to the X-Ray Spex single "Oh Bondage Up Yours!" backed with "I'm a Cliché," a record made in 1977. It's one of the precious pieces of vinyl I bought at Bleeker Bob's, the first store in New York to stock punk records, both imported and homegrown. At the time, buying singles was a crapshoot: You knew nothing about the bands since most of them had barely been together long enough to make a record. Every week there were a dozen singles by bands you'd never heard of. You picked out the ones with the best covers, the most shocking names, the colored vinyl—and for every ten you bought, eight were good, and of those eight, four would be incredible—a few life-altering.

"Oh Bondage . . ." starts like this: An adolescent, lightly congested voice comes out of an echoing void. "Some people think little girls should be seen and not heard, but I think OH BONDAGE UP YOURS ONE TWO THREE FOUR!"[1] On the final word, a sloppy drum roll, and the band has already started, too fast and crashing into each other: guitar, bass, and drums at once, topped by a bleating saxophone that's playing something that's not melody exactly and isn't a riff either, mostly two notes alternating like a siren. Buoyed by the band, the singer (Poly Styrene, born Marianne Elliott-Said, who was nineteen when this was recorded) starts bellowing about being tied up, being a victim, being a "slave to you all." She's a teenage mixed-race girl, and her voice is shouting desire and disgust; she's squawking the lines someone wrote for a slut in a porn flick and shattering them into a new kind of life, a life that is dazzling and sickening at once. I want to scream along, display myself in all my confused wanting, to be a little girl who is seen *and* heard.

The 1970s were a time when the obscene was the last refuge of the sane. A bloated culture made by corporations paraded itself everywhere as common sense and sensual bliss at the same time. Collective political action had collapsed into a morass of "self"-cultivation that blinded people to the extent of their oppression. Cities festered in anger, poverty, and debris that no normal person wanted to live around. So that left all the other people, the abnormals, to make anything they wanted out of the crap that was left lying around. Those people made hip-hop, punk rock; they made art of cellophane and dime-store kitsch. They made performances in which they braved the city streets for a year, or they found old stag movies and made them into art events by running them over and over again. Buildings were abandoned, and populations were left to shift for themselves. The explosion of innovation that marked the art worlds of the early 1960s had cooled and condensed into batches of new establishments, but there was another generation ready to take up the strategies that had been abandoned, an artistic generation for whom reaching for the scissors and glue was more natural than reaching for the paintbrush or the typewriter.

It's hard today to understand the unique valences of collaging—how difficult it was then. Now "cut" and "paste" are computer keyboard commands that carry no charge at all, since they are always accompanied by the possibility of the command "undo." Before the digital age, cutting always carried with it the acknowledgment of loss: To cut up and recombine entailed a leap of faith since the resulting thing might never be as good as the thing you destroyed to make it. But what about now, when every act of destruction can be erased as soon as it's enacted?

2. Fan

I first heard about Kathy Acker's work from a teacher. In 1980 I was an art major at Bard College, satisfying an English requirement by taking a tutorial with the poet Robert Kelly. I had said that I was going to be writing "performance scripts," but having forgotten that writing plays actually entailed sitting down and writing, I wasn't making much headway. One afternoon, I found myself in front of Robert explaining an elaborate system I had worked out for a puppet show, whose script would change from performance to performance because it would be composed of small sections that would be reconfigured by spinning a segmented wheel over and over again at the performance's beginning. While I had charted out several of the narrative snippets that would be grist for this chance operation, I hadn't bothered to actually write any of them. I had probably gotten the idea from making film loops with found footage in the previous years, but I hadn't made the leap from found footage to found text. I was, in a word, winging it: a twenty-year-old with a lot of ideas culled from other artists but with very few of the work habits that might make those ideas anything other than vague possibilities. That didn't stop me from explaining those possibilities to Robert, who finally responded to my meanderings with an astute and patient suggestion: "There's a writer whose work I think you'll like. Her name is Kathy Acker."

> Even prior to college, I was an art-world baby. When I was fourteen years old, I would sneak out of my high school in order to hang around with the downtown avant-garde filmmakers and painters who were probably far more fascinated by my schoolgirl uniform than by any other aspect of whatever's called "me."[2]

Shortly after talking to Robert, I was back in New York City and tracked down two books: *The Childlike Life of the Black Tarantula by the Black Tarantula* and *The Adult Life of Toulouse Lautrec by Toulouse Lautrec*. The covers were confusing. Only by repeatedly checking the spine and the copyright page was I able to determine that these were Kathy Acker books. The editions are on my table in front of me right now. They are squat and simple in design, obviously the products of a small press. They reminded me of the artists' books I used to go downtown to buy at Printed Matter, and of the Grove Press edition of *My Secret Life by Anonymous*, a pornographic Edwardian memoir that my parents had on their living-room shelf and that I used to sneak into my room and masturbate to.

To say I read Acker's books with growing enthusiasm would be an understatement. They were the first books in years that I read in the same way I listened to favorite albums: over and over, until the pauses between songs were as much a part of the experience as the songs themselves. I read them like they were letters written to me. Why did I love those two small books? In part because they contained passages like this:

"You're a raving maniac!!" I screech at the top of my lungs. I can't believe artists can do everything! Artists can know all the joy and misery
and terrifyingness and usefulness because artists don't have to suffer!
Even though I can barely walk; I'm always in pain; I'm always hungry.

All I think about is sex. At night, nights, I lie alone in bed; I see
the right leg of every sexy man I've ever seen on the street, the folds of
cloth over and around the ooo ooo. . . . I ache and I ache and I ache. I
feel a big huge hole inside of my body. I see a man I like about to stick
his cock in my hot pussy.[3]

Here was someone who wrote about artists and about fucking, two
things I thought about a lot. Someone who had a middle-class New York
upbringing like mine and who read porn and was willing themselves out of
their family and into some new, different social configuration that meant
escape and also meant the possibility of making things, of being around
other people who made things. She induced in me a state that I can only
refer to as cunt envy. The artists she wrote about were the ones whose work
I had sneaked out of high school to look at, and she wrote with alternating sympathy and disdain about their moneygrubbing, their tribal rituals,
and glamorous poverties. Like the characters in her books, I, too, walked
around New York looking to get a show and to get laid, hanging around the
porn bookstores in Times Square fingering books like *The Gay Whores* while
checking out the crotches of my fellow patrons.

Kathy Acker books placed the act of reading at their center. They made
me think that my own reading wasn't useless, that it could be generative,
that I could "find" text in the same way that I found footage for my films or
images in the old *National Geographics* I cut up to make cassette cases or
postcards to send to my friends. I had read William Burroughs and Samuel
Delany years earlier; both had confounded me. It wasn't until reading Acker
that I understood that other writers' narratives could be chopped up and
reconfigured to suit my needs. While her books were formally familiar to
me because of the art I'd seen growing up, the stories they told and the images they contained were of those things I aspired to.

Throughout the 1970s, while artists reinvented cities' failing industrial landscapes as new places for making work, gay men colonized those
spaces as a sexual terrain, living out pornographers' fervid scenarios. Acker
shows that the exultation of that freedom is only a prelude to further ambiguities. Her characters often escape the family, but like the singer in the
Velvet Underground's "I'm Set Free," they often find they are "set free to

find a new illusion."[4] Her strategy of fracturing and remaking culture presents writing as a way of moving through the world, one that never ceases. Stories don't conclude; they simply breed more stories.

I've often thought about why Acker's work has so much appeal for queer readers. In her literary world, there are two groupings: family, which is the birthplace of the state; and friends, a confederation known variously as pirates, artists, whores. In part, they are her version of Burroughs's Wild Boys. Her characters are engaged in one long escape from the family/state into the band, the tribe. For queers, the option of family is foreclosed, so the band is all we have left. To be marked by one's sexuality, indeed, to be marked as sexual first and foremost is the fate that her characters offer themselves up to: "Sex in public: the streets made themselves for us to walk naked down them take out your cock and piss over me."[5]

It's belaboring an already overstated point to connect Acker's work with punk. After a while, it was a liability for her to be saddled with the tag *punk writer* because it so narrowly defined her. It is useful to remember, however, how much punk was a music shaped by the art that predated it, art that was modest and homemade like Fluxus, austere and repetitive like minimalism, or strategy based like conceptualism. One of her earliest romantic involvements was with P. Adams Sitney, the leading theorist of New York's avant-garde film scene. As much as Acker's work is indebted to the cutups of Burroughs, it also resembles the found footage films of Bruce Conner, Ken Jacobs, and Peter Kubelka. Indeed, her heroines, questing for self-knowledge, could easily have stepped out of Maya Deren's *Meshes in the Afternoon*, a film where the female protagonist embarks on an ambiguous journey of self-definition/destruction. (Indeed, it might be interesting to study the varieties of Deren's influence on Acker, including both of their writings on Haiti.) In the early 1970s, the boundaries between the worlds of visual art, performance, and film were much more permeable than they are now. Artists crossed them easily and passed ideas back and forth readily. In New York, at least, much of what was later called *punk* was first identified as *art rock*. "I remember, when I was fifteen, Jack Smith telling me that what he most wanted to do was build a huge dome somewhere in North Africa. Whoever entered this dome would tell Jack his or her dreams and instantaneously Jack would make a movie of this dream or series of dreams. Movie would be shown twenty-four hours a day."[6]

What marks Acker as an artist of her generation is the way she combined formal editing strategies that had previously been used to produce an effect of intellectual distance with content of overwhelming intimacy. This part is the lesson she learned from the Marquis de Sade, but it is also present in much of Bruce Conner's work. It is also the technique of hip-hop: A record is in itself an utterly alienated and impersonal thing. The needle touches it, and it plays. The best you can hope to do is consume the music like a reader consumes a book. But by disrupting the expected use of the record by replaying the bass line over and over, by changing the sound levels, by extension and compression, the record is made back into a musical instrument. Acker remakes the possibilities of text into her instruments, by treating text as a thing, a material to be sliced up and pushed around. She skins the characters and narratives she finds and constructs her own suit out of them.

In a way, reading Acker regresses me, bringing me back to the desire to be in the land of make-believe. This is, of course, the same effect as pornography, a form that makes a place for us to escape into. Porn novels are like fairy tales before Charles Perrault got his hands on them: episodic, morally ambiguous, repetitive, more interested in the arrangement of the characters than in emotional depth or forward narrative motion. For the most part, they were written anonymously by people who had to churn them out on a schedule. (In the late 1970s, I went to a porn publisher looking for work drawing covers of the books. What I remember vividly of that visit is a row of rumpled men seated at typewriters turning out the novels. Each typewriter was being fed paper off of larger rollers; I presume the hacks were being paid by the inch.)

In the end, the puppet show I tortured Robert with never got made, and the tutorial is marked "incomplete" on my transcripts to this day. But in pointing me to Acker, Robert gave me something that every artist needs: an ideal audience, a person I could treat like a confidant and an ally even though she didn't have the slightest idea that I was alive. I wanted to turn my work into a dialogue, to insert it into a larger discussion, to be part of the world of artists I had admired growing up. Encountering Kathy Acker's work made me feel I could do that. In the twenty-five years since his suggestion, I've had occasion to thank Robert mentally for uttering that sentence. I'm doing so again now.

3. *Low*

In 1990 I finally worked with Kathy. It is more accurate to say that I purchased her attention. I had been living in San Francisco since 1984 and, over the years, had gotten to know a few people who were also friends of hers.

Because of that, I had also come to think of myself as some part of the tribe that I had been so entranced with growing up. Back in New York, the cluttered broken collage aesthetic of the late 1970s and early 1980s had yielded to work that reveled in machined polish and theoretical gloss. The new work claimed to expose the hollowness of commodity culture and paradoxically produced fabulously successful commodities. For the first time, it was possible to make a decent living as an American artist: to appear in magazines, to purchase a country home, to approximate chic. I was preparing my first solo show in New York and persuaded my gallery there to hire Kathy to write a catalog essay. Once she agreed, we met. I showed her a bunch of slides of my work and talked to her in the standard way I talked to everyone about what I thought I was doing, and then she interviewed me. Did I have any recurring dreams? What was my childhood like? I told her about growing up on the West Side in New York City, with parents of differing races; about my younger sister; about being an art nerd in high school. Our talk was hedged by my overeagerness and her diffidence.

Months later, she sent in her text for the book. When I read it, I was puzzled. I thought the parts of it that looked more like fiction were somewhat successful, and the parts that were written as traditional art criticism, with their references to the mythic and to American optimism, were labored and off the mark. More than that, I wasn't seeing myself in the story. There wasn't even anything gay in it. I wanted to tell her that it was okay, she didn't have to write an "art essay"; all she had to do was transform me, make me over into one of the desperate, smart, horny outsiders who populated her books; all she had to do was understand through looking at my work that I had read her work and I had understood. In 1990 I was so impatient to get through that door that I tried cutting the line. I wanted Kathy to take me seriously, for me to reside in her thoughts in a way that would echo how she resided in mine. The book that resulted from our collaboration is a slim hardback similar in format to the earliest of the books of hers I had bought in art school, except that this one was full of color reproductions of things I had made.

Chain-store chain-smoke
I consume you all
Chain-gang chain-mail
I don't think at all

Oh bondage up yours

Oh bondage no more
Oh bondage up yours
Oh bondage no more[7]

It doesn't work that way. Even though queers can choose their tribe, artists can't choose their clan—the clutch of people who will see their work for what it is and value it—any more than one can choose the person who's going to fall in love with you. Artistic communication is more complex than simple identification. My own convictions about the similarities in what we did were no guarantee that she would see it that way. I hadn't reckoned on the one thing that we perhaps had most in common: the highly cultivated narcissism we each used to make our work.

At the time, the project felt like a misfire. But one of its results was that we became friends. Soon after, she moved to San Francisco, and I saw her a great deal more. She came to the Thanksgiving dinner my boyfriend and I hosted. I read her new books as they were published, with varying degrees of enthusiasm. We both began to teach at the San Francisco Art Institute and chatted in its coffee shop about various tattooists. As a friend, she was charming, flirtatious, vital, and infuriating by turns. I think it was a marker of how far our friendship had progressed that I finally saw the ugly side of her competitiveness: At one point we had both been asked to be guest lecturers at a school in the East Bay. She seemed uncomfortable sharing the spotlight. During my talk, she publicly corrected me with a tiny flourish of meanness. That day, I gave her a drawing; she barely acknowledged it. By the mid-1990s we saw little of each other. I moved back to New York, hearing shortly after about her illness.

4. Heard

I started this essay with the charge to talk about the relation between Kathy Acker's work and that of visual artists, in part through a history of our collaboration on *Low*. But that's an awfully simple word, *collaboration*, masking as it does the crosscurrents of influence, erasure, devotion, and competition. Instead, I'd rather substitute two questions: What did she make of my work? What did I make of hers?

After I learned that Kathy had died, I picked up a copy of *Low* and reread her essay. In it, she wrote about innocence, hysteria, American optimism, Hansel and Gretel, and William Blake. At the end is a transfiguration of one of the dreams she had asked me about: a dream in which I wander around in the American Museum of Natural History until the dioramas begin to fill with water, the animals moving inside the murk, the glass shattering, leaving me floundering waist-deep in sharks. I see now how she captured much of what I have become as an artist. Her writing was more predictive than descriptive. When it was written, I valued cleverness, the operation of my own mind through my work. I wanted my ideas taken seriously as part of an art historical argument. In time, I've come to value more and more the emotional life of my work. I care less about ideological positions and more about inhabiting the moment of creation, manifesting my pleasures through making. I used to wish to be thought of as an adult. Now my work seems more and more to revolve around the images and stories of childhood, my own and others'.

In 1998 I had a small, two-room exhibition that I titled *Feeder2 and corollary*. In the first room of the show, I built a cabin, seven by seven by ten feet, out of steel and gingerbread. In the second room were four things: two prints of a blurred photograph of a snow-covered cabin, a vitrine containing a six-pack of bottles of Brer Rabbit brand molasses, and a one-hour videotape in which I am fed over and over again by another man.

The cabin (*Feeder2*) was large enough for adults to enter if they crouched under the doorway. Children ran right in. The smell of gingerbread, enticing in the gallery, turned thick and buttery once you got inside the house. Its temptation proved too much for many people, who broke off chunks of the piece to nibble on. The first *Feeder* was a piece I had made for the show in 1990, a large steel cage with a waist-high slot. In her essay Kathy turned it into the "animal-restraining cage" that the witch locks Hansel into. The shape of "Feeder" is that of the witch's cookie hut but also that of the prototypical American log cabin, the one Abe Lincoln was born in, that of Uncle Tom's.

You need molasses to make gingerbread, but the bottles in the back room are linked together like a six-pack of soda pop. On the video, a shirtless Black man encourages(?) forces(?) me to eat donuts, pizza, sandwiches, watermelon, chocolate. He pours milk down my throat. Is this care, subservience, slavery, abuse? Am I being nourished, punished, infantilized, fucked, reduced to a hole to be filled? After seeing the tape, one had to pass the gingerbread house again to exit. I like to think that the show began to ask the question: What happens when we get what we want? Is this what bliss looks like, smells like?

It's a question Kathy taught me to ask.

I like to think that this is how I finally returned the volley of her writing about me: I used her thoughts and images as a blueprint for my liberation and as a brick to smash the illusion that that liberation embodied. It had never occurred to me to look at the Hansel and Gretel story, to inhabit it, until I reread that essay and let those words work on me. Ultimately, that is how artists work together, by allowing each other's ideas to work on them. I no longer believe that I can find safety in a three-minute punk squall. But I can add my voice to that noise; I can make something that echoes that call. I'm sorry that Kathy was never able to see the ways in which I tried to make use of what she gave me. Sometimes that's how collaboration happens: blindly, in halting fragments that spill through time.

I had told her about a dream, and she made a book out of it, a book that also embodied the dream I hadn't dared to tell her about—the dream of belonging. Her writing is partially the fulfillment of Jack Smith's plan: the arena where dreams are confessed and made into gigantic art to be seen round the clock, the palace of wonder.

I hope that this essay contains the monstrousness of my desire. It is part of my story that all I've ever wanted to be is a character in a book. I've come to know, through experience, that that isn't as nice a feeling as I thought it would be and also that getting one's wishes fulfilled carries with it a responsibility to a work whose final form can barely be guessed at.

Thrash me crash me
Beat me till I fall
I wanna be a victim
For you all

Oh bondage up yours
Oh bondage no more
Oh bondage up yours
Oh bondage no more

Repeat first verse[8]

Notes

1. "Oh Bondage Up Yours!" by X-Ray Spex. Poly Styrene, recorded live at the Roxy Club. Virgin Records Ltd., 1977. 331/3 rpm. https://youtube.com/watch?v=aTfgWegud7o.

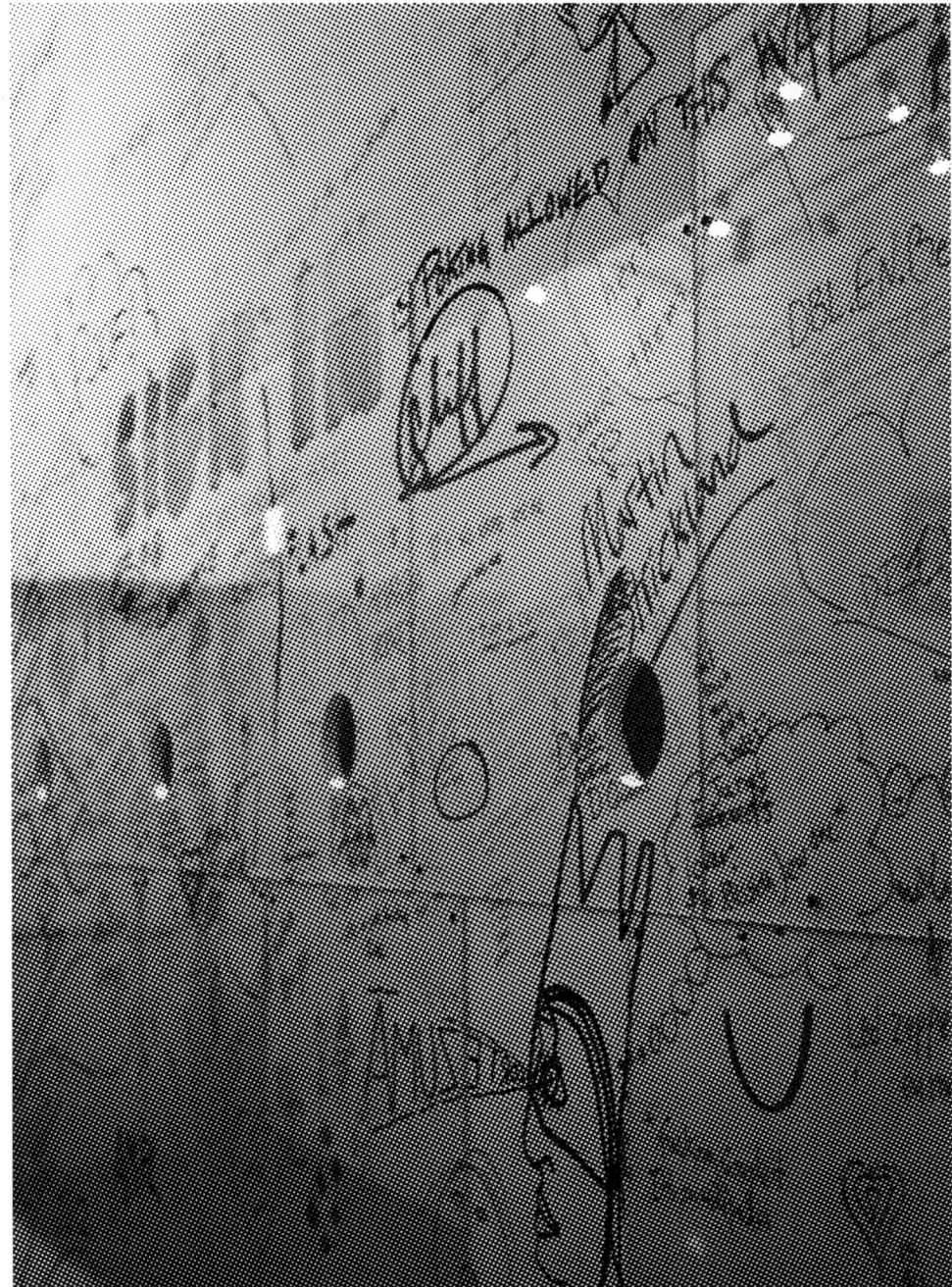

2. Kathy Acker, "Critical Languages," in *Bodies of Work* (London: Serpent's Tail, 1997), 83.

3. Kathy Acker, *The Adult Life of Henry Toulouse Lautrec* (New York: TVRT Press, 1975), 6.

4. "I'm Set Free" by Lou Reed, recorded March 1, 1969, Track 7, *The Velvet Underground*, T.T.G. Studios, LP.

5. Kathy Acker, *Great Expectations* (New York: Open Book/Station Hill Press, 1982), 113.

6. Acker, "Critical Languages," 83.

7. "Oh Bondage Up Yours!" by X-Ray Spex. Poly Styrene, recorded live at the Roxy Club. Virgin Records Ltd., 1977. 331/3 rpm. https://youtube.com/watch ?v=aTfgWegud7o.

8. "Oh Bondage Up Yours!" by X-Ray Spex.

JIM HODGES: "THEME FROM MANTRAP"

Jim Hodges: 1991, 1992, *2007*

It's a scene from innumerable movies, TV shows, and cartoons: In the attic, in the basement, in the swamp, in the ruined castle, the heroes, flashlight in hand, peer into the darkness. While strings on the soundtrack thrum discord, they step forward cautiously, feeling their way, and all at once it happens: They plunge face-first into the ancient cobwebs that fill the space. Spinning, shocked, they attempt to brush the sticky web from their eyes, spit it out of their mouths, and disentangle themselves. In the film, it's a small shock that sets you up for the bigger one to come as they blunder into the claws of the monster. In these works of Jim Hodges, that moment is restaged and posited as the climax, the point in which rapture and disgust collide, as an encounter with questions of representation, material desire, and symbol.

Tidy, shimmering, and reserved in affect, these pictures are easy to overlook. Originally, Hodges installed them in the margins, tucked them into the corners of galleries, too high or low for normal viewing. In group show situations, this often meant that Hodges's work was one you would find last, the unexpected surprise that made you reconsider the whole. When you finally become aware of them in space and get up close enough to see them, their seeming fragility makes you nervous, painfully aware of your own bulk and awkwardness. They are visual and conceptual conundrums: a fragile, organic thing mimicked by a sturdy machine-made one; an animal's functional nest made from a human's adornment. The chains are representations of spiderwebs, and yet they are often combined with items like jeans that have not been transformed into representations of anything else, that simply seem to be themselves. This combination of the worked and the unworked in one piece ensnares us in the tangles of its syntax. In *No One Ever Leaves* (1992), are we supposed to pretend to believe the scenario that the piece posits at first glance? That someone left their jacket in the corner and some spider wove a web over it? Obviously not. Yet it is also true that while we believe that Hodges made the chain into a web, we are not at all sure that he "made" the cast-aside jacket. So the piece combines two different experiences of time: the abrupt gesture of shucking off and dropping the jacket, and the patient construction of the web. What are the two doing together? Is the web woven in memorial to that quick gesture? Is the jacket the bait in the trap, the dense skin that a tick wraps himself in to entice us? Look again: It's incorrect to speak of the jacket and the web as separate things. On closer examination, we see that the web is anchored to the jacket as well as the wall. From a structural point of view, they depend on each other for support and need to be read as one unit. Hodges consistently works back and forth between formal rigor and symbolic density. He is inspired both by the structural clarity of Richard Serra and by the narrative allusiveness of Paul Thek.

When the Dadaists blasted open the material possibilities for sculpture at the beginning of the twentieth century, they forced a confrontation with the notion that artists transformed materials. No more imaginings that marble could be made flesh or bronze, cloth. That sleight of hand was reserved for sideshows and waxworks. The sculptors of the early 1960s embraced this eclectic material palette, incorporating neon, rubber, fabric, dirt, and a host of other substances, but avoided the associative implications embedded in those materials. Instead, they substituted a narrative of process: That lead is there in that configuration as the result of a material process, not because of a symbolic imperative. That is what the lead did when I acted on it, and the associative chain stops there.

It fell to Hodges's generation of sculptors, inspired, in part, by artists like Joseph Beuys, Carolee Schneemann, and Bruce Nauman, to combine the formal structuring concerns of the 1960s generation with the excavation of the narrative implications of varied materials. A material like rubber could no longer be imported from the outside world simply as a formal choice; it remained saturated with all of the associations it had outside of the gallery, and those associations became fair game for the orchestrations of the artist. Consequently, the dense symbolism in Hodges's work arises in two ways: through the piece's imagery and through its material associations.

My Studio Is a Dungeon Is the Studio

First, imagery: A chain is both a line and a volume, flickering between two and three dimensions. A chain is a serial structure based on a module, the link. Its ultimate size is not predetermined; it can be added to indefinitely. In this way, it bears some formal resemblance to the grid, which rose to prominence as a compositional strategy in the art of the 1960s. But unlike the grid, it cannot be presumed to be an associatively neutral form. The chains that Hodges uses admit to their history as both adornments and constraints. They are both the chains of the Fourteenth Street jewelry shops and the Eleventh Avenue dungeons, the chains of dandies and rough trade.

Fashioned into a web, the chain becomes a way of delimiting space without filling it. While we may be unable to physically occupy the space on the other side of the web, we can still explore it visually. This is a way of structuring a sculpture in which inside and outside exist in uneasy relation to each other, and it is this permeability that marks much of Hodges's work. The psychological message of this formal strategy is that the "I" that makes this work is as fragmented and provisional as the viewer that encounters it. Hodges's work is rife with veils, mirrors, punctures, and shadings. In its unassuming way, his work piles together contradiction in order to produce a figure of doubt.

The web is the emblematic structure of postmodernism. The ability for any juncture in the web to become a hub, a leaping-off place to other associations and connections, marks a break with left to right, up and down systems of information organization. We think of webs as social organizations that privilege connectivity instead of hierarchy.

The materials: These are not simply webs but quite specifically spiderwebs. Cobwebs are one of the symbols of age and disuse. Cobwebs are sticky and excreted. Spiders weave webs to capture food and attract mates. The vibration of the web's strands transmits information to the spider about their prey. Some spiders rebuild them every day. But these webs are bright, new, and formed from machine-made metal. They are fixed in space and change at a rate so slow as to be invisible to us. Prior to embarking on these pieces, Hodges was making drawings on Scotch tape, a material he felt to be less pretentious than traditional materials and more available to his own inflection. Inevitably, people raised questions about the tape's permanence. In part, the metal cobweb is his riposte. But the image also forms a continuum with his previous themes: connection, humility, adhesion. Enticement and trapping, reflection and adornment, community and isolation—all of these are elements in Hodges's emotional alchemy.

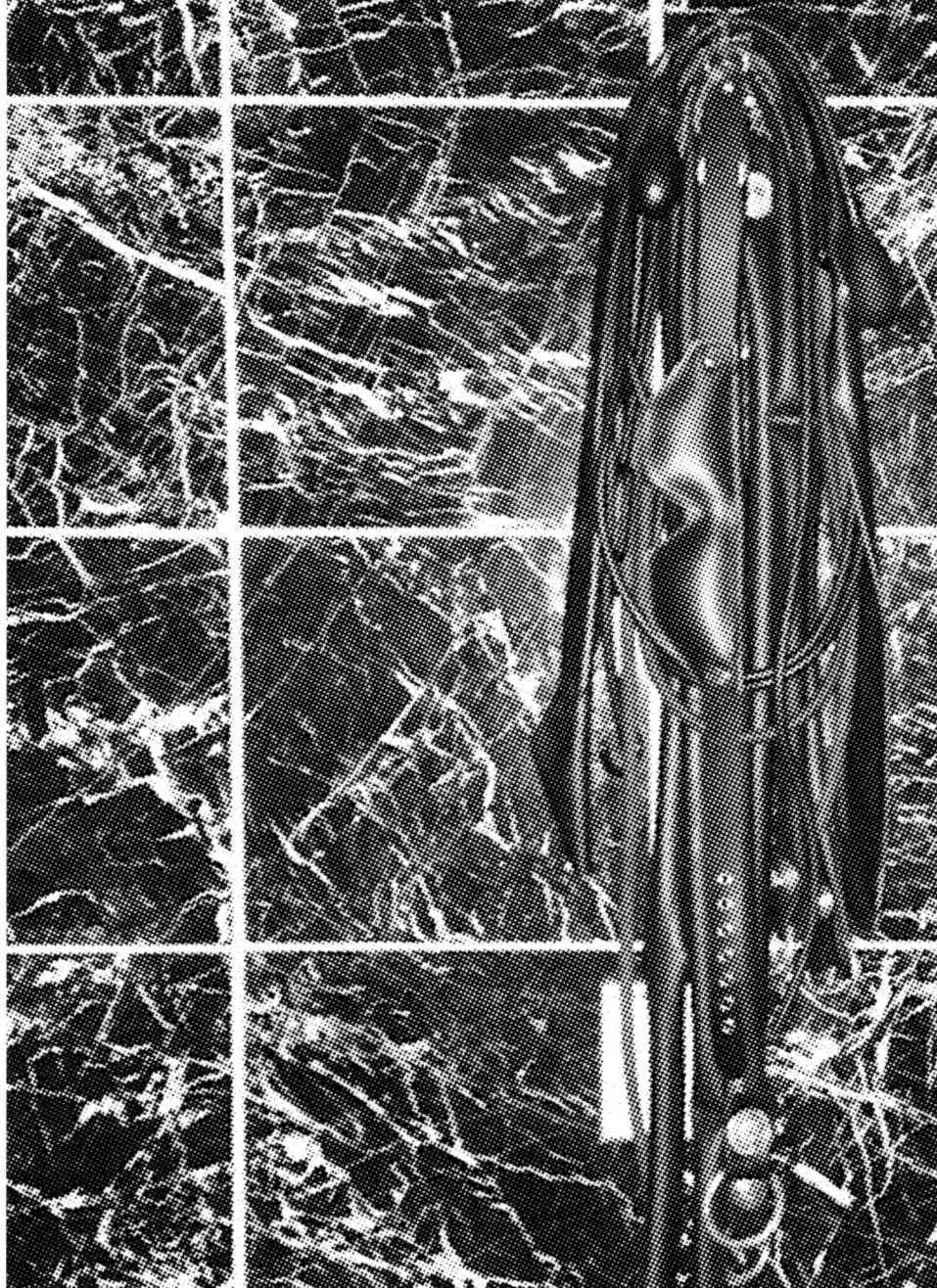

By combining the metal with clothing, store-bought rope, cardboard boxes, Hodges is inviting us to a tactile immediacy. One set of materials is familiar to us; we remember how it feels. The other is familiar in composition but exotic in configuration. In the midst of trying one on mentally, we come up against what it might mean to try to fit into the other.

Finally, space: In these pieces the web forms a plane between us and something else. In *Gate* (1991), what lies on the other side of the chilly curlicues of the metal web is a glowing, empty blue room. New age Nirvana? VIP lounge? Endless blue sky? Gallery back room? The space beyond is pure enticement. We want to be there, but the gate stops us from entering. Once it is considered on its own terms, however, the blue room is a cell. Even if we could gain access, when the gate closes behind us, we will have no place left to go. Above, I mentioned the permeability of Hodges's structures and their psychological implications. When it comes to space, Hodges used his experiences both as an art handler and as a gay man in the New York of the 1980s to examine the collision between longing and identification across spatial barriers. In Vito Acconci's *Seedbed*, the artist and the viewer occupy the same space and different spaces simultaneously. Separated by a plywood ramp while in the same room, they are enacting the dilemmas of proximity and distance that characterize urban life. There is sexual desire, anonymity, violence, exhilaration, and disregard. This was the emotional spectrum of gay cruising—the feeling one got wandering through the clubs in the Meatpacking District, where any alcove and any stranger might combine into a private heaven or, conversely, an express ride to desolation. Hodges dramatizes the poignant moments in which our hopes and desires lead us to the ambiguous embrace of the tenderest traps.

INTERVIEW BY JESSE PEARSON

Vice, *2008*

Another moment of coming out. When I did this interview, I had been running an MFA program for Bard College for six years and had been active in New York's kink scene for almost a decade. —NB

This person right here is an artist and a professor and a bear, a pipe man, and an S&M switch and—what in hell does all that mean? We don't know. Let's talk to them and find out.

Jesse Pearson You were telling me that you're about to go away for a very special weekend. . . .

Nayland Blake It's basically this annual gathering of gay men. It's been going on for something like twenty years at this point.

Pearson Does it have a name?

Blake It does, but I'm a little wary of saying it.

Pearson That sounds kind of *Eyes Wide Shut*–ish.

Blake Well, it's an invitation-only thing, and this is my first year going.

Pearson Ah, so you don't want to get kicked off the list for next year.

Blake Exactly.

Pearson OK, then let's talk about these photos that Kern took of you. For example, the garbage man shot. You actually have a garbage man fetish. All of the gear in that photo is your own, and it's all authentic New York Department of Sanitation stuff. Why do you like to dress up as a trash collector?

Blake I keep coming back to the way that appearance is not an index of identity. I think that identity is kind of a performative thing.

Pearson And these events you go to are full of people who are into playing with identity.

Blake Yeah. You asked me what the people at these events look like. The answer is that they kind of just look like America. Sometimes it feels like the vibe is suburban, but then it's like suburban kinky. I find myself starting to wonder what's really going on in the houses that you drive past in the suburbs.

Pearson A lot of people have wondered that. David Lynch comes to mind.

Blake Yeah. It's not as easily defined as we'd like to imagine.

Pearson I fear that behind all those closed doors, the ones where you wonder what kind of crazy shit is going on, there's actually nothing going on. I feel like sexual self-repression is a big thing for a lot of Americans.

Blake I don't know. But we are in a really funny time because, in part, of the internet. A lot of the S&M organizations around the country have seen a decline in membership. If you look at New York in terms of gay bars and leather bars and stuff like that, there's been a big drop. A lot of people attribute that to the fact that people just hook up online now. You don't have to go to a bar anymore.

Pearson I used to wait for the bus outside of this place in the Meatpacking District. It was called the Hellfire Club. I think it was also called the Manhole. There were two signs there. Anyway, it's gone now. That makes me sad. I liked the fact that that place even existed.

Blake Oh yeah, I spent a lot of time in there. (*Laughs.*) I used to go to cigar-play parties there.

Pearson You told me before that you're a "pipe man." What's that?

Blake It's basically someone who fetishizes pipes, and sometimes cigars, as part of sex.

Pearson And how does that work?

Blake One of the things that a lot of kinky people are into is breath control. That's where you're muffling someone's breathing or somehow controlling their oxygen intake. One of the ways to do that is by feeding them the smoke from a cigar. Another thing is to use the heated end of a cigar or the heat from the bowl of a pipe on people's bodies.

Pearson Do they get burned?

Blake Some of them like to, but you don't really have to. You can get someone really warmed up without them being in any danger of being burned.

Pearson There's a big trust thing inherent in all of this stuff.

Blake You need to have a real discussion about what you want to do and what you're willing to do before any of it happens. Also, I think part of the reason why these events tend to skew toward older men is because when you're really young, just fucking is enough.

Pearson Right. When you're twenty, fucking is plenty. At thirty, you have to start getting weird.

Blake And you also might not have the negotiating skills at twenty. Like you're so eager for it that you don't necessarily think before agreeing to do something. The older people who have been around these scenes for a while are very comfortable with talking about what they want to do.

Pearson A lot of people with more traditional values would say that S&M is perverted or unnecessary, but I've always suspected that maybe you guys are just evolved beyond the rest of us. There's some kind of deep self-honesty that comes along with getting into kinky shit. You guys are psychologically advanced!

Blake (*Laughs.*) There's also the whole concept of aftercare. You do a scene with somebody, and then you check in with them to make sure they're OK. And people have any number of ways of putting a stop to something if it's not going right.

Pearson Are there really safe words, or is that an urban legend?

Blake Oh yeah, totally.

Pearson Do you have one?

Blake It all depends on who I'm playing with. When I first started getting into this, I was really nervous and intimidated, and I would talk to someone and be like, "We need to agree on a safe word." A couple of times, people were like, "You know, um, 'stop' seems to work."

Pearson Right, unless your deal is rape role-playing or something.

Blake Yeah, if you're really going to do a scene that's about being overcome. But generally the amount of negotiation and discussion is much more involved in the kink scene than in the regular scene. No offense, but I can't fathom how women deal with meeting straight guys.

Pearson We're not great communicators. I guess in a lot of traditional relationships, there can be a lack of a certain kind of talk.

Blake And tied up with that is this hope that it's going to "work out." Like you'll meet the magically right person, and they'll do everything right, and you'll just know. One of the things that's interesting about the kink community is that it's very self-policing. If someone is an asshole, word gets around.

Pearson Is there a flip side to that? Are there people about whom everyone says, "Listen, if you want to get tied up real fucking good, you have to meet this guy Joe?"

Blake There are people whose skills are valued, and there are a lot of classes and skills-acquisition things at these events. For instance, with something like caning—hitting someone with a cane—you need to know what you're doing. You need to know where you can hit somebody safely. People who are really good at doing things have a full dance card regardless of what they look like, what gender they are, whatever.

Pearson It's like how you need a special license to drive an eighteen-wheeler.

Blake Yeah. So somebody who's a really good rope person will have women, men, everyone, getting in line to get tied up.

Pearson Do you think people who *aren't* getting into all this stuff are missing out on something? Or are some people only meant to do in-out, in-out, drop-a-load-and-call-it-a-day sex?

Blake I can only speak for myself. It's very tied to my artwork, which is always about learning stuff about myself. But there are also people who are in the kink scene for whom it's all about reaffirming a really rigid role, like they're a master and that's that. So, for some people, it can be a really great experience, but for other people, I don't know. . . .

Pearson Can it get constricting or limiting?

Blake Yeah, if you're not an introspective person, you won't get any more benefit out of it than anything else that you do.

Pearson Tell me more about your garbage man thing.

Blake I grew up lower middle class, and I'm kind of overeducated, and my tendency is to fetishize working-class guys. I think the garbage man is hot. And one of the good things about being queer is that you can fetishize something but still end up looking like it. Also, I've always had a hard time with certain aspects of the leather community that are based on military power structures. It's a rigid notion of social behavior. I find it laughable, but a lot of the guys are into military and police uniforms. I'm too much of a pseudo-hippie, so, for me, wearing the garbage man outfit is a piss-take on the kink-scene guys who do the military thing.

Pearson But still, it's also sexually gratifying for you to dress up in the garbage man gear.

Blake Yeah.

Pearson Isn't it hard not to start cracking up when you're role-playing?

Blake That's the thing. You have to figure out how to do it. It can be like being in a bad comedy skit. But you don't have to have a scenario that's like a one-act play.

Pearson So you'll just have characters to portray and go from there?

Blake Yeah. And the role might be about doing something else.

Pearson Like what? Give me a specific scenario and make it dirty.

Blake Like there could be a scenario where the prissy queen guy comes out to yell at the garbage man for always dumping stuff from the trash can on the curb. And then the tables get turned, the garbage man throws the queen in the back of the truck, drives him off someplace, and fucks him.

Pearson Ouch.

Blake The goal in that scenario is to transfer the power and humiliate this upper-class guy. That might be what he's getting off on.

Pearson And the ultimate goal is to service whatever psychological thing you want to satisfy.

Blake Exactly. That might be about humiliation; it might be about finally being able to ask for what you want. . . . One of the things that's interesting to me is thinking about what the roles that I gravitate toward say about me.

Pearson Like the garbage man in relation to the class situation in which you grew up.

Blake And I think also it goes back to my performance work. I did one where I was being fed for an hour. I didn't have a role except having to eat whatever it was the audience gave me. The performance was more about the feelings of everybody in the audience.

Pearson But there was also an endurance thing for you.

Blake In some ways, yes. It was interesting. It varied from person to person. Some of them were tender, and some were really sadistic.

Pearson What were they feeding you?

Blake Pizza, doughnuts, fruit, vegetables. It would all be spread out on a table. I'd sit in front of it, shirtless, with a sign next to me that said, "Please Feed."

Pearson Good one.

Blake It was like at the zoo: "Please don't feed the animals." It had that sort of inflection.

Pearson What were your first experiences with going beyond one-on-one straight-up sex?

Blake I'm not so sure how much my parents knew about this, but in my teens I used to sneak off to porn theaters in the city a lot. This was in the mid-1970s when Times Square was at its sleaziest. I saw and participated in a fair amount of sex at those places. And then, I also read a lot of stuff, like William Burroughs, in my teens. A big influence on me later on was Kathy Acker.

Pearson What about S&M? How did you learn about all that?

Blake Well, there was *Drummer* magazine.

Pearson What's that?

Blake It was an early gay S&M mag.

Pearson When you were going to the theaters at Forty-Second Street when you were young, were you already intellectualizing sex?

Blake No, but there was an overlap in that Times Square scene and the art scene. One of the first places I saw a Keith Haring drawing was at this porn theater I used to go to all the time. Then, once I knew what Keith looked like, I started seeing him around that scene.

Pearson A lot of art films that included graphic sex had no other outlet but those places. I guess it's a function of just being in New York City, but it doesn't surprise me that the communities of so-called perverts and artists overlapped a lot.

Blake I have a kind of highfalutin theory about it.

Pearson Let's hear it.

Blake I think that the rise of leather culture in the mid-1960s through the 1970s paralleled the rise of performance art. People like Marina Abramović and Vito Acconci were basically born out of the same impulse as the leathermen, but one was taking place inside the art world, and one was taking place in the underground. Many of the same issues were being looked at. You can talk about leather culture as being the anonymous folk art version of the supposedly more respectable gallery work.

Pearson I like that way of looking at it.

Blake It's also no coincidence that both of those things were being cracked down on in the 1980s by Ronald Reagan. It's that sort of cultural surge, that way of playing with power and trying to expand the body's limits, that was met with all this backlash and repression later on.

Pearson It seems like this impulse is nowhere in the art world right now. Nobody is carrying on that tradition, and I don't know why. I had a really good theory about it a second ago, but I forgot it.

Blake Well, for one, it's really hard to sell. Also, ideas no longer really occur in the art world. Ideas have been turned into style. The social implications of all of that body work have been stripped away, and now it's just seen as a style of art making. It's a style that's down right now, but it will be up later on.

Pearson Shit, so there are no ideas in the art world right now?

Blake It's really pervasive. I lay the blame for it on the internet. Here's another way to tie the leather world and the art world together—there was a time when to be interested in either of those things, you had to put your body on the line. In other words, you had to show up to the gallery or the club.

Pearson And now everything can be seen on the internet a couple of minutes after it happens. It's the same thing with music. It's way easier to be a poser and a dilettante with the internet as a research tool for more effective bullshitting.

Blake And that's one of the reasons why I'm loathe to talk much about the event I'm going to this weekend. I think it's great that there are still some things in society that you have to be initiated into. You have to make a commitment to it to be able to see it.

Pearson Sometimes I wish the internet would die, and we could just use the phone and the mail and zines and mixtapes again. Maybe that means I'm getting old.

Blake Some of the work I'm doing now involves these things that I make totally anonymously and leave out on the street. I've been doing things like drawing on garbage, making little pieces that I leave out, sort of as gifts for people. I don't document them with photographs or anything.

Pearson That's awesome. Nowadays, if there isn't a photo of something on Flickr, it's like it never existed.

Blake On the internet, we have all this information, but it doesn't necessarily have any value for us because we didn't work for it. You turn

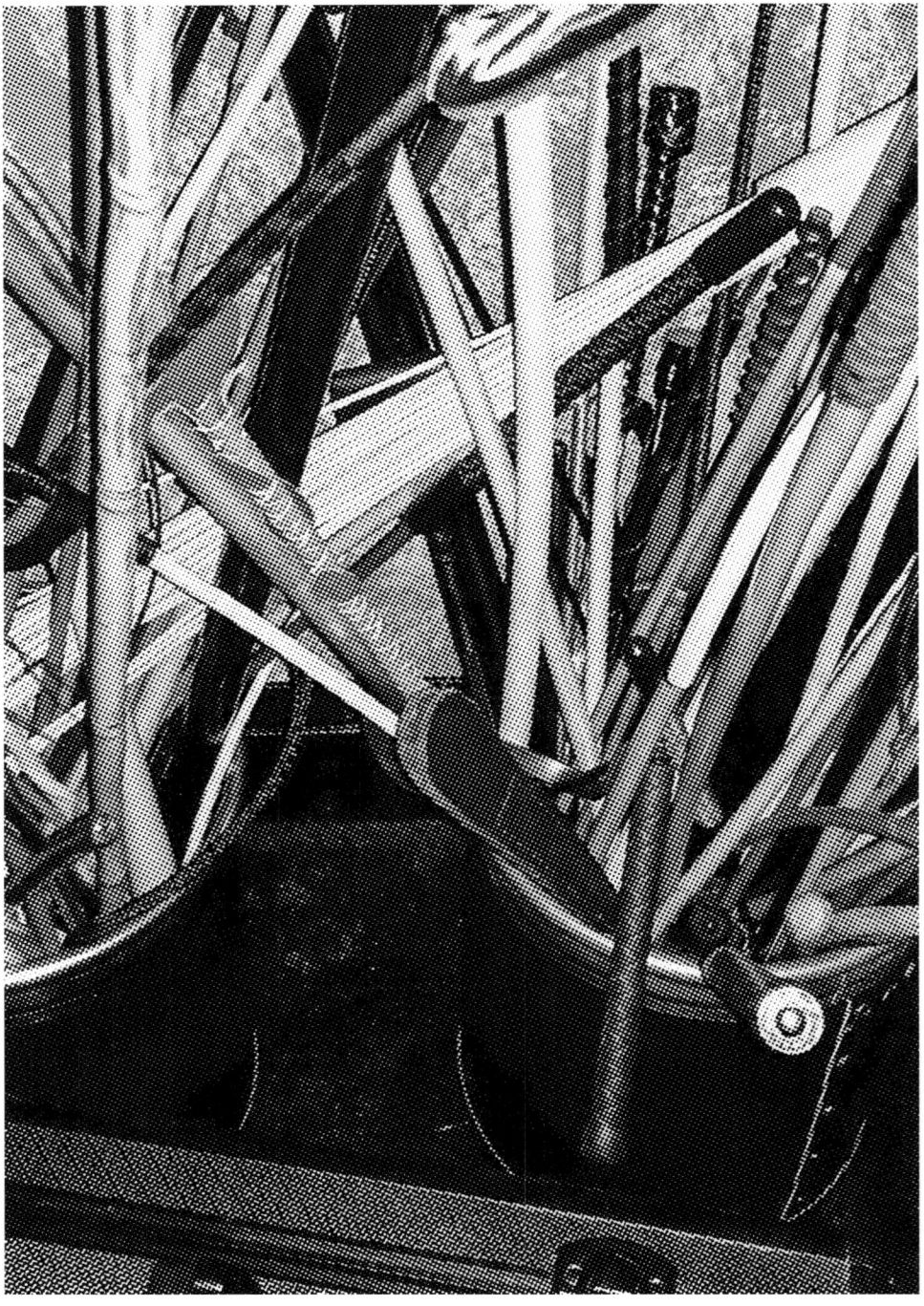

on the tap, and information comes out. We don't know what the consequences of that will be yet.

Pearson OK, so you're an S&M switch, you're a pipe man, you do the garbage man thing . . . are you a bear too? I mean, what else are you?

Blake I guess I can come out publicly as bi now, although I'm not really using the word *bi*. I'm using *pan*. But yeah, for the past few years, I've been with both men and women.

Pearson I would imagine that after living in the queer world for so long, admitting that you've been sleeping with women could be just as scary as coming out for the first time years ago.

Blake Completely. Yeah. There definitely are people who are freaked out. I have friends who are confused by it and friends who are into it. And yeah, the bear thing? I'm fine with that identity. One of the reasons I started identifying as a bear in the late 1980s was because those were the guys who were around the leather scene in San Francisco but weren't tidy enough to really be a part of it. Bears were the outcasts of the leathermen.

Pearson And then they became such a dominant thing—a bear world of their own.

Blake It's been interesting to watch the way that identity became fossilized really quickly. It was like, "Who's a bear? Who's not a bear?" It was instructive for me because I'd seen it happen around punk rock too.

Pearson It's similar to the way a lot of alternate cultures organize themselves, and it's a fucking bummer. What starts as a refuge for weirdos becomes just another set of rules. The misfit kids from high school move to New York or San Francisco or wherever so that they can be among people they can have fun with, but then they create their own microcosms of the shitty world that marginalized them. It makes me want to puke.

Blake These identities get postulated by people who are trying to break out of categories and escape that trap, but once that space of freedom is opened up, it gets filled up with all these other people who want to police the border. I've always found myself disappointed in that. It's much more interesting when the boundary is kind of fucked up.

NANCY GROSSMAN:
MISRECOGNIZED

Nancy Grossman: Tough Life Diary, *2012*

In the wake of pop art came a return to an expanded notion of the figurative. A group of artists—Lucas Samaras, Leon Golub, John Chamberlain, Nancy Spero, Bruce Conner, Lee Bontecou—began to reinsert images of their own and others' bodies into their work as both symbolic and visceral events. For each of these artists, the object was not entire unto itself and inert; it also produced meaning through the activities of its maker. The object bridged the symbolic and the social body called into meaning by the actions of the artist. In a subtle way, these works were performative, either tied to private ritual or postulated as social utterances, calls to action. Why, then, are these artists often seen as sui generis, often receiving only fitful critical attention?

The split in post-1960s art often got expressed as a division between representation and abstraction, but the deeper divide separated warm from cool: the pop artists and their conceptual descendants actually ended up on the same side as the abstract-process artists all the way down through moments like "pattern and decoration." What united them all was a cool disengagement that became the default stance for contemporary art from the 1960s onward. This disengagement allowed every kind of activity to come under the scrutiny of the art world because it arrived as a specimen, safely divorced from consequence and effect. Against this bulwark washed successive tides of engaged work, much of it attempting to grapple with the vagaries of social injustice and psychic distress.

What does it mean to be a warm artist in a cool age?

It means in part that the misreadings that all work is subject to can be particularly disfiguring. To the extent that Nancy Grossman's work has become emblematic of a time, it has endured just such misreadings. The leatherheads, in their graphic power and profound isolation, are easily mistaken for artifacts from a sexual community rapidly devolving into a "lifestyle" as it grew in visibility.

What does it mean when one's work is made emblematic in spite of oneself? Grossman's work was taken up and championed by a group of gay men who misread the ideas and desires in the work through their hunger for the types of representation they lacked. But in doing so they flattened the possible readings of the work into simple celebration and titillation. A similar thing happened in the attempts to tie John Chamberlain's work to critiques of American car culture. Sometimes your champions do you no favors.

Nancy Grossman has too discerning an eye, too much artistic intelligence, to simply be a fetishist.

Grossman's work uses the trappings of leather fetishism and S&M in the same way that Piranesi used the architecture of the dungeon: as a stage to act within, a vehicle for the exploration of human emotion that cannot be rendered into language, an armor against disengagement.

What you need in making the work is far from what they need to read the work.

Today, when even the most arcane devices of S&M are available to us with a few mouse clicks, we can stop taking Grossman's work as an invitation to or evidence of sexual activity and begin to ask what her objects point at through S&M's language.

One trajectory of collage runs through Max Ernst into Joseph Cornell, the other through cubism into Robert Motherwell and, possibly, Richard Serra. The detail invites us in, and the block pushes us out.

Romare Bearden filtered Motherwell's chunky scraps through the minds of generations of quilt makers, creating poems of Black body and urban space. Grossman's collages start from a similar place but veer off in the direction of a planar mosaic. While Bearden appeals to our urge to reconfigure the fragmented space into narrative, Grossman doesn't rely on an external anecdote but, instead, moves the eye back and forth from drawn line to creased paper to punctured surface to dyed edge, bringing us above and below the surface, making us aware of the construction of the thing in front of us. Her collages are not windows to be seen through, even when she presents an imagery of landscape; we are meant to see the land itself as a skin, creased and permeable.

An invitation to mystery: Grossman's surfaces compel because of the universe that seethes beneath them. What is important is not the skin but the way it is shaped by the crazy, fractured, fighting heart beneath.

Grossman doesn't offer us a way out, no palliative notion that we can somehow slip through this world with our cool intact.

My journey into Nancy Grossman's work won't result in a truer reading by any means, but I act on the belief that it is helpful to watch each other wrestle.

What is the appeal of the cool? I think of the postwar world as traumatized into a vast distrust of all earnestness, aghast at the bloodbaths perpetrated by regimes that deployed every type of symbolic panoply, willing to treat human beings as symbols (of impurity, reaction, decay) and take the step of erasing those offensive symbols. That trauma remains in our language of casual irony and unearned pessimism. We have a fear of investing ourselves emotionally and symbolically. I've talked above about the ways in which "cool" triumphed in the art worlds of the 1960s, bringing attention and approval to artworks that took disengagement as their starting place. People's distrust of symbolic investment on the mass scale led them to reject the earnestness of group social action, but at the same time, they embraced symbolic meaning on the individual scale. They became concerned with what they meant on an individual basis and devised a methodology for investigating those meanings in concert with others. When these investigations took place in the art world, it was called *performance art*. When it took place in private, it was called *kinky*. In both places, it became the way people turned social distress and convulsive anger into acts of personal wounding, marking confinement, aggression. The meanings of these acts remain highly contextual in a way that for the most part kept them safe from the commercialization of the ensuing years.

But here is a different story I've been thinking of.

The Strap On

Queer sexuality is so threatening because it unmasks the ideology that lurks behind the word *natural*. It says that natural sex is insufficient, that it needs human technology, artistry, to make it answer every need. It is tempting to talk about sex as "mere sex" when talking about art.

The 1960s ended with ongoing images of the body in extremis, ecstatic or brutalized. The notion that one might achieve meaning through imposing such states on one's own body remains for most far too threatening as a type of symbolic enactment. A decade later, when men began to die

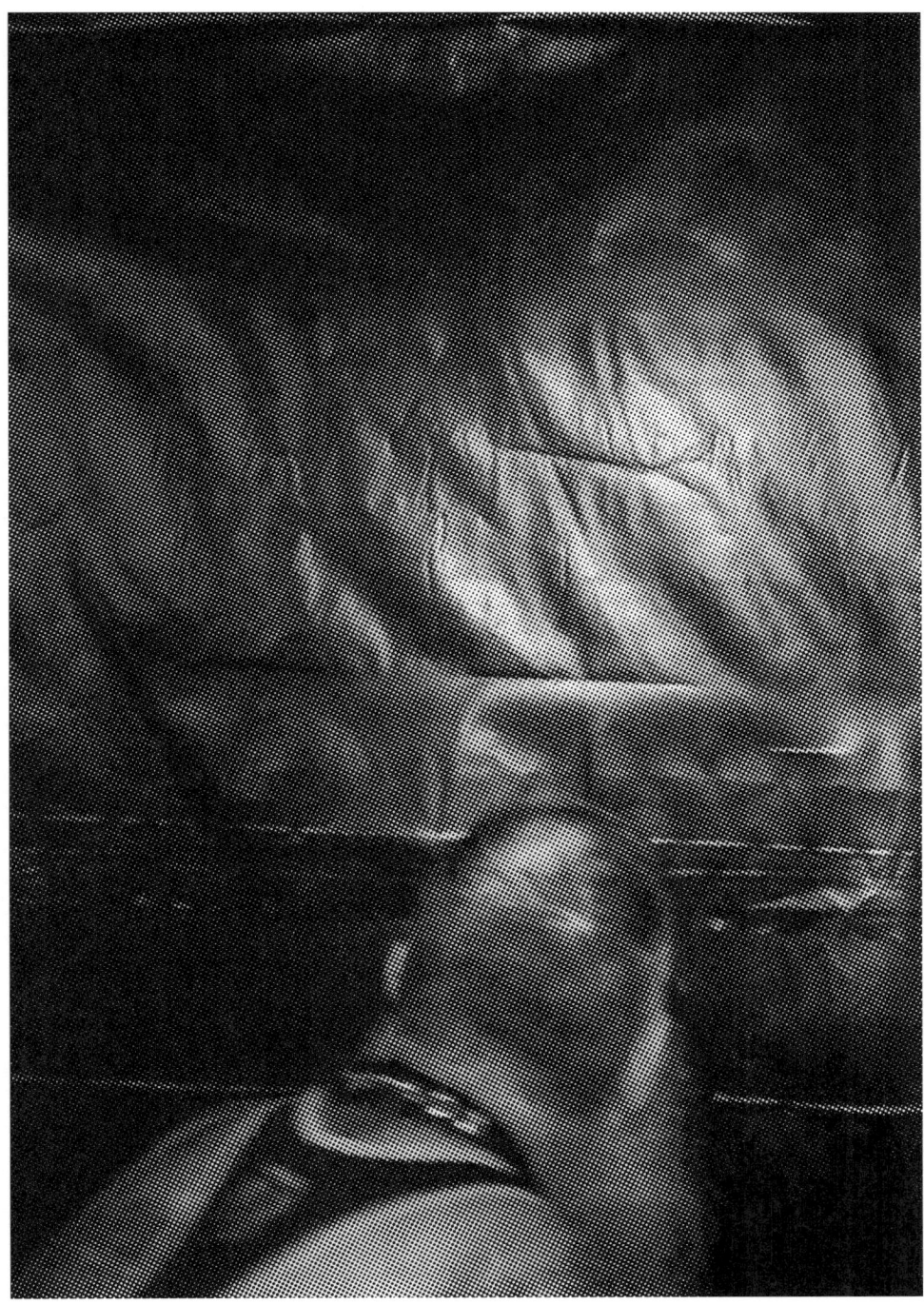

from a virus transmitted through sex, it was in part seen as the inevitable outcome of such "unnatural" practices.

At one time, Grossman's work used materials that could easily be confused with the trappings of these practices. But sculpture gains meaning not only from what it depicts but also from how it is made. It embodies through showing us not just bodies but the trace of construction, the impression of the hand, the logic of how a piece holds together and holds itself up.

Looked at in this light, Grossman's pieces come much closer to armor and prosthetics than to restraint and fetish. They provide a buffer, a series of layers between our core and the world. They are things we tie onto ourselves with a swagger to mark our difference and channel our fury. Nature gives us one face, and we make ourselves another. Her horns, harnesses, zippers, straps, reins, and skins mark us as beasts but not animals. We can partake of the flesh, but we ask what it means to do so, something no animal does. Her hides are organized as no animal's pelt ever is. And the restless tracing of her line across the surface of a rubber tube or torn piece of paper marks the path of human thought, human longing, and choice. If this is sex, it is sex that is decided on, pleasure taken with forethought at the highest level. Strapped in, strapped on, we confront the massive brutality of the world's misrecognitions.

FREE! LOVE! TOOL! BOX!
WORKBOOK

Yuerba Buena Center for the Arts brochure, 2012

My exhibition Free! Love! Tool! Box! *at the Yerba Buena Center for the Arts allowed me to bring together curating, performing, and teaching within the context of Yerba Buena's history. I wanted to honor that location's history as a site of the rise of leather culture in San Francisco, the nonprofit arts, and—thirty years later—the queer punk moment. I did not want an explanatory text to tell people what they should think about the show; I wanted to provide them with ways to activate it. Hence the workbook. The questions in it reflect my own teaching practice of posing possibilities rather than providing conclusive answers. The show's physical form changed over the months that it was up, bringing together the spaces of creation and display. —NB*

Where do you feel safe?
What is the best thing about your body?
What is liberation?
Do you want to change our world? Where would you start?
What was the last thing you created? Where did you do it?
When was the last time you felt free?
What is your most powerful piece of clothing and why?
Describe a beautiful thing from your past.

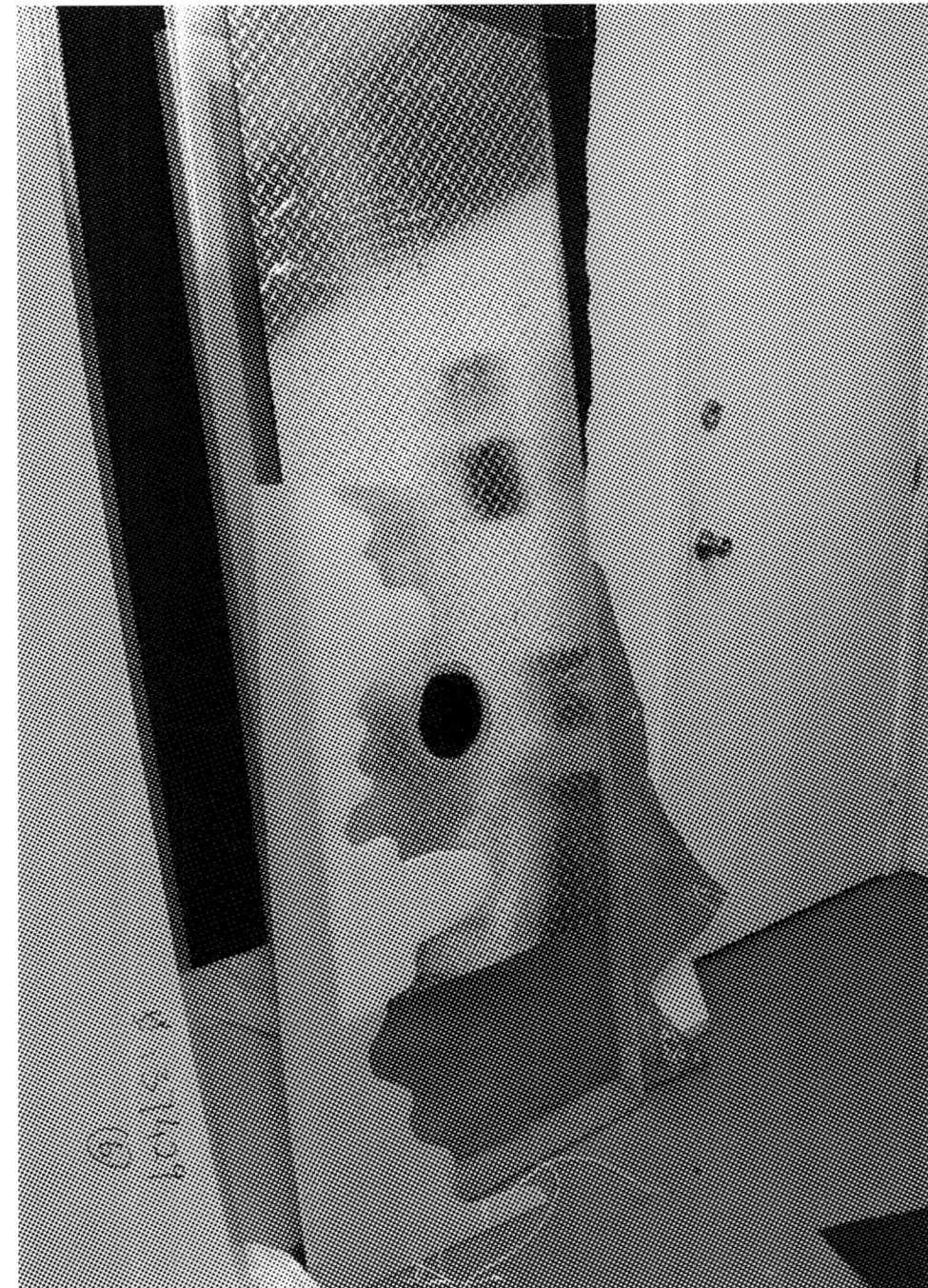

ANTHONY FRIEDKIN: "AND *I'M* CARMEN MIRANDA"— WHAT LIBERATION LOOKS LIKE

Anthony Friedkin: The Gay Essay, *2014*

It is said that we cannot truly retain the memory of pain, but surely joy is even more difficult to recall. Pain, struggle, and striving seem, because of their gravity, more appropriate subjects than pleasure for memory and reconsideration. When we ask photography, especially documentary photography, to be our memory and conscience, to capture and record truth, it is almost always images of struggle and pain that we are thinking of. Recent photographic theory has revolved around two concepts: the slipperiness of photography's claim to veracity and the moral implications of recording and witnessing what Susan Sontag called "the pain of others." These discussions make little room for emotions other than suffering, and when they do, it is more often than not to point out the failure of projects that attempt to turn photographic subjects into symbols of universal humanity. Pleasure, joy, and ecstasy all seem less noble, undeserving of serious discussion. Perhaps because these states seem more situated in our bodies, we distrust them.

It is this thinking that has dogged the political struggle of queer people since its inception. Because it is so difficult to argue for sexual pleasure, to argue for the truth of our bodies, the lesbian and gay communities have had to make a different argument, one based on a notion of equal rights, a rational argument that takes as its template the American civil rights movement of the 1950s and 1960s. This story of struggle, one whose roots stretch all the way back to the Enlightenment, has been portrayed with certain kinds of images: sober depictions of adverse conditions, humanizing pictures of members of minority groups, portraits of community leaders and organizers, and pictures caught on the fly at street protests.

There is a different story that laces its way through the photographs of *The Gay Essay*, and it is a story of joy, of facing an indifferent and hostile world with something other than a grimace. Anthony Friedkin's pictures, made during the crucial years just after Stonewall, trace the emergence of a public gayness, a new face on the streets of America, one with a history as rich as that of the years preceding the rumblings of gay liberation.

My first encounter with these pictures was utterly by accident: As I began work on another project, one involving the early years of the leather scene in San Francisco, International Center of Photography curator Brian Wallis suggested that I might want to look at Anthony Friedkin's pictures. They appeared, at first blush, casual, exploratory, and not particularly revealing. *The Gay Essay* contains examples of the types of pictures I mention above, pictures firmly within the civil rights documentary tradition, an approach that first saw print in *Life* magazine's groundbreaking article "Homosexuality in America," published on June 26, 1964, with pictures by Bill Eppridge. Friedkin's pictures seemed to cover ground similar to Eppridge's: the cities of Los Angeles and San Francisco, and their fledgling bars and community centers, streets, and adult theaters—peeks into worlds heretofore hidden from straight eyes.

I wasn't especially interested in the community leaders and the civil rights story that is told in these pictures and that in large part was already defined by the *Life* article: cops harassing, leaders organizing, spokespeople being anointed, and parades and the bigots who attend parades to yell. Certainly, Friedkin captures in these photos the stuff that passes from news into history. But these pictures do not really give us a sense of what is at stake for the people caught up in these public events. It is Friedkin's other pictures—the pictures of the people who will never be stars, except to one another, people who win their freedom and love day by day—it is these pictures that caught my compassion and made me look again.

And as I spent more time with Friedkin's work, I began to see a transition: first in the spaces that Friedkin seemed to be shooting, and then in the attitudes of the people who inhabited those spaces. The volcanic events of Stonewall and the Summer of Love lay between Eppridge's pictures and Friedkin's. Groups had begun speaking about lesbian and gay liberation. As

I started looking for stories that were obscured by the standard one, I began to ask myself this question: What does liberation look like?

First, its precursor: A portly man stands silhouetted against the LA sun, his shadow slanting onto a wall with a rendering of Michelangelo's *David* (with an appliquéd fig leaf) and a series of signs:

A Warehouse of Wild and Wooly Adult Entertainment!
All Male Film Festival
2 Hours in Gay Color!
For Men Only!

He is almost past the entrance, hands shoved into pockets, face obscured by shadow. He could be entering or leaving, but in either case, his diffidence is palpable.

And next, an image presumably from inside the Wild and Wooly Warehouse: Two men sit, backs to the camera, in seats that seem to have no space between them, and at the center of the picture is a grainy, chopped-down rectangle of hardcore action.

In both pictures, Friedkin's clear eye and sturdy compositions make specific editorial points; the men are squeezed into the frame, faceless, either because they are turned away from us or because of their shadows. The focus is the porn theater itself as a location that is both cheap and cramped. The men are merely exemplars, the older one looming slightly over the younger one. And even the street outside feels like an interior; there is no sky, no horizon. In these images, as in many of his pictures, Friedkin brings us into a world that is a confined safe haven in the midst of a hostile environment.

People's attitudes in other pictures are marked by wariness, defiance, or determination: the guarded calculation of a hustler displaying the goods; a gallant butch cowgirl next to the men's room at a bar; a line of female impersonators at the "Queen's Ball," fully confident in their illusion and ready for the stage; or Reverend Troy Perry, resolute in the ashes of the church he founded.

Each of these photographs inhabits a role that seems to be offered by the camera itself, presenting an identity that, however controversial, is still recognizable: entertainer, activist, whore. They are embodiments of types. At the point that Friedkin undertook his project, two forces were at work in gay life. The first was the recognition of these types; the second was the development of a new, self-aware gay style.

Photography itself exists in the space of contradiction: It captures the unique moment that is occurring in front of the lens at the instant the shutter opens. In that sense, each photographic image is sui generis. Yet photography also tells us stories by showing how that unique moment is also a typical one, how it resembles images we have seen before it. When we are the subjects of photographs, we collude in this process; we have become so habituated to the camera that we arrange ourselves in ways that are familiar to us because such ways are derived from all the other pictures we have seen. We are addressing an audience, and at the time that Friedkin was shooting this project, that audience was rarely a sympathetic one.

And that is when my enthusiasm for these pictures began to grow: I started to look at those pictures where Friedkin photographed people whose audience *is* sympathetic, where couples or groups of people are enacting their queerness for one another, and not for the world at large.

A group of these pictures was shot at a performance by San Francisco's Cockettes, the extended commune/performance troupe that melded flower power and camp into a style that was a rebuke to any hope that gay people would fit into the wider world. Friedkin's pictures catch the thrill of the people who hope to transform their world through the smallest gestures. Here are some of my favorites:

A fabulous couple standing in line outside the Palace Theater, all tossed-on finery and buzzing anticipation: one with bangles and a proper clutch, frizzy hair, and a glittered goatee. Another nonchalant in an old band jacket, fishnets, and a garter. If this is drag, what is the role that they are putting on? Who is being impersonated? No one. Instead, genders are being mashed up, played with, made elastic, and revealed to be a matter of personal style. This couple is dressed for themselves and each other.

The Cockettes' shows were notoriously ramshackle, closer to "happenings" than to polished performances, and the charm of that slapdash approach is visible in Friedkin's picture of Pristine Condition, who sports necklaces of candy corn, Bette Davis eyebrows, and an improbable bunch of feathers bursting from her head. The picture captures a sweetness that seems very different from the measured self-presentation of his image of Michelle, a female impersonator at the C'est La Vie Club in North Hollywood. Pristine is not perfecting an illusion; she is part of a scene where the roles of audience and actor are almost interchangeable. Michelle is part of a show, and she has craft and a very specific type of femininity that she projects. She uses her position in front of Friedkin's camera to connect to a long line of Hollywood glamour queens. More important, one image is drawing on the known of the typical, and one is fusing together fragments to create something new.

My Studio Is a Dungeon Is the Studio

Another couple: In contrast to the stalwart butch cowgirl in the bar, there is a picture of pure adoration: One woman, an ankh medallion around her neck, indulgently looks on while her charming trick(?) partner(?) girlfriend(?) swaggers against the wall, cigarette dangling. This is what freedom looks like: sweetness, silliness, and defiance. Yes, the woman in the cropped jean jacket is putting on a show—part for the camera, but, more important, for her pal—and the acceptance that she has won from both parties makes her irresistible.

In another picture, both women playfully bump crotches against a wall outdoors, and the first woman's look of love is undiminished, even amplified, perhaps, by the bravery of flirting and taking your pleasure however you want it, right there in the street. The difference between the way these women light up the street and the shadowed, guarded faces of the men in and around the porn theater is the mark of history being made; it is exactly what liberation looks like.

As the 1970s wore on, the various parts of the gay and lesbian community fragmented and, as some would put it, matured. For the most part, this meant that as the various communities drew further apart, they developed more coherent internal identities. "Gay and lesbian rights" replaced "gay liberation," and earnestness replaced frivolity. There was a possibility of achieving a place in society, and that possibility brought with it the temptation to conform to society's expectations.

The flimsy nature of that possibility was revealed when the AIDS epidemic showed how far society was from any real acceptance of queer people. It also made clear to a new generation the power that comes from controlling and articulating your own image. Streets around the world once again became a forum for people to make visible their own truths. By the late 1980s, gay pride parades had transformed into crosses between funeral marches and political rallies. The poster and the placard, the T-shirt and the sticker, became the locales of people's declarations and self-advertisements.

I had the opportunity to think about Friedkin's pictures once again this past summer as I worked on *Knee Deep in the Flooded Victory*, a project for the International Center of Photography. In it, I tried to draw parallels among several bodies of work that were part of the CENTER'S collection: Friedkin's work of the early 1970s, queer protest posters of the early 1990s, and my own performances and zines exploring the state of queer identities today. I was thinking about the street as a stage, the palace where we still have the ability to break down and reconfigure identities, the place where the pageant might still have power. I was also thinking about the ways that

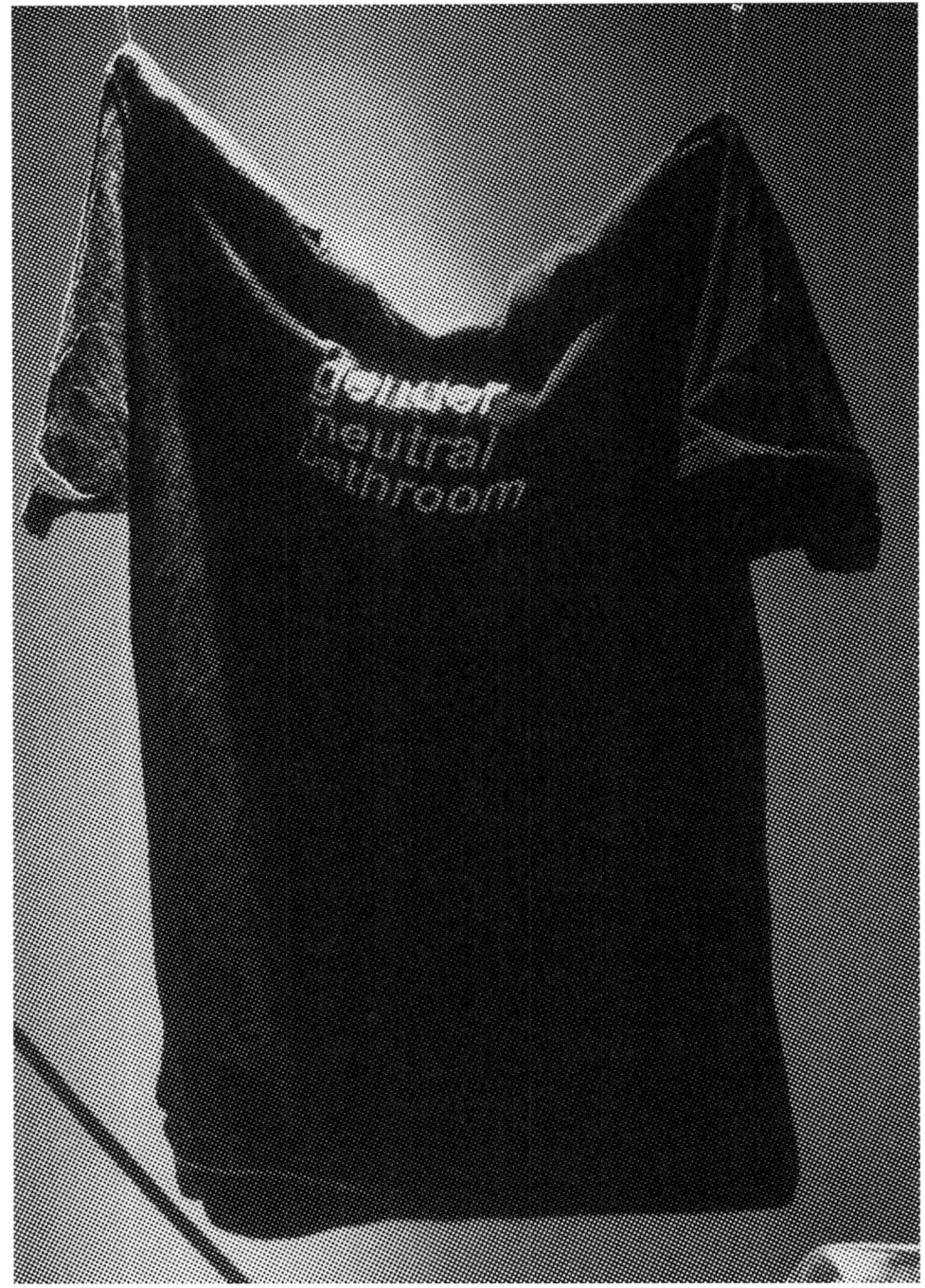

museums can activate their collections so that they can work as engines for social change.

Among the many items included in this installation were two posters by lesbian collectives: one by New York's Fierce Pussy and one by San Francisco's Girl with Arms Akimbo. Both exhibit the kind of self-defining queer voice that I spoke of earlier, the voice that I both hear and see in some of Friedkin's pictures.

The Girl with Arms Akimbo poster juxtaposes a photograph of two naked women wrapped in a seated embrace with the single word "SAFE" at the bottom of the frame. First, this is a reference to safe sex, but beyond that, it is an assertion of the safety and joy found in the arms of a lover, and beyond that, it is a declaration that the streets where the poster was displayed are places where same-sex couplings, and the representation of queer bodies, are safe. It shows the way that we create our own safety through acknowledging our truth.

On the Fierce Pussy poster is another declaration: "I AM A stone butch androgyne femme tomboy girlfriend sapphic deviant AND PROUD." Here again is a place where the stereotype is shattered and recombined: My pride comes from being all these things, from containing multitudes, from wearing identities in succession, and from discarding them at will. The relish behind this series of terms is the same one that I detect in the eyes of the lesbian couple in Friedkin's pictures.

And finally, I chose a protest sign from an ACT UP action: a card that bears Ed Koch's famous front-page declaration "I'm Heterosexual," followed with an anonymous protester's riposte: "And *I'm* Carmen Miranda." This is a long, long way from the shadowy men ducking off the street into the wild and woolly world of all-male adult entertainment. These four words aimed at a politician widely believed to be closeted are unshakable, puckish—the kind of frivolous, wacky response that so quickly fades from memory. It is a moment in history when an individual confronts society and refuses to accept its terms. It is the only kind of history that matters to me.

These explosions of joy and these flowerings are fleeting, and yet they are exactly what was historically important about gay liberation. They are declarations of something new on the streets and in the lives of Americans. The chance to be unconfined, to make ourselves look and to love how we choose, to find pleasure on our own terms—all this potential sings out to us through Friedkin's images, and it is all the sweeter for how quickly it can be forgotten. We may define ourselves by our struggles, but it is in the compilation of our joys that we fly free.

Anthony Friedkin

QUEER AT CAA

Previously Unpublished, delivered at the College Art Association, 2015

For the past few years, I've been engaging in a performance practice that has involved a series of collaborators and that has taken place in campgrounds and hotels and basements and apartments around America. In each of these performances, I and my collaborators devise a script, secure props and costumes, and train for our various roles. Some of my collaborators have been trained in the arts. Some have not but bring other skills to bear on the work. In each instance, the recipients of the performance are the same as the performers.

I'm not going to show them to you, but if I did, it would look like you were viewing kinky queer sex.

That's because it is kinky queer sex.

I want to talk about some things I've learned through this performance practice in these past years.

What I've learned as a kinky queer: Nobody can fuck for you. Typing isn't fucking, and it certainly isn't a way to fuck things up.

Here is the invitation sent to the participants on this panel:

Each speaker will have approximately twenty minutes to present their own cultural point of view regarding the state of the arts from the position of theory, aesthetic practice, politics, economics, genres, genders, sexuality, spirituality, etc. This is a specially commissioned panel in honor of the hundredth year of the founding of the College Art Association (CAA). You each represent crucial points of reference and intersection regarding the contemporaneous concerns in the arts industry, whether mainstream, global or on the edge.

In other words, I'm here to talk about what's important to me in art these days. I should be doing this from my position as an educator. This is the College Art Association after all. But I want to talk as an artist. After all, I teach because it helps me make my work. Not only financially but because I'm a little dim, and I need to be reminded about what my problems are.

The problem is representation.

By definition: to represent, to stand in for.

The pathos of the stand-in, always waiting for their big break on the ideological stage.

Representation is built on absence. The real event is always delayed, coming. Our representatives speak for us but are not us.

This is the problem.

Or to re-present: to present over again, to give the known, to reassure. Let me know you are really whatever, so we can finally get the uncertainty between us over with.

It is laudable that our society strives for fairness. It is not laudable that the justification for that fairness is so often an essential sameness.

When we submit to the regimes of representation, we occupy the mental space that W. E. B. Du Bois delineated so clearly as double consciousness: "It is a peculiar sensation, this double-consciousness, this sense of always looking at one's self through the eyes of others, of measuring one's soul by the tape of a world that looks on in amused contempt and pity. One ever feels his twoness, —an American, a Negro; two souls, two thoughts, two unreconciled strivings; two warring ideals in one dark body, whose dogged strength alone keeps it from being torn asunder."[1]

The civil rights model and representational politics in this country lead us to ask the following questions: Where's my slice of the status quo? Is it the same size as my neighbor's? Is it predicated on an assumption that I am supposed to be both myself and the representation of a social group, an abstraction?

Our difference is acknowledged but only as a way of pointing to our essential sameness. It is that sameness that gives us a claim on fundamental rights.

We are allowed to be different in every way except when we wish to step outside our role as a representative.

Further, as an artist, I am charged with making this dual nature legible to a mainstream. I am given the task of identifying my issues and then providing the remedial course in them to a public that can then decide whether they have been discussed long enough. Trends, in either an art market or an academic one, are predicated on a notion that issues can be raised and resolved. In order to be heard, you must format your utterances to that system. Fuck the status quo. I don't want my fair share of ignorance, jingoism, and billionaire worship. I'm not waiting outside the chapel to get my love validated. I got into the cocksucking racket because I thought I wouldn't have to worry about any of that crap. To move from the toleration of variation to a love for the alien in all of its flowering should be our goal.

I want our difference to make things different; if it doesn't, it's been squandered.

Difference means change; queer difference means unexpected change.

The work of sexual liberation remains unfinished. The sexual revolution is almost entirely consumed but unconsummated. The artworks that emerged at the same time were also predicated on a radical idea of presentness. They were boring and uncomfortable as often as they were brilliant and transformative.

Ideologies issue from bodies, from our bodies, which are not abstractions but wondrous facts, existing not in the realm of abstraction but in specific locations at specific times.

The information age banishes the specific, providing access to everything except those things that matter.

In a society that asks us to stand in for ourselves, we must not submit to the regime of double consciousness, which is the regime of representation.

I'm supposed to talk about the current art scene, so I'll talk about what I see there: a bifurcated world where two markets, one financial and one intellectual, both collaborate to make the specific experience of artists irrelevant and interchangeable.

We talk about the dematerialization of the art object. It's time for the dedocumentation of art. We live in an age where people are trained to experience art through the document and to make art that can immediately be reduced to that document. Performances that are reduced to photographs, videos that are endlessly looped tableaux—unmoored from any temporal urgency.

We are the existence of sex in public. We don't have to be behaving sexually for that to be the case.

We are the reminder that the term *natural* is a mask for ideology. That identity is an ongoing pageant, not some sacred core of who we are.

In this society, it is our job to contradict—to speak against, to speak across. Even when things are nice. Because someone has to do it. It is something all societies need: the disruption of the commonsensical, the rational, the disembodied.

We are hated because we remind people that pleasure is possible, that anyone can decide to take it. That it is a *choice*, a choice that many don't have the courage to make for themselves. As such, for many, we are the reminder of their cowardice.

Queer isn't who you fuck; it's how you fuck them. It isn't what you do; it's how you do it. It isn't what you depict; it's how you transform consciousness through the action of your will. That is what it means to make art.

Queer culture is not a style of culture, nor is it an adjunct to our lives that we can detach like a Lego. We cannot stop talking about it or making work about it simply because some publication imagines that it has been resolved.

Queer culture is the manifestation of our will in the world. Our transformation of reality.

Your dirty pictures are our history. Your embarrassments our monuments.

So, when you start taking them down or when you ask us to do it differently, you are not just rearranging our decor. You are attempting to make us disappear. When an art-buying public turned away from "identity-based work," it presented the world with the image of people growing tired of their own ignorance being pointed out to them after they had loudly demanded to be educated. "We're tired of inclusion; what else have you got?"

The removal of David Wojnarowicz's *A Fire in My Belly* from the exhibition at the National Portrait Gallery was not about artistic freedom (which, in this society, is the freedom to be supposedly irrelevant); it was an attempt to rewrite American history in an American history museum.

Representation is a losing game, one where our own pleasure is put on hold while we make our case to a rigged jury. To beg for their tolerance. I'm supposed to believe that if a platoon of straight comic fans is persuaded to be slightly less homophobic because they see two superheroes kiss, it's more important than for one queer person to fully be themselves. I call shenanigans on that shit.

Because, to our straight allies, we are here to remind you of the fact that you are making a choice every time you fuck. And to encourage you to

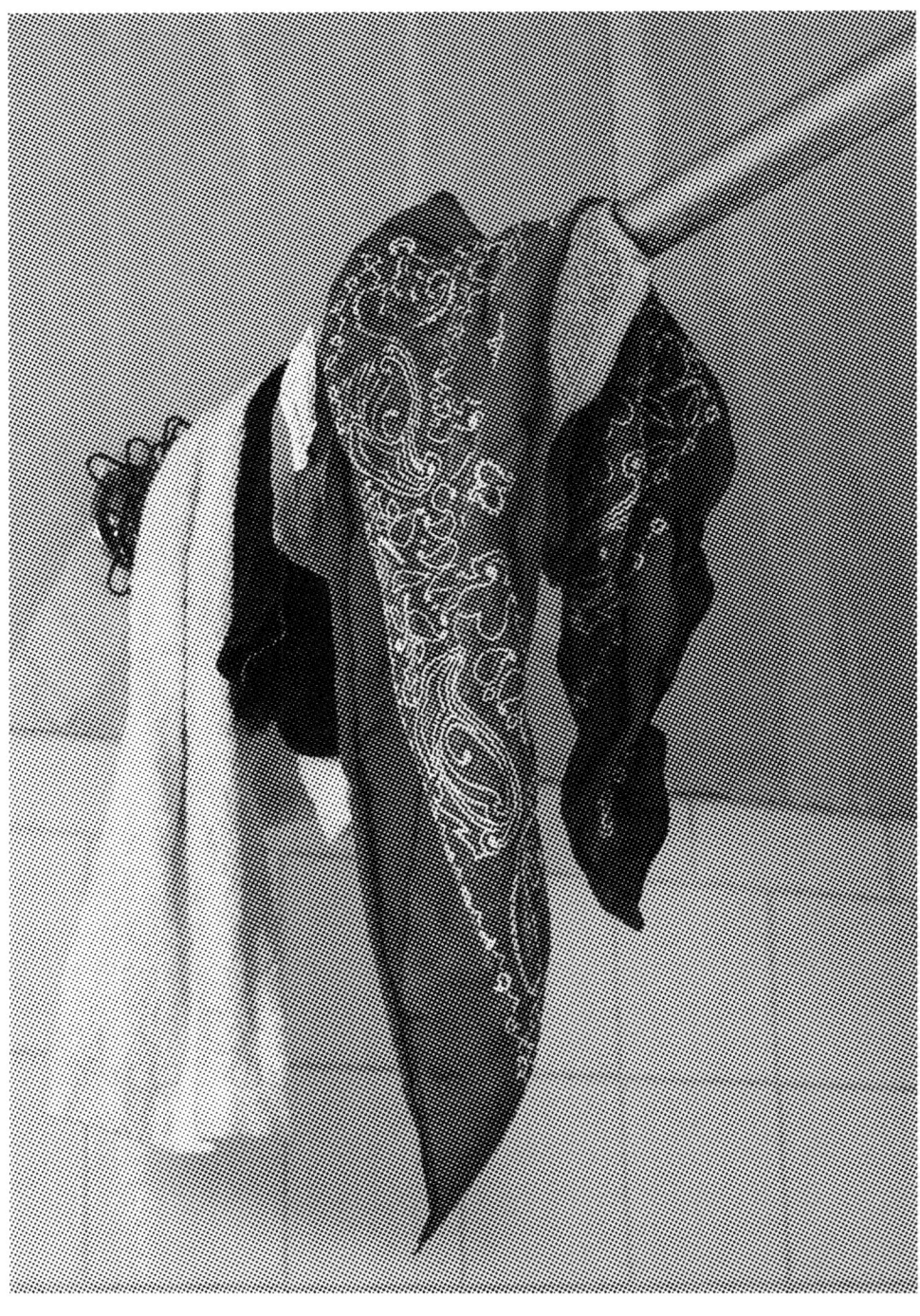

make bolder ones, not by buying sex toys, but by bringing your whole self to the persons you are fucking.

These days I teach photographers, and I've come to regard photographic documentation as the enemy of artistic thought. It is time to abandon the document, to show it for the false currency it is. We understand art through proximity, through our own risk—not by browsing and scrolling. What is the art fair experience, if not that of a three-dimensional trip through a Google image search? Attention accrues to the loudest, and the most looked-at becomes somehow the most pertinent.

What can we do now?

Present, not represent.

These pieces are embodied in the midst of a rhetorical landscape that has become increasingly disembodied.

Represent no one. Be yourself present, and make us a present of your pleasure.

Embody queer, don't represent it. Do this in your work, your teaching, your career.

Make things different.

Refuse to buy in; refuse the status quo; stop standing in for an idea, an abstraction.

Stop standing in the wings waiting for your big break in a show that we didn't write and that isn't meant for our amusement. Stop waiting to add your special stripe to the rainbow.

Stop hoping. Start transforming.

Notes

1. W. E. B. Du Bois, *The Souls of Black Folk: Essays and Sketches* (Chicago: A. C. McClurg, 1903), 3.

SAMWISE GAMGEE CRIES, WITH PADDING

Previously Unpublished, 2017

This is a performance script written for the New Narrative Conference. It hearkens back to the earlier text-based scripts from the 1980s and 1990s. —NB

1   I am service oriented.

2   And a list is the desperation of those of me who can't master form but want to be held by somebody else or hang out about to compare distances.

3   And Sam is, I am, longing for the Shire where I could decode every potato down to the dirt that whelped it and the chip it aspired to.

4   And I wanted to be a loved object understood always to be talking back before rings and stupid elves and the stupid thieving elfin.

5   And I couldn't sit as the bewitching character whose blankness gave birth to the absorbed reflector's agonized, flowering insides.

6   I have a sturdy hobbit torso.

7   And so am practical, not theoretical, which is the name that I gave to people that stick *the* in front of every noun to wish for meaning. The Body, The Lovers, The Discourse.

8   And so Sam: adjacent to meaning

9   "I don't care how much there is as long as it's firm."

10 And if I had made a lettered list, you would have some sense of how long I was going to go on for.

11 And in this version, Samwise is a child of identical cousins and the Riddler and Gomez Addams. Movies.

12 And so: Dungeons, Cigars, Train Wrecks, Lithium, Henchmen, Hot Dogs, Crêpes Suzette.

13 And so well we aren't available to history until I am become inert and as Missy says: Lose Control.

14 And so I can't help it, I regard with suspicion every person who hides their fine feet within shoes.

15 And on another hand, I should start a "to un-do list."

16 And Sam was and I am jealous of Sméagol's bifurcation, the way that their treachery and inner turmoil seems to captivate F to the exclusion of All others, so un-do. That's right It's better than yours I could teach you.

17 And so I petulantly say, "Hey, I carried the ring too, Me too. At least until F pulled it back."

18 Is there colorism in the Orc community?

19 And so the dwarves braiding each other's beards, hands sliding through hardened hands.

20 And mom was in an Amityville Horror, the one with the lamp, so I am an heir to stories too.

21 And if Middle Earth has run different races, does that dissolve prejudice or stand for a world built separate must be scrubbed?

22 Service oriented so in the years since F's departure, I've lapped piss off the floors of a subterranean club (now closed) known as the Manhole, but that was for cameras, so maybe it doesn't count or maybe it counts more, costar.

23 And I've been the mayor of Hobbiton eight times.

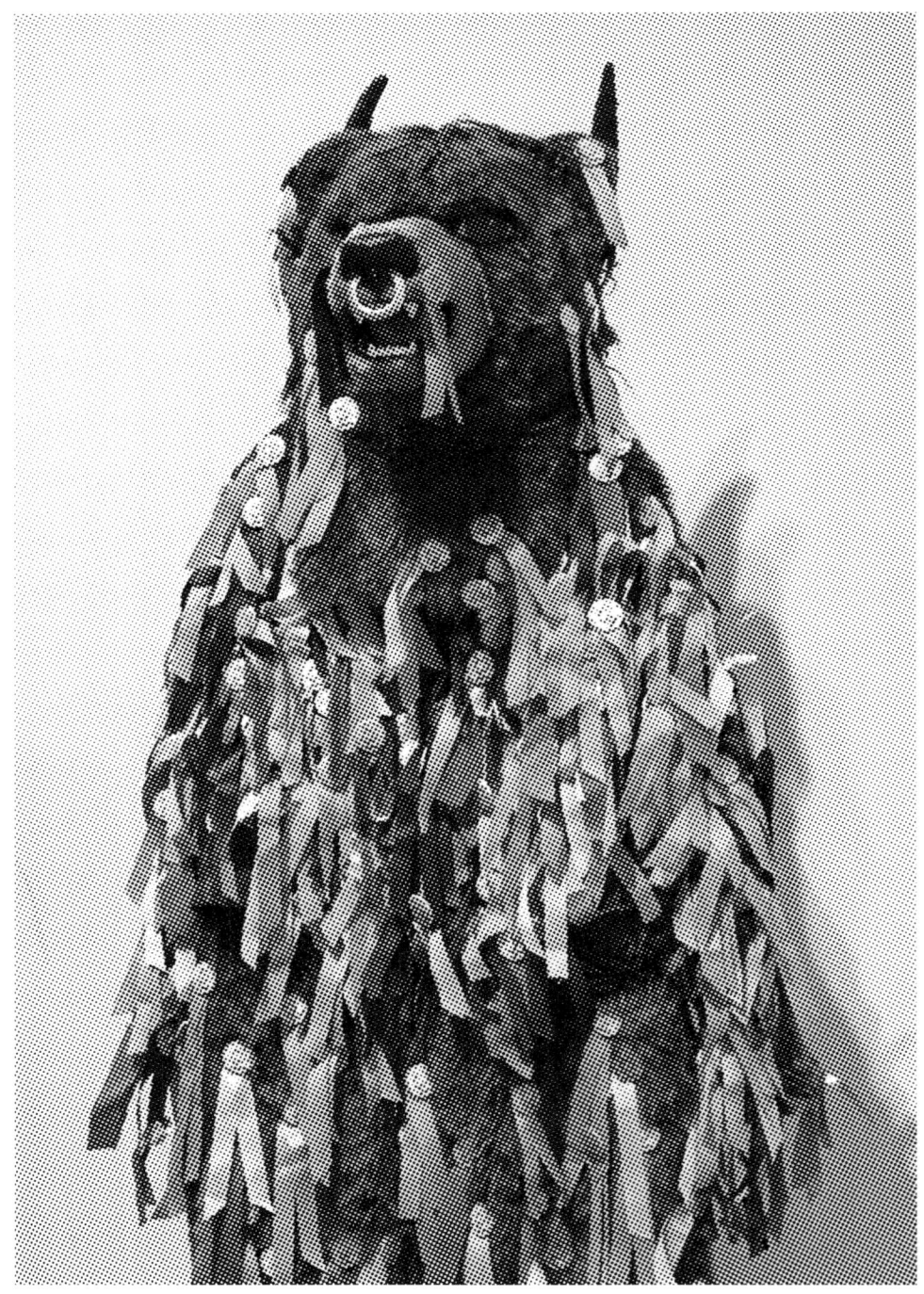

24 And I'm sorry I've forgotten how paragraphs work, out of peevish-
ness, but the men who left the piss smoked cigars, and the floor
was gritty on the tongue.

25 I Sam, I was, I am, F's batman, serving but called a switch.

26 And so service oriented, so when M, El Rey Nomo, suggests I put
on a chicken suit or that I have glory hole duty or that those clamps
belong on my balls, it all happens, and when L the Princess says be
daddy, or when J the Boss Lady says be dolly and presses my clit, I
think, "Let's see where this is going" because that's where stories
are minted, and I could hitch a.

27 And if this was a lettered list, I could have stopped with the last
one, but I'd have to charge.

28 And so Initials solve nothing, except and including who oh who
will ever write the history of flirtation and socialism and sarcasm.

29 And every aside is a middle on this earth.

30 And then F goes west, stretched thin and underbuttered, and I
that is Sam turn to Bywater and go on, and there is yellow light,
and there is fire within.

31 And, Well, I'm back.

INTERVIEW BY
TINA HORN

Mel *Magazine, 2018*

I learned about the furry fandom in the late 1990s but did not become an active participant until 2013. It's a culture where people are designing new identities for themselves through the creation of costumes, images, and stories—a rich cultural exploration that has pretty much bypassed the gallery-based art world. The sorts of transformations people imagine with and for each other in furry allow me to rethink the possibilities for my own body and gender. —NB

Tina Horn Gnomen, your "fursona," is a genderqueer anthropomorphic bear/bison. In the New Museum exhibition, you wear a Gnomen suit and instigate "encounters" with museum attendees. You and I have been at private play parties together where you're running around in a dinosaur costume. How is that exhibitionistic play related to this project? What's the difference between wearing a full-body costume at an art museum and doing it at a kinky play party? What is the relationship between your fursona and your libido versus your art or your identity?

Nayland Blake The short answer is that for me there isn't a difference: Almost as long as I've been making art, it has been part of the continuum of my sexual expression and vice versa. The only difference is the venue. In practice, however, there are types of interactions I can expect at a play party that I can't expect in a museum. But you'd also be surprised at how often people have confided to me in the midst of one of my performances that they find the situation "hot." So there is a strong libidinal component in our experience of art that we rarely get the chance to acknowledge. Part of my public performance work is about giving people the chance to experience and admit that.

For the New Museum show, Gnomen is riding the elevators with a tray full of badges and ribbons. There's a sign saying: "Pick up a button, tell your secret to the button, pin the button on Gnomen." The idea is that by the end of the show, Gnomen will be wearing the evidence of all of these secrets, all of these intimacies in the form of the ribbons. So the interaction is very structured, which allows people to feel safe in following the rules in public. In a private play party, you have the chance for more in-depth negotiation and thus improvisation.

Also, at private play parties, wearing an animal suit can be my way of cutting the superserious atmosphere of the "scene." Last summer, I hosted a queer orgy and did so as "Safety Skunk," which allowed me to outline the rules of conduct for the party in a way that was still also playful.

Horn How did you develop Gnomen's identity, and how much do you know about him? Is your Gnomen persona related to your personal fantasy life, or was he designed expressly for this art project? Do you have other fursonas?

Blake I met Gnomen about four-and-a-half years ago. I was very curious about folks who were part of the furry fandom and wanted to explore it further. A friend gave me some guidance around various furry sites, and after being on there for a while, various parts of Gnomen's personality began to make sense, and I got a clear image of what their appearance and attitudes would be. At that point, I began drawing them myself and also commissioning other artists to make art of them. Gnomen allows me to inhabit possibilities that are difficult for me: They are shorter than me, for example, and fatter. Their genitals can change; they can be turned into a stuffed animal or a rubber flotation device.

I think of Gnomen and my other fursonas as distinct from previous work I made when I wore bunny suits or made drawings of animals: Gnomen isn't a costume but more of a body that I can feel is coextensive with my own. As for personality: Gnomen is finicky and bossy with more of a sense of their own dignity, which makes them a good foil for debasement and mockery. All of these are aspects that have revealed themselves to me through the process of asking other people to make work with the character.

Horn How was the Gnomen suit made?

Blake The suit is unusual in that most fur suits are custom-made, commissioned from artists who do that for a living. I was initially trying to go that route, but the timing didn't work out. I still have plans to commission another suit, but the suit that's in the New Museum show is a premade bear suit that a friend of mine had that I have personally customized. I added the nose ring, the horns, and the hooves, and got a bespoke waistcoat from JCRT, a pair of clothing designers. In most furry circles, this wouldn't pass muster, and I've been trying to be clear that for me this isn't representative of what most fur suits are.

Horn What kind of interactions have you experienced at the New Museum so far? Have you mostly been in the elevators, or have you been roaming the galleries and café? What kind of interactions are you hoping will happen but haven't yet?

Blake After spending time in the suit, I realized that it isn't practical for me to move around all that much. I have low visibility and need to have someone spotting me during the performance, so I have stayed mostly in the museum's large elevator. This has a few benefits: First, as I arrive at each floor, there's a big reveal as the doors open, so it's a bit more theatrical. It also forces people to interact with me a bit more as they get in and out, but they also have the chance to act like this is business as usual and just pretend that they are totally cool with sharing the space with a big, hairy, ribbon-covered animal.

Reactions have been varied. Some people are excited to get close to Gnomen; others have something like a phobia where they can't even look at Gnomen. Children up to two years old seem to like it the most, and after that age, they get shy and uncertain. Most times, women will be the ones to initiate contact. Most men hide out. One thing that I enjoy the most is that most of the folks who work security at the museum enjoy Gnomen being there and are waving hello and being supportive. The two things I hear most often are "I don't have any secrets," said when people see that they are supposed to tell secrets to the buttons provided, and "I don't want to hurt you," said when people go to pin

My Studio Is a Dungeon Is the Studio

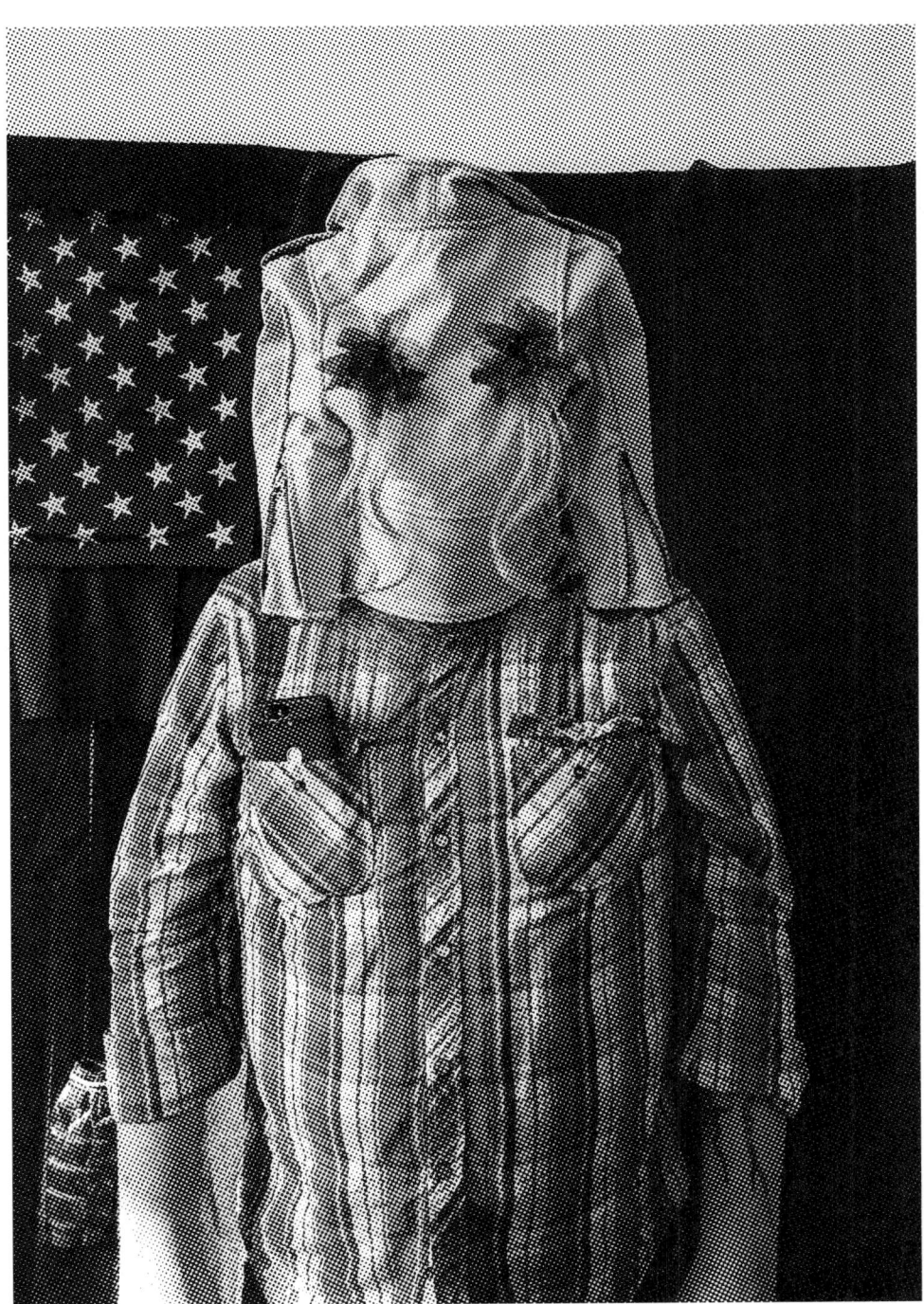

the buttons on. In both cases, people are saying it more for the benefit of those around them, which is very interesting to me. I'm seeing the way that people are responding to a request for intimacy by performing.

Horn How do people react differently to the Gnomen suit when it's hung up in the gallery as opposed to you when you're wearing it? For example, when I saw it hung up, it kind of reminded me of the taxidermy bears in certain kinds of rustic lodges/bars, and your presence felt sort of there but not there simultaneously. Do you have to be wearing the suit in order for Gnomen to be present in the gallery? How does this relate to the artist/art relationship, and the fursona/human relationship?

Blake I don't have much of a sense of how people are reacting when I'm not there, but I imagine that it's much like the way I reacted to the display of armor or costumes at the Metropolitan Museum in New York when I went as a child: by trying it on with my mind, by playing mental dress-up. One thing that has changed over the course of the show is that Gnomen is covered with more than six hundred secrets, so they are looking more festive and burdened at the same time. I don't think I have to be present for Gnomen to be active as a possibility, in the same way that I don't have to be watching a Daffy Duck cartoon to think about what Daffy might do in a specific situation. In truth, Nayland is as absent inside the suit as outside: People can't speak to me as Nayland when I wear it.

Horn What does it mean that Gnomen can change sex and gender at will? Is this something Gnomen is doing during your performance? Is there a way to tell? How is this related to your genderqueer identity? Is it a sort of supernatural affirmation? Or fantasy fulfillment? Is this none of my business?

Blake Working with and experiencing Gnomen has been a way for me to articulate and understand the shifting nature of my own gender identifications. So, yes, being inside of Gnomen has meant that there are moments when I feel those things shift, but I think the most important part is that Gnomen stands for me as a figure of having the body and pleasures that I want. In the time that I've been involved with kink, I've learned to experience sensation and connection in very different ways, to listen to the possibilities of my body. Gnomen and my other fursonas are my attempt to visualize those sensations on my own terms.

100 ASSIGNMENTS:
TOWARD A CURRICULUM

Previously Unpublished, 2020

I've taught for thirty years in colleges, residencies, and sex parties. I've come to view teaching as a necessity, a way of putting back into the world the culture and ideas the world has poured into me. The bedrock of teaching art is the assignment. And the basis for my own work as an artist is being able to give myself assignments. The right assignment at the right time can answer a need we haven't been able to articulate to ourselves. The assignments we need tell the story of how we view the work and the world, even if they tell it slant. I give my students assignments that were given to me directly in school as well as others that I've gleaned from the writings of artists and thinkers in various fields. Finding a good assignment provides a thrill. I give them to people for various reasons—to build a particular skill or to perhaps lead someone to a different sense of how they could look at what they do. Some of these I've honed over years of classes in various disciplines; some are for no one but myself. When I doubt what I do or am unable to get myself to work, the only thing that has got me out is a self-administered assignment. They have been my technique for creating myself. Good assignments are not easy to come up with, but one principle that has helped me comes out of recovery: Take the action, and let go of the result. Many times people attempt to use assignments to force people to come to a conclusion, to predetermine the outcome. Good assignments awaken us to the breadth of possibilities available to us rather than narrow things down to one possibility. They are the scaffolding we build to touch the unexpected and wild within ourselves. They are how we stretch. There is no right or wrong answer. There is only the next thing to do.

While these assignments will not turn someone else into me, they will provide the practitioner with a path to the deviations within themselves. —NB

1   Reconstruct, without photographs, a childhood toy, including what it felt, smelled, and tasted like.

2   Design a sculpture to be taken internally.

3   Make a crown. Give it away.

4   Purchase an issue of a magazine that you have never opened before. Treat it as the only surviving artifact of a vanished civilization. Use it to reconstruct the attitudes and values of that civilization. Create your own artifact as part of that civilization.

5   Draw the feeling of someone—a relative—lying on top of you and snarling while you struggle to get up.

6   Combine two pieces of your clothing into a garment that neither was designed for.

7   Find a collaborator. Have them touch you fifty times over a period of two hours.

8   Draw the previous US presidents from memory. Draw the next ten from your imagination.

9   Make a piece using only materials you have obtained by barter, without currency.

10 Make a guardian packet: a bundle to be worn under your clothing to keep you safe. It must have ten elements. Wear it for a week.

11 Holding your arms out from your sides, measure the distance from your left to your right hand. Make something that is that length, plus two feet.

12 Make daily drawings that cannot contain words.

13 Build your divination deck. Include the activity of adding a new card on your birthday.

14 Design your dream body: How many limbs does it have? How many holes? What is it covered with? Scales? Fur? Where is it most sensitive? What part is it proudest of? What kind of bed is most comfortable for it?

15 Describe your dream body to an audience and ask them the question of how they would care for it. Make drawings of their responses.

16 Build a sculpture that produces the pleasure of being ignored.

17 Make a hopeful piece.

18 Try again if your piece is about how hope never works out.

19 Carve a block of wood and say goodbye to every piece you take from it.

20 Say goodbye to yourself until the word loses all meaning. Then sing it.

21 Describe the subjecthood your upbringing has granted you and ask where you are dissatisfied with it.

22 Draw the feeling of when your genitals feel wrong for how you want to masturbate.

23 Make a piece that lies to you about your heritage.

24 Write a five-hundred-word explanation for a piece you will never make.

25 Cast your elbows, knees, crotch. Use the resulting fragments to make one smiling face, one frightened face, and one asleep face.

26 Masturbate and note the exact qualities of the image or scenario that tips you into orgasm.

27 Every time you take a photograph, shift six inches to the side and take another.

28 Paint a family food onto the side of a building.

29 Once a week, make ten drawings, each one by four inches. Leave these drawings as bookmarks in nooks on the shelves in second-hand stores.

30 Take a vinyl record and drill a hole 9/32″ in diameter one inch from its center. Using this as the new spindle hole, play the record and record it, using the recording as the basis for new musical compositions.

31 Practice drawing feet and hands.

32 Tell the story of your family, once as a triumph and once as a tragedy. In both tellings, only whisper.

33 Pick a favorite album. Make one piece for each song.

34 Sit near a wall and trace your shadow. No, the other one.

35 Learn how to program a game for the original Game Boy.

36 Make a piece, and hang it in your home. After one year, revise it. Repeat the process for the next four years.

37 Purchase a potato. Take fifty photographs of it, trying to make each as different from the previous ones as possible.

38 Make a sculpture that confines you until you are comforted.

39 With a chisel, carefully nick the laminate from a dresser you have found that was discarded. Gouge the particle board that is revealed until the entire surface looks fuzzy.

40 Wash until a shape is changed.

41 Fix a problem from a previous piece in a new piece.

42 Tell lies. Enjoy the taste of them.

43 Walk until the ideas come.

44 Draw the feeling of people turning away from you in embarrassment when you ask for help.

45 List your failings; make a piece for every item on the list.

46 In a public library, find a favorite book. Count ten books to the left and then use that book as the basis for four new pieces.

47 Using scrap fabric, make a flag for the country you will establish after you leave this one.

48 Design two traps.

My Studio Is a Dungeon Is the Studio

49 Create a pedestal for a famous sculpture.

50 Make a banner for each of your friends.

51 Install shelves on the street. See what ends up on them.

52 Make a performance for just one person. Show it only to them. Do not document or make any other record of it.

53 Have someone sew ribbons to your skin.

54 Design a holiday and the parade that celebrates it.

55 Every day: a painting made of ten strokes. Its surface can be any size or material; strokes can be any length.

56 Make a drawing about the statement "I am inside myself."

57 Take the technique of a sundae as the basis for a sculpture.

58 Design a monument to another artist.

59 Build the components for a piece that will be finally assembled ten years in the future.

60 Make note of every joke your family tells about itself. Rewrite them as songs.

61 Draw on yourself with bruises.

62 Draw the feeling of those around you.

63 Remember the potato you took fifty photographs of? Eat it and write a description of how it tastes on a shirt.

64 Wear that shirt and ask fifty other people to take a photograph of you in it.

65 Paint a recipe—no words.

66 In ten photographs, show how a particular person does their job. Only do this with their consent.

67 Write two lists of fifty items each: "In my work I always _____" and "In my work I never _____." For each of the next ten weeks, pick five of your "nevers" and do them.

68 Design a barrier. A sonic one.

69 Take *Hamlet*. Present the narrative of the play in ten found images. Edit the play to one hundred lines.

70 Practice drawing with feet and hands.

71 Find a painting made before 1600; re-create one object depicted in it in three dimensions.

72 Stash pieces where they will not be found until at least ten years after your death.

73 Find a black bag. Cut a hole in it. Put a white bunny in the bag.

74 For a day hold every door open for at least six people before you go through it.

75 Create a drawing across a city by tracing your steps. Scribble. Every ten blocks, observe something and draw it.

76 Sculpt a self-portrait where every part of your body that you feel is vulnerable is rendered at twice its normal size.

77 Draw what you miss.

78 Script a performance of your cowardice.

79 Make ten paintings on the theme "I forgive you." Send them to ten people picked at random.

80 Narrate the apocalypse as love at first sight.

81 Destroy all the documentation you have of a past piece.

82 Make a piece that everyone will call "intimidating." Make a piece that everyone will call "generous." Show them together and try to guess which is which. Contemplate the extent to which those words are the same.

83 Set up a collection point for other people to donate things that will cover over a piece that you have made.

84 Draw the stacks of books in your home, bringing out the way that they represent a weight that confounds any other small bit of progress in your life. Draw the impossibility of moving them and the ache inspired by that realization.

85 Define your race and then betray it.

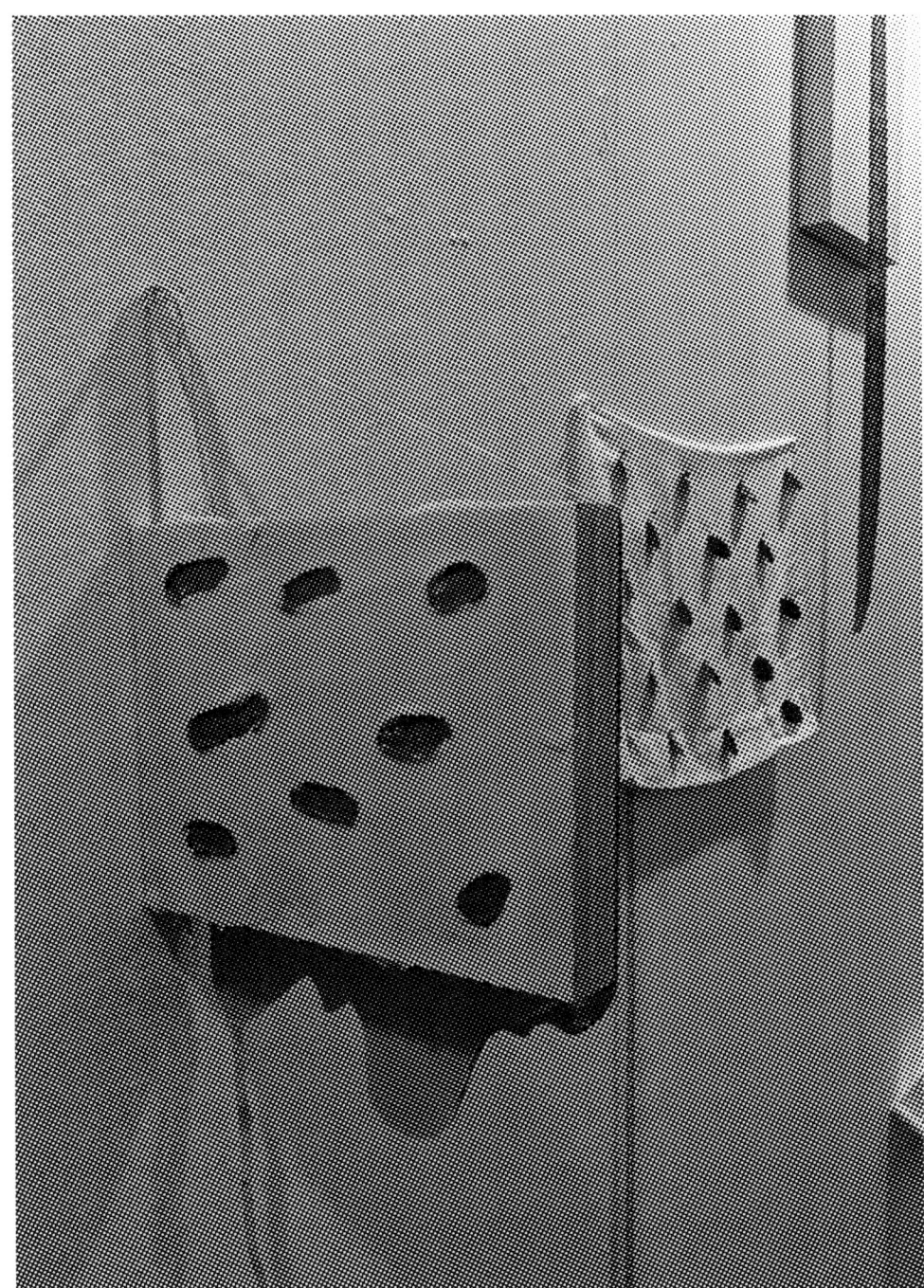

86 Make guardian packets (see assignment 10) for five of your closest friends.

87 Design a piece that will provide a thank you for the person who cleans an exhibition space. Make it.

88 At a paint shop, find the color that is the fury you feel when on a vacation with your partner knowing that you will break up with them once you return home. Purchase enough of the color to paint your bedroom. Every morning pour some on the floor and walk through it.

89 Cover up a tattoo.

90 No beards without dresses; no dresses without beards.

91 In any room, measure a space three feet in from the walls. Move any previous contents of the room into this new boundary. Spend three days within this new collection of objects. On the second day, request that collaborators make paintings to record your situation from the periphery. On the fourth day, clean yourself and the contents of the condensed room. On the fifth day, replace the contents of the room with the paintings.

92 Write fan mail.

93 Create a T-shirt; then form the band to go with it.

94 Gather a list from friends of ten words they associate with *private*. Wear those words publicly.

95 Go to an exhibition. Note the name of each piece. Go home and draw each piece from memory and your list of names.

96 Take your initials. Draw a self-portrait using the letterforms as the only mark you can make.

97 Once a week, create one object to furnish your Utopia.

98 Devise assignment 99.

100 Do what you have left undone.

SHAMBLING MONSTROSITY
SEEKS MAD SCIENTIST

Previously Unpublished, 2021

A return to the early collage performances. I was asked to do something for a Scooter LaForge show; I adore Scooter's work and was so happy to be asked. This piece is my coming out as monstrous, as wanting to own the monstrousness of my own body and the body that I would desire and to be kind of honest about that. In this way, it relates to the later performance In My Dream Body. —NB

Me: six-foot, two-inch, 258-pound griz bear bottomed mulatestto mutt thing with newly trained clot occasional ingrown hairs and many that are outgrown as well, smoker happily forgetful drinker and little tiny pocket packer on intoxicants, pretty CORNY popped, post palatable depressed, wearing thin and wearing finery, an aspiring preacher without a flockING who would build a cavern of wonders to rival Ludwig if they didn't shit where they ate. I learned everything I know worth knowing from fistfeminists and now I am a gender-neutral bathroom. Preferred pronouns are grumble, lubricate, and omnivore. Trained by year on year of after-school cartoons moving drawings where everything became everything else anvils falling to boys and girlfriends named goo with no block to their heads hosted by ranchers or at least men in rooms with bales of hay who hold their dummies on their laps and play the straight man to chunks of wood while in ice cream castles adorned with neon boos rabbits dispense manicures of bowled mousetraps and the children clap with anxiety, I have learned that there are no wrong holes and arrange my expansive and deeply recolonized terrain accordingly.

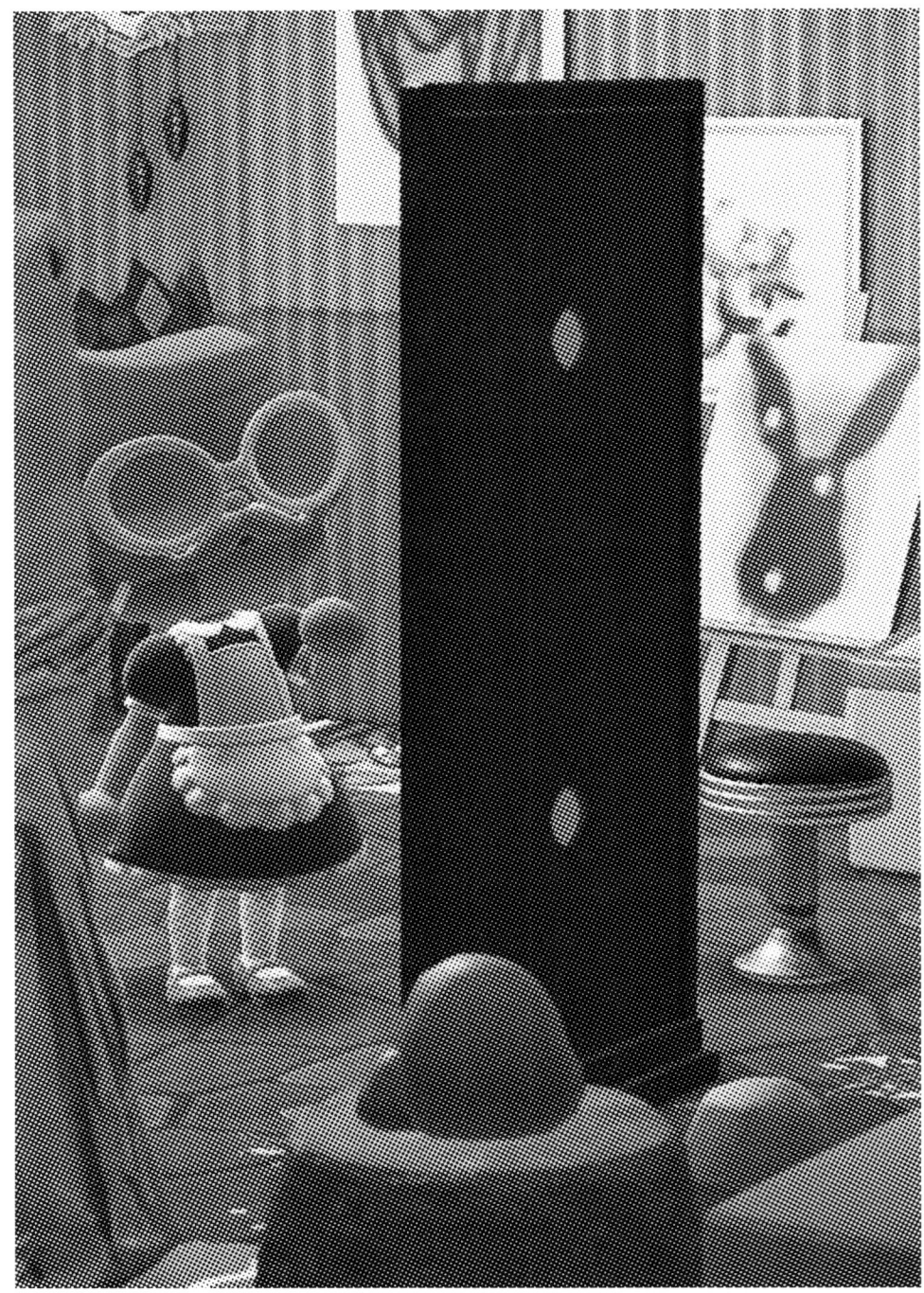

Looking for researchers welding electricity and assistants with a taste for grave robbing and fly gobbling (because of all the little lives therein) who leap before they lock and nestle their pestle. You may be single double or legion, just be ready to cast me out. You can have your own fungeon or say to me my placards or yours? We will flee and forgive the tiresome townsfolk together until we reach the rutted ruins of this country's comfortless dream nooks when we will turn and tentacles entwined beg them to present their pitchforks and torches which we will mount until they are extinguished and blunted or the patriarchy ends, whichever comes first.

Serious Replies Only! I AM A FAT FEMME PHONY, YOU BE THE SAME. DON'T WASTE MY TIME OR YOUR OWN.

EMBARRASS, HUMILIATE, DEGRADE, OBJECTIFY: BASICS OF PSYCHOLOGICAL STATUS PLAY

Previously Unpublished, 2022

I teach in "official" academic settings, and for nearly twenty years, I've taught in kink settings—at gatherings and dungeons around the country. This is the outline for one of my kink classes, but it is also me teaching art, trying to answer the questions: How can we produce meaning in our lives? How can we awaken to the creative possibilities in the moment? It also explores the question of why anyone would want to be humiliated. Kinky people know that what they do is dangerous and that they are the only ones to whom they can look to keep one another safe. They can't rely on the state or the family. The fact is that all sex and all creativity is just as dangerous. The tools developed by kinky people would be helpful in an art world that professes an interest in social movements and interactions but remains quite naive about how to cultivate trust and safety. Because I move across the borders of those worlds, I try to bring the approaches together. S&M communities are communities of trust. You gain trust in that community by being a safe player and being clear about what it is that you're going to do and how you're going to do it. And by achieving consent. And if you lose those things, then you don't play. People don't want to play with you. —NB

What's Psychological Status Play?

I call these types of play *psychological* because they can be engaged in with only your mind and mouth. And all of them involve the ideas of fluctuating status on the part of the subject of the play. *Subject* rather than *bottom*.

A word of caution: Psychological play is both subtler and more difficult than physical play, in that the potential damage is both slower to be seen and longer lasting. It's my belief that it is also much more rewarding, requiring greater empathy and intimacy between the players. So I don't believe that these types of scenes are pickup play. They require prior negotiation and postplay follow-up.

Why are we drawn to it?

Humans are primates, animals that have evolved elaborate social structures. Place, in hierarchy, is important. Every social gathering is a parade of social and psychological behaviors. We play with psychological pain for the same reason we play with physical pain: to know what lies on the other side of what we fear.

Defining Terms

Embarrass: To cause confusion and shame to; make uncomfortably self-conscious; disconcert; abash.

Humiliate: To cause (a person) a painful loss of pride, self-respect, or dignity; to mortify; to make humble.

Degrade: To reduce (someone) to a lower rank, especially as a punishment. "He was degraded from his high estate."

Objectify: To treat as an object.

The first three are actions, types of play; the third is a technique that may be employed in inducing the other states.

Distinctions Between Terms

Embarrassment is a social behavior, a response when a social norm has been violated and one feels implicated in the violation. One can be embarrassed by the acts of other people. While the feeling of embarrassment may be acute, it does not challenge one's core: I may be embarrassed to not know the answer to a question, but it is not immediately implied that I am a stupid person. Embarrassment has to do with how we are perceived at the moment. Embarrassment also seems tied to the accidental and is thus easily forgiven by others. Often, embarrassment is something that we signal socially to others: We blush, we giggle, we are expressing and releasing tension. In part, we are asking for help. It is not a serious change in status to be "confused," as the definition says. Societally, it can be acceptably flirtatious to remark on this, which means that we are noting the temporary change in status, but we have not violated a societal norm. At least in the West, it is acceptable to note embarrassment as a way of increasing intimacy. In play, we might deliberately use a crude term to provoke an embarrassed reaction in our subject.

Humiliation makes one humble and has more to do with one's beliefs about oneself. It involves behaviors and situations that *might* have implications for the person as a whole. I expose myself in public; does that mean that I am a flasher? Humiliation also reinforces a positive core value (paradoxically). My top orders me to piss myself in public: In the eyes of others, I am somehow incontinent or incompetent, but since I know that I am doing it on orders, my core value of myself as a submissive has been reinforced. Oddly enough, I've done a good thing in the context of my relationship (following orders) even though I've done a bad thing in a public sense (pissing myself). Many religions incorporate humility and becoming humble as a spiritual tool. Silence, restrictive clothing, and the renunciation of worldly goods and achievements are all tools that make us humble but do not make us "bad people." Failure, in a social sense, is a good way to produce humiliation. Many cuckold scenes are humiliation scenes. More on this later.

To degrade someone is to attack a core belief. Degradation works only if the person believes in the grading system they are being repositioned within. If someone is a sex worker, it is professional for them to ask for money for sex, not degrading. If you believe that you are better than a whore, then having to ask for payment for sex is degrading. You cannot bust someone down from sergeant to private if they are outside of the military and thus not part of the system of rank. Degradation also implies a longer-lasting change in status. Plenty of people would work in a kissing booth for an afternoon without suffering any change in self-image, but if they had to do it day in and day out, if they became "that chick who works at the kissing booth," then their status would change in a deeper way. If you want to degrade someone, you have to know what they view as essential about themselves. In our society, people are closely identified with their jobs, where they live, their family position, their sexuality. Is the person a vegetarian? If so, what do they feel about meat eaters? By forcing them to eat meat, you may be degrading them. As men or butches, what do they feel about feminine people? Is forcing them to act feminine degrading them?

My Studio Is a Dungeon Is the Studio

Remember that we are dealing with someone's core, and when that is attacked and questioned, their reactions can be violent and unexpected.

Many people ask to be degraded when what they want is to be humiliated.

Be careful: The prefix *de-* means "to take away from." Every time you degrade someone, you are taking something. They are not giving it up voluntarily. You may feel that that is a good use of your power, but I believe that everything you take in a D/s (Dominance and submission) relationship, you then have a responsibility for. It's just like if you take my stereo: Once you have it, you have to figure out if you are going to store it, sell it, or whatever. Any of those decisions has an implication for further down the line. You can just give it back at the end of the scene, but if you are going to do that, you have to decide *how* you do so because that also has many implications. How do you return me to myself? Restore my rank? What gesture, what words, will do that?

Objectification is more of a technique to be employed in these scenarios. An object may automatically seem like a step down in status, but it isn't always: It may be a useful object or a sacred object—a beloved dolly or a trusted tool.

An example of these things in action: *Silence of the Lambs*
(At this point, I play the scene of Clarice Starling's first encounter with Hannibal Lecter from *Silence of the Lambs* and then break down what happens.)

Migs: "I can smell your cunt!" while masturbating. He attempts to degrade Starling: "You are nothing but a cunt, and I know it."

Lecter asks for ID, directs her into moving "closer . . . closer." He alludes to her rank: "You're not real FBI."

Lecter humiliates Starling by asking her to repeat what Migs said.

She says, "He said he could smell my cunt." By obeying, she is gaining intimacy with Lecter and reinforcing core identity traits (I am honest and strong; I can repeat this without believing it).

He is humiliating her by humbling her into the role of patient to his doctor. His concluding line of the exchange, "I, alas, cannot," followed by the elaboration of everything he can smell, is a subtle compliment, implying a desire for her and an interest in her. But he expresses this interest in a socially acceptable form. It is part of Lecter's menace that he understands social norms and expectations so much more completely than his adversaries ("and don't lie or I'll know"). He seduces Starling by demonstrating that he can see her as she is and still value her. Thus, the points when he chooses to punish her are all that more painful. "You know what I see when I look at you? A rube . . ." (He also, I believe, sees her as queer, or, at least, not interested in sex with men's "sticky fumblings in the backs of cars.")

When Starling leaves, Migs hits her in the face with his cum, successfully (in his eyes) degrading her at that point. He proves that she's just "a cunt" there to take his load. Lecter calls her back and expresses regret—"I detest all coarseness"—(or something like that) and later punishes Migs by making him swallow his own tongue.

How to Play This Way

1. Know Your Scene

Take some time to ask some questions, just as I did at the beginning; clarify your terms so that you are speaking about the same objectives.

I'm a big fan of a standard questionnaire.

So:

Have they played with humiliation before?

If so, what do they mean by the term? What happened, and how did they react to it?

Were they embarrassed or humiliated as a child?

If so, by whom, and how, and about what? You are looking for both things to aim for and things to steer away from.

What are the things they value? Ask them about what they value in others and how others see them.

Who do they believe they are better than? People are trained not to reveal this information directly, so you have to listen carefully for it.

What are their core beliefs about themselves—those things they would hate to lose?

Ask about clear, must-avoid phrases and areas.

Ask how they react to embarrassment socially. Some people get chatty, some silent.

2. Know Your Setting

Gain an understanding of the social structure of the situation. What are the rules of where you will play? What is expected of people? Asking someone to expose their genitals in a dungeon may not produce much effect. Asking someone in a restaurant to go to the bathroom, remove their stockings (or, in the case of men, to put them on), and return to the table may not look

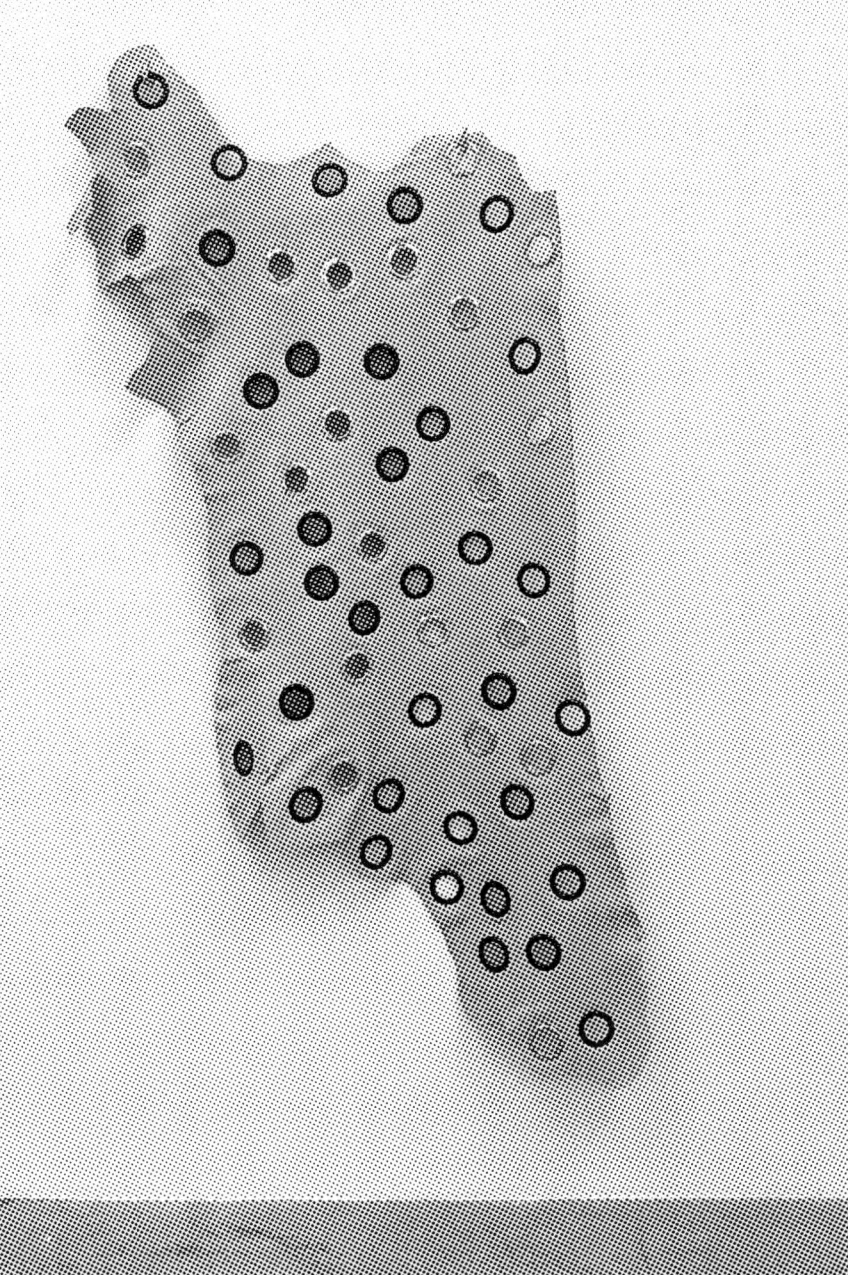

different to the casual observer but can produce a strong feeling of humiliation because of its implied public nature.

Use the rules of the situation to produce failure in the subject. If they are expected to speak, make sure they can't. Don't let them use their hands. Don't overreach: If it's a public situation, what will happen if they meet someone who could create a real problem for them? Have a plan.

Acknowledging someone's embarrassed appearance but refusing to help can move them to humiliation: "Why the act? We both know what a pig you are. Why shouldn't other people know as well?" Think about body language and other gestures of help.

Social structures exist to provide people with reassurance. You want to take that away. Stand too close. Get impatient. Don't give agreement signals.

3. Know the Goal

The goal is to get your subject to expose a truth about themselves but not the ultimate truth about themselves. Most people have an identity that they want to inhabit and an identity that they fear inhabiting. The importance of witnesses.

What to watch out for:

Breakdowns. People may well not know their own limits. Be ready to provide reinforcement of core values through activities. Since this is a kind of social play, it requires social activity to come out of it. Public praise, demonstration of competence. This goes for bottoms too. Have something ready to do. What is the reward?

Check back in, and provide empathy. Have an exit interview: What worked for them, and what didn't? Often, things we think of as hot in the abstract are not once we experience them. Or we may be surprised when a "minor" aspect of the scene really works for us. Think about how you can do more of that the next time around.

IN MY DREAM BODY:
FOR JORGE ZONTAL AND
GENERAL IDEA

Previously Unpublished, delivered at **General Idea: Ecce Homo,** *2022*

Every morning my alarm sounds: a batch of animal chirps and tweets and gentle susurrations of wind—insistent voices of nature that compete with what actually comes through the windows of whatever place I'm sleeping. As I reach to swipe it off, I am battling time, hoping to fix in my mind the memory of the previous night's dream. I am pulling together textures and imagery into sentences I will repeat to myself hopefully in the minute before Google Assistant greets me, tells me about my schedule, and starts to play me the day's news.

Since February 2021, I have distilled the previous night's dream into a tweet and a journal entry. Frustrated with not being able to recall my dreams, I decided to force the issue by returning to a practice I had in my early twenties and through that practice rewriting myself thus: "I am a person who remembers their dreams." And so, each morning, I write a sentence that starts with "In my dream." Enacting that daily revision, hauling the night's fragments into narrative, has allowed me to dawdle on the threshold, to become sensitive to everything that is going on in my consciousness at the day's boundary.

Through that sensitivity, I have come to see that, at the same time as I clutch at my slippery dreams, I am also pulling together a body—from sensation, from memory, from shame and joy. I am re-membering myself. Each

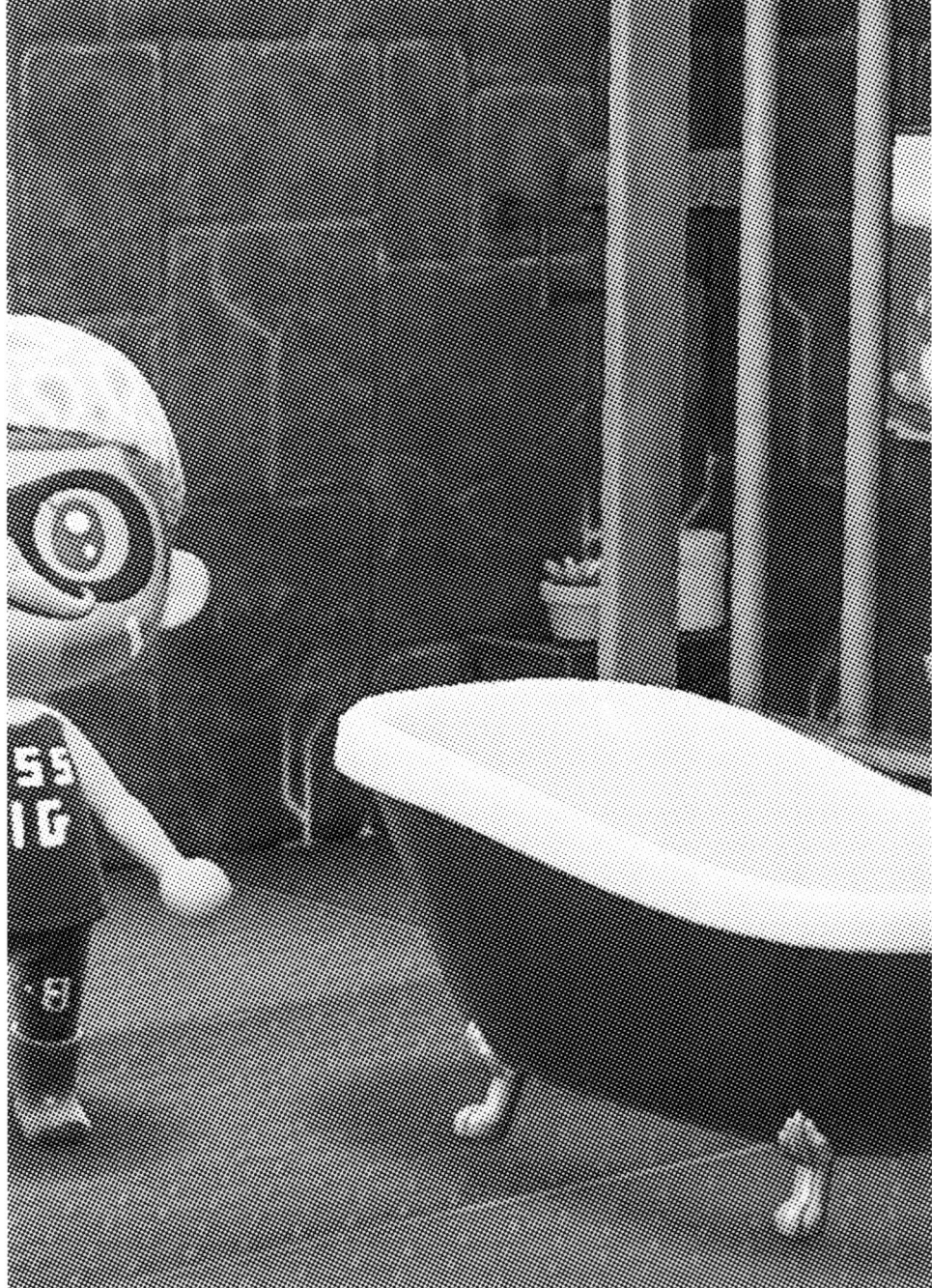

night, my body dissolves, contorts, loses coherence. It becomes a terrain and the monsters that roam that terrain. It is not my "self" because it knows that it predates that self, and it knows that it will be there—fragmented and stuffed—at the end, when the self, that parade of social response and reflection, has fled into death.

Each night unraveled, each morning knitting together dream and body. So why not acknowledge that each day's body is as chosen as each day's dream tweet? Why not a dream body? A body that reveals itself in narrative slippage and ellipsis, a body sung eccentric? I say, "There is the body I have, and the body I wish I had." But it's really the body I *say* I have, and I can say something different. To do so, I need maps and examples. Targets and aspirations.

And so, to Jorge's/General Idea's drawings. Drawings made out of a collective will using an individual hand, issuing from a compiled body, one with bad or, perhaps, the best boundaries. This compiled work offers me the maps to my dream body, that vagabond commune of delights. I'll say a few things about it as it congeals in my consciousness this morning, using the language of my tweets:

In my dream body I fill every frame with a boisterous quaking fat.

In my dream body each orifice has a welcome mat, and every lump has a cozy place to nestle.

In my dream body there are no cops, and every bristle and pimple is a possibility.

In my dream body my eyes are down here, buddy.

In my dream body lines are thick and flesh baggy saggy for you to heft deliciously.

In my dream body revulsion is the happy sister to revolution.

In my dream body one of my mouths is filled with flames, and one of my assholes is a roach.

In my dream body there is no room for you, but there is always room for you and you and you.

In my dream body the waves crest, and each wave has a boat, and each boat has a little man in it, and each little man is always found forever and waving.

In my dream body the Halloween costume wears it.

In my dream body the tailor's knees buckle at the many many possibilities.

In my dream body the jowls are windows to the soul.

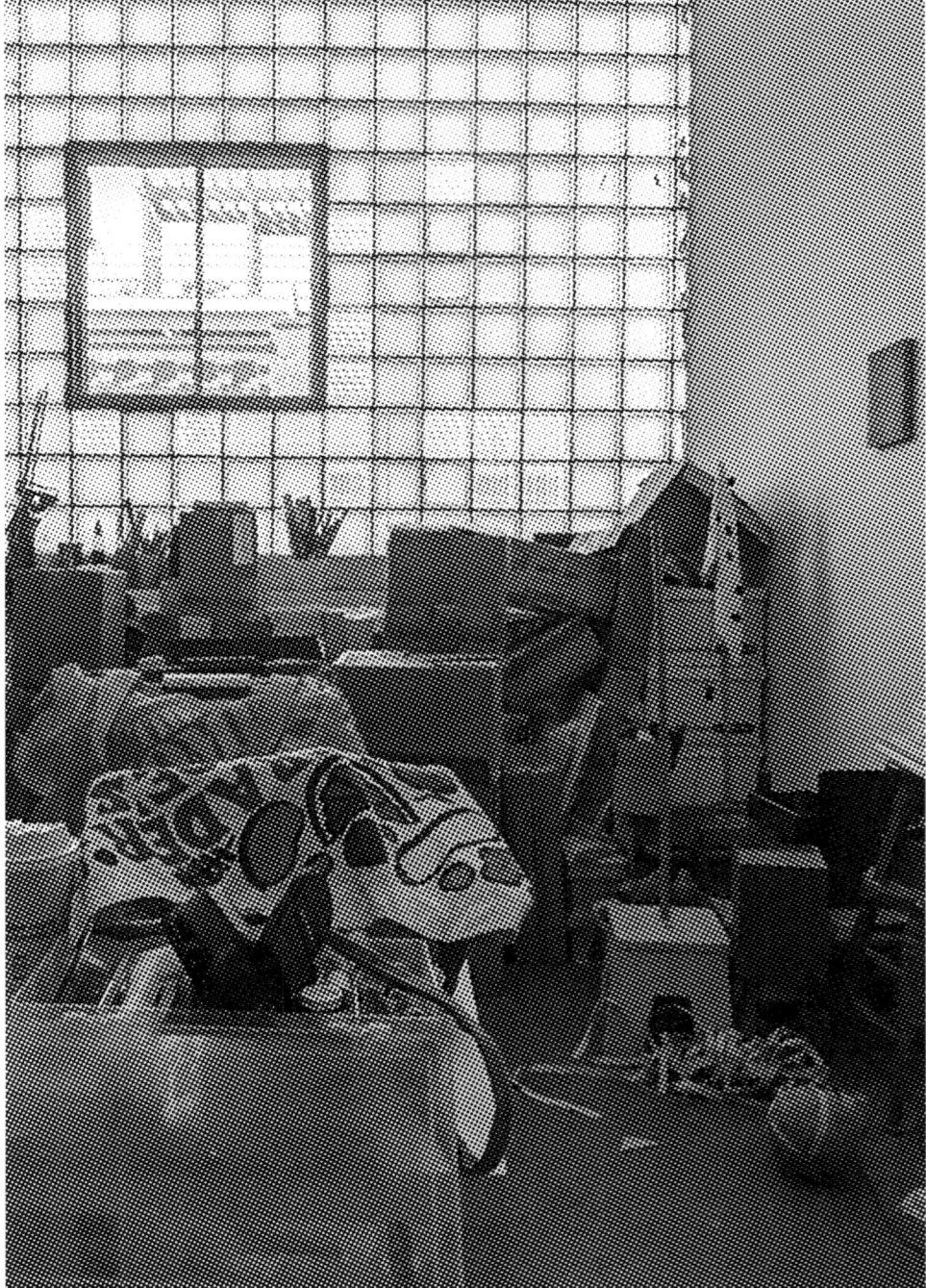

In my dream body the inside is always on the verge of, as Diana Ross would put it, "comin' out, wanting the world to know, and getting to let it show."

In my dream body no ticket is refundable, but every seat is a box.

In my dream body the droop and the dribble hold hands beneath the "they-might-be-tits" until they applaud my graceful shudders and welcome me into the day.

YUMMY, SLURP! THE PIPPA
GARNER STORY

Pippa Garner: $ELL YOUR $ELF, *2023*

I was seven years old when I hit the jackpot. After weeks of staking out the gumball machines at the local grocery store and cadging nickels from my parents at every opportunity, I had a plastic capsule in my hand, and in that capsule was my new mascot: a hairy, rotund figure with popping eyes, a feral grin, notched ears, and patched overalls with the letters "R.F." appliquéd to the front that identified what my new treasure was: a Rat Fink.

Created by car customizer and countercultural antihero Ed "Big Daddy" Roth in 1963, Rat Fink was a character initially conceived as an answer to the oppressive blandness of the 1950s iteration of Mickey Mouse. In place of Mickey's smooth, rounded outlines, staid family-friendly success, and suburban leisure clothing, the Fink is all jagged lines and antisocial aggression. He looks like he smells bad, even if you don't notice the flies buzzing around his clearly unwashed feet. He's probably a speed freak in both senses of the word. The card that was stuck to the front of the gumball machine was a marvel of advertising: A group of Rat Fink key fobs are surrounded by phrases like "I'm sloppy," "I'm vicious," "I'm selfish," "I'm dirty," "I'm dangerous," "I'm nasty"—the whole thing surmounted by the phrase "Rat Fink: That's Me!" Seven-year-old me could not resist that siren call, somehow sensing that I had more in common with the monstrous rat than with the milquetoast mouse.

Every notion of progress, whether it be social or aesthetic, creates the possibility of its shadow at the moment of its conception. That shadow, composed of everything that "progress" must repress to assert its own positivity,

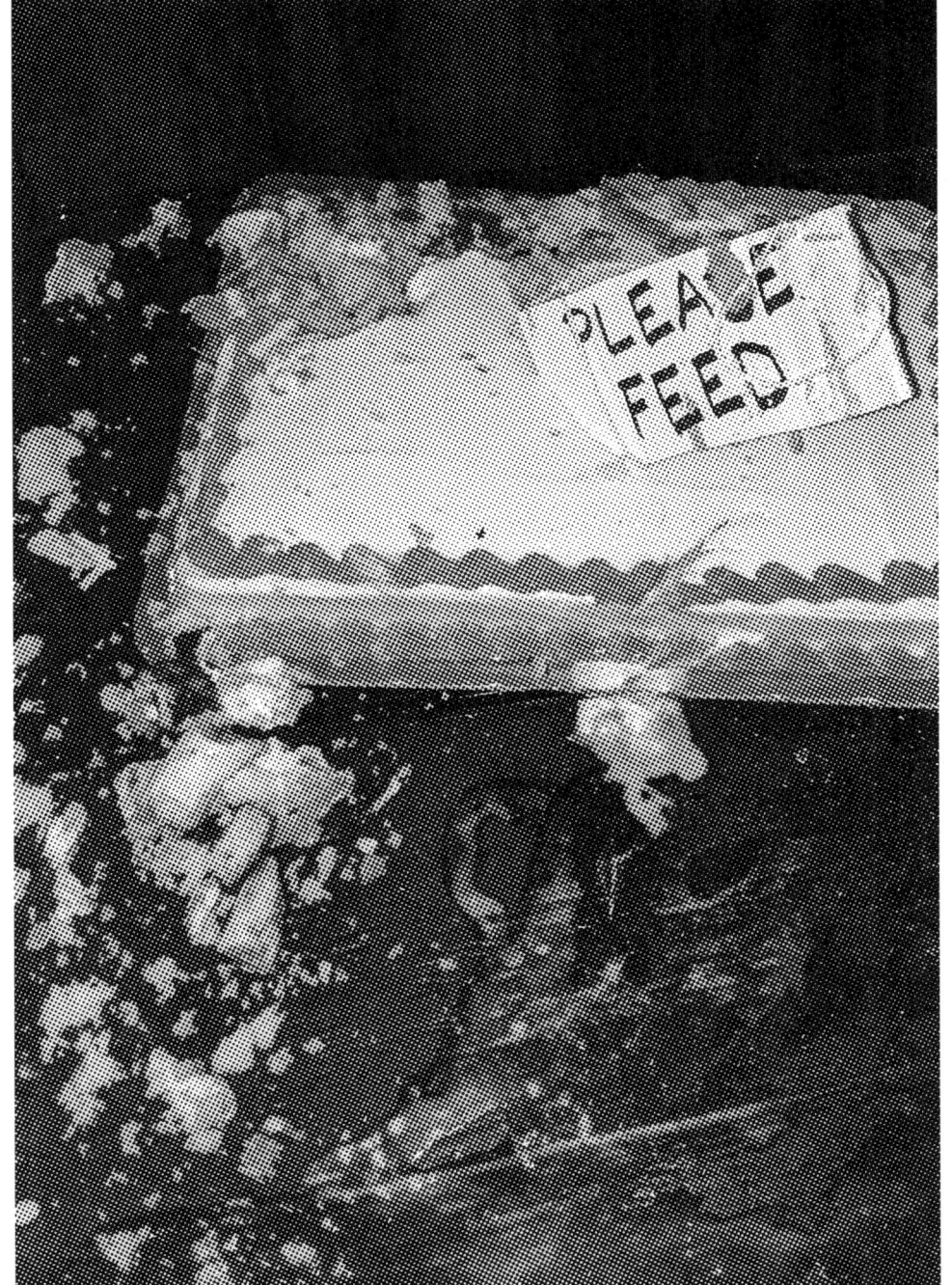

resides within culture as a place of potential power, a location that can correct the stupidity and brutality that often walks alongside forces of "progress." The flush of economic power that the United States experienced in the aftermath of World War II jump-started a positivist cultural imperialism built on extravagant consumer culture and social conservatism. American capitalism positioned itself as the antidote to global communism as well as all kinds of social deviance. American automobiles, in particular, were advertised as symbols of freedom, virility, and triumphant individuality, in spite of their merely being mass-produced, mass-marketed commodities. And these symbols of supposed progress called forth their shadow: a counterculture of the customized, the antisocial, the hybridized, and the monstrous.

Custom car culture was the freaky, dirty reaction to the gloss of American consumerism. It was dirty, handmade, unshaven, and misshapen, created by ne'er-do-wells in greasy garages who pillaged old junkers and created rococo missiles out of the parts they found there. Custom car culture was twinned with the rise of "sick culture," the impulse that mostly played out in comedy and print media, encompassing creators like Charles Addams, Basil Wolverton, Lenny Bruce, and many more. Sick culture was surrealism's pop culture wing, delighting in monsters, grotesque bodies, and goofball cynicism. *Mad Magazine* was its most visible publication, trailing in its wake imitators like *Cracked*, *Think*, *Help!*, *Frenzy*, and *Humbug*. Big Daddy Roth was the figure that forged the connection between custom car culture and sick culture, creating visions of goon-eyed hot-rodders whose bodies were as weird as their wheels.

The counterculture of the 1960s and 1970s produced its own narratives of progress, built around bodily autonomy and liberation. In a funny way, the monsters of sick culture were tamed and mellowed into hippies for whom progress required nothing more than the twinned platitudes of peace and love. The possibilities of social revolution postulated by the New Left, the civil rights movement, and the women's movement all were absorbed and transmuted into new varieties of soothing consumerism.

The commonality running through and linking all these developments is the sophisticated burbling of America's most evolved cultural language: advertising. Since World War II, American advertising has worked to sell the world on visions of prosperity, safety, stability, and conformism couched in a rhetoric of individualism. It has called for change, as long as change meant continuing to buy the same stuff. It has preached "togetherness" as an antidote to collective action and has sold jeans, cigarettes, shotguns, and computer operating systems, all called "Maverick."

Enter Pippa Garner, child of an ad man, whose early life reads like a train-ing course in mainstream identity: midwestern childhood, employment in an auto factory, stint in the military, college for auto design, job as an illustra-tor for *Car and Driver* magazine. And yet, while steeped in the language and locations of advertising, Garner managed to see the shadows it birthed. As she says in an interview from 2021, "The advertising, consumerism, in the background in my life, was very much gender-oriented. There were things for women and things for men. It was all-out masculinity or all-out femininity, macho or made up. And if you didn't feel that yourself, you felt uncomfort-able. That was what they wanted, so that you would buy their products."[1] She saw the outfit that society had measured her for and knew that it didn't fit.

To begin with, she used the tools and language of mid-century American consumerism to call forth the monstrous and hybrid. She started customiz-ing cars. Her approach was markedly different from that of the detailers and hot-rodders of an earlier generation. The Southern California scene, for all of its macho bluster, produced cars that were as camp as the outfits of any drag queen: acid yellow, candy-flaked, curving bodies topped by plexi-domes and dripping with chrome; flame jobs as carefully applied as any shadow and eyeliner. In contrast, Garner's vehicles present as midwestern butch. If you sell a car as just an extension of a guy's dick, she asked, why not a car with a dick? That proposal didn't go over well at automotive design school: They expelled her. She took on the identity of a tinkerer, a putterer, a customizer whose subversions could pass muster as mere eccentricities: "Hey, that idea's so crazy it just might work!" Watch her deftly deadpan her way through an interview with that pillar of the American mainstream, Johnny Carson, pre-senting a series of gadgets that solve problems that, on further reflection, are all problems of gender, alienation, loneliness, and social anxiety. Her patter is quiet and reserved: She's not pushing for jokes; she's letting the ideas do the work. (Now imagine what she could do with that temple of entrepreneurial pomposity, *Shark Tank*.) Her work at this point seems to me to be related to several other strains of subculture that employed similar imagery, like the Church of the SubGenius and DEVO.

If I can customize my car's body, then why can't I customize my body? It's a simple question, and Pippa was not alone in asking it. Throughout the 1980s, several communities converged around the idea of body modifica-tion as performance art, spiritual quest, or personal adornment. In the Bay Area, these explorers overlapped with the expanding tattoo culture and the leather scene, an interaction documented in the RE/Search publication *Modern Primitives*. Most of these modifiers weren't thinking about gender, and even though there was an increasing number of visible trans people, they were discussed as being in transition from one side of a gender binary to another. The idea that it might be possible to walk away from a binary altogether was rarely brought up until the next decade, when the concept of gender as performance began to gain purchase.

Pippa brought a customizer's sensibility to the problem of her gender, experimenting with her body's chemistry, looking at surgery and tattooing. Creating a new self. In this sense, she is her most utopian work. But as I said, every utopia spawns a shadow, and it is the way that Pippa has voiced that shadow that moves me most. To understand that, we need to return to advertising once again.

Behind every physical thing that advertising encourages you to consume there lurks another thing it is trying to sell you: the notion that your self is something that expresses its essence through the act of consumption and not through the act of creation. This conflation of selfhood with consumption is a sophistry so pervasive that it allows people to measure their social actions in relation to what they term their "brand." We have internalized capitalism's transactional ontology so completely that we become willing advertisements for ourselves and by extension our communities. And so we get the Minority Role Model, precursor to, among other nightmares, the Influencer. Minorities are offered the chance for the basic human dignity they are owed, so long as they behave themselves and spout the same positivism as the mainstream. They are supposed to inspire with their courage, overcome the odds, express gratitude for the scraps.

Like any sensible monster, Pippa rejects that position too, refusing to be looked up to, to repackage her pain and desires into uplift and inspiration. My favorite works of Pippa tackle this state of affairs directly: How do we demand what we want when all we can use is the debased language of advertising and we know how debased that language is? I'm talking about the series of personal ads she has posted in various queer publications since her transition and the sloganizing T-shirts she continues to make. These ads bounce between disdain and desperation, exuberance and raucous humor, all in the space of a few well-turned phrases:

SEX CHANGED DEVIL GIRL

> I AM the battle of the sexes—the worst traits of man and woman convoluted into one demented soul. Step into my lair and you are lost irretrievably. Even reading this is dangerous. Yummy, slurp![2]

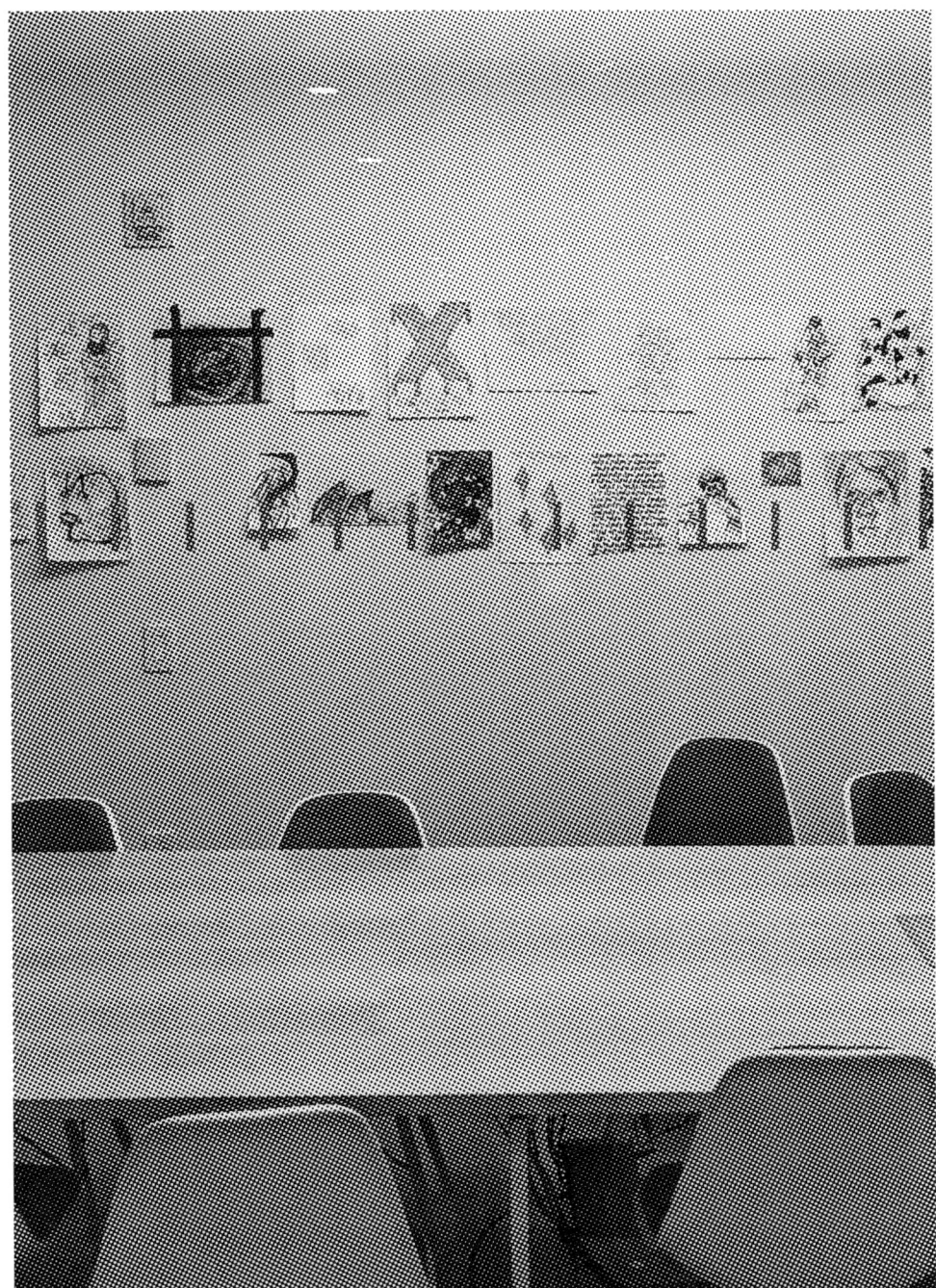

This is masterful writing and as wonderful a piece of gender demolition as I have ever encountered. In these pieces Garner reveals the inadequacies of another positivism, one based in her position as a trans woman. She refuses to settle for being a role model and demands that the world meet her terms. It's as if Rat Fink were asking me out on a date and daring me to be worthy of the honor.

That Pippa tinkers with her gender to please herself is her greatest power. That she is self-satisfied, remaking her body and her self as she sees fit while retaining her skepticism regarding all organized positivism, is the thing that makes her work even more important today. Her choices and her honesty about those choices remind me of the difference between real human autonomy and the manufactured nonchoices dished up by our contracting society. Pippa is irredeemable. That makes her precious.

Notes

1. Hayden Dunham, "Pippa Garner and Hayden Dunham on the Struggle of Being Inside Bodies," *Interview*, May 19, 2021, https://www.interviewmagazine .com/art/pippa-garner-and-hayden-dunham-on-the-struggle-of-being-inside -bodies.
2. One of Pipa Garner's personal ads (an art work).

MY STUDIO IS A DUNGEON
IS THE STUDIO

Previously Unpublished, 2024

A joke I first heard forty years ago goes Q: How do you know the artists at a New York party? A: They're the ones in the corner talking about real estate.

I grew up in a city, and my conceptions of selfhood and culture were shaped by city life: its randomness, its density of information, its performative nature. When I think about making art, it is always tied to the specificities of its destination: What space will it end up in? What are the potentials for complicating the experience of that space through my actions? What is the space's history? Its official function? How has that function been subverted, enriched, eroticized? What are its textures, its sounds? What do people expect to find there, and how can they be surprised?

I ask these things in a material way. I call myself a sculptor because I believe that we encounter ideas through the physical world, and my job is making and transforming objects. I call myself a performance artist because I am one of those physical objects in the world, and I explore my ideas through the ways that I perform embodiment.

From very early on, I have had the vision of a utopic space: a living space where art could be created, where it could be displayed, and where it could generate more art. An environment that grew and changed through the actions of its occupants. I've spent a lot of time daydreaming about that space, and over the years I have had the chance to try to concretize various versions of those dreams. I'd say that all my work is an attempt to call that utopia into being.

PRIVATE C
MEMBERS ONLY
835

Where did I get the idea? In one version, I am four years old, and I am in the basement of a building on West 101st Street in Manhattan. My father is the superintendent of the building, and he and I are pouring enamel paint across the surface of a sheet of plywood. We are making art. Later this painting will hang in my family's various living rooms, sometimes giving me nightmares when the random drips and swirls come together to show me a charging bull or distorted skull. Later still this painting will be part of my piece *Ruins of a Sensibility* (c. 1972–2002) and will hang in various galleries and museums, providing a backdrop to a DJ setup where people can spin records from my collection and provide a soundtrack for the other viewers in the space.

In another version, I am a child watching this: Season 1, Episode 14, "Art and the Addams Family."

First of all, their house is a museum. It begins with Grandmama on a painting binge. Entranced, she throws fistfuls of oil paint at a canvas set up in the living room. Gomez loves this so much he summons an art critic to advise her. From the heights of his disdain, the critic tells her to "try lessons," so once he leaves, Gomez calls Spain to summon Picasso to be her new teacher. In Spain, Sam Picasso is about to hang himself, but the offer of a job from Gomez Addams is enough for him to throw some things in a shabby case and hop a liner. (The show never bothers with the actual logistics of how people travel; they pop in and out of scenes as needed). Once in the Addamses' house, Picasso starts trading art lessons for a constantly refilled plate of food. Grandmama is delighted with Picasso, even though, when the art critic comes back, he denounces him as a fraud. The Addamses decide that they will champion his work, and to help him make more of it, they lock him up in the family's "playroom" with their iron maiden, a bed of nails, and various shackles. His attempts to escape are met with assertions that he must suffer for his art. Eventually, Wednesday enters the dungeon through one of the tunnels Pugsly has made all over the house and agrees to show Picasso the way out in exchange for him letting her paint. He doesn't get far, but when he is captured, the playroom is filled with Wednesday's paintings, and, thinking that he made them, Gomez again summons the critic, who is so struck with Picasso's (Wednesday's) genius that he purchases all the pieces on the spot and vows to champion Picasso to the art world. At the end, Morticia, Grandmama, and Wednesday are all painting away, as Gomez beams.

In another version, it is 1967, and I am watching this: Season 2, Episode 57, "Pop Goes the Joker."

Alfred is at an art gallery shopping for his boss, Bruce Wayne, who also lives in a mansion on the edge of the city with a cave in the basement. The Joker bursts into the gallery and begins spraying the paintings with red and green paint from a hose. Alfred phones Bruce, who arrives at the gallery in his guise as Batman, accompanied by his ward Robin. They beat up the Joker but stop when the artist having the show praises the sprayed paintings as true art and begs the Joker to share credit for them. No crime has been committed, so Batman retreats. In Bruce's cave, Robin is reading the *Gotham City Art News* and sees that the Joker has been invited to compete in the Gotham City International Art Contest. Batman and Robin attend the contest undercover since Bruce is rich like Baby Jane Towser, the young socialite who organized the event. During the contest the various artists (1) pour paint from cans, (2) roll around in a paint-filled wheelbarrow and then imprint the canvas with their paint-covered bodies, (3) encourage a monkey to throw blobs of paint at the canvas, and (4) paint with their bare feet. The Joker holds a palette and with a fluttering wrist waves a brush back and forth over a blank canvas. When time is up, he titles the untouched result *Death of a Mauve Bat* and, at Baby Jane's insistence, is declared the winner. Baby Jane is now his muse, and he opens an art school for wealthy women, allowing wealthy bachelor Bruce Wayne to also enroll. At the school, the Joker Art Institute and Lair of Artistic Instruction, the various students are re-creating a bowl of fruit with welded steel tubing, pink Silly Putty, and barbed wire, which the Joker claims is "the medium of the future." Bruce Wayne, champion of realism, is carefully shaping a still life from clay, which disgusts the Joker, and he reveals his true plan: kidnapping the wealthy students and ransoming them for their valuable art collections. Word gets back to Robin, and he shows up at the Joker's studio to fight him, only to get captured. The Joker takes Robin and Bruce Wayne downstairs and ties Robin to his latest invention: the Mobile, a sculpture composed of whirling "razor sharp palette knives" that look like machetes that will soon slice him to bits.

So, two stories about art, rich people, critics, galleries, art lessons, art as a scam, the physicality of paint, mansions, museums, playrooms and caves, studios, and torture devices. Suffering and paint.

Batman got his start in *Detective Comics*, and one version of him is described as "The World's Greatest Detective." In the 1960s show, he does figure things out, but as time has gone on, he is mostly known for owning a lot of fancy stuff, training as a martial artist, and brooding about his tortured inner landscape, especially the death of his parents. His villains all have a motif that they base their crimes around: cats, eggs, books, or birds. His detection turns on identifying the motif and anticipating where they will strike next. In Gotham City, crooks are either two-bit henchmen or relentlessly "on brand." The popularity of Batman's villains has led to a change in crime-centered stories across popular culture, shifting them from whodunnits or howdunnits to whydunnits, where the criminal act, usually serial murder, must be interpreted, understood, decoded. The methods of interpretation are those of the critic, no longer an arbiter of taste but now a chief explainer of why someone would want to do the sorts of things these killers do. The contemporary serial killer narrative is a version of the dilemmas of interpreting contemporary art. The Joker in Tim Burton's *Batman* makes this explicit, butchering his lover's face and declaring it art. In movies like *Se7en*, *The Cell*, and *Silence of the Lambs*, crime scenes are, in effect, exhibitions, confronting the detective with dilemmas of self-expression carved into the victims' bodies.

Batman lives in a castle with a cave underneath it. The Addams Family lives in a mansion on the outskirts of town with a graveyard and swamp on the premises alongside their catacombs and playroom/dungeon. Batman's adversaries set up shop in the spaces left in Gotham's decay—"abandoned" fun houses, chemical plants, libraries, greenhouses. How many amusement parks and warehouses did Gotham City once support? So many have been left to villains, who quickly install their own talismans and props, redecorating them as reflections of their own manias. The Addams Family doesn't have adversaries so much as it has a bemused détente with the rest of the world. The complicated decay of their house, a sanctuary from the rational order that reigns beyond their gate, is carefully cultivated. These spaces, with their jumbles of history, art materials, and criminality, became my dream homes.

A foundational rhetorical trope of the eighteenth century was the conflation of visual clarity and enlightenment. The space of knowledge and reason was figured as well lit and open. This rhetoric began a reconfiguring of the ideal artist studio. The studio shifted from being an artisan's workshop and became a well-lit space of the mind. Artists may still lead marginal lives, but now they lead them in garrets—their studios stuffed into attics.

And what of dungeons? While often associated with medieval castles and keeps, the dungeon as a trope in the popular imagination is mostly an invention of Gothic literature. The Gothic arose as the Enlightenment's shadow: emotional, cluttered, dark, in love with obscurity, secrecy, and the night. The Gothic dungeon's closest historical relative is the oubliette, a cell where one is placed to be forgotten. So, a binary: light and thought on high, emotion and body and darkness down low. The dungeon is the place where all that has been forgotten gathers its power.

By the time of my childhood, these two figures, studio and dungeon, began to take on particular meanings in the city I grew up in.

In 1960s New York, deindustrialization and white flight had left swaths of the city empty and forgotten by the supposedly rational people. These material economic conditions also laid the groundwork for people to formulate new self-definitions around being an artist. Bigger spaces to work meant a different kind of art was being made, and art galleries, the space where art was viewed, began to change as well. In 1971 New York passed the first of its loft laws, enshrining the notion of live/work space as a hallmark of the urban art world. In 1976 Brian O'Dougherty began to publish essays analyzing the ways galleries were shaping themselves to sell this new art, formulating the notion of "the White Cube," essentially a space of pure opticality stripped of the specific history of its site.[1] He described the way that the popularity of the White Cube as a placeless space, a space that can be everywhere, also ushered in a new transnational style in art, one that is especially amenable to a reinvigorated commercial art market. Alongside the growth of this market was the growth of an international art lifestyle, one where every city with former industrial cores transmuted them into art centers, where the notion of live/work took hold as a new bourgeois ideal. The abandoned factory—the site of deviant criminality in *Batman* and the ignored place of potential for artists in the 1960s—was now a gold mine, a space ripe with development possibilities for speculators who had learned to sell the trappings of a postindustrial art world to the same white people who had fled "urban decay" a couple of decades earlier. Art and artists had become both the narrow end of the wedge that split neighborhoods apart and then the slightly inconvenient speed bumps on the gentrification highway while "lofts and studios" grew ever more popular. The whiteness of these spaces often applied to the people presumed to live there as well, as artist gentrification became a handy way of disrupting working-class neighborhoods—often those where people of color lived.

At the same time, other "useless" spaces became the gathering places of the sexually and socially marginalized. In the 1960s leftist philosophers linked psychological conformity with political fascism. People began to explore possibilities for social and personal freedom by subjecting their bodies to various extreme states. As the shipping industry declined, the docks became a prime cruising spot and home to any number of leather bars.

Forgotten factories, slaughterhouses, and warehouses became romantic grottoes and gathering places for a sexual underground. With subterranean names like Mineshaft, Manhole, and Waterworks, the landmarks of the city's sexual life mirrored the shifting locations of the art neighborhoods. And any number of artists circulated through both. When someone was being nailed to a car in a gallery, it was called *performance art*. When it happens in a dungeon, it's called *kink*.

I became aware of both of these worlds as I entered high school, ranging beyond my parents' apartment to the city beyond, learning about art at SoHo galleries, and kink at Times Square and Christopher Street bookstores. The thrill of taking over an abandoned space and making it my own loomed in my mind as a possible way to have my combined dream location. I collected books on building your own furniture and rehabilitating lofts alongside the Grove Press editions of William Burroughs and the Marquis de Sade. Samuel Delany's *Dhalgren* introduced me to the pleasures of pansexual urban and narrative fragmentation. I bring up books because writing has structured my erotic and artistic life.

For much of my life, I described myself as heady, verbal, brainy, and not very physical. This is only partly true: I certainly had a hard time picking up physical skills when other people were trying to teach me, my own anxiety compounding on itself so that I couldn't find ease and grace in moving my body, but I don't think I was any more awkward than other kids—simply more self-conscious and wanting to perform correctly under other people's scrutiny. The weight of other people's judgments of my body became a source of shame and anxiety, particularly after one of my relatives began a pattern of teasing and aggression that I finally came to be able to call abuse. Their behavior—tickling me, lying on top of me and growling, jumping out of corners, making snarling noises as I went up to bed in their house at night—skirted the explicitly sexual in a way that allowed them to continue in full view of the rest of the family with only a few remarks of "cut it out" or "leave the kid alone" offered when things went on too long. They taught me two things: that my body was theirs to play with and that no one in my family was coming to save me. Eventually, I figured out an escape: I dissociated, leaving my body under them, enduring it while my mind wandered off. I did a similar thing in the lake at camp when two older boys put their hands in my bathing suit and declared that I must be a girl, before forcing me to feel them up. In both situations, I can remember distinct sensations: the cold of the water the three of us were paddling in and the fabric of the couch I was pinned on, and I can also see the scenes as a bystander, wondering what they would mean when they were finally over. One horror of abuse is that it makes you a secondary character in your own narrative. In effect, my abuser scared me out of my own body many years ago, compounding a mind/body split that led me to favor the mind over all. Over time, I came to see my body as a problem that had to be solved: the paleness of my skin invalidating my identity as Black; my fat and my softness as unlovable, something to be starved away and controlled; my penis as undeniable evidence of a maleness that I loathed enacting.

Eventually, I went off to art school and then another art school and from there to advanced education in the artist's life in San Francisco, a city whose simple embrace of self-reinvention I am continually grateful for. In San Francisco the recently christened art neighborhood of SoMa also overlapped with the city's gay leather neighborhood. I started making art that tried to overlay those two experiences on top of each other, finding narratives to fit the technologies and props of BDSM. I saw what those two worlds had to offer each other, and I tried to help others see it.

In the past forty years, the spaces for art and sex have become even more contested in the face of two developments: the dismantling of the public sphere begun in the United States under Ronald Reagan and the rise of digital telecommunication technologies, especially as they have accelerated in the past two decades. Privatization of space and industry means less space for the irrational, the unprofitable. Twice in my lifetime, I have seen marginal people create places of cultural resistance and power for themselves out of dire circumstances by occupying places and modes deemed useless and abandoned by the mainstream. And both times, I've seen those strategies attacked by the political right and gobbled up by speculators. In the 1980s and 1990s, the Bay Area still had cheap space where artists and queers could get together. Those spaces allowed me to explore bodily autonomy and gender complication in the midst of the sex panic surrounding HIV-AIDS. AIDS activism led to Queer Nation and Queer Theory. I began to see the ways that my selfhood was the meeting place for various discourses about Blackness and whiteness, about performances of maleness and femaleness, about health, about fatness. I wasn't the only person doing this, and I was excited by all the ways that events, zines, and spaces were producing a deprofessionalized knowledge that pointed away from assimilationist politics and toward new possibilities. In the early 1990s, I began teaching in various art schools and cocurated the largest show I've ever worked on, trying to bring together the various communities I moved within in spaces where they would not normally be welcome.

In 1996 my partner and I moved back to New York, and shortly afterward, the Bay Area experienced what came to be called "the tech boom." Friends and neighborhood businesses were priced out of the city overnight. Similar things were happening everywhere. At the same time, the internet began to be spoken about as a "place" to be, a place independent of the individual computer you might be working on, and particularly a place that was increasingly image based. Spaces for queer sexuality might be disappearing in the physical world, but chat rooms and mailing lists allowed people to connect across distances. Chatting became blogging, and online publishing created a different kind of narrated self, performed for an audience that could be anywhere. Individual blogs and websites condensed into social platforms like LiveJournal and ultimately Facebook, and being online began to present itself as a kind of inevitability. Throughout the early 2000s and into the 2010s, smartphones made physical space more porous as we carried little doors to online space with us everywhere.

That online space had two important characteristics: It was privately owned by people who planned to profit from it, and by 2009 it was overwhelmingly photographic. Advertising became the path to profit, and the online self began to be talked about as "a brand." By the middle of the 2010s, artists were being advised on how to cultivate "engagement" for their online presence, with very little understanding of the fact that anything they posted to Instagram or Facebook no longer exclusively belonged to them and in fact was simply the window dressing meant to lure eyeballs to the various sites' ads. We were being made bystanders in our own lives, submitting to modes of address that masqueraded as connection. *Engagement* as a term of business has no moral value, and these services work to foster emotions that keep us engaged regardless of the cost to ourselves. The two most effective ones seem to be envy and outrage. The speed and ubiquity of online posting makes us reactively sort into tribes to cling to moral certitude and punish ambiguity. Online media speculators and real estate speculators share the same belief: It doesn't matter what happens in a space or what lives are lived there, as long as the value of that space increases. Numbers must go up. Everything must be productive.

In 2016, forty years after O'Dougherty's "White Cube" essays, Kyle Chayka published "Welcome to Airspace,"[2] an essay that examined the interior design aesthetic of businesses like Airbnb, WeWork, Apple, and Blank Street Coffee—an aesthetic that has proved to be effective at suggesting a lifestyle that is transnational and profoundly ahistorical. Chayka's essay captured the crucial moment when this aesthetic was moving beyond an online visual style and was beginning to reconfigure actual material spaces. I call this new placeless space "the White Tube." The White Tube is an ideological space that inhabits various specific spaces worldwide but is first and foremost an online phenomenon. It is a space of white-painted brick walls, Edison bulbs, and reclaimed wood. It emerged as a parody of the idea of live/work space. It has the trappings of loft life, brimming with creative potential, but without mess. It is a live/work space where neither living nor working takes place. It is a space that presumes the laptop, even when laptop use is restricted by the owner. It is a space where the screen and the camera have merged into the mobile phone, and social media pokes holes between privacy and publicity. What do we imagine we will do when we come to occupy these spaces? First, we will get on our phones to tell other people that we are there. When each person is a broadcaster, every place is a "location," a backdrop. Oddly, this recalls the earliest days of the photo studio, where painted sets imitated parks and parlors. Or perhaps the theme park, where adventure is digested into preordained experience. The idealized occupant of the White Tube is not an artist or a worker, even though the White Tube masquerades as a workspace. The occupant of the White Tube is a "creative," a generator of "content." And what is "content" as opposed to "art"? Content is a collection of words and images made to fill a predetermined container. Art has the capacity to overflow or break down all sorts of containers, awakening us to the arbitrary nature of containment itself. Content presents itself as a kind of creativity that can be recuperated into "productivity." It can be measured and rationalized, defined, and distributed. Art is often unproductive, reveling in opacity and frustration. In the same way that the White Cube presents itself as a neutral backdrop that occurs anywhere, the White Tube hides its ideologies behind a vision of easy cosmopolitanism and whimsical hedonism. The White Cube demolished history and regionalism in art making and viewing, and the White Tube attempts to do the same for neighborhoods and lives. Both Cube and Tube are containers that turn their contents into perfect objects for capital: ubiquitous, transient, and interchangeable. As a form of social relation, they are abusive, tricking us into believing we are presenting our own narrative when really we've become the mouthpiece for theirs. They lead us to disembodied opticality. They present a vision of a future life that is inhuman and spectral, where little matters but everything has to make sense.

I am house hunting. I've always been a renter, but now the circumstances of my life have conspired to make it seem like purchasing property is the smart thing to do. Every previous change of living space for me has had the undercurrent of "Where might I be permitted to live?" A renter does not command space: They are allowed until they aren't. Last year, my landlord decided that they would retire and sell the Brooklyn building that both of us had been living in for the past two decades. Now I can't shake the feeling that I am searching for the setting where the remainder of my life will play out. And so I have to ask what I want those remaining years filled with. This is leading me to want this fantasy house that has everything I could possibly need until what I need is a grave. I want a space where I can define myself until where I end up defines me.

As I search through house listings, I'm alternately thrilled and crushed by the possibilities of the spaces on offer. Here's where I can make a mess. In this one, the neighbors are too close, and noise might carry. Here's where I would suffer the drudgery of caring for a yard. Behind everything is my desire for it to have both a studio and a dungeon. I'm looking for my utopian space again, in a world that has shifted profoundly.

And so let's go back to dungeons. I talked above about being scared out of my own body by abuse (I almost typed "my abuser" there, but I loathe the formulation that they are bound to me in any special way). For years, my subsequent life as an artist was heavily based in reading, research, and narrative. As I moved into public performance, I acted out a prismatic self that was the product of and mouthpiece for a variety of fragmented narratives, many from pop culture. I am, as we used to say in the 1990s, anti-essentialist. This work culminated with my 1997 theater piece *Hare Follies*, and at the end of that experience, I felt I had gone as far as I could go with talking, writing, and thinking through my issues. It was time for me to turn to a different type of learning: to learn from my body.

The performances I made changed; I stopped speaking in them, instead existing in them as a subject that is acted on, without explaining the meaning of those acts to an audience. I was "bottoming in the scene," and as I did more of that, I decided that I needed to go back to school to learn the emotional lessons locked in my body. That school was what we call the *kink scene*, a very broad coalition of people—an extended Addams Family, if you will—spread through a network of nomadic dungeons around the world. Not everybody who participates in the scene is there for the same reasons I am (self-understanding), but there are many who are, and it has been my distinct pleasure to learn from and with them for over twenty years. They have allowed me to return to embodiment with a sense of joy and surprise at all that my body can provide for me. They have opened up new possibilities for what I can mean to myself.

Let's talk about the spaces where meaning can happen, the spaces that inform my making: One is empty, white, brimming with illumination and possibility at the top of five extratall stories of stairs. A studio. The other is dim, cluttered with tools and toys, filled with sound, but set up so that sound cannot escape. A dungeon. I need both because very different things happen in each, and one without the other leaves me arid and incomplete.

These spaces are mindsets made physical, but neither is permanent. Over the years, I've had many studios and played in many dungeons. In apartments and campgrounds, in suburban houses owned by pro dommes, in hotels and alleys; these spaces have coalesced and dispersed as various people willed it.

The dungeon is not a place of solitude. Being alone in the dungeon is pointless. The dungeon is where we can discard the selves we portray all day long and howl at their shreds. The dungeon is where we can take a piece of leather and invest it with supreme importance before taking it inside of our bodies and then laughing at the story we just made up for each other.

So the dungeon is a theater, a place where the actors and the witnesses are the same people. We conjure the dungeon together by agreeing to act in a certain way within its confines.

The dungeon is for two or more. The studio is for one. The studio is supposedly a place where you are free to "make a mess," and yet a quick look at the in situ portraits of contemporary artists in their studios shows them to be neat, rationalized workspaces where every paint rag breaks your heart with its elegance. Thus, the "studio visit" is an activity of intimacy afforded to special customers. Visitors are granted access to the space of private exploration.

I can't bear studio visits because then I have to engage in the theater of artistic production: tidy some stuff up, lay out other stuff so that it *looks* like I'm working. My actual working process barely looks like anything is happening. Work is either made or inchoate. The work is happening in my head. The conventions of appearing to work are just another version of the White Tube. This is one of the reasons why it's nearly impossible to make a film about an artist: It's not the action of the activity that gives a work of art its meaning.

There are no visitors in the dungeon. Looky-loos are actively discouraged, though you might find a role there as a self-declared voyeur, given that you had negotiated your presence with the other participants. But that's the point: By negotiating, you have become another participant. Voyeur, not flaneur. You are implicated in and responsible for sustaining the theater.

My Studio Is a Dungeon Is the Studio

It's a potluck: If you want to get nourishment, you have to bring something for the table. I can't fall apart in the ways I need to if someone isn't matching my level of risk.

If I went back to the dungeon for my second master of fine arts degree, what lessons have I learned there? Here are a few:

1   Pain is a sensation, one among many that my body is capable of and that I can understand better by sitting with it instead of putting all my energy into avoiding and muting it. I enjoy taking pain for another person and being praised for doing so. The fear of pain and the conflation of discomfort with pain often make us justify harming each other.

2   When you spend much of your time as a hyperverbal authority figure, being turned into a mute, useful object for someone else's amusement can be a lot of fun.

3   When someone is doing something to me that is harming me and that I haven't agreed to, I don't have to dissociate and leave my body to survive the experience. I can tell them to stop, and other people will show up to help me.

4   Intense emotional and physical experiences require prior negotiation and consent, as well as aftercare: a time to discuss the impact of what has happened.

5   I love my fat and the fat of other people. I love softness, heft, sturdiness, abundance, puckering, dimpling, stretch marks, massive thighs, plump fingers, people who take up space, the sheer sweet volume of fat people. I love raucous fat people laughing in the dungeon. I love serene fat people bound to platforms.

6   I have to be very cautious when I name things; we have built a society around the idea that naming certain body parts provides correct and incorrect ways to use those parts and that the organization of those parts implies an essential meaning about the person attached to them. I mean gender. Around 2007 I started describing myself as gender gaseous in my online profiles, and I think it still fits me. We'd be in a much better situation if we could think of our genders as weather systems rather than as bedrock. In the past few years, my genitals have been sending very mutable signals about

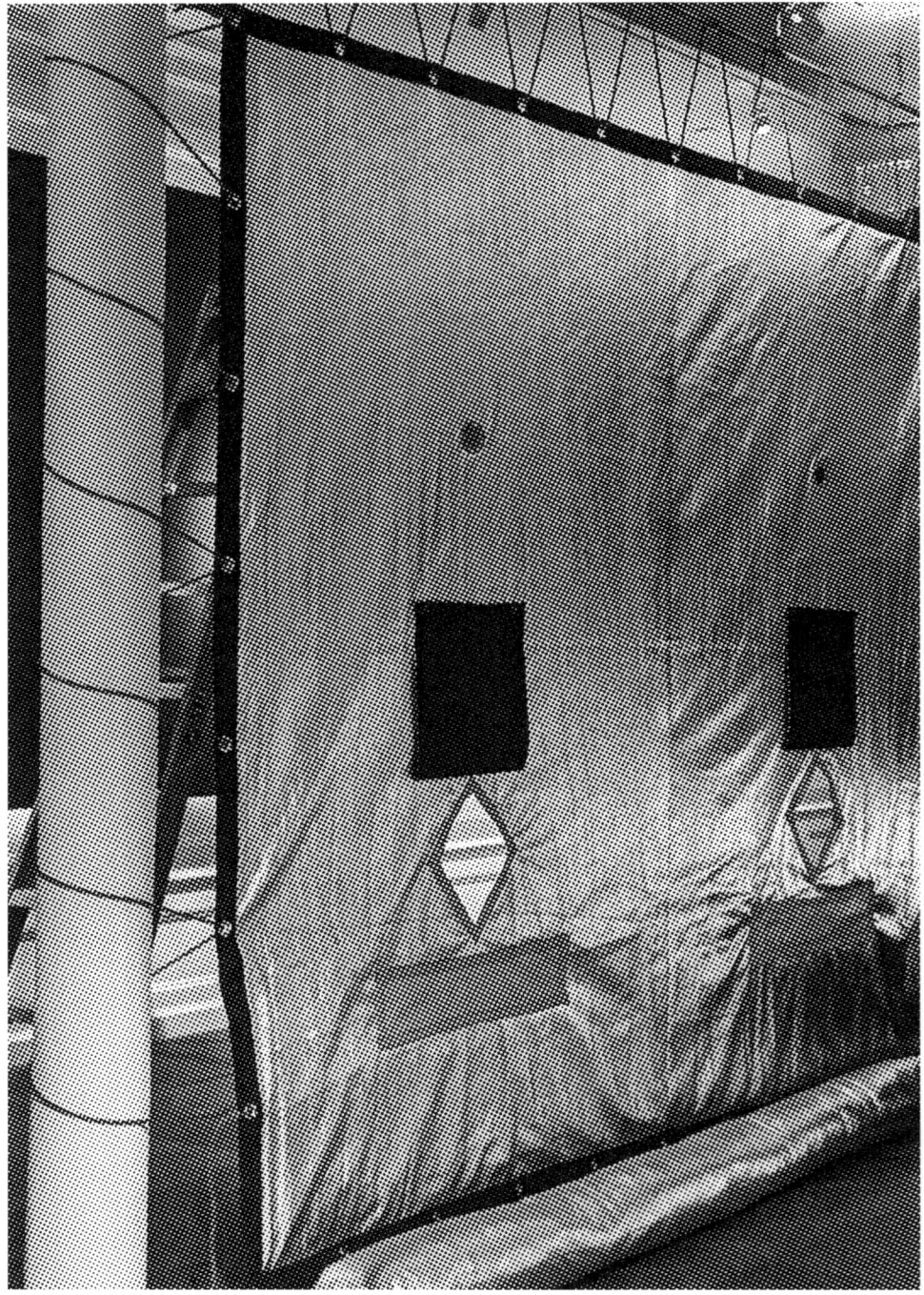

what they want to be called and how they want to be handled on any particular day, and while I have been wary of saying that that makes me transgender, it has confirmed for me that the current gender binary, like so many others, is not useful for me as a way of understanding myself.

7   I am an animal, sometimes several, sometimes fantastical, and there are many others eager to celebrate that fact with me.

All of these are lessons that I take with me into the studio.

So here I am, at age sixty-four, the inheritor of so many social, political, emotional, and physical traditions: urban design, the transatlantic slave trade, minimalist aesthetics, the Gothic novel, roadside taxidermy, comic books, and on and on and on. I'm looking for a way to house and honor and perpetuate all of them and a place where I can yet discover those legacies that are still dormant within me.

The best place is the place where I could make a mess, be a mess, and be loved for both.

Notes

1. Brian O'Dougherty, *Inside the White Cube: The Ideology of the Gallery Space* (Berkeley: University of California Press, 2000).

2. Kyle Cayka, "Welcome to Airspace," *The Verge*, https://www.theverge.com /2016/8/3/12325104/airbnb-aesthetic-global-minimalism-startup-gentrification, August 3, 2016.

CONTRIBUTORS

Jarrett Earnest is a writer, curator, and editor living in New York and the author of *What It Means to Write About Art: Interviews with Art Critics* (2018) and *Valid Until Sunset* (2023). His work has appeared in publications around the world and regularly in the *New York Review of Books*.

Nayland Blake is an acclaimed interdisciplinary artist living in New York who has exhibited, lectured, and published widely in the international art world since the 1980s. They are a professor and codirector of the Studio Arts Program at Bard College.

INDEX

Abbott, Tank, 210

"The ABCs of Art Institutions" (public talk), 4

Abdoh, Reza, 11

Abramović, Marina, 256

abstract expressionism, 206

abstraction, 2, 141; gender and, 143; representation and, 150, 260, 275–76

abstract thought, 229

abuse, 153, 325–26, 329

Acconci, Vito, 154, 249, 256

Acker, Kathy, 7, 234, 238–42, 256; Blake on, 12; at CalArts, 3; *The Childlike Life of the Black Tarantula*, 3, 213, 235; queer relation to, 237

ACT UP action, 273

The Addams Family (television show), 321, 323, 329

Adler, Amy, 154

Adonis Theater, 191

The Adult Life of Toulouse Lautrec by Toulouse Lautrec (Acker), 235

advertising, 314, 316, 327

aesthetic culture, 141

aftercare, 252, 331

Against Nature (exhibition), 136

Aguilar, Laura, 153

AIDS crisis, 32, 150, 151–52, 271, 326; Gran Fury relation to, 161; postmodernism relation to, 148; representation relation to, 119–20

Albers, Josef, 206

Albert, Francis, 47

Alexander and Bonin, New York, 220

Alfred (fictional character), 322

alienness, 156

allegory, 105

Altamont (venue), 61

alternative art spaces, 102–3

alt-porn movement, 85

Alvarez, D-L, 5

amateur porn, 94

ambiguity, 229, 236

ambisexual representation, 202

American culture, 106, 199

An American in Paris (film), 87

American Museum of Natural History, 219, 240–41

America's Sexiest Home Videos, Volume One (film), 94–95

anality, 115, 125

anal sexuality, 162

Andrews, Terry, 213

The Andy Warhol Diaries (Wolfe), 159

Angelo, Tony, 88

Anthology Film Archives, 191

antihistoricism, 25

Antin, Eleanor, 214–15

Arbus, Diane, 157

archetypes, 221

Arena (Kelley, M.), 198

Arnaz, Desi, Jr., 66–67

"Art and the Addams Family" (television show episode), 321

art establishment, 194–96

Artforum (magazine), 11–12, 39

art history, 9; respect and, 23; Smith, J., relation to, 196
Art in America (magazine), 39
artistic communication, 240
artistic hierarchy, 142
artistic worth, 193
Artists in Action series, 10–11
artist's statement, 230, 232
artist studio, 11, 323, 330
art practice: of Gobel, 215–16; meaning in, 15, 17, 205
art rock, 237
ashi (fictional character), 110, 113
"Assessing My Work" (Blake), 3
assignments, 289–94, 296
assimilation, 23, 201
Astin, John, 45
authority, 18, 106, 331; domestication relation to, 40; fascism relation to, 29; of hierarchy, 26; uniforms relation to, 95
autoerotic asphyxiation, 135
avant-garde art scene, 202
avid (fictional character), 110, 113

Baby Jane Tosier (fictional character), 322
Baby Makes 3 (image), 158
Bacher, Lutz, 104–5
Baking Bread for the Boys (painting), 222
Ball, Lucille, 66
Bamber, Judie, 152, 190, 225–27, 229
Banana Pudding (sculpture), 162
Bard College, 2–3, 18, 234, 250
Barrymore, Drew, 77
Barthes, Roland, 130
Bat Dude and Throbbin' (film), 93
Batman (fictional character), 322–23
Batman (television show), 321–23
Baudrillard, Jean, 76, 130
Bay Area, 103, 108, 326–27. *See also* San Francisco
Bay Area Conceptualism (exhibition catalog), 6
Bay Area Reporter (newspaper), 4–5, 85
Bay Guardian (newspaper), 39
BDSM, 5, 326
The Beach Bar Nightmare (film), 101
Bearden, Romare, 261
BEAR (magazine), 5
bears, 216, 259

Beautiful Book (photograph collection), 158
The Beautiful Book (Smith, J.), 198
beefcake, 24, 201
Benedict, Matthew, 220–22, 224
Ben Hurry (film), 100–101
Bergman, Ingmar, 46
Berkeley Art Museum, 6, 9, 32, 136
Beuys, Joseph, 215
bi, 259
biases, 230
The Big Chill (installation), 106
Big Dog Dawson (fictional character), 84
Big Uterus (exhibition), 105
big words, 232
Bijou Video, 86–87
Bill of Rights, US Constitution, 123
Billy Budd (fictional character), 220
Bizango (Haitian secret society), 219
"Bizarre Love Triangle" (song), 81
Black body, transgression relation to, 119
black humor, 159
Black Mountain College, 206
Blackness, *Hare Follies* relation to, 11
Blacula, 180
Blacula (film), 11
Blair, Nicky, 46
Blake, Nayland. *See specific works and topics*
Blanchot, Maurice, 124
blaxploitation, 11
Bleckner, Ross, 151–52
Bleeker Bob's, 233
Bleep (installation), 115, 118, 121, 122
Blind Spot (painting), 151
blogs, 327
bloopers, 93–94
bodies, 76, 232, 291, 309, 329; in *Big Uterus*, 105; Black, 119; capitalism relation to, 316; dissociation and, 325–26; lambada and, 65; Schreber relation to, 116; *Workstation* relation to, 114
bodily autonomy, 326
body hair, 88
body modification, 315
La Bohéme, 77
Bohemia, 141
Bonaduce, Danny, 77
Book of Splendors (play), 2
Borofsky, Jonathan, 2
Boucicault, Dion, 11

Bowie, David, 156
Brains (magazine), 5
Brakhage, Stan, 191
Breakfast at Tiffany's (Capote), 51
Brecht, Stefan, 192
Breer, Robert, 191
Brennan, Walter, 77
Brentwood Studio, 86
Br'er Rabbit (fictional character), 9, 133
Brer Rabbit (molasses), 241
Breton, André, 121
Brian Ridley and Lyle Heeter (bondage picture), 127
The Bride Stripped Bare by Her Bachelors, Even (Duchamp), 155
Brillo boxes, 159
Britain, 115, 123–24, 145
Brooklyn Academy of Music (BAM), 10–11, 169–87, 189
Brooks, Romaine, 156
Bruce Wayne (fictional character), 322
bruise, 226
Bubbles (Sill), 7
Bugs Bunny, 9
Bunny Butt (zine), 8, 165
"The Bunny Hop" (song), 11
Burroughs, William, 2, 236, 237, 256, 325
Burton, Scott, 152
Burton, Tim, 323

Cadmus, Paul, 23–24
Cage, John, 152, 206
Caja, Jerome, 159
California: Bay Area, 103, 108, 326–27; Hollywood, 100–101, 270; Southern, 2, 161, 227, 315. *See also* San Francisco
California Highway Patrolman (CHP), 96
California Institute of the Arts (CalArts), 2–3, 15, 21
Callas, Maria, 101
camp: in car culture, 315; of Duchamp, 125; gay men and, 93; gay sensibility relation to, 128; queer relation to, 200–201
caning, 253
Cantarel (fictional character), 33, 35
capitalism, 68, 75, 194, 314; bodies relation to, 316; desire relation to, 130, 146; rot relation to, 199
Capote, Truman, 50–52
Car and Driver (magazine), 315

car culture, 261, 314–15
career ambition, 15
Carnival (musical), 56–58
Carson, Johnny, 315
Carving (sculpture), 214–15
"The Case of Paranoia Running Counter to the Psychoanalytic Theory of the Disease and Some Neurotic Mechanisms in Jealousy, Paranoia, and Homosexuality" (Freud), 116–17
castration, 117, 122
Catholic saints, 221
celebrities, 74, 77
Cell Mates (film), 100
center-vagina-flower, 151
C'est La Vie Club, 270
chains, 246–47
Chamberlain, John, 261
Chardin, Jean Siméon, 226
Chayka, Kyle, 327–28
Chekov (fictional character), 67
chemical weapons, in Vietnam, 73
Chicago, Judy, 150–51
The Childlike Life of the Black Tarantula (Acker), 3, 213, 235
Christianity, 221
Christopher Street, New York, 44, 191–92, 325
Christopher Street (magazine), 27
Church of the SubGenius, 315
cigars, 96
City of Hares (installation), 133, 135
civil rights movement, 267–68, 314
Clarice Starling (fictional character), 303–4
Clift, Montgomery, 209
climax, 245
Clinton, George, 197
close-up, in porn, 93
clothing industry, 39
Cochrane, Chris, 10–11, 169
Cockettes, 270
Cocteau, Jean, 32
collaboration, 240, 242, 274, 290
collage, 55, 234; of Grossman, 261; of Johnson, Ray, 206; New Narrative movement relation to, 8; in New York, 239; "Polysexuality," 6, 13–14
collective will, 309
College Arts Association (CAA), 274–75
colonialism, 65

coming out, 129–30, 250, 259, 297, 311
Coming to Power (Samois), 5
commercial art spaces, 103
commodification, 3, 103, 146
commodity culture, 239
communication, 40, 253
communism, 314
community, 200; of bears, 216; critical
   writing relation to, 40; cultural identity relation to, 139; first-generation
   activities and, 149; gay, 25–26, 31,
   42, 157; gay culture and, 147, 149–50;
   S&M relation to, 300; women's art
   movement and, 143
conceptual art, 103–4, 108
conceptualism, 103, 105, 150, 237
Confidence-Man (fictional character), 220
conformity, fascism relation to, 324
connectivity, 247
Conner, Bruce, 238
conservatism, 23, 24, 64, 314
consumer culture, 145, 151, 314
consumer hedonism, 144
consumerism, 191, 314, 315
consumption, selfhood and, 316
containment, 328
contemporary culture, 200–201
content, 328
Conversations Part III (Acconci), 154
"cool," 262
Cooper, Dennis, 121, 122
cops: in porn, 96–97; queens and,
   43–44, 52
Corcoran, 143
core beliefs, 304, 306
Corinne, Tee A., 160
Cornell, Joseph, 162, 196, 206, 261
"correct attitudes," 25
cosmopolitanism, 328
CougarCash, 88
counterculture, 142–44, 314
Crane, Margaret, 106
Creative Management Associates, 56
crime, victims of, 124
critical writing, 38–40, 42
Crossfire (McMarty), 161
Crowley, Aleister, 58
cruising, 27, 249, 324–25
Cruising (film), 7, 43–44, 49
cultural identity, 42, 139
cultural imperialism, 314

cultural quietism, 145
culture, 23, 40, 76, 138; aesthetic, 141;
   American, 106, 199; car, 261, 314–15;
   commodity, 239; consumer, 145, 151,
   314; contemporary, 200–201; counter,
   142–44, 314; of furry fandom, 284;
   leather, 256, 265; omni, 65; postmodernism relation to, 139–40; power in,
   254, 312, 314; queer, 139–40, 146,
   277; of San Francisco, 192; selfhood
   and, 319; teaching relation to, 289;
   Western, 39, 42. *See also* gay culture
culture wars, 38
cunt envy, 236
Curtis, Ian, 81
Cut Piece (Ono), 11
cutting, 234
cutups, 237

Dadaists, 246
Dahmer, Jeffrey, 115, 118, 122
dance halls, 77
"Danceland," 61
Danny Partridge (fictional character), 75
La Danse Interdit (The Forbidden
   Dance), 65
Darth Vader (fictional character), 219
Dashiell, David Cannon, 8, 104–5, 109
David (sculpture), 269
Days of the Greek Gods program, 100
Dear World (zine), 71
death, 118, 120, 193
decapitation, 122
decay, 193
degradation, 301–3
Delany, Samuel, 236, 325
Deleuze, Gilles, 32, 116
Delos, Kate, 157–58
Del Rio, Vanessa, 88
DeLuise, Dom, 92
dematerialization, 276
Democratic Convention, 104
Deren, Maya, 2, 191, 237
De Salvo, Donna, 205
Des Barres, Pamela, 8
desire, 12–13, 130, 132, 146
Detective Comics, 322–23
DEVO, 315
Dhalgren (Delany), 325
Diary of a Witch (Leek), 7
A Different Light bookstore, 43

"The Difficulties That Afflict Us in Art
   School" (Blake), 15–17
disco, 77–78, 81–82
disengagement, 260–61
dissociation, 325–26, 331
diva, 77–78, 82
divination deck, 290
Divine Horseman (Deren), 2
documentary photography, 267, 279
domestication, 40, 194
double consciousness, 275–76
double-think, 106
Dough Boys, 222
Dracula (fictional character), 179–84
drag, 150, 155, 270; anal sexuality and,
   162; identity relation to, 153–54;
   Smith, J., relation to, 202
drawn porn, 22–23
dreams, 237, 240–42, 307, 309, 311
Drummer (magazine), 256
Du Bois, W. E. B., 275
Duchamp, Marcel, 6, 32, 34, 117, 155–56;
   camp of, 125; Fluxus relation to, 142;
   Johnson, Ray, and, 207, 209; meaning
   and, 140–41; transvestism and, 35, 37
Duke, Patty, 7
"dumb" work, 18
dungeons, 261, 300, 323–24, 329–31
Dutch still life, 226
Dylan, Bob, 63

earnestness, 262, 271
Edison, Thomas, 193
editing strategies, 237–38
Eisenman, Nicole, 158–59
Elesby, Sally, 162
Elliott-Said, Marianne, 233–34
ellipsis, 140
Elvis Herselvis (Drag King), 154
Elwood (fictional character), 165–66, 168
embarrassment, 301–4, 306
embodiment, 32, 227, 229, 269, 329
empathy, 301, 306
encounter-reflection-elucidation, 39
engagement, 327
England, 115, 145
enlightenment, visual clarity relation
   to, 323
"Enough Is Enough" (song), 77
Enterprise (fictional starship), 64
enthusiasms, 232

ephebe, 31
ephemera, 199
Eppridge, Bill, 268
Ernst, Max, 261
erotic imagination, 100
Erotophobia (exhibition), 136
Erzulie, 2
escapism, 145, 238
essentialism, 147, 149, 150
Eureka Bound (film), 86–88
Evans, Walker, 154
exhibitionistic play, 284
explicitness, sexuality relation to, 129
expressionism, abstract, 206
Eyes Wide Shut (film), 250

Facebook, 327
Fading Flowers (Morton), 151
failure, 302
fairness, 275
faith, 15, 222, 224
Falk, Harry, 44–45, 48–49
fame, 74
familial identity, 139
fan clubs, 207
fan fiction, of *Star Trek*, 5–6
Fanny's Hill (film), 101
fantasy drawings, 24
fascism, 27–29, 324
fat, 215, 331
faux-naïf touches, 20
Fecteau, Vincent, 158
feedback effect, 103
Feeder2 and corollary (exhibition), 11,
   241
Feeder (sculpture), 241
Feher, Tony, 161–62
Fellows (Officer), 220
felt, 215
The Female Eunuch (Greer), 7
femaleness, 326
feminine pursuits, 215
Ferraro, Geraldine, 104
fetish, 130, 155–56, 264; camp relation
   to, 201; commodification of, 146; foot,
   127; garbage man, 251, 254; leather
   and, 261; perversion and, 120; pipe
   man, 251–52; for uniforms, 95
Fierce Pussy (lesbian collective), 273
figurative art, 260
File (zine), 146, 158

A Fire in My Belly (exhibition), 277
first drafts, 230
first-generation activities, community and, 149
"The First Radical Art Show of the Eighties" (*Village Voice* article), 192
The First Time (film), 91–92
Fizeek Art Quarterly (magazine), 31
Flaming Creatures (film), 158, 191–92; drag in, 202; *Rose Hobart* compared to, 196; vampirism and, 193
Flechsig (Doctor), 117
Flesh Journals (Hammond), 152
Flux Divorce Box (Hendricks), 157
Fluxus, 142–43, 157, 237; gallery/museum system relation to, 150; modernism relation to, 144; punk compared to, 146; queer relation to, 149; women's art movement and, 145
Foley, Suzanne, 102
folk art, 20, 195–96, 213, 256
foot fetishism, 127
The Forbidden Dance (*La Danse Interdit*), 65
Foreman, Richard, 2, 7
forgetfulness, 17
form: gender and, 143; women's art movement relation to, 149
formalist aesthetics, 104
Foucault, Michel, 121, 123
found footage films, 237
Free! Love! Tool! Box! (exhibition), 12–13, 265
Freud, Sigmund, 32, 34, 114, 116–17, 155
Friedkin, Anthony, 268–71, 273
Friedkin, William, 7, 43
A Friend of Dorothy, 1943 (painting), 158
Fritscher, Jack, 97
Frying, Dawn, 106, 108
fucking, 99–100, 236, 252; queer relation to, 274, 277, 279; sex compared to, 87
functionality, 126
Funt, Allen, 93
furry fandom, 284–85

Gacy, John Wayne, 121, 122
gainer/encouragers, 11
gallery/museum system, 150, 206
the Gallows, 133, 135
Gange, John, 115–30
garbage man fetish, 251, 254

Garland, Judy, 139; as diva, 78, 82; Minelli relation to, 55, 56–58, 60, 63
Garner, Pippa, 315–16, 318
Gate (sculpture), 249
"gay and lesbian rights," 271
gay bars, 251
gay community, 42, 157; placeless community relation to, 31; sexual courtship in, 25–26
gay culture, 4; coming out and, 129–30; community and, 147, 149–50; music industry relation to, 76–77; postmodernism relation to, 128; Stonewall relation to, 201; Tom of Finland relation to, 22–23; in West Village, 191
Gay Erotica from the Past (film), 100
The Gay Essay (photograph collection), 268
gay identity, 4, 21, 24
gay liberation, 268–69, 271, 273
Gay Liberation Front, 157
gay men, 89–92, 120, 151, 236; AIDS crisis and, 148; *Bay Area Reporter* relation to, 85; in *BEAR*, 5; bears, 216; camp and, 93; *Cruising* relation to, 43–44; disco relation to, 77–78; Minelli relation to, 60; placeless community for, 31; representation of, 3, 261; Tom of Finland and, 23; uniforms for, 27
gay politics, 23
gay power, 145
gay pride parades, 271
gay sensibility, 22, 138; camp relation to, 128; gaze relation to, 120; modernism and, 117, 124–25
gaze, 31, 124; gay sensibility relation to, 120; porn relation to, 27
gender, 318, 326, 331, 333; Fluxus relation to, 142–43; as performance, 316, 326; physicality and, 214–15; queer relation to, 153
gender binary, 316, 333
gender norms, 154
General Idea, 158
generalities, 230
Geneva Protocol, 73
gentrification, 324
Germany, Nazi, 25, 27–28
Gilbert & George, 157
gingerbread, 241

Girl with Arms Akimbo (lesbian collective), 273
Glass, Phil, 90
The Glow (Stanwood), 7
Glück, Robert, 8
Gnomen, 284–86, 288
Gobel, James, 214–16, 218
Gober, Robert, 10, 156
Goldin, Nan, 157
Gomez Addams (fictional character), 321
Gorge (video performance), 11
Gothic literature, 323–24
Gover, Robert, 155
Grandmama (fictional character), 321
grand opera, 77–78
Gran Fury (artist collective), 161
Greek sculpture, 119
Green Box, 125
Greer, Germaine, 7
Gregg, Pam, 9, 136
grief, 151
Grossman, Nancy, 152–53, 190, 261–62, 264
the Grotto, 133
group epiphanies, 138
group shows, 245
Grove Press, 235, 325
Guardian (newspaper), 129
guardian packet, 290, 296
Guattari, Félix, 116
guilt, 15
Guston, Philip, 210

Haitian Vodou practices, 2, 219
Halkan Council, 64, 67
Hamlet (Shakespeare), 294
Hammer, Matt, 90
Hammond, Harmony, 152, 157–58
Hammons, David, 197
Hampton, James, 195
Han, Donna, 158–59
Hannibal Lecter (fictional character), 303–4
Hansel and Gretel (fictional characters), 241–42
Happenings (Kaprow), 195
The Happy Hooker (Hollander), 7
hardcore porn, 31
Hare Follies (performance), 10–11, 169–87, 189, 329

Haring, Keith, 160, 256
Harry, Debbie, 77
Hawkins, Richard, 159–60
Head (Grossman), 153
Hebdige, Dick, 5
hedonism, consumer, 144
Hellfire Club, 251
Hells Angels, 61
Helms, Jesse, 211
Hendricks, Geoffrey, 157
Henson, Mike, 99
Hernandez, Jaime, 210
Hesse, Eva, 152, 159
heterosexuality, 129, 141, 162
Hewicker, Scott, 152–53
H (fictional character), 165–66, 168
Hideous Sun Demon (film), 101
hierarchy, 26, 193, 247, 301
high art, 23, 128
high conceptualism, 105
Him (fictional character), 213
Hindley, Myra, 122
hip-hop, 238
history, 9, 138, 230, 277
history paintings, 227
The Hitchhiker (Hockney), 160
Hite, Saul, 50
HIV. *See* AIDS crisis
Hockney, David, 120, 160
Hocquenghem, Guy, 32, 116, 125
Hodges, Jim, 159–60, 190, 245–47, 249
Hoffbauer, Patricia, 10–11, 169
Hollander, Xaviera, 7
Hollywood, 100–101, 270
Holzer, Jenny, 160
home craft, 215
home video, 88, 92
homoerotic content, 129
homophobia, 148, 161
Homosexual Desire (Deleuze, Guattari, and Hocquenghem), 116
homosexuality, 24, 65, 115, 201, 211; in *Cruising*, 43; grand opera relation to, 77–78; lesbians and, 5, 144, 146, 150, 271, 273; meaning and, 6, 63; Minelli relation to, 54; modernism relation to, 124–25; paranoia relation to, 32, 116–17. *See also* gay men
"Homosexuality in America," 268
horizon, 225
Horn, Roni, 161–62

House Un-American Activities Committee, 141
Houston-Jones, Ishmael, 10–11, 169
Howard-Howard, Margo, 7
"How Does It Feel?" (song), 211
How It Is Organized (exhibition), 120
"How I Wrote Certain of My Books" (Roussel), 34
Huberland, Kathy, 155
Hugo, Victor, 121
Hujar, Peter, 157
humanism, 146–47, 220
humiliation, 255, 301–4, 306
humility, 302
Hunt, Robert, 59

Iceland, 161
Ice-T, 211
idda (fictional character), 111
idea art, 103, 160
ideas, 257
identity, 259; cultural, 42, 139; drag relation to, 153–54; furry fandom relation to, 284; gay, 4, 21, 24; of Gnomen, 285–86, 288; mainstream, 315; performance of, 251, 277; queer and, 271, 273; witnesses relation to, 306
identity politics, 137, 149
ideology, 277
Idol, Ryan, 99
idolatry, 222
iell (fictional character), 109–11, 113
illness, 151
"I'm a Cliché" (album), 233
impermanence, 206
impotence, 122
"I'm Set Free" (song), 236–37
I'm with the Band (Des Barres), 8
In a Different Light (exhibition), 9–10, 136, 162, 190
Independent (newspaper), 129
individualism, 314
information age, 276
In Sandy's Room (photograph), 153
Instagram, 327
Institute of Contemporary Art (ICA), 121
intellectual production, 75–76
interactive art, 106
Internal Erotic (Nagy), 151
internalized racism, 169

International Center of Photography, 268, 271
internet, 257, 259, 327
intimacy, 226, 330; embarrassment and, 302; in performance, 286, 288; status play and, 301
Invert, Oracle (installation), 105
investments, 103–4
irony, 200–201, 262
"It's Raining Men" (song), 81

Jack Hanley Gallery, 198
Jacobs, Ken, 196
Jagger, Mick, 61
James, Darius, 11
James Bond (fictional character), 3
Jenkins, Michael, 152
Jerico Video, 99–100
Jett, Joan, 139
Johns, Jasper, 2
Johnson, Lady Bird, 61
Johnson, Ray, 190, 205–7, 209
Johnson, Ricky, 88
Johnston, Jill, 157
Johnstone, Stephen, 116–30, 132
Joker Art Institute and Lair of Artistic Instruction, 322
The Joker (fictional character), 321–23
Jokes (exhibition), 104
Jorge/General Idea, 309
journalists, 73–74
joy, 267, 273
Joy Division, 81
Judd, Donald, 7
Judy and Liza (Spada), 7
Jurassic Park (film), 204
Just Pathetic (exhibition), 120

Kahlo, Frida, 151, 153, 159
Kake (fictional character), 26, 28–29
Kaprow, Allan, 195
Kass, Deb, 154
"Kathy Acker" (Blake), 12
Katz, Alex, 218
Kaz, 210
Keaton, Michael, 98
Keith Partridge (fictional character), 71–72, 74–75, 78, 84
Kelley, Kitty, 7
Kelley, Mike, 121, 197–98
Kelly, Robert, 3, 234–36

Kennedy, Jack, 50, 56
Kennedy, Jacqueline, 50
Kilimnik, Karen, 158, 198
Killing for Company (Cooper), 121, 122
kink, 6, 169, 288, 329; negotiation relation to, 252–53; performance compared to, 262, 325; queer sex and, 274; social-sexual space and, 11; status play, 12–13, 301–4, 306; teaching of, 300
Kinky Gelinky, 129
Kipper Kids, 157
Kirk (fictional character), 64–66, 67
Kirkwood, Gene, 45
Kissinger, 72–74
kitsch, 23
Knee Deep in the Flooded Victory (installation), 271, 273
Knight, Chad, 99
Koch, Ed, 273
Kristeva, Julia, 130
Kruger, Barbara, 160

Lacan, Jacques, 124
Lacy, Suzanne, 157
Lake, Tony, 72
lambada, 65
Land of Pasaquan (sculpture garden), 195
language, 104, 106, 262
Lanigan-Schmidt, Thomas, 158, 159
The Large Glass (Duchamp), 34–35
La Rue, Chi Chi, 93, 95
The Last Star (Kelley, K.), 7
Laurie Partridge (fictional character), 71–72, 78–79
leather, 26–27, 261, 330; bars, 251; culture, 256, 265
LeDray, Charles, 157
Led Zeppelin Live, 79
Lee, Peggy, 96
Leek, Sybil, 7
legacy, 204
Leibowitz, Cary, 159
leisure, 153, 218
Leonard, Zoe, 152, 161
Leprechaun 5 (film), 211
lesbians, 5, 144, 146, 150, 271, 273
Le Va, Barry, 159
Levine, Sherrie, 154
Leyendecker, J. C., 221–22
libertarian notions, 146–47
libido, 89

Librium, 81
Liddell, Siobhan, 161–62
Life (magazine), 158, 268
Lincoln, Abraham, 25, 241
Linklater, Richard, 123
lithium, 68
live/work space, 324
Locke, Richard, 88
Locus Solus (Roussel), 32–53, 35
loft laws, 324
London, 115, 145
Lonesome Bear (fictional character), 84
Looking Glass (sculpture), 221
"Losing My Mind" (song), 76–78, 81–82
Lovecraft, H. P., 222
Low (Acker), 12, 240
lubricious power, 28
Lucifer (sculpture), 221
Lucky Lady (film), 54
Lynch, David, 251
lynching, 135

Maakies (comic), 211
Made in Hollywood U.S.A. (film), 101
Mad Magazine, 314
Madonna, 129
mail art movement, 146
mainstream art world, 10, 142, 144, 162, 199
mainstream identity, 315
Major Arcana, 221
Mandingo (film), 11
Manetti, Nick, 97–98
the Manhole, 251
Mapplethorpe, Robert, 127, 153, 201–2
Marcel Duchamp Club (collage), 207, 209
marginalized artists, 32, 138–39
Marine Jake, 96
Marky Mark, 129
Marsh, Reginald, 23
Marshall, Tanner, 97
Martin, Eddie Owens (St. EOM), 195
masochism, 130. *See also* S&M
Masonic ritual, 222
Masonite cutouts, 226
Massachusetts, 1, 24–25
masturbation, 291
Matisse, Henri, 24
"The Maze" (*Rigid Video, Vol. 1* episode), 88
McDermott & McGough, 158

McLaren, Malcolm, 145

McMarty, Marlene, 161

meaning, 260, 262, 264, 300, 330; in art practice, 15, 17, 205; Duchamp and, 140–41; gay sensibility relation to, 125; homosexuality and, 6, 37; queer relation to, 138–39

Meatpacking District, New York, 249, 251

Mekas, Jonas, 194

Méliès, Georges, 193

Melville, Herman, 219, 220

memory, 105, 190–91, 267, 307, 309

The Merv Griffin Show (television show), 66

Meshes in the Afternoon (Deren), 237

Metropolitan Museum of Art, 288

Michael's Thing (newspaper), 191

Michelangelo, 269

Michelle (female impersonator), 270

Mickey Mouse (fictional character), 312

Migs (fictional character), 303–4

Milch gallery, London, 115

military power structures, 254

Millett, Kate, 157

Millionaire, Tony, 211

Mind over Matter (show), 119, 124

Minelli, Liza, 43, 54, 59, 70, 82; fame and, 74; Garland and, 55, 56–58, 60, 63; the Pet Shop Boys relation to, 76–78, 81

minimalism, 237

Minority Role Model, 316

minstrel show, 118

Mister Shane (fictional character), 74–75

modernism, 55, 141, 162; gay sensibility and, 117, 124–25; perversion and, 115; women's art movement relation to, 144

Modern Primitives (publication), 315

molasses, 241

Mona Lisa (painting), 35

monobrow, 88

Montez, Maria, 196, 200

Montez, Mario, 193

Moorman, Charlotte, 2

moral ambiguity, 121

morphology, 198

mortality, 148

Morton, Ree, 151

Motherwell, Robert, 261

moticos (collage), 206

Moyer, Carrie, 157

musicians, 61

music industry, gay culture relation to, 76–77

My Death My Life by Pier Paolo Pasolini (Acker), 3

Myron (Vidal), 213

My Secret Life by Anonymous (memoir), 235

My Studio Is a Dungeon Is the Studio (visual essay), 14 319?

"My Way" (song), 47

Nagy, Peter, 151

Naked Lunch (Burroughs), 2

narcissism, 240

narratives, 25–26, 227, 307, 309; of counterculture, 314; serial killers and, 323

National Endowment for the Arts (NEA), 129

National Geographic (magazine), 236

National Portrait Gallery, 277

Nazi Germany, 25, 27–28

negotiation: in dungeons, 330–31; kink relation to, 252–53; in status play, 301

Negrophobia (James), 11

neoclassicism, 25, 27–28

neo-Expressionism, in New York, 147–48

New Bedford, Massachusetts, 1

The New Candid Camera (film), 92–93

New Langton Arts, 6, 9, 136

New Left, 68, 76, 314

New Museum exhibition, 284–86

New Narrative movement, 8, 280

New Order, 81, 82

New York, 39, 148, 169, 236; Alexander and Bonin in, 220; Bleeker Bob's in, 233; Christopher Street in, 44, 191–92, 325; collage in, 239; Fierce Pussy in, 273; Meatpacking District in, 249, 251; Metropolitan Museum of Art in, 288; neo-Expressionism in, 147–48; punk in, 145; street art in, 160; Times Square, 147, 255–56, 325; West Village, 191, 201; white flight in, 324

New York Correspondence School (NYCS), 207, 209

New York Department of Sanitation, 251

Nilsen, Dennis, 115, 118, 121, 122

Nixon, Richard, 72–73

nonbinary, 6, 333

noncompetitive behavior, 76
nonprofit arts organizations, 32, 103, 149, 265
No One Ever Leaves (sculpture), 246
No Rest for the Wicked (film), 101
North Hollywood, C'est La Vie Club in, 270
Novak, John, 101
nudist colonies, 56

objectification, 301, 303
objects, 104, 215, 260, 331
obscurity, 205
occult practices, symbols in, 222
The Octoroon (play), 11
O'Dougherty, Brian, 324, 327–28
Oedipus complex, 65
"Oh, Sister" (song), 63
"Oh Bondage Up Yours!" (song), 233–34
O'Keefe, Georgia, 151
Oldenburg, Claes, 159, 160, 195
Old Reliable (porn company), 94, 96
omni-culture, 65
Onassis, Jackie, 154
"100 Assignments" (Blake), 12–13, 289–96
One Woman Show (Lacy), 157
Ono, Yoko, 11
On Our Backs (magazine), 5
Operation Spanner, 123–24
Opie, Catherine, 152, 161
oppression, 234
orgy, 109–11, 160, 285
Orgy (exhibition), 159
Ormudz, 35
otherness, 155
Other Voices, Other Rooms (Capote), 50–51
Otterson, Joel, 156
oubliette, 323–24
outline, 111
OUT/LOOK (magazine), 4, 21
Out of Hand Screwing Screw Ups (film), 93–95
outsider status, 191
"Over the Rainbow" (song), 197
oz (theatrical place), 109–11, 113

Pacific Ocean, 227, 229
Pacino, Al, 43–44, 49, 46
Page, Jimmy, 61, 79–81

pain, 267, 331
paintings, 103, 215, 294, 296, 321; of Bamber, 225–27, 229; photography compared to, 227. See also *specific paintings*
Palace Theater, 270
Palm Drive Video, 96–97
pansexual, 259, 325
paranoia, 32, 96, 116–17, 222
Paris student revolts, 145
Parker, Al, 95
Parks, Robert, 88
Partridge Family, 71–72
passing, 11, 154, 202
"pattern and decoration," 260
Pay for Your Pleasure (installation), 121
Pekka (fictional character), 26
Peraldi, François, 6
perception, 225
performance, 255, 274, 276, 293, 294, 329; body modification as, 315; gender as, 316, 326; of identity, 251, 277; intimacy in, 286, 288; kink compared to, 262, 325; leather relation to, 256; puppets and, 235
Performance Principle, 76
"Performance Script" (1990) (Blake), 7, 43–54
performance scripts, 7, 13, 65–68, 70, 234
permeability, 247, 249
Perrault, Charles, 238
Perry, Troy, 269
personal ad, 216
perversion, 115, 117–18, 127; fetish and, 120; pleasure and, 125; sex relation to, 123
Peter, a Young English Girl (painting), 156
the Pet Shop Boys, 76–78, 81
Pfaff, Judy, 2
phallus, 115, 124–25, 130, 202
Phase Four, 213
The Philosopher's Suite (installation), 114–15
Philosophy in the Bedroom (Sade), 115
Photographs #27, 160
Photographs #42, 160
photography, 227, 269–70, 291, 327; documentary, 267, 279; on internet, 257; porn in, 22–23
photorealist style, 24
photo studios, 328

physicality, gender and, 214–15
physique magazines, 31
Picasso, Pablo, 207
Pictures Generation, 3
Pier 39, 91
Pierce, William Luther, 11
piercings, 123
Pierre (Melville), 219
pinup pictures, 31
pipe man, 251–52
pirating, 22
placeless community, 31
pleasure, 34–35, 111, 113, 151, 158, 277;
cruising relation to, 27; desire compared to, 130, 132; perversion and,
125; porn relation to, 5, 21, 211; sex
and, 264; of S&M, 28
Plywood (sculpture), 10, 155
Pogo the Clown, 121
Police Wrestling (film), 96–97
political struggle, 67–68, 267–68
politics, 106, 194
Pollock, Jackson, 209
polymorphous perversity, 118
"Polysexuality" (*Semiotext(e)* issue), 6,
13–14
pop art, 141, 260
"Pop Goes the Joker" (*Batman* episode),
321–22
Pop Shop, 160
porn, 87–88, 93, 184; at Adonis Theater,
191; amateur, 94; cops in, 96–97; escapism and, 238; gay identity relation
to, 4; gaze relation to, 27; hardcore,
31; novels, 238; in photography, 22–23;
pleasure relation to, 5, 21, 211; queer
relation to, 5; sadism in, 29; theaters,
85–86, 191, 255–56, 269; uniforms in,
95–96. See also *specific works*
"Pornography by Women for Women,
with Love" (Russ), 5–6
positivism, 316, 318
postminimalism, 150, 151
postmodernism, 55, 247; AIDS crisis relation to, 148; culture relation to, 139–
40; gay culture relation to, 128
postplay follow-up, in status play, 301
post-structuralist theory, 104
power, 43, 68, 145; in culture, 254, 312,
314; lubricious, 28; relationships, 60;
uniforms relation to, 95

Powerpuff Girls (television show), 213
Presences (Hammond), 157–58
Printed Matter, 235
Priola, John J., 151
Pristine Condition, 270
privatization, 326
production, intellectual, 75–76
productivity, 328
"Program" (Blake), 1
progressive aesthetic, 103–4
protomodernism, 220
Prudhomme, Paul, 92
Pruitt-Early, 157
PS1, 200
psychedelia, 158–59
*Psychoanalytic Notes on a Case of Auto-
biographical Paranoia* (Freud), 114
Pugsly Addams (fictional character),
321
Punch, 122
Punch Agonistes (installation), 115
punk, 82, 145–46, 149, 259; Acker rela-
tion to, 237; queer and, 150, 265
puppets, 60, 235, 238
Puppy Potter (fictional character), 84

queens, 43–44, 51, 52, 93
"Queen's Ball," 269
queer, 3–4, 12; Acker relation to, 237;
camp relation to, 200–201; Fluxus
relation to, 149; fucking relation to,
274, 277, 279; gender relation to, 153;
identity and, 271, 273; mainstream art
world relation to, 10; meaning relation to, 138–39; memory relation to,
190–91; political struggle and, 267–
68; porn relation to, 5; punk and, 150,
265; science fiction relation to, 156;
sexuality and, 262, 327
queer art history, 9
queer culture, 139–40, 146, 277
queer difference, 276
queer expression, 21
Queer Mysteries (installation), 8, 109
Queer Nation, 326
queer practice, 138; in theater, 141–42;
tribal affiliations and, 139
queer sensibility, 9, 162
queer sex, 153, 262, 274
Queer Theatre (Brecht), 192
Queer Theory, 326

queer visibility, 161
queer zines, 146

rabbits, 8–9, 133, 165, 171–78, 183–84
racial duality, 119
racism, 118, 169
Rat Fink, 312, 318
Ray, Elizabeth L., 7–8, 58–59
Ray Johnson (presentation), 209
Reagan, Ronald, 256, 326
Reage, Pauline, 8, 165
*Reconstructed Score from John Cage's 4
    Minutes and 33 Seconds* (Tudor), 152
Reed, David, 27
Reichman, Brett, 151
Rejection Quintet (Chicago), 150–51
René Magritte (Johnson, Ray), 209
rent, 194, 200, 328–29
representation, 28, 111, 277, 279; ab-
    straction and, 150, 260, 275–76; AIDS
    crisis relation to, 119–20; ambisexual,
    202; of gay men, 3, 261; in paintings,
    229; safety and, 273; S&M and, 127–28;
    of women, 104–5
resistance: to art establishment, 194;
    lambada and, 65; leisure relation to,
    153
respect, 17, 23
Restraint (sculpture), 114
Restraint 6 (sculpture), 126
Reuben Kincaid (fictional character), 71,
    74–75, 78, 84
revolutions, 200
Reynolds, Burt, 54
Rico, 94
Rigid Video, Vol. 1 (film), 87–88
Rinder, Lawrence, 136–37
Rivera, Diego, 153
Rizzo, Jilly, 47
Roberts, Greg, 88–89
Robin (fictional character), 322
Rocco, Pat, 101
rock concerts, 79
Rockwell, Norman, 24–25
Rockwell Museum, 24–25
Rodchenko, Alexander, 154
the Rolling Stones, 61
Romantic sublime, 130
Rose Hobart (film), 196
Ross, Diana, 311
rot, 193, 198–99

Roth, Ed "Big Daddy," 312, 314
Rough Riders, 222
Roussel, Raymond, 6, 32–35, 116
Roy, Camille, 71
Rrose Sélavy (guise of Duchamp), 35
Rude Screen (sculpture), 221
Rugoff, Ralph, 120
Ruins of a Sensibility (installation), 321
Russ, Johanna, 5–6

Sabbats, 56
Sacher-Masoch, Leopold von, 130
Sacred Arts of Haitian Vodou (exhibi-
    tion), 219
"The Saddest Story I Know"
    (performance), 8–9, 55–63
Sade, Marquis de, 29, 115, 118, 237–38,
    325
sadism, 29, 80, 130. *See also* S&M
safety, 273, 300
Safety Skunk, 285
safe words, 252–53
Saget, Bob, 94
sailors, 96
saints, Catholic, 221
St. EOM (Eddie Owens Martin), 195
Salle, David, 96
salon painting, 25
Samaras, Connie, 156
Samdi, Bawon, 2, 219
Samois, 5
Sam Picasso (fictional character), 321
Samwise Gamgee (fictional character),
    280–81, 283
San Francisco, 3–4, 8, 89, 270, 273, 326;
    bears in, 259; culture of, 192; Jack
    Hanley Gallery in, 198; leather culture
    in, 265; Pier 39, 91
San Francisco Art Institute, 8, 109, 240
San Francisco Museum of Modern Art,
    Space, Time, Sound at, 102
Sanrio, 158–59
sarcoma lesions, 152
Saret, Alan, 159
Scheherazade, 213
Schrade, Nick, 88
Schreber, Daniel Paul, 6, 32–33, 114–16;
    paranoia relation to, 116–17; transves-
    tism and, 35, 37
The Schreber Suite (installation), 6,
    32–33, 114–16

science fiction, 1–2, 8, 109, 156
Scooter LaForge show, 297
Score 10 (film), 98–99
Scotch Tape (film), 191
Scott, Mr. (fictional character), 67, 68
scrutiny, 325
sculptural material, 215, 246–47, 249
"secret heat," 35
Secret of Rented Island (Smith, J.), 198
Seedbed (sculpture), 249
Segar, E. C., 210
self, 3, 152
self-cultivation, 234
selfhood, 316, 319, 326
self-mockery, 159
self-pity, 82
Self-Portrait (photograph), 152
Self-Portrait with Cropped Hair (painting), 153
Self-Portrait with Whip (photograph), 153
self-repression, 251
Semiotext(e) (journal), 6, 13–14, 39
sensationalism, 122–23
sensitivity, to dreams, 307
serial killers, 115, 121–22, 123, 323
Serra, Richard, 246, 261
Seven Deadly Sins (exhibition), 105
Seven Marks (exhibition), 106, 108
sex, 93, 237, 256, 276, 300; fucking compared to, 87; gay sensibility relation to, 125; perversion relation to, 123; pleasure and, 264; punk relation to, 145–46; queer, 153, 262, 274
Sex Pistols, 145
SEX (shop), 145
sexual bondage, 114, 126–27
sexual courtship, in gay community, 25–26
sexual deviance, 141
sexuality, 153, 192; Acker relation to, 237; anal, 162; explicitness relation to, 129; queer and, 262, 327; Tom of Finland relation to, 22
sexual liberation, 276
Shakespeare, William, 294
Sharits, Paul, 191
Sherman, Cindy, 198
Shirley Partridge (fictional character), 71–72, 74–75, 78–79
signature style, 20
signs, communication with, 46

Silence of the Lambs (film), 303–4
"silent pervert," 117–18
Sill, Beverly, 7
Simulationist artists, 130
Sinatra, Frank, 46–48
Sinatra, Frank, Jr., 74
Siobhan and I: sex (black bra) (photograph), 157
Sisters of Mercy, 81
Sitney, P. Adams, 237
Situation (exhibition), 9, 136–37
skin, 152
Slacker (film), 123
Slater, Craig, 99
Sludgemaster, 211
S&M, 7, 114, 251; community relation to, 300; *Drummer* and, 256; lesbians and, 5; pleasure of, 28; representation and, 127–28; in *Rigid Video, Vol. 1*, 88; social-sexual space in, 11; *Workstation* and, 125–26
Sméagol (fictional character), 281
Smith, Jack, 2, 7, 158–59, 190–92, 204, 213; art establishment relation to, 194–96; camp relation to, 201; death and, 193; drag relation to, 202; dreams and, 237, 242; Kelley, M., compared to, 197–98; Kilimnik relation to, 198; mainstream art world relation to, 199
Smith, Sandy, 48
Smith, Wayne, 71
social activism, 146–49
socialist realism, 24, 25, 201
social liberation movements, 76, 143–44, 145
social platforms, 327
social-sexual space, 11
social structures, 304, 306
societal norms, 301–3
societal pressures, 17
sociopolitical history, 104
Sock Monkey (comic), 211
Soft Drum Set (Oldenburg), 159
Solnit, Rebecca, 8, 109
Sondheim, Stephen, 77, 82
Sontag, Susan, 267
Sophia (fictional character), 166, 168
soundtrack, 86, 88
Space, Time, Sound (exhibition), 102
Spada, James, 7
Spartacus (film), 101

Spectacle (exhibition), 104
Spock (fictional character), 64–65, 68
Stalin, Joseph, 25
Stanwood, Brooks, 7
Star Trek: The Next Generation
    (television show), 92
Star Trek (television show), 5–6, 64–65,
    67
status play, 12–13, 301–4, 306
status quo, 275–76, 279
Steel, Jim, 98
Stefanino's, 46
Stefano, Joey, 94
Stein, Gertrude, 162, 209
Steiner, Rick, 210
Sterling, Matt, 99
Stewart, Alan Breck, 58
Stine, Les, 97–98
Stockbridge, Massachusetts, 24–25
Stockhausen, Karlheinz, 197
Stoller, Robert, 127
Stone, Chris, 99
Stonewall, 145, 149, 201, 268
Store (Oldenberg), 160
The Story of Harold (Andrews), 213
"The Story of H (Excerpt)" (Blake), 8,
    165–68
Story of O (Reage), 8, 165
straight allies, 277, 279
straight men, 44, 129, 130, 162
Strangers at Play (film), 101
street art, 148, 160
Streisand, Barbra, 77, 154
Studio 54, New York, 54
"studs," 87–88
style, 257
subcultural activities, 129
Subculture (Hebdige), 5
suffering, 78, 267, 321
Sulu (fictional character), 65–66, 67
Summer, Donna, 77
Summer of Love, 268
Summertime Blues (film), 89–91
Sun Ra, 197
Surge Studios, 94–95
Sylvester, 78
symbols, 28, 222, 246, 262
synecdoche, 152

tableaux, 7, 29, 126–27
Tambov, 59

tarot, 105, 221
tattoo culture, 315
Taylor, Elizabeth, 7, 61
teaching, 289, 300
tech boom, 327
Temporarily Untitled (exhibition), 108
Test Piece (Hesse), 152
Teviotdale, 60
texture, 26–27
theater, 141–42. *See also* performance
Thek, Paul, 246
theory writing, 44–45, 32
"The Three Case Histories" (Freud), 32
Three's a Crowd (film), 101
*Throne of the Third Heaven of the Na-
    tion's Millennium General Assembly*
    (installation), 195
Tight Right White (Abdoh), 11
TIME (exhibition), 106
Time Magazine, 106
Times Square, 147, 255–56, 325
The Times Square Show (1980), 2, 192
To Have and Have Not (film), 77
To Live and Let Die (movie), 3
Tom of Finland, 4, 21–24, 31, 85; fascism
    relation to, 28–29; narratives and,
    25–26
touch, 225–26
Toys "R" Us, 221
trans, 6, 316, 318, 333
transformation, 204, 284
transgression, 65, 119, 202
transvestism, 35, 37
trauma, 262
Travis, John, 87
Traylor, Bill, 213
tribal affiliations, 139, 327
true crime, 115, 121
Truisms (Holzer), 160
The Trumps (sculpture), 221
trust, 252, 300
Tudor, David, 152
The Turner Diaries (Pierce), 11
Two Slaves (film), 100

Übermensch, 28, 29
Uhura (fictional character), 67
Uncle Tom, 241
underground film scene, 194
underground publications, 5
Underworld, 100

Underworld (comic), 210
Uniformed Fantasies (film), 95–96
uniforms, 27–28, 95–96, 254
uniqueness, 200
Untitled (Mona Lisa with Coil) (collage), 207
US Constitution, Bill of Rights, 123
US Navy, 23
utopia, 195, 198–99, 216, 218, 319, 329

vacations, 218
vaginas, 226
vampirism, 193
VanderGriff, Bob, 57–58
vaudeville, 202
Velvet Underground, 145, 236–37
the Ventures, 101
V-8 (film), 97–98
victims, of crime, 124
Vidal, Gore, 213
Vietnam, chemical weapons in, 73
viewers, 137, 232
viewing, intimacy of, 226
Village Voice (newspaper), 192
vintage goods, 221
virginity, 37
virility, 76
vision, 225, 229
visual clarity, enlightenment relation to, 323
Vivid Video, 89–90
Vodou, 219–20
void, 152
vulnerability, 226

Walking Fingers Bonanza, 84
Wallis, Brian, 268
Warhol, Andy, 145, 154, 158, 159, 160, 206–7
Washington, DC, 161
Washington, George, 25
The Washington Fringe Benefit (Ray), 7–8
Waters, John, 122
Wednesday Addams (fictional character), 321
weirdness, 114
"Welcome to Airspace" (Chayka), 327–28
Western culture, 39, 42

Weston, Edward, 154
West Village, New York, 191, 201
Westwood, Vivienne, 145
Wexner Center for the Arts, 205
What I Believe (painting), 24
"the White Cube" (O'Dougherty), 324, 327–28
white flight, in New York, 324
"the White Tube," 328, 330
Whitney's, 205–6, 209
Wild and Wooly Warehouse, 269
Wild Hunt, 58
Willis, Bob, 101
Wilson, Millie, 156
Winet, Jon, 106
witchcraft, 58
witches, 55–56
witnesses, 306
Wojnarowicz, David, 277
Wolfe, Steve, 159
Womanhouse (installation), 155–56
women, 147; Fluxus relation to, 142–43; representation of, 104–5
women's art movement: community and, 143; Fluxus and, 145; form relation to, 149; lesbians in, 144
women's liberation movement, 76, 143–44
women's music movement, 146
Wood, Ed, 202
Wood, Robin, 43
the Workshop, 133, 135
Works Progress Administration (WPA), 23
Work Station #5 (1989) (installation), 7
Workstation (sculpture), 114, 125–26, 128
World Championship Wrestling (WCW), 210
writing, 44–46, 42, 32, 230, 234

Xenakis, Iannis, 197
X-Ray Spex, 233

Yerba Buena Center for the Arts, 265
Young Gay Men (YGM), 89–92

Ziegler, Ron, 73
zines, 5, 146
zombification, 193